High-Performance Algorithmic Trading Using AI

Strategies and insights for developing cutting-edge trading algorithms

Melick R. Baranasooriya

www.bpbonline.com

First Edition 2024

Copyright © BPB Publications, India

ISBN: 978-93-65895-872

All Rights Reserved. No part of this publication may be reproduced, distributed or transmitted in any form or by any means or stored in a database or retrieval system, without the prior written permission of the publisher with the exception to the program listings which may be entered, stored and executed in a computer system, but they can not be reproduced by the means of publication, photocopy, recording, or by any electronic and mechanical means.

LIMITS OF LIABILITY AND DISCLAIMER OF WARRANTY

The information contained in this book is true to correct and the best of author's and publisher's knowledge. The author has made every effort to ensure the accuracy of these publications, but publisher cannot be held responsible for any loss or damage arising from any information in this book.

All trademarks referred to in the book are acknowledged as properties of their respective owners but BPB Publications cannot guarantee the accuracy of this information.

To View Complete
BPB Publications Catalogue
Scan the QR Code:

www.bpbonline.com

Dedicated to

My beloved wife, **Sachika Imali Semage**
and
My cherished son, **Nich Olin Baranasooriya**

About the Author

Melick Rajee Baranasooriya, an accomplished Enterprise Architect and Co-founder of an AI Startup. He brings extensive international experience in establishing digital technology footprints, delivering financial solutions, aligning enterprise technologies, and driving digital strategies, architectural governance, and data-driven decision-making. His expertise spans capital markets, trading, and index domains, with significant engagements in fintech, edtech, legaltech solutions, and government sectors.

He holds a Master's and two Bachelor's degrees in Information Technology, alongside the globally recognized TOGAF 9.2 Enterprise Architecture certification. Recognized as a technology leader, he is honored with the Microsoft Most Valuable Professional award and actively collaborates with global communities and enterprises. His achievements in areas like data science and IoT demonstrate his capability to address complex challenges with innovative solutions.

About the Reviewers

- **Devon Y.P. Chan** is a Technical Lead at Forex Forest Algorithmic Trading, where he has been driving innovation since 2018. With a strong focus on developing quantitative trading strategies, Devon ensures the creation of low-latency, high-frequency cross-platform trading environments using deep learning and cloud computation. His expertise has been instrumental in managing large-scale projects for government departments and commercial enterprises in Hong Kong. A graduate of HKUST with a dual degree in Computer Science and Quantum Physics, Devon's achievements include winning first place in the Microsoft Challenge at QC Hack 2021. Passionate about integrating cutting-edge technologies into financial applications, he continues to push the boundaries of what's possible in algorithmic trading.

- **Juergen Weichenberger** has 20+ years of experience in advanced analytics, data science, database design, architecture, and implementation on various platforms to solve Complex Industry Problems.

  Industrial Analytics, a field that Juergen has significantly influenced, is the fusion of manufacturing, production, reliability, integrity, quality, sales- and market-analytics. By combining skills and experience, he has created the next-generation AI & ML solutions for clients, revolutionizing the industry.

  He is driving a team and gaining knowledge to extend the limits of AI and ML beyond what is currently possible. He holds more than 15 patents and is working on new innovations. He is working with his partner ecosystem to enrich the accelerators with modern ML/AI techniques. Integrating robotic equipment will allow him to create next-generation solutions.

Acknowledgement

I am deeply grateful to everyone who supported me throughout the writing of this book. First and foremost, I want to express my heartfelt thanks to my loving wife, whose constant encouragement and understanding were indispensable in this journey.

I am also indebted to those who provided behind-the-scenes support. Special acknowledgment goes to Devon Chan and Juergen Weichenberger for their meticulous technical insights, which greatly enhanced the quality of this work.

I would also like to extend my gratitude to the team at BPB Publications for their unwavering support and understanding. Their patience and flexibility in allowing the book to be published in multiple parts were invaluable. This approach was essential, as it enabled us to thoroughly explore the expansive and dynamic field of image processing research without overwhelming the reader.

Preface

This book is your comprehensive guide to Algorithmic Trading and **Artificial Intelligence (AI)** in Finance, designed to equip both beginners and seasoned professionals with essential knowledge and practical skills. Beginning with an exploration of Algorithmic Trading's evolution and the transformative impact of AI, Chapter 1 lays the foundation by tracing historical developments and highlighting key innovators. From there, chapters 2 and 3 delve into the core of AI in finance, covering fundamental concepts and practical applications. Readers will gain insights into how AI and **Machine Learning (ML)** revolutionize trading strategies, empowering them to navigate complexities with confidence.

Data Processing and Analysis take center stage in chapter 4, equipping readers with the tools to extract actionable insights from vast datasets. Through real-world examples and step-by-step guidance, this chapter ensures readers master crucial techniques in data handling and analysis critical for informed trading decisions. Python enthusiasts and algorithm developers will find chapters 7 and 8 invaluable, offering deep dives into Python tools and libraries essential for financial modeling and algorithm development.

The book also highlights real-world case studies in chapter 9, showcasing AI's practical applications in diverse trading scenarios. Lastly, chapter 11 looks forward, exploring emerging technologies like quantum computing and blockchain, shaping the future landscape of algorithmic trading. Whether you are a seasoned trader or a tech enthusiast entering the world of finance, this book serves as your indispensable guide to mastering Algorithmic Trading and AI in the modern era.

Chapter 1: Introduction to Algorithmic Trading and AI - This chapter introduces algorithmic trading and explores the impact of **AI** and **ML** in modern finance. It covers the evolution of algorithmic trading, key innovators, and various trading styles and timeframes. AI and ML's role in trading strategies and decision-making is highlighted, along with insights into risk and return management. Readers gain a comprehensive understanding of algorithmic trading, preparing them to navigate and utilize this dynamic field effectively.

Chapter 2: AI and Machine Learning Basics for Trading - This chapter explores **AI** and **ML** in finance and trading. It covers AI and ML fundamentals, types, and techniques, followed by real-world applications like algorithmic trading, sentiment analysis, high-frequency trading, and fraud detection. The chapter also examines AI and ML frameworks, libraries, popular algorithms for trading, and their advantages in trading algorithms. Readers will learn to build a simple AI-powered trading system and gain insights into model selection and evaluation, providing a comprehensive view of AI and ML in finance and trading.

Chapter 3: Essential Elements in AI Trading Algorithms - In this chapter, you will learn to create effective AI-driven trading strategies, from formulating and validating models to optimizing performance. We will delve into evaluating model effectiveness, fine-tuning for better results, and addressing challenges like overfitting and underfitting. You will also explore enhancing model interpretability and explaining AI insights. Discover how AI transforms portfolio management and asset allocation, integrating with traditional strategies for enhanced trading outcomes. Gain a holistic understanding of AI trading algorithms to apply them confidently in real-world scenarios.

Chapter 4: Data Processing and Analysis - This chapter discusses the essential skill set required for successful algorithmic trading: data processing and analysis. Divided into multiple sections, it equips readers with the expertise necessary to navigate through various stages of data analysis. From understanding data sources to handling real-time feeds, each section offers a comprehensive exploration of key concepts and techniques. Through practical examples and illustrations, readers will gain proficiency in pre-processing, feature extraction, visualization, and time series analysis. By the chapter's end, they will possess the knowledge and tools to make well-informed trading decisions based on data-driven insights.

Chapter 5: Simulating and Testing Trading Strategies - This chapter explains the dynamic world of algorithmic trading, where success lies in effectively evaluating performance and managing risks. We begin with backtesting, scrutinizing strategies on historical data, and forward-testing, deploying algorithms in real time. Performance metrics and evaluation techniques will be uncovered to aid in making informed decisions. We then address risk management and mitigation strategies crucial for safeguarding investments. Furthermore, the chapter explores walk-forward analysis, custom backtesting environments, stress testing, and scenario analysis to validate strategies thoroughly. Lastly, we delve into the transformative journey from paper trading to live trading, ensuring a seamless transition towards a profitable trading experience.

Chapter 6: Implementing AI Models with Trading Platforms - This chapter embarks on an insightful journey through some of the most popular trading platforms available today, dedicating a comprehensive examination of the intricacies of the popular trading platform MetaTrader 5 and integration processes for institutional platforms. As artificial intelligence continues to reshape trading strategies and methodologies, we will delve into the process of embedding AI models within these platforms, ensuring they not only operate efficiently but also adapt and evolve. However, the sophistication of these tools demands rigorous oversight; hence, we'll discuss the methodologies to monitor and maintain these deployed AI models. Recognizing the pivotal role of robust infrastructure, the chapter also explores cloud-based solutions tailored for trading, ensuring agility without compromising on security. Lastly, in an era where data breaches can lead to significant financial and reputational harm, we underscore the imperativeness of safeguarding trading algorithms, highlighting best practices to ensure their security and privacy. Dive in to stay ahead of the curve in this confluence of technology and trading.

Chapter 7: Getting Prepared for Python Development - In this chapter, you will learn about the key tools and libraries essential for advanced Python programming, particularly in data-driven environments. We will start with an exploration of Python's numerical libraries, which are fundamental for performing complex mathematical computations efficiently. Next, we will delve into Python's financial libraries, which are critical for conducting detailed financial analysis and algorithmic trading. You will also gain proficiency in using Python's visualization tools, which enable clear and impactful data representation, crucial for data science and analytics. Finally, we will cover version control using Git, empowering you to manage your code effectively and collaborate with others on development projects. By mastering these topics, you will enhance your technical toolkit and be better prepared to tackle a variety of programming challenges.

Chapter 8: Leveraging Python for Trading Algorithm Development - In this chapter, you will learn how to develop efficient trading algorithms using Python. We will begin by exploring the development of trading algorithms, utilizing Python's extensive libraries and tools for financial modeling. Practical strategies for troubleshooting and debugging will be covered, ensuring your algorithms are not only effective but also resilient. Emphasis will be placed on unit testing and maintaining high standards of code quality, which is crucial for reliable trading operations. You will also gain insights into performance optimization, including parallelization techniques to enhance execution speed. Finally, we will cover Python best practices tailored specifically for algorithmic trading, enabling you to implement robust and effective trading strategies. By the end of this chapter, you will have a comprehensive understanding of how to leverage Python to develop sophisticated trading algorithms and ensure they are efficient, reliable, and high-performing.

Chapter 9: Real-world Examples and Case Studies - In this chapter, we will cover the real-world applications of the concepts explored thus far, bringing theoretical knowledge to life through compelling case studies. The introduction sets the stage, emphasizing the practical relevance of **artificial intelligence (AI)** in finance. The chapter is structured to provide a seamless flow, beginning with a comprehensive explanation of the topic at hand. The subsequent case studies serve as illuminating examples, covering diverse applications such as AI-enhanced momentum trading, machine learning for mean reversion, sentiment analysis for trading signals, portfolio optimization with AI, and AI-driven market-making strategies. These real-world scenarios not only illustrate the adaptability of AI in financial settings but also offer valuable insights for readers aiming to bridge the gap between theory and implementation.

Chapter 10: Using LLMs for Algorithmic Trading - This chapter explores the pivotal role of **Large Language Models (LLMs)** in algorithmic trading, focusing on their transformative impact through advanced **Natural Language Processing (NLP)**. LLMs, including **Generative Pre-trained Transformers (GPT)**, revolutionize financial analysis by decoding market sentiment and enhancing predictive models. We examine their integration into trading strategies for sentiment analysis, their effectiveness in forecasting market behavior, and their contributions to optimizing risk management strategies. This exploration equips readers with insights into leveraging LLMs for enhanced decision-making in financial markets.

Chapter 11: Future Trends, Challenges, and Opportunities - This Chapter explores how AI, ML, quantum computing, blockchain, and DeFi are transforming algorithmic trading. It covers emerging trends in AI and ML, discusses challenges and ethical considerations, and highlights quantum computing's potential for enhancing trading efficiency. The role of blockchain and DeFi in improving transparency and security is examined alongside evolving regulatory frameworks. This chapter equips readers with insights into leveraging these technologies for innovative and secure algorithmic trading strategies in the future financial landscape.

Code Bundle and Coloured Images

Please follow the link to download the
Code Bundle and the *Coloured Images* of the book:

https://rebrand.ly/724c68

The code bundle for the book is also hosted on GitHub at **https://github.com/bpbpublications/High-Performance-Algorithmic-Trading-Using-AI**. In case there's an update to the code, it will be updated on the existing GitHub repository.

We have code bundles from our rich catalogue of books and videos available at **https://github.com/bpbpublications**. Check them out!

Errata

We take immense pride in our work at BPB Publications and follow best practices to ensure the accuracy of our content to provide with an indulging reading experience to our subscribers. Our readers are our mirrors, and we use their inputs to reflect and improve upon human errors, if any, that may have occurred during the publishing processes involved. To let us maintain the quality and help us reach out to any readers who might be having difficulties due to any unforeseen errors, please write to us at :

errata@bpbonline.com

Your support, suggestions and feedbacks are highly appreciated by the BPB Publications' Family.

Did you know that BPB offers eBook versions of every book published, with PDF and ePub files available? You can upgrade to the eBook version at www.bpbonline.com and as a print book customer, you are entitled to a discount on the eBook copy. Get in touch with us at :

business@bpbonline.com for more details.

At **www.bpbonline.com**, you can also read a collection of free technical articles, sign up for a range of free newsletters, and receive exclusive discounts and offers on BPB books and eBooks.

Piracy

If you come across any illegal copies of our works in any form on the internet, we would be grateful if you would provide us with the location address or website name. Please contact us at **business@bpbonline.com** with a link to the material.

If you are interested in becoming an author

If there is a topic that you have expertise in, and you are interested in either writing or contributing to a book, please visit **www.bpbonline.com**. We have worked with thousands of developers and tech professionals, just like you, to help them share their insights with the global tech community. You can make a general application, apply for a specific hot topic that we are recruiting an author for, or submit your own idea.

Reviews

Please leave a review. Once you have read and used this book, why not leave a review on the site that you purchased it from? Potential readers can then see and use your unbiased opinion to make purchase decisions. We at BPB can understand what you think about our products, and our authors can see your feedback on their book. Thank you!

For more information about BPB, please visit **www.bpbonline.com**.

Join our book's Discord space

Join the book's Discord Workspace for Latest updates, Offers, Tech happenings around the world, New Release and Sessions with the Authors:

https://discord.bpbonline.com

Table of Contents

1. **Introduction to Algorithmic Trading and AI** 1
   Introduction 1
   Structure 1
   Objectives 2
   Overview of algorithmic trading 2
       Types of algorithmic trading strategies 4
   Rise of AI and ML in finance 5
   Evolution of algorithmic trading 6
   Key players 7
   Trading styles and timeframes 8
   Risk and return in algorithmic trading 9
   Conclusion 10

2. **AI and Machine Learning Basics for Trading** 11
   Introduction 11
   Structure 11
   Objectives 12
   Introduction to artificial intelligence 12
       Definition and history of AI 12
       Types of AI: Narrow AI, General AI, and Superintelligent AI 13
       AI techniques: Expert systems, rule-based systems, and neural networks 14
       AI in finance and trading 14
   Introduction to machine learning 15
       Definition and history of ML 15
       Types of ML: Supervised, unsupervised, and reinforcement learning 16
       ML techniques: Regression, classification, clustering, and dimensionality reduction ... 17
       ML in finance and trading 18
       Real-world applications of AI/ML in trading 19
           Algorithmic trading and portfolio management 20
       Sentiment analysis for news and social media 20

High-frequency trading and market making..21
　　　Fraud detection and risk management...22
　AI/ML frameworks and libraries for trading 23
　Popular AI/ML algorithms for trading...25
　　　Time series forecasting: ARIMA, GARCH, and LSTM 26
　　　Classification algorithms: Logistic regression, SVM, and random forests 28
　　　　　Example of using Random Forests to determine price movement 29
　　　Reinforcement learning: Q-learning, DDPG, and PPO..31
　　　　　Deep Deterministic Policy Gradient in trading and finance 31
　　　　　Proximal Policy Optimization 32
　　　Natural language processing: Sentiment analysis and topic modeling 32
　　　　　Sentiment analysis 32
　　　　　Topic modeling...33
　　　Advantages of using AI/ML in trading algorithms 35
　　　　　Improved accuracy and predictive capabilities 35
　　　　　Adaptability to market changes 36
　　　　　Automating complex decision-making processes 37
　　　　　Reducing human biases and errors 37
　　　　　Enhancing risk management 38
　　　Building a simple AI-powered trading system: A walkthrough 39
　　　　　Defining the problem and selecting the data 39
　　　　　Preprocessing and feature engineering...39
　　　　　Feature engineering..40
　　　　　Selecting and training the ML model...40
　　　Testing and evaluating the model..41
　　　Integrating the model into a trading strategy..41
　　　　　Backtesting and optimizing the strategy..42
　　　AI/ML model selection and evaluation 42
　Conclusion...43

3. Essential Elements in AI Trading Algorithms 45
Introduction 45
Structure 45
Objectives 46
Formulating trading strategies with AI 46
Training and validating AI models 47
Evaluating AI model performance 51
Fine-tuning and optimizing AI models 53
Handling overfitting and underfitting 57
Model interpretability and explainability 59
AI for portfolio management and asset allocation 61
AI-driven risk management 61
Combining AI with traditional trading strategies 63
Conclusion 65
Multiple choice questions 65
Answers 66

4. Data Processing and Analysis 67
Introduction 67
Structure 67
Objectives 68
Data sources for algorithmic trading 68
Stock exchanges and financial data providers 68
Alternative data sources and indicators 73
Technical indicators and charting tools 77
Popular financial data APIs 83
Data preprocessing and cleaning 85
Handling different data formats 86
Data quality assessment and validation 87
Feature extraction and selection 91
Analyzing historical successful/failure trading patterns 98
Working with real-time data feeds 103
Handling and processing real-time data 104

Overview of EDA in algorithmic trading 105
  Data visualization techniques for trading analysis 106
    Common visualization types 106
  Handling missing and incomplete data 111
  Time series analysis techniques 113
  Conclusion 114

5. **Simulating and Testing Trading Strategies** 115
  Introduction 115
  Structure 115
  Objectives 116
  Backtesting: Historical data testing 116
    Implementing backtesting: Techniques and tools 118
    Pitfalls of back testing 121
  Forward-testing: Testing algorithms in real-time 122
    Real-time data: Acquisition and handling 123
    Forward-testing procedures: Steps and best practices 124
    Analyzing forward-testing results 126
  Performance metrics and evaluation techniques 128
    Sharpe Ratio, Sortino Ratio, Drawdown 128
    Evaluating strategy: Profit Factor, expectancy, risk of ruin 131
    Benchmarks and comparisons: Benchmarking against market indices 133
    Robustness of performance metrics: sensitivity analysis 135
  Risk management and mitigation 137
    Types of trading risks 138
    Risk metrics and models: VaR, CVaR, stress tests 139
    Mitigation strategies: Diversification, hedging, position sizing 140
  Walk-forward analysis for strategy validation 141
    Conducting walk-forward analysis 142
      Analyzing walk-forward results 144
  Building custom backtesting environments 145
    Components of a backtesting environment 146
    Constructing a custom backtesting environment 148

Stress testing and scenario analysis	149
Developing stress test scenarios	*150*
Interpreting stress test results: Impacts and actions	*152*
Paper trading and transition to live trading	154
Analyzing paper trading results	*155*
Transitioning to live trading	*156*
Conclusion	159

6. Implementing AI Models with Trading Platforms 161

Introduction	161
Structure	161
Objectives	162
Overview of popular trading platforms	162
Choosing the right trading platform	*165*
MetaTrader 5 integration	166
Setting up MetaTrader 5 for algorithmic trading	170
Using MQL5 for scripting trading algorithms	171
Testing and optimizing AI strategies on MetaTrader 5	174
Institutional trading platform integration	176
Compliance and regulatory considerations	*178*
Development of AI models for trading	*179*
Monitoring and maintaining deployed AI models	186
Cloud-based trading infrastructure	190
Key components of a cloud-based trading system	*190*
Security and reliability considerations	*191*
Ensuring security and privacy	192
Ensuring data privacy	*194*
Conclusion	195
Multiple choice questions	195
Answers	*196*

7. Getting Prepared for Python Development 197

Introduction 197
Structure 197
Objectives 198
Python for finance 198
    Numerical libraries 198
        NumPy 199
        Pandas 201
        SciPy 205
    Financial libraries 209
        Quantlib 209
        Pyalgotrade 211
        PyAlgoTrade backtesting 211
        Zipline 213
        pyfolio 217
    Visualization tools 220
        Matplotlib 221
        Plotly 223
        seaborn 226
    Additional libraries and tools 228
Version control and collaboration with Git 229
    Git basics 230
        Cloning 230
        Committing 230
        Pushing 230
        Pulling 231
        Branches 231
        Merging 231
        Resolving conflicts 231
        Pull requests 232
Conclusion 232

8. Leveraging Python for Trading Algorithm Development 233

- Introduction 233
- Structure 234
- Objectives 234
- Developing trading algorithms using Python 234
  - *Momentum* 235
  - *Statistical arbitrage* 238
  - *Mean reversion* 241
  - *Pairs trading strategy* 242
  - *Trend Following strategy* 244
  - *Volatility Breakout strategy* 245
  - *Machine learning-based strategy* 246
  - *Options trading strategy* 248
- Troubleshooting and debugging 249
  - *Latency and execution timing* 249
  - *Market data quality and cleansing* 250
  - *Slippage and order execution* 251
  - *Intelligent order routing algorithms* 251
  - *Limit and stop orders* 252
  - *Algorithmic logic errors* 253
  - *Overfitting and model selection* 253
- Unit testing and code quality 255
  - *Python unit testing tools* 256
    - *unittest* 256
    - *pytest* 257
  - *Code quality tools* 258
    - *flake8* 258
    - *black* 258
    - *isort* 258
- Performance optimization and parallelization 259
  - *Profiling Python code* 259
  - *Parallel processing* 261
- Python best practices for algorithmic trading 263

  pip 264
  conda 264
  virtualenv 265
 Conclusion 266

9. Real-world Examples and Case Studies 267
 Introduction 267
 Structure 267
 Objectives 268
 Case study 1: AI-enhanced momentum trading strategy 268
 Case study 2: Machine learning for mean reversion 276
 Case study 3: Sentiment analysis for trading signals 280
 Case study 4: Portfolio optimization with artificial intelligence 283
 Case study 5: AI-driven market-making strategies 286
 Conclusion 288

10. Using LLMs for Algorithmic Trading 289
 Introduction 289
 Structure 289
 Objectives 290
 Introduction to Large Language Models 290
  Tools and libraries 293
 Integration of LLMs in algorithmic trading 294
 Natural Language Processing for market sentiment analysis 295
 Predictive modeling with Large Language Models 296
 Use of GPT for sentiment analysis in trading 297
 Risk management strategies with LLMs 300
 Conclusion 301

11. Future Trends, Challenges, and Opportunities 303
 Introduction 303
 Structure 304
 Objectives 304

Emerging trends in AI and ML for trading 304
    TensorFlow and Keras in AI-based trading... 307
Overcoming common challenges in AI-based trading 308
Preparing for the future of algorithmic trading.. 309
AI-based tools for alternative data analysis 310
Ethical considerations and potential pitfalls 311
Impact of quantum computing on algorithmic trading 312
    Quantum algorithms in finance... 312
Decentralized finance in trading.. 314
    Smart contracts and automated trading 315
Evolving regulatory landscape for AI-driven trading 317
    Global regulatory variations and challenges.. 317
    AI in compliance and risk management 318
    Regulatory Technology innovations.. 318
    Legal frameworks governing AI trading.. 318
    Future policy directions and discussions.. 319
Conclusion.. 319

References... 321

Index 331-336

CHAPTER 1
Introduction to Algorithmic Trading and AI

Introduction

This chapter provides a comprehensive introduction to the dynamic world of **algorithmic trading**, exploring its evolution, the revolutionary integration of **artificial intelligence (AI)** and **machine learning (ML)**, and the key players shaping its future. We will discuss the core aspects of algorithmic trading, examining various trading styles, timeframes, and the balance of risk and return. Additionally, we outline the objectives of this book, clarifying its intended audience and the prerequisites needed to fully engage with the material presented. By unpacking the intricacies of algorithmic trading and its technological advancements, this chapter sets the stage for a deeper understanding of how modern finance is being transformed by these powerful tools.

Structure

In this chapter, we will discuss the following topics:

- Overview of algorithmic trading
- Rise of AI and ML in finance
- Evolution of algorithmic trading
- Key players

- Trading styles and timeframes
- Risk and return in algorithmic trading

Objectives

The objective of this chapter is to furnish readers with a foundational understanding of algorithmic trading, emphasizing its development, the impact of AI and ML, and the pivotal entities driving its progress. We aim to demystify the concepts and methodologies underpinning algorithmic trading, illustrate its evolution over time, and highlight the influence of technological advancements in finance. The chapter is designed to cater to a spectrum of readers, outlining the necessary background knowledge and the target audience, while also exploring diverse trading styles, timeframes, and the critical relationship between risk and return. Through this chapter, readers will gain a holistic view of algorithmic trading, equipping them with the knowledge to navigate and leverage this field effectively.

Overview of algorithmic trading

Algorithmic trading, also recognized as *automated or black-box trading*, leverages advanced computer algorithms to execute trades based on predefined criteria, such as timing, price, and volume, aiming to outperform human trading capabilities in terms of speed and efficiency. This innovative trading strategy seeks to capitalize on minute discrepancies in market prices and other opportunities that require rapid execution, which would be challenging, if not impossible, for human traders to exploit due to the physical limitations of speed and time.

The strategic foundation of algorithmic trading lies in its ability to analyze vast quantities of data, interpret market trends, and execute orders at lightning-fast speeds, thereby maximizing profit opportunities while minimizing the risk of significant human errors. By automating the trading process it ensures a disciplined and consistent approach, devoid of emotional or psychological biases that often affect human traders.

Emerging in the 1970s, the concept of algorithmic trading has evolved dramatically with the digital age, especially in the 21st century. Its adoption was propelled by the advent of high-frequency trading and an increase in algorithm-based strategies among hedge funds and institutional investors. The evolution of this trading form is tightly intertwined with technological advancements, particularly in computational power and speed, allowing the execution of complex trading algorithms and the management of multiple, simultaneous trades across diverse markets with minimal latency.

As a cornerstone of modern financial markets, algorithmic trading contributes significantly to market liquidity and efficiency. It has transformed trading floors from bustling, noisy environments to sophisticated, computer-driven operations, where decisions are made in fractions of a second, a testament to the profound impact of technology on financial markets.

An efficient algorithmic trading system is built on several crucial components, each playing a vital role in the system's overall functionality:

- **Market data feed**: This is the foundation of an algorithmic trading system. It provides real-time or delayed price and volume information that the system uses to make informed decisions. For example, a market data feed might supply the system with the latest stock prices, enabling the algorithm to determine whether to buy or sell based on predefined criteria.
- **Strategy logic:** This is the core of the trading system, the algorithm itself, which defines the trading strategy. It processes the market data to make trading decisions. For instance, a simple strategy logic might be programmed to buy a stock when its 50-day moving average crosses above its 200-day moving average and sell it when the opposite occurs.
- **Execution system**: Once the strategy logic decides on a trade, the execution system is responsible for carrying it out in the market. This component ensures that trades are executed quickly and efficiently, minimizing slippage (the difference between the expected price of a trade and the price at which the trade is executed). For example, if the strategy logic determines it is time to buy 100 shares of a particular stock, the execution system handles the order placement, ensuring it is executed at the best possible price.
- **Risk management**: This crucial component monitors and controls the risk associated with trading activities. It ensures that the trading system adheres to predefined risk parameters, such as maximum drawdown or value-at-risk limits. For instance, if a trading system has a rule not to risk more than 2% of the portfolio on a single trade, the risk management component would ensure that this rule is enforced, possibly by adjusting the size of the trades or stopping trading altogether if the limit is breached.

Each of these components is essential for the smooth operation of an algorithmic trading system, ensuring that it makes informed decisions, executes trades efficiently, and operates within set risk parameters. This table concisely encapsulates the dual-edged nature of algorithmic trading, highlighting its capacity to optimize trading efficiency while also underscoring the need for vigilance regarding its broader market implications.

Following table delves into the multifaceted world of algorithmic trading, highlighting its capability to optimize trade execution and reduce transaction costs, while also presenting significant challenges and benefits:

Aspect	Benefits	Challenges
Trade Execution	Executes trades at the best possible prices, enhancing profitability.	Complexity and sophisticated infrastructure can be prohibitive for some traders.
Transaction Costs	Reduces costs by minimizing human intervention.	Concerns about market fairness and integrity, potentially giving an unfair advantage to some.
Strategy Testing	Enables back testing on historical and real-time data to refine strategies.	Potential for market manipulation through the exploitation of algorithmic speed and complexity.
Decision Consistency	Eliminates emotional and psychological influences, ensuring consistent trading.	Can exacerbate market volatility, especially during turbulent market conditions.

Table 1.1: Benefits and challenges of algorithmic trading

Types of algorithmic trading strategies

There are numerous types of algorithmic trading strategies, each designed to exploit different market conditions or achieve specific investment objectives. Some common strategies are as follows:

- **Trend-following strategies**: Such strategies capitalize on the ability to identify and utilize market trends for profit. A classic example is the moving average crossover strategy. When a short-term moving average (for example, 50-day) surpasses a long-term moving average (for example, 200-day), it might signal a buying opportunity, suggesting the trend will persist upwards. If the short-term average falls below the long-term average, it could signal a selling point.

- **Mean reversion strategies**: These strategies are predicated on the belief that prices will return to an average or mean level over time. The Bollinger Bands strategy is a key example, where the price tends to return to the middle band, a moving average, after reaching the outer bands, which represent standard deviations from the average. Traders might buy or sell based on the asset's deviation from these bands, expecting a return to the average.

- **Arbitrage strategies**: This approach exploits the price discrepancies of identical assets in different markets. For instance, if the price of a stock varies between two exchanges, a trader could buy at a lower price and sell at a higher price, thus securing a guaranteed profit. This is evident when a stock like Apple has a slight price difference between the **New York Stock Exchange (NYSE)** and **London Stock Exchange (LSE)**.

- **High-Frequency Trading (HFT)**: HFT strategies involve executing numerous orders at incredibly fast speeds. Latency arbitrage is a prime example where traders gain an edge by executing trades slightly quicker than others, thanks to superior network infrastructure, thus exploiting brief price differences before they are available to the wider market.

Rise of AI and ML in finance

The emergence of AI and ML marks a significant milestone in the evolution of technology, exerting a profound influence on multiple industries, particularly in the realm of finance. AI is essentially the creation of machines endowed with the capability to emulate human cognitive functions, enabling them to think and learn autonomously. ML, a specialized branch of AI, is concerned with the design of algorithms that equip computers with the capacity to assimilate and infer from data autonomously, without the need for explicit programming.

In the sphere of trading, the application of AI and ML technologies is revolutionizing the process by enabling the analysis of extensive datasets, recognition of complex patterns, and execution of predictive modeling with efficiency and precision that surpass human capability. These advanced technologies leverage statistical methodologies to imbue computer systems with the ability to incrementally improve their task performance, drawing on data insights, without the necessity for direct programming intervention. This capability not only enhances the efficiency and accuracy of financial operations but also opens up new avenues for innovation and strategy in the financial sector.

AI and ML are transforming the financial sector, offering innovative solutions in trading, risk management, and customer engagement. In the trading domain, AI-infused systems are capable of sifting through extensive data sets rapidly, facilitating immediate and informed decision-making where institutes leverage ML to optimize trade executions, thereby substantially lowering transaction costs.

When it comes to risk management, AI and ML stand out by offering a more nuanced and precise assessment of potential risks compared to conventional methodologies. An example is Credit Suisse, which integrates ML algorithms to identify early indicators of market irregularities, enabling them to preemptively address potential threats.

In the realm of customer service, AI is making significant strides, offering real-time, tailored financial advice through chatbots and AI-powered advisory services. Bank of America's virtual assistant, Erica, exemplifies this trend by providing personalized investment guidance to clients instantly. These advancements underscore the transformative impact of AI and ML on the financial industry, streamlining operations, enhancing risk assessment, and improving customer interaction.

Incorporating AI and ML into trading operations significantly boosts both efficiency and effectiveness. These advanced technologies are capable of sifting through market data, timing trades for optimal execution, and uncovering trends that may elude human traders, thereby enhancing the potential for increased returns.

Additionally, AI and ML bring a new dimension to trading strategies by assimilating a broad spectrum of variables and data points, which are typically too complex for human traders to analyze concurrently. This enhanced analytical capability fosters the development of more dynamic and resilient investment approaches, which can mitigate risks and amplify profitability prospects.

While AI and ML revolutionize trading with their numerous advantages, they also introduce specific challenges and limitations that need careful consideration. A significant concern is the opacity of certain ML models, commonly referred to as the 'black box' issue. This opacity makes it challenging to understand or trust the rationale behind specific decisions or predictions made by these models, leading to difficulties in interpreting their outputs.

Moreover, AI and ML systems depend heavily on large datasets for learning and making accurate forecasts. The integrity of this data is vital; if the data is flawed, it can result in inaccurate models and unreliable outcomes. Another risk is overfitting, where a model becomes too attuned to the nuances of the training data, including its noise, and fails to generalize to new, unseen data, affecting its performance in real-world applications.

Evolution of algorithmic trading

The transformation of financial markets began to accelerate with the advent of electronic trading in the late 20th century, marking a departure from traditional floor trading towards digital platforms. This change has had significant repercussions for the markets, facilitating the rise of algorithmic trading and the subsequent incorporation of AI into trading methodologies. Electronic trading heralded a new age of speed and efficiency, with trades being executed in mere milliseconds. The shift towards computer-driven trading has notably increased trading volumes and market liquidity. It also enabled the emergence of **high-frequency trading (HFT)** strategies that leverage small price discrepancies at rapid speeds, thus boosting market liquidity and efficiency.

The utilization of electronic trading platforms has allowed for the extensive collection and analysis of market data, setting the stage for quantitative models in trading. The advent of algorithmic trading, which employs mathematical models to carry out trades based on set criteria, became increasingly prevalent. The capability to swiftly process and analyze large volumes of data has been pivotal in the development of these algorithmic strategies, enabling traders to make more informed decisions and execute trades more proficiently.

Electronic trading's impact on the market is profound, influencing not only transaction speed and efficiency but also market structure and dynamics. For example, while electronic trading has contributed to enhanced market liquidity and reduced transaction costs, it has also sparked concerns regarding market stability and the risk of systemic issues, highlighted by incidents like the 2010 Flash Crash.

Additionally, electronic trading has democratized market access, allowing a wider array of participants to engage in trading, thus intensifying competition and spurring innovation. This has encouraged the creation of novel trading strategies and technologies.

With ongoing advancements, electronic trading is becoming increasingly integrated with AI and ML, signaling a new phase in trading evolution. AI-driven algorithmic trading can analyze intricate market data and execute trades with precision and speed unattainable by humans, representing a significant advancement in market participants' ability to interpret, predict, and react to market movements.

In essence, the rise of electronic trading has acted as a pivotal force in reshaping financial markets, fostering the development of algorithmic trading, and paving the way for AI integration. As technology progresses, the influence of electronic trading is set to deepen, further revolutionizing the financial market landscape.

Key players

Everyday investors and casual market participants are increasingly turning to algorithmic trading to improve their investment approaches. This modern trading method employs computer algorithms to execute trades with a speed and frequency beyond human capability. The integration of artificial intelligence in trading has revolutionized the field, granting casual traders access to advanced analytical tools that were previously exclusive to large institutional investors. Casual traders are now using algorithmic trading to exploit market inefficiencies or to place large orders in a manner that reduces their impact on the market. For example, research has shown that algorithmic trading can enhance market efficiency by narrowing the gap between the buying and selling prices, offering advantages that casual traders can use to improve their trading outcomes. Moreover, platforms such as *Robinhood* [121] and *E*TRADE* [122] have made algorithmic trading more accessible, enabling casual traders to apply automated strategies based on set conditions. These platforms incorporate AI-powered analytics to provide forward-looking insights, helping traders to make better-informed decisions.

Institutional traders and hedge funds are pivotal players. These organizations harness advanced algorithms and artificial intelligence to sift through extensive data, pinpoint trading prospects, and conduct transactions at the most favorable prices. A prime example is Renaissance Technologies, a notable hedge fund, which utilizes mathematical models and statistical methods to inform its trading strategies, showcasing the effectiveness of algorithmic trading for institutional entities. Firms such as *Two Sigma* [58] and *Bridgewater Associates* employ artificial intelligence to analyze a broad spectrum of data, ranging from market dynamics to news reports, in order to forecast trading decisions. The integration of AI allows these hedge funds to quickly adapt to evolving market scenarios and detect nuanced patterns that could suggest upcoming market trends.

Trading intermediaries and digital trading environments play a crucial role in popularizing algorithmic trading. They supply the essential framework and resources that enable both retail and institutional traders to execute their algorithmic trading plans. For example, Interactive Brokers provides a variety of algorithmic trading options that its customers can leverage for more efficient trade execution. Platforms like *MetaTrader* [96] and *NinjaTrader* [123] offer users the ability to create and modify their own trading bots and to test these systems with back-testing tools. This empowers traders to develop, evaluate, and deploy their algorithms. Such platforms support a spectrum of algorithmic strategies, ranging from straightforward automated trading setups to intricate models powered by artificial intelligence that can dynamically adjust to fresh data.

Fintech firms specializing in AI are leading the charge in merging artificial intelligence with financial offerings, creating groundbreaking solutions that redefine algorithmic trading. Entities such as *QuantConnect* [63] and *Alpaca* [124] are at the forefront, offering cloud-based services that facilitate the creation, testing, and execution of trading algorithms through the use of ML and advanced data analysis. These innovative fintech enterprises are broadening the accessibility of AI tools for traders, enabling them to evaluate market tendencies, forecast future price shifts, and streamline trading processes. A case in point is *Kensho Technologies* [125], which leverages AI to scrutinize financial news and economic analyses instantaneously, offering traders timely insights that can shape their trading tactics. In essence, the amalgamation of AI with algorithmic trading is transforming the financial landscape, affecting everyone from solo investors to large hedge funds and fintech firms. The integration of AI and algorithmic trading methods is increasingly becoming a vital factor for securing a competitive edge and improving outcomes in the market.

Trading styles and timeframes

Algorithmic trading has revolutionized the approach to various trading styles, adapting strategies across different timeframes with precision and efficiency unattainable by human traders. This section will discuss how algorithmic trading and AI have been integrated into the core trading styles scalping, day trading, swing trading, and position trading and explores the significance of timeframes ranging from intraday to monthly in shaping trading algorithms:

- **Scalping** is a trading style characterized by extremely short holding periods, often minutes or even seconds, aiming to capture small price changes with high-volume trades. Algorithmic trading excels in this style, as AI can quickly analyze market conditions and execute a large number of trades at a speed beyond human capabilities. For example, AI algorithms can analyze tick-level data to make split-second decisions on trade entries and exits [35].

- **Day trading** involves entering and exiting positions within the same trading day. Algorithmic traders use AI to identify patterns and trends that emerge during the day, executing trades based on predefined criteria without the need to hold any positions overnight. This reduces the risk associated with overnight market fluctuations.

- **Swing trading** captures gains in a stock within an overnight to several weeks timeframe. AI-driven algorithms in swing trading analyze short- to medium-term price patterns and market momentum, making decisions based on a broader set of data points than day trading or scalping.

- **Position trading** is a longer-term strategy where traders hold positions for weeks, months, or even years. While algorithmic trading is often associated with high-frequency strategies, AI can also enhance position trading by analyzing long-term trends and incorporating a wide range of macroeconomic data into the decision-making process.

The choice of timeframe is crucial in algorithmic trading, as it influences the data set used for analysis and the speed at which trading algorithms need to operate. Intraday trading involves a timeframe within a single trading day, requiring algorithms to process information rapidly and make immediate decisions.

- **Daily trading** algorithms analyze data on a day-to-day basis and make decisions at the close or open of the trading day. This style benefits from avoiding overnight market risk and focuses on the patterns that emerge within the trading day.

- **Weekly and monthly timeframes** extend the horizon of the analysis. Algorithms operating on these timeframes analyze longer-term trends, incorporating broader market movements and fundamental analysis into their strategies. While the execution speed is less critical here, the complexity of data analysis increases, as algorithms must discern sustainable trends from short-term fluctuations.

In summary, the integration of AI and algorithmic trading across various styles and timeframes has profoundly impacted the trading landscape. By leveraging vast datasets and executing trades with precision and speed, AI-driven algorithms have opened new possibilities for traders and reshaped traditional trading strategies.

Risk and return in algorithmic trading

Algorithmic trading, while offering substantial opportunities for optimizing returns, also introduces unique risks that must be meticulously managed. This section explores the critical aspects of risk management in algorithmic trading and discusses the evaluation of returns and performance metrics, essential for assessing the effectiveness of trading strategies.

Risk management is a fundamental component of algorithmic trading, as the speed and automation of trades can amplify both gains and losses. Effective risk management strategies are essential to safeguard against significant financial losses and ensure the longevity of the trading algorithm. One of the primary risk management techniques in algorithmic trading is the implementation of stop-loss orders. These orders automatically sell a security when its price reaches a predetermined level, thus limiting potential losses.

Moreover, risk management in algorithmic trading involves the careful design of algorithms to prevent catastrophic failures, such as those resulting from software bugs or system glitches. This includes the establishment of circuit breakers that halt trading in response to extreme market volatility or significant losses within a short timeframe.

Diversification is another key risk management strategy, where algorithms are programmed to trade across various assets or markets to spread risk. By not overconcentrating on a single asset or market, the algorithm can reduce exposure to specific economic events or market conditions.

Assessing the performance of algorithmic trading strategies is crucial for understanding their effectiveness and making informed adjustments. Returns are a primary metric, but they must be evaluated in the context of the risk taken to achieve them.

The Sharpe ratio, for instance, is a widely used metric to assess the risk-adjusted return of an investment. It provides insight into the amount of excess return obtained per unit of risk. A high Sharpe ratio indicates a more efficient investment in terms of risk-return trade-off.

Additionally, the **Sortino ratio**, which differentiates harmful volatility from total overall volatility, is another critical metric for evaluating the performance of trading strategies. It focuses on the downside risk, offering a clearer view of the strategy's risk-adjusted performance in relation to negative returns.

Drawdown, which measures the decline from a peak to a trough in the value of an investment or trading account, is another vital metric. It helps in understanding the potential loss that could occur in a worst-case scenario, providing insights into the strategy's risk profile.

By closely monitoring these metrics, traders and investors can gauge the effectiveness of their algorithmic strategies, making necessary adjustments to optimize performance while managing risk.

In conclusion, managing risk and evaluating returns are pivotal in algorithmic trading. Effective risk management strategies are essential to protect against significant losses, while comprehensive performance metrics provide the insights needed to refine and optimize trading strategies, ensuring sustainable profitability in the fast-paced world of algorithmic trading.

Conclusion

In conclusion, this chapter has provided a thorough exploration of algorithmic trading, detailing its emergence, the transformative role of AI and ML, the evolution within the sector, and the key influencers. We have navigated through the objectives of this book, identified the target audience, and discussed the nuances of various trading styles, timeframes, as well as the intertwined nature of risk and return. In the next chapter, we will discuss trading and high-performance algorithmic trading using AI, providing readers with actionable insights and advanced strategies to enhance their trading performance using artificial intelligence and ML techniques.

CHAPTER 2
AI and Machine Learning Basics for Trading

Introduction

In this chapter, we will provide an in-depth exploration of **Artificial Intelligence (AI)** and **Machine Learning (ML)** in the realm of finance and trading. We will start with an introduction to AI and ML, covering their fundamentals, types, and techniques. Next, we will discuss real-world applications of AI and ML in trading, such as algorithmic trading, sentiment analysis, high-frequency trading, and fraud detection. We will then delve into the various AI and ML frameworks, libraries, and popular algorithms for trading, followed by a thorough examination of the advantages of using AI and ML in trading algorithms. Additionally, we will walk you through the process of building a simple AI-powered trading system and provide insights on AI and ML model selection and evaluation. By the end of this chapter, you will have gained a comprehensive understanding of the role of AI and ML in the ever-evolving world of finance and trading.

Structure

- Introduction to artificial intelligence
- Introduction to machine learning
- AI/ML frameworks and libraries for trading
- Popular AI/ML algorithms for trading

Objectives

This chapter provides an overview of AI and ML in trading, covering their concepts, historical development, and applications. It explains how machine learning enables computers to make informed decisions without explicit programming. Various algorithms like supervised, unsupervised, and reinforcement learning are discussed, showcasing their use in analyzing financial markets. The chapter introduces specialized frameworks and libraries for trading and their importance. It explores popular platforms, and insights into their features and advantages. Additionally, the chapter presents popular AI/ML algorithms like decision trees and neural networks, explaining their principles and challenges. Overall, readers gain a solid foundation to implement AI/ML techniques in real-world trading scenarios.

Introduction to artificial intelligence

Artificial Intelligence (AI) pertains to the creation of computer systems capable of executing tasks that typically necessitate human intelligence, such as recognizing visual information, understanding spoken language, making decisions, and translating languages. In this segment, we will offer an overview of AI, encompassing its description, historical evolution, various categories, methodologies, and its utilization within the realms of finance and trading.

Definition and history of AI

AI involves creating computer systems capable of undertaking activities traditionally needing human intellect, including visual understanding, voice identification, decision-making, and translating languages. AI has grown to encompass a range of subfields, including machine learning and deep learning. Machine learning involves the development of algorithms that allow computer systems to learn from data and improve their performance over time, without being explicitly programmed to do so. On the other hand, deep learning involves using artificial neural networks with many layers, which enables the computer system to learn more complex and abstract patterns from the data.

The concept of AI has its roots in the 1950s, when computer scientists began to explore the possibility of creating machines that could simulate human intelligence [1]. However, the field of AI experienced several setbacks and periods of stagnation over the following decades, leading some to question whether AI was simply an unattainable dream. Nevertheless, recent years have seen an explosion in the development of AI technologies, driven in large part by advances in machine learning and the availability of large datasets.

The history of AI is characterized by a series of key breakthroughs and milestones. One early milestone was the development of the perceptron algorithm in the late 1950s, which enabled machines to learn from examples and make predictions based on input data [2]. Another key breakthrough was the development of expert systems in the 1970s, which allowed machines to make decisions based on complex rules and knowledge [3]. In the 1990s and early 2000s, the development of machine learning algorithms such as support vector machines and neural networks further advanced the field of AI.

Today, AI is a rapidly evolving field with many exciting applications in areas such as healthcare, transportation, and finance. While there are still many challenges to be overcome, including the ethical implications of AI and the potential for job displacement, the continued progress and development of AI is expected to significantly impact how we live and work in the coming decades.

Types of AI: Narrow AI, General AI, and Superintelligent AI

AI can be broadly classified into three types: Narrow AI, General AI, and Superintelligent AI. Narrow AI, also known as weak AI, is designed to perform specific tasks and operate within a defined domain. A common example of narrow AI is image recognition software used in social media platforms. Another example is virtual assistants like Apple's Siri or Amazon's Alexa, which can perform a variety of tasks like setting reminders, making calls, or answering questions.

On the other hand, General AI, also known as **strong AI**, is designed to operate and think like humans in multiple domains. It can understand and respond to natural language, perform complex reasoning and decision-making, and learn from experience. However, creating General AI has proven to be a significant challenge, and no fully functional General AI system exists today. Prominent examples of General AI in popular culture include the robot Ava from the movie Ex Machina or the androids in the TV series Westworld.

Lastly, Superintelligent AI refers to machines that can surpass human intelligence and operate beyond human understanding. It is often associated with the concept of Singularity, a hypothetical point in the future when AI becomes capable of recursively self-improving, leading to an explosion of technological progress. While Superintelligent AI remains a topic of speculative discussion, some experts warn of the potential risks associated with its development, including existential threats to humanity.

While Narrow AI is the most prevalent type of AI today, General AI and Superintelligent AI are still in the early stages of development. As a result, the capabilities of these two types of AI are currently limited. However, significant advances in machine learning and deep learning have led to remarkable breakthroughs in areas like image and speech recognition, natural language processing, and autonomous systems. As technology continues to evolve, we will likely see the emergence of more sophisticated AI systems with broader capabilities and potentially unprecedented impact on our lives.

AI techniques: Expert systems, rule-based systems, and neural networks

AI techniques have been revolutionizing the field of finance and trading, enabling the development of sophisticated models that can analyze vast amounts of data and generate actionable insights. Three key AI techniques used in machine learning are expert systems, rule-based systems, and neural networks. Expert systems are designed to mimic the decision-making processes of human experts by using a knowledge base and a set of inference rules to make decisions based on input data. On the other hand, rule-based systems use predefined rules to make decisions, without necessarily incorporating expert knowledge. Neural networks, modeled after the human brain's structure, use layers of interconnected nodes to learn patterns in data and make predictions.

Each AI technique has its own set of advantages and disadvantages. Expert systems, for instance, can be useful when there is a well-defined problem and a clear set of rules to follow, but may not be able to adapt to new scenarios without significant modifications. Rule-based systems can be faster and more efficient than expert systems but may be limited by the number of rules and may not be able to handle complex decision-making processes. Neural networks, on the other hand, are able to learn complex patterns in data and adapt to new scenarios but may require a large amount of data and computational resources.

In finance and trading, AI techniques can be used for a variety of tasks, such as predicting stock prices, identifying market trends, and detecting fraud. For example, neural networks have been used to predict stock prices based on historical data, with some studies showing improved accuracy compared to traditional statistical models [4]. Rule-based systems can be used for automated trading, where trades are executed based on predefined rules and market conditions. Expert systems have been used in fraud detection, where a set of rules can be used to flag potentially fraudulent transactions based on various factors, such as transaction amounts and locations.

Overall, understanding the strengths and limitations of different AI techniques is crucial for developing effective models for finance and trading. By leveraging the capabilities of different AI techniques and applying them to specific problems, traders and investors can gain a competitive edge in the market.

AI in finance and trading

AI has been revolutionizing the finance and trading industry with its numerous applications, ranging from algorithmic trading to risk management and fraud detection. One of the most significant advantages of using AI in finance and trading is its ability to process large amounts of data in real-time and generate valuable insights for traders and investors. For instance, high-frequency trading algorithms (algo trades) have become popular in the financial industry, where trades are executed at a high speed to take advantage of even the slightest fluctuations in prices.

In addition to algorithmic trading, AI has also been used for risk management in finance. AI-based systems are used to identify and mitigate potential risks in financial transactions by analyzing large amounts of data in real-time, detecting anomalies and unusual patterns, and predicting potential risks based on historical data. For example, BlackRock's Aladdin platform uses AI to manage risk across the firm's investments [5].

Moreover, AI has given rise to the development of robo-advisors, online platforms that provide clients investment advice and portfolio management services. These platforms use AI algorithms to analyze client data and provide personalized investment recommendations, often at a lower cost than traditional financial advisors. Wealthfront, for example, uses AI to create personalized investment portfolios for its clients [6].

Despite the many benefits of AI in finance and trading, several challenges are associated with its implementation. For instance, the lack of interpretability of some AI models can make it difficult to understand how decisions are being made, while the potential for bias in AI models can lead to unfair or inaccurate decisions. To address these challenges, it is essential to carefully design and test AI models before deploying them in real-world settings.

In conclusion, AI has numerous applications in finance and trading, and its use has the potential to significantly improve decision-making and efficiency. By leveraging AI techniques such as expert systems, rule-based systems, and neural networks, financial professionals can gain a competitive edge in the market and better manage risk and fraud.

Introduction to machine learning

Machine learning (ML) is a rapidly growing field that is transforming the way we approach many different areas of technology and business. At its core, ML is about teaching computers to learn from data, enabling them to make predictions and decisions based on patterns and insights that are difficult for humans to identify on their own. In this section, we will provide an introduction to ML, starting with a brief history and definition of the field. We will then explore the three main types of ML - supervised, unsupervised, and reinforcement learning - and the techniques commonly used within each category. Finally, we will examine some of the ways that ML is being applied in finance and trading, highlighting the ways in which this technology is revolutionizing industry and helping investors to make better decisions. By the end of this section, readers should clearly understand what ML is, how it works, and some of the keyways it is being used to drive innovation and growth in a wide range of fields.

Definition and history of ML

Machine learning (ML) is a field of study focused on the development of algorithms and models that enable computers to learn and improve from experience, without being explicitly programmed. This approach has become increasingly important in recent years due to the explosion of data in various fields, including finance and trading. The ability of ML to process and analyze large amounts of data has the potential to significantly improve decision-making and efficiency in these domains.

The history of ML can be traced back to the early days of computer science, where researchers began developing algorithms that could learn from data. However, it was not until the 1990s that ML started to gain traction as a field of study in its own right [7]. Since then, ML has become a key area of research and development, with numerous applications in various fields, including natural language processing, computer vision, and robotics.

There are three main types of ML: supervised learning, unsupervised learning, and reinforcement learning. Supervised learning involves training a model using labeled data, where the input and output values are known. On the other hand, unsupervised learning involves training a model using unlabeled data, where the goal is to discover patterns or structure in the data. Reinforcement learning involves training a model to make decisions in a dynamic environment, where the model receives feedback in the form of rewards or punishments based on its actions [8].

ML techniques such as regression, classification, clustering, and dimensionality reduction have numerous applications in finance and trading. Regression is used to predict continuous numerical values, such as stock prices, while classification is used to predict discrete values, such as whether a stock will increase or decrease in price. Clustering is used to group similar data points together, while dimensionality reduction is used to reduce the number of features in a dataset. By leveraging these techniques, financial professionals can gain valuable insights and make more informed decisions.

Types of ML: Supervised, unsupervised, and reinforcement learning

ML is a subfield of AI that focuses on algorithms and statistical models, enabling computer systems to learn and improve their performance through experience. There are three main types of ML: supervised, unsupervised, and reinforcement learning, each of which has distinct characteristics and applications [9].

Supervised learning is the most common type of ML, where a model is trained on labeled data to make predictions or decisions. The labeled data consists of input-output pairs, with the input being a set of features and the output being the desired result or label. The algorithm's primary goal is to learn a mapping function that can accurately predict the output for new, unseen data. Some applications of supervised learning include image classification, spam detection, and medical diagnosis. For instance, a model can be trained to recognize different types of objects or animals based on a labeled dataset in image classification.

Conversely, unsupervised learning handles data without labels, enabling algorithms to identify underlying structures or patterns without prior information about the desired outcome. Common methods in unsupervised learning include clustering and dimensionality reduction. Unsupervised learning finds applications in areas such as anomaly detection, customer segmentation, and natural language processing. For instance, unsupervised learning techniques like clustering algorithms can be employed to categorize similar traders or investors based on their trading patterns, which can then be used to develop tailored trading strategies or investment recommendations.

Reinforcement learning is a type of ML where an agent learns to make decisions by interacting with an environment, receiving feedback in the form of rewards or penalties, and adjusting its behavior accordingly. Reinforcement learning aims to maximize the cumulative reward over time, which often involves exploring various strategies and learning from mistakes. Applications of reinforcement learning include robotics, game playing, and recommendation systems. For instance, an algorithmic trading system can use reinforcement learning to learn from past trading experiences and modify its behavior to maximize profits while minimizing risk.

Comparing the three types of ML reveals several key differences. Supervised learning is well-suited for tasks with clear input-output relationships and ample labeled data. However, obtaining labeled data can be costly and time-consuming, limiting its applicability in certain situations. Unsupervised learning is advantageous when labeled data is scarce or when the underlying patterns in the data are unknown. However, it can be challenging to interpret the results, and the lack of a ground truth makes evaluating the model's performance difficult. Reinforcement learning is useful in dynamic, interactive environments where the optimal solution may change over time. However, it often requires extensive exploration and can suffer from slow convergence. Additionally, reinforcement learning may struggle with the *credit assignment problem*, which involves determining which actions contributed to a specific outcome [10].

Each of these ML types has its strengths and weaknesses, and the choice of the appropriate method depends on the specific problem and the available data. Supervised learning excels in its predictive accuracy and interpretability when sufficient labeled data is available. In contrast, unsupervised learning can reveal hidden patterns and structures in the data, making it useful for exploratory analysis and data pre-processing. Reinforcement learning, although computationally expensive, is well-suited for solving complex, dynamic problems that require adaptability and decision-making capabilities.

ML techniques: Regression, classification, clustering, and dimensionality reduction

ML techniques are broadly classified into four categories: regression, classification, clustering, and dimensionality reduction. Each technique has unique characteristics and applications, particularly in finance and trading [11].

Regression is an ML technique that focuses on predicting continuous-valued outputs given a set of input features. There are various types of regression, including linear regression, logistic regression, and **support vector regression (SVR)**. Applications of regression in finance and trading include predicting stock prices, portfolio optimization, and forecasting macroeconomic indicators.

On the other hand, classification involves predicting discrete output labels or classes based on input features. Common classification techniques include decision trees, k-nearest neighbor, **support vector machines (SVM)**, and neural networks. In finance and trading, classification algorithms are applied in areas such as credit risk assessment, bankruptcy prediction, and algorithmic trading.

Clustering is an unsupervised ML technique that aims to group data points based on their similarity, without any prior knowledge of the output labels. Clustering algorithms include k-means, hierarchical clustering, and DBSCAN. In finance and trading, clustering is used for tasks such as customer segmentation, portfolio diversification, and market microstructure analysis.

Dimensionality reduction is another unsupervised ML technique that reduces the number of input features while preserving the essential information or structure in the data. Common techniques include **principal component analysis (PCA)**, **t-distributed stochastic neighbor embedding (t-SNE)**, and autoencoders. Applications of dimensionality reduction in finance and trading include financial data visualization, feature selection for prediction models, and noise reduction in high-frequency data[12].

Comparing the different ML techniques reveals several advantages and disadvantages. Regression is well-suited for modeling relationships between variables and predicting continuous outcomes. However, it often assumes linear relationships and can be sensitive to outliers. Classification is useful for predicting discrete outcomes and offers a wide range of algorithms with varying levels of complexity and interpretability. Nonetheless, classification performance can be affected by class imbalance. Clustering is advantageous when the inherent structure of the data is unknown, but the results can be sensitive to the choice of distance metric and initial conditions. Dimensionality reduction is valuable for data compression and visualization, but it can be challenging to select the appropriate technique and determine the optimal number of reduced dimensions.

ML in finance and trading

ML has rapidly gained prominence in the world of finance and trading, transforming various aspects of the industry by improving efficiency, accuracy, and decision-making processes. ML applications in finance and trading cover a wide range of areas, including algorithmic trading, risk management, and fraud detection.

Algorithmic trading, for instance, employs ML techniques to automatically execute trade orders based on predefined rules or strategies. ML models can analyze vast amounts of historical and real-time market data, enabling them to accurately identify trading opportunities and predict market movements. In risk management, ML algorithms can analyze complex financial data, such as credit histories and financial statements, to assess and quantify the risk associated with investments, loans, and other financial products. Furthermore, ML techniques have proven effective in fraud detection, as they can identify patterns and anomalies in financial transactions, potentially mitigating the impact of fraudulent activities on businesses and consumers.

The benefits of incorporating ML in finance and trading are numerous. ML models can process vast amounts of data at high speeds, allowing them to adapt to changing market conditions and offer real-time insights. Additionally, ML algorithms can uncover complex patterns and relationships in financial data, enabling more accurate predictions and better-informed decision-making processes. Moreover, the automation of tasks through ML can reduce human errors, emotional decisions and biases resulting in more objective and consistent outcomes.

However, there are also challenges associated with using ML in finance and trading. The performance of ML models heavily depends on the quality and relevance of the data used for training, which may be susceptible to noise, missing values, or other inconsistencies. Moreover, the black-box nature of some ML algorithms, such as deep neural networks, can make it difficult to interpret and explain their predictions, raising concerns about transparency and accountability. Lastly, the rapid pace of technological advancements in ML can create a competitive landscape, where organizations must continuously invest in research and development to stay ahead of their competitors.

Examples of successful applications of ML in finance and trading include **high-frequency trading (HFT)** and robo-advisors. HFT is a form of algorithmic trading that uses sophisticated ML algorithms to execute a large number of orders within fractions of a second, capitalizing on small price discrepancies in the market. Robo-advisors, on the other hand, are automated investment platforms that leverage ML algorithms to create and manage investment portfolios based on the clients' risk preferences and financial goals, offering a cost-effective alternative to traditional financial advisors.

Real-world applications of AI/ML in trading

AI and ML are rapidly transforming the world of trading, providing investors with new tools for making more informed decisions and improving portfolio performance. In this section, we will explore some of the real-world applications of AI and ML in trading, focusing on four key areas: algorithmic trading and portfolio management, sentiment analysis for news and social media, high-frequency trading and market making, and fraud detection and risk management. Each of these areas represents a critical component of modern trading, and AI and ML have the potential to revolutionize the way we approach each of them. In the following section, we will delve into each of these applications in more detail, exploring how AI and ML are used to create smarter, more efficient trading systems that can help investors achieve better results in an increasingly complex and fast-paced market.

Algorithmic trading and portfolio management

The advent of AI and ML has revolutionized the field of finance, particularly in the areas of algorithmic trading and portfolio management. These technologies have enabled financial professionals to develop and deploy advanced trading strategies, optimize portfolios, and manage risk more effectively.

In the realm of algorithmic trading, AI and ML have been employed to develop predictive models that can generate trading signals based on historical and real-time data. These models can analyze large volumes of data, uncover hidden patterns and relationships, and make accurate predictions about the future behavior of financial assets. For instance, hedge funds such as Renaissance Technologies and Two Sigma Investments have successfully utilized AI-driven models to develop quantitative trading strategies that have consistently outperformed traditional investment approaches (Patterson, 2010).

One notable example of AI-driven algorithmic trading is the use of deep learning techniques, such as **recurrent neural networks (RNNs)** and **long short-term memory (LSTM)** networks, to predict stock prices or other financial time series data. These models can capture complex temporal dependencies and adapt to changing market conditions, making them well-suited for predicting financial asset prices and generating profitable trading signals for long data sequences.

AI and ML have also been applied to the field of portfolio management, where they can assist in asset allocation, risk management, and financial evaluation. One example is the use of **reinforcement learning (RL)** algorithms, such as **Q-learning or deep Q-networks (DQNs)**, to optimize portfolio allocation by learning to make investment decisions based on historical and real-time data.

In addition, AI-driven techniques have been employed to manage risk in investment portfolios more effectively. For instance, unsupervised learning methods such as clustering or **principal component analysis (PCA)** can be used to identify and group assets with similar risk characteristics, enabling portfolio managers to diversify their holdings and reduce portfolio risk.

AI-powered portfolio management has also been successful in the context of robo-advisory services, where AI-driven algorithms are used to provide personalized investment advice and portfolio management services to individual investors. Companies like Betterment and Wealthfront have utilized AI to create low-cost, automated investment platforms that offer tailored asset allocation and rebalancing strategies based on each investor's unique risk profile and investment objectives [13].

Sentiment analysis for news and social media

Sentiment analysis, also known as opinion mining, is a powerful AI/ML-driven technique that has gained significant traction in the financial sector, particularly in trading. This approach involves extracting, processing, and analyzing textual data from news articles, social media platforms, and other online sources to gauge the sentiment or opinions surrounding financial assets, such as stocks, commodities, and currencies.

The ability to assess the sentiment associated with financial assets is crucial for traders, as it can help them anticipate market trends, identify trading opportunities, and manage risk more effectively. AI/ML techniques, such as **natural language processing (NLP)**, text mining, and deep learning, have been employed to develop sentiment analysis models that can analyze large volumes of unstructured textual data and generate actionable insights for trading.

For example, researchers have demonstrated the potential of using AI-driven sentiment analysis to predict stock price movements based on the sentiment extracted from financial news articles [14]. In a seminal study [14], found that negative sentiment in the news was associated with lower stock returns, highlighting the potential value of sentiment analysis for trading and investment decisions.

Social media platforms, such as Twitter, have also emerged as a valuable source of sentiment data for traders, as they can provide real-time insights into the opinions and emotions of market participants. AI/ML techniques have been employed to analyze the sentiment of tweets related to specific financial assets, with researchers finding a strong correlation between social media sentiment and stock price movements [15].

A notable real-world application of sentiment analysis in trading is the use of AI-driven algorithms to develop sentiment-based trading strategies. For instance, MarketPsych, a financial technology company, offers a sentiment data feed that incorporates information from news articles and social media sources, which can be integrated into trading algorithms to generate buy and sell signals based on the prevailing sentiment [16].

Furthermore, hedge funds and asset management firms have begun incorporating AI-driven sentiment analysis into their investment strategies, utilizing models that can process vast amounts of textual data and predict market trends based on the sentiment of market participants. One such example is the Point72 Asset Management fund, which has integrated sentiment analysis into its investment process to better understand market dynamics and identify potential trading opportunities [17].

High-frequency trading and market making

High-frequency trading (HFT) is a specialized form of algorithmic trading that involves the execution of a large number of orders at extremely high speeds, often in the order of milliseconds or microseconds. HFT firms leverage advanced technology, including AI and ML algorithms, to analyze market data in real-time, identify short-lived trading opportunities, and capitalize on small price discrepancies or span across different markets or assets.

AI and ML have been instrumental in enhancing the capabilities of HFT firms, enabling them to develop sophisticated trading strategies that can adapt to changing market conditions and exploit fleeting inefficiencies more effectively. For instance, deep learning models, such as **convolutional neural networks (CNNs)** and reinforcement learning algorithms, have been employed to predict short-term price movements or market imbalances, providing valuable trading signals for HFT strategies[18].

Market making is another area within trading where AI and ML have demonstrated significant potential. Market makers are financial institutions or individuals who provide liquidity to markets by continuously offering to buy and sell financial instruments at specified bid and ask prices. The primary objective of market makers is to profit from the bid-ask spread while managing their inventory risk and exposure to adverse price movements.

AI/ML-driven techniques have been employed by market makers to optimize their quoting strategies, manage their inventory, and assess market conditions more effectively. For example, reinforcement learning algorithms, such as Q-learning or policy gradient methods, have been used to develop adaptive market-making strategies that can learn the optimal bid and ask prices based on historical and real-time data [19].

In addition, unsupervised learning methods, such as clustering or anomaly detection, have been applied to monitor market conditions, identify unusual trading patterns, and detect potential market manipulations, such as spoofing or layering. By incorporating AI/ML techniques into their market-making activities, financial institutions can improve their pricing efficiency, better manage their inventory risk, and enhance their overall trading performance.

One notable example of AI-driven HFT and market making in practice is Virtu Financial, a leading global market-making firm that utilizes advanced technology, including AI and ML algorithms, to provide liquidity and execute trades across multiple asset classes and markets[20]. Virtu's success in HFT and market making can be attributed to its ability to process and analyze vast amounts of data in real-time, identify short-lived trading opportunities, and manage risk effectively, highlighting the power of AI and ML in transforming the landscape of trading.

Fraud detection and risk management

The integration of AI and ML into the financial sector has proven particularly beneficial in the areas of fraud detection and risk management. By leveraging these advanced technologies, financial institutions can identify suspicious activities, minimize losses, and safeguard their operations more effectively.

Fraud detection is a critical aspect of the financial industry, as fraudulent activities can lead to significant financial losses and damage to a firm's reputation. AI and ML techniques have been employed to develop fraud detection models that can analyze large volumes of transactional data, identify unusual patterns, and flag potentially fraudulent activities for further investigation.

One example of an AI-driven fraud detection technique is the use of unsupervised learning methods, such as clustering or anomaly detection algorithms, to group transactions based on their similarity and identify outliers that may indicate fraud. Supervised learning techniques, such as **support vector machines (SVMs)** or random forests, have also been employed to develop classification models that can distinguish between legitimate and fraudulent transactions based on historical data.

Deep learning models, such as autoencoders or **recurrent neural networks (RNNs)**, have been applied to fraud detection, demonstrating their ability to capture complex relationships and patterns in the data that may be indicative of fraudulent activities. Furthermore, AI-driven fraud detection models can be continuously updated with new data, allowing them to adapt to changing fraud patterns and maintain their accuracy over time[21].

Risk management is another crucial aspect of the financial sector, as financial institutions need to assess and manage various types of risks, including market, credit, and operational risks. AI and ML techniques have been utilized to develop risk management models that can analyze vast amounts of data, identify potential risk factors, and estimate the likelihood of adverse events.

For example, AI-driven techniques have been applied to credit risk assessment, where ML models such as logistic regression, decision trees, or neural networks are used to predict the probability of default for individual borrowers based on their financial data and credit history. Additionally, AI and ML models can be employed to estimate value-at-risk (VaR) and other risk measures, enabling financial institutions to manage their exposure to market risk more effectively [22].

AI and ML techniques have also been applied to operational risk management, where they can be used to identify potential risk events, assess their potential impact, and prioritize mitigation efforts. For instance, **natural language processing (NLP)** algorithms can be employed to analyze unstructured data, such as emails or internal documents, and identify potential risks or vulnerabilities that may not be evident from structured data alone.

AI/ML frameworks and libraries for trading

AI and ML are transforming the world of trading, enabling investors to make more informed decisions and achieve better results. To harness the power of AI and ML, traders need access to a range of frameworks and libraries that can help them to develop, train, and deploy these cutting-edge technologies. In this section, we will explore some of the most popular and widely used frameworks and libraries for trading, starting with Conda, a popular package management system that allows traders to easily install and manage a wide range of software packages. We will then delve into some of the most popular ML frameworks and libraries, including TensorFlow and Keras, PyTorch, scikit-learn, pandas and NumPy, Gensim and NLTK for **natural language processing (NLP)**, and OpenAI Gym and RLlib for reinforcement learning. Each of these frameworks and libraries offers unique capabilities and advantages, enabling traders to build sophisticated models and algorithms to help them gain an edge in the markets. By the end of this section, readers should have a clear understanding of the different AI/ML frameworks and libraries available for trading and be able to choose the ones best suited to their specific needs and goals:

- **PyAlgoTrade (https://gbeced.github.io/pyalgotrade)**: A Python library for backtesting trading strategies that provides a range of tools for technical analysis, event-driven backtesting, and optimization.

- **Quantopian (https://github.com/quantopian)**: A platform for developing and testing trading strategies that provides access to historical market data, backtesting tools, and a community of developers and traders.

- **TradingView (https://www.tradingview.com)**: A web-based platform that provides tools for backtesting trading strategies using historical market data, as well as a range of other features such as real-time charting, alerts, and social trading.

- **TradeStation (https://www.tradestation.com)**: A platform for developing and testing trading strategies that provides access to historical market data, backtesting tools, and a range of other features such as real-time charting, alerts, and automated trading.

- **Amibroker (https://www.amibroker.com)**: A platform for developing and testing trading strategies that provides access to historical market data, backtesting tools, and a range of other features such as real-time charting, alerts, and automated trading.

- **Conda (https://docs.conda.io)**: A popular package manager and environment management system that simplifies the installation and configuration of Python packages and dependencies.

- **TensorFlow (https://www.tensorflow.org) and Keras (https://keras.io)**: TensorFlow is a popular open-source machine learning framework developed by Google that provides a wide range of tools for building and deploying machine learning models. Keras is a high-level API that runs on top of TensorFlow and simplifies the process of building and training deep learning models.

- **PyTorch (https://pytorch.org)**: An open-source machine learning framework developed by Facebook that provides a range of tools for building and deploying deep learning models.

- **scikit-learn (https://scikit-learn.org)**: A popular open-source machine learning library that provides a range of algorithms for classification, regression, clustering, and dimensionality reduction.

- **NumPy (https://numpy.org) , pandas (https://pandas.pydata.org) , and SciPy (https://scipy.org)**: These are Python libraries that provide tools for data manipulation and analysis, including arrays, data frames, and statistical analysis.

- **Zipline (https://github.com/quantopian/zipline) and backtrader (https://www.backtrader.com)**: These are Python libraries that provide tools for backtesting trading strategies using historical data.

- **Ccxt (https://docs.ccxt.com) and Alpaca (https://alpaca.markets)**: These are Python libraries that provide API-based trading interfaces to cryptocurrency and stock trading platforms.

- **Matplotlib (https://matplotlib.org) , Seaborn (https://seaborn.pydata.org) , and Plotly (https://plotly.com/python)**: These are Python libraries that provide tools for data visualization, including line plots, scatter plots, and heat maps.

Overall, the combination of these tools and libraries provides a comprehensive set of tools for backtesting, analyzing, and deploying trading strategies using machine learning and other advanced techniques.

Popular AI/ML algorithms for trading

This section explores some of the most popular and widely used AI/ML algorithms for trading. We began by discussing time series forecasting algorithms such as ARIMA, GARCH, and LSTM, which are used to analyze historical data and make predictions about future trends. We then moved on to classification algorithms such as logistic regression, SVM, and random forests, which are used to identify patterns and classify data into different categories.

Reinforcement learning algorithms, such as Q-learning, DDPG, and PPO, were also discussed in this section. These algorithms are used to train agents to make decisions based on feedback from the environment, enabling them to learn and improve over time. Finally, we explored natural language processing algorithms such as sentiment analysis and topic modeling, which are used to analyze text data and extract insights about public sentiment and market trends.

Overall, the algorithms discussed in this section represent some of the most powerful and versatile tools available to traders today, offering new ways to analyze data, make predictions, and automate decision-making processes. By incorporating these algorithms into their trading strategies, traders can gain a competitive edge in the fast-paced and ever-evolving world of finance.

Time series forecasting: ARIMA, GARCH, and LSTM

Autoregressive Integrated Moving Average (ARIMA) which stands for Autoregressive Integrated Moving Average, is a popular statistical method used for time series forecasting, particularly in the context of finance and trading. The technique is based on three main components: **autoregression (AR)**, **differencing (I)**, and **moving average (MA)**. The AR component describes the relationship between an observation and a number of its lagged values, while the MA component models the relationship between an observation and a residual error from a moving average model applied to lagged observations. The I component refers to the differencing applied to the time series to make it stationary, a key assumption for the ARIMA model [23].

ARIMA models have been widely applied in finance and trading, particularly in the areas of stock price prediction, foreign exchange rate forecasting, and commodity price modeling. For instance, ARIMA models were employed by Adebiyi et al. (2014) to predict the closing stock prices of the Nigerian Stock Exchange, finding that the models provided accurate short-term forecasts. Similarly, Meese and Rogoff (1983) used ARIMA models to predict the future values of major exchange rates, outperforming more complex structural models in out-of-sample forecasting accuracy.

Generalized Autoregressive Conditional Heteroskedasticity (GARCH): The GARCH model is a widely used statistical tool for modeling and forecasting the volatility of financial time series data. The GARCH model is an extension of the **Autoregressive Conditional Heteroskedasticity (ARCH)** model introduced by Engle (1982). The main distinction between the two models is that GARCH incorporates both the autoregressive component and the lagged conditional variance in the estimation process, whereas the ARCH model only considers the latter.

GARCH models have found extensive applications in trading and finance, particularly in the realm of volatility forecasting. This is because accurate volatility forecasts are crucial for risk management, option pricing, and portfolio optimization. For instance, GARCH models have been employed to estimate and forecast the volatility of stock market returns, currency exchange rates, and commodity prices. One notable real-world example is the use of GARCH models by financial institutions for calculating the **Value-at-Risk (VaR)** metric, which estimates the potential loss of a portfolio over a given time horizon at a specific confidence level [24].

Long Short-Term Memory (LSTM): LSTM is a type of **recurrent neural network (RNN)** architecture that was introduced by *Hochreiter* and *Schmidhuber* (1997). It is specifically designed to address the vanishing gradient problem, which occurs when training traditional RNNs on long sequences of data. The vanishing gradient problem arises due to the exponential decay of gradients during the backpropagation process, leading to difficulties in learning long-range dependencies in the data. LSTM networks overcome this issue by incorporating memory cells and gating mechanisms that allow them to retain and selectively update information over long sequences.

LSTM networks have found numerous applications in trading and finance, particularly in the areas of stock price prediction and portfolio optimization. One of the main advantages of LSTM networks in financial time series analysis is their ability to capture complex non-linear relationships and long-range dependencies that are often present in financial data. For instance, researchers have employed LSTM networks to predict stock prices based on historical price data and various technical and fundamental indicators. Furthermore, LSTM networks have been utilized to optimize portfolio selection by predicting the future performance of different assets and determining the optimal asset allocation to maximize returns and minimize risk [25].

Example of Time Series forecasting in Meta stock using ARIMA Model

The code performs time series forecasting using an ARIMA model on the historical closing prices of a stock. The data is downloaded using the finance library and split into train and test sets. An ARIMA model fits the train data and is used to make test data predictions. The mean squared error is calculated as a measure of the model's accuracy. Finally, the actual and predicted prices are plotted using Matplotlib. The specific stock used in the example is Facebook (ticker symbol "FB"), but this can be replaced with any other stock of interest:

```
1.  import pandas as pd
2.  import numpy as np
3.  import matplotlib.pyplot as plt
4.  from statsmodels.tsa.arima.model import ARIMA
5.  from sklearn.metrics import mean_squared_error
6.  import yfinance as yf
7.
8.  # Load your dataset (replace the ticker symbol with your stock of
    interest)
9.  ticker = "META"
10. data = yf.download(ticker, start="2016-01-01", end="2022-03-27")
11.
12. # Use the closing price for the ARIMA model
13. closing_prices = data["Close"]
14.
15. # Split the data into train and test sets
16. train_data = closing_prices[:int(0.8 * len(closing_prices))]
17. test_data = closing_prices[int(0.8 * len(closing_prices)):]
18.
19. # Fit the ARIMA model (p, d, q) - you may need to find the optimal
    values for your dataset
```

```
20. model = ARIMA(train_data, order=(1, 1, 1))
21. model_fit = model.fit()
22.
23. # Make predictions on the test set
24. predictions = model_fit.forecast(steps=len(test_data))
25.
26. # Calculate the mean squared error
27. mse = mean_squared_error(test_data, predictions)
28.
29. # Plot the predictions against the actual values
30. plt.figure(figsize=(10, 6))
31. plt.plot(test_data.index, test_data, label="Actual Prices")
32. plt.plot(test_data.index, predictions, label="Predicted Prices")
33. plt.legend()
34. plt.xlabel("Date")
35. plt.ylabel("Stock Price")
36. plt.title(f"ARIMA {ticker} Stock Price Forecasting")
37. plt.show()
38.
39. print("Mean Squared Error:", mse)
```

Classification algorithms: Logistic regression, SVM, and random forests

Logistic regression: Logistic regression is a method used to predict the chance of something happening (binary outcome) based on some factors. It is an extension of a technique called linear regression, which is used for continuous outcomes. For example, logistic regression can be used to predict the probability of a person getting a disease based on their age, gender, and other factors. The technique uses a function that converts the combination of the factors into a probability value between 0 and 1.

In the context of trading and finance, logistic regression has been applied to various tasks, such as credit risk assessment and bankruptcy prediction. For instance, logistic regression can be employed to predict the probability of a borrower defaulting on a loan based on factors such as income, credit score, and debt-to-income ratio [26]. Financial institutions can use this information to assess the creditworthiness of potential borrowers and make lending decisions. Similarly, logistic regression has been utilized in bankruptcy prediction models, which aim to identify companies at risk of financial distress based on financial ratios and other firm-specific characteristics[27]. These models can provide valuable information to investors, creditors, and regulators, helping them make informed decisions related to investment, lending, and regulatory oversight.

Support Vector Machines (SVM) in trading and finance: SVM is a versatile machine learning algorithm that has gained significant attention in the field of trading and finance due to its effectiveness in classification and regression tasks. SVM focuses on finding an optimal hyperplane that separates two classes of data with the largest margin possible, ensuring better generalization and classification performance. In recent years, SVM has been applied to various financial problems such as algorithmic trading, market trend prediction, and risk management with promising results.

SVM has demonstrated remarkable success in various financial applications, including algorithmic trading and market trend prediction. In algorithmic trading, SVM has been used to predict stock price movements, allowing for the creation of automated trading strategies. For example, *Cao* and *Tay* (2001) successfully applied SVM to forecast the daily stock prices of IBM and Boeing, outperforming other techniques such as artificial neural networks and linear regression. Additionally, *Ince* and *Trafalis* (2007) employed SVM to predict the direction of the S&P 500 index, achieving superior accuracy compared to traditional methods.

Random Forests in trading and finance: Random forests is a robust ensemble learning technique that combines multiple decision trees to improve predictive accuracy and prevent overfitting. The method has been widely employed in trading and finance to tackle various problems, including fraud detection and financial distress prediction, due to its capability to handle large amounts of data, high-dimensional feature spaces, and intricate interactions among variables.

Random forests have been extensively applied in trading and finance for various purposes, such as fraud detection and financial distress prediction. For example, *Phua, Lee, Smith,* and *Gayler* (2010) employed random forests to detect credit card fraud, achieving high detection rates and outperforming other techniques, including logistic regression and neural networks. The ability of random forests to capture complex patterns and interactions among variables renders them well-suited for detecting fraudulent activities in large, high-dimensional datasets.

Another notable application of random forests is predicting financial distress in companies. *Sun* and *Li* (2012) used random forests to predict corporate bankruptcy and found that it outperformed other machine learning algorithms, including support vector machines and artificial neural networks. The high accuracy of random forests in predicting financial distress can be attributed to its ability to handle noisy data and nonlinear relationships among variables, which are commonly observed in financial data.

Example of using Random Forests to determine price movement

This is a Python code that downloads historical stock data for Apple (AAPL) from Yahoo Finance using the **yfinance** library. It then computes two technical indicators - **simple moving average (SMA)** and **exponential moving average (EMA)** - for trading signals. Next, it defines the target variable as a binary value representing whether the stock price increased or decreased. The data is then split into training and testing sets using the **train_test_split** function from the **sklearn.model_selection** module. The **RandomForestClassifier** from the **sklearn.ensemble** module is used to train a Random Forest model on the training data. The model is then used to make predictions on the testing data, and the accuracy of the model is calculated using the **accuracy_score** function from the **sklearn.metrics** module. Finally, the accuracy of the model is printed to the console:

```
1. import yfinance as yf
2. import pandas as pd
3. import numpy as np
4. from sklearn.model_selection import train_test_split
5. from sklearn.ensemble import RandomForestClassifier
6. from sklearn.metrics import accuracy_score
7.
8. # Download historical stock data
9. ticker = 'AAPL'
10. stock_data = yf.download(ticker, start='2010-01-01', end='2021-09-30')
11.
12. # Compute technical indicators for trading signals
13. stock_data['SMA'] = stock_data['Close'].rolling(window=14).mean()
14. stock_data['EMA'] = stock_data['Close'].ewm(span=14, adjust=False).mean()
15. stock_data.dropna(inplace=True)
16.
17. # Define target variable (price increase or decrease)
18. stock_data['Target'] = np.where(stock_data['Close'].shift(-1) > stock_data['Close'], 1, 0)
19.
20. # Prepare data for training and testing
21. X = stock_data[['SMA', 'EMA']]
22. y = stock_data['Target']
23. X_train, X_test, y_train, y_test = train_test_split(X, y, test_size=0.2, shuffle=False)
24.
25. # Train the Random Forest model
26. rf_model = RandomForestClassifier(n_estimators=100, random_state=42)
27. rf_model.fit(X_train, y_train)
28.
29. # Make predictions and calculate accuracy
```

```
30. y_pred = rf_model.predict(X_test)
31. accuracy = accuracy_score(y_test, y_pred)
32.
33. print(f'Accuracy of the Random Forest model: {accuracy:.2f}')
```

Reinforcement learning: Q-learning, DDPG, and PPO

Q-Learning in trading and finance: Q-learning is a widely used reinforcement learning algorithm that allows agents to learn optimal policies by interacting with an environment. The technique has garnered significant attention in the domain of trading and finance, with applications ranging from optimal trading strategies to portfolio management.

Q-learning has been applied to various problems in trading and finance, including the optimization of trading strategies and portfolio management. In one study, *Huang, Zheng,* and *Zhao* (2017) employed Q-learning to develop an optimal trading strategy for stocks in the Chinese market. The Q-learning agent successfully devised a trading strategy that outperformed benchmark indices and other trading algorithms by learning from historical stock price data.

Another application of Q-learning in finance is portfolio management. *Deng, Gao,* and *Yang* (2019) developed a Q-learning-based portfolio management system to allocate funds among a set of assets. The Q-learning agent dynamically adjusted the asset allocation based on market conditions, with the goal of maximizing expected returns while minimizing risk. The authors found that the Q-learning-based approach yielded superior performance compared to traditional portfolio management strategies, such as mean-variance optimization and risk-parity allocation.

Deep Deterministic Policy Gradient in trading and finance

Deep Deterministic Policy Gradient (DDPG) is a reinforcement learning algorithm that combines the strengths of both deep learning and policy gradient methods to solve problems. DDPG has been applied to various complex problems in trading and finance, such as multi-asset trading and portfolio optimization. DDPG is based on the actor-critic framework, which consists of two neural networks, an actor and a critic, working together to learn an optimal policy [28]. The actor network learns the policy, determining the best action to take in a given state, while the critic network evaluates the value function of the state-action pairs, providing feedback to the actor network to improve its policy.

DDPG has shown great promise in tackling continuous action space problems in trading and finance. One notable application is multi-asset trading, where the agent must decide on the allocation of assets in a portfolio to maximize returns while minimizing risk[28]. The continuous action space in this problem, represented by the percentage of each asset in the portfolio, makes DDPG an ideal candidate for solving it.

Proximal Policy Optimization

Proximal Policy Optimization (PPO) is a modern, advanced **reinforcement learning (RL)** algorithm that has gained significant popularity in recent years due to its sample efficiency and ease of implementation. PPO is an actor-critic algorithm that operates on the same fundamental principles as other policy optimization methods. It aims to improve the policy iteratively by optimizing a surrogate objective function derived from the estimated advantage of the actions taken by the agent during training.

In the context of trading and finance, PPO has the potential to address various challenges, including risk-sensitive strategies and high-frequency trading. For instance, PPO's trust region optimization can be employed to develop risk-sensitive strategies that balance expected returns with risk management [29]. By incorporating risk measures, such as the Sharpe ratio or the **Value-at-Risk (VaR)**, into the objective function, PPO can adapt its policy to consider the expected returns and associated risks.

Moreover, PPO's sample efficiency and scalability make it a suitable candidate for **high-frequency trading (HFT)** applications, where rapid decision-making is crucial. HFT firms often operate on short time horizons, executing thousands of trades per second. PPO's ability to learn quickly from limited data samples can be advantageous in these scenarios, enabling the agent to adapt to rapidly changing market conditions and exploit short-lived opportunities.

Natural language processing: Sentiment analysis and topic modeling

In this section, we will discuss about natural language processing. We will learn about sentiment analysis and topic modeling.

Sentiment analysis

Sentiment analysis, also known as opinion mining or emotion AI, is a subfield of **natural language processing (NLP)** that aims to determine the sentiment, emotion, or opinion expressed in textual data. Sentiment analysis involves extracting, identifying, and classifying opinions and emotions from text, often in terms of polarity (positive, negative, or neutral) or specific emotions, such as joy, sadness, or anger. In the context of trading and finance, sentiment analysis plays a crucial role in uncovering hidden patterns and trends that may affect market dynamics and investment decisions.

In trading and finance, sentiment analysis has been employed to predict stock price movements based on news articles and social media data. For instance, researchers have used sentiment analysis to measure the impact of financial news articles on stock prices, finding that the sentiment of news content can influence short-term stock returns [30]. Social media platforms, such as Twitter, have also been explored as sources of market sentiment, with studies showing that tweet sentiment can predict stock market movements.

Topic modeling

Topic modeling is an unsupervised machine learning technique used to discover hidden thematic structures within large collections of documents. This method allows for the extraction of underlying patterns or *topics* from unstructured text data, making it easier to analyze and interpret large volumes of textual information.

In the realm of trading and finance, topic modeling has been applied to various types of textual data, such as financial news, earnings call transcripts, and regulatory filings. For instance, topic modeling has been used to analyze financial news articles, revealing thematic structures that can be used to monitor market trends and inform investment decisions[31]. In a similar vein, researchers have employed LDA to analyze earnings call transcripts, discovering latent topics that can help predict stock price movements[32].

Furthermore, topic modeling can be applied to regulatory filings, such as 10-K and 10-Q reports, to identify risk factors and assess the financial health of publicly traded companies [33]. By leveraging topic modeling techniques, investors can gain a deeper understanding of the factors driving the performance of individual stocks or entire market sectors, ultimately leading to more informed investment decisions.

Example of using Topic Modeling

This Python code demonstrates how to preprocess financial news headlines using the NLTK library and train an **Latent Dirichlet Allocation (LDA)** model to extract topics from the text.

The code first imports the necessary libraries, including NLTK, Gensim, and WordNetLemmatizer. It then defines a list of sample financial news headlines, which will be preprocessed and used to train the LDA model.

The `preprocess()` function defined in the code tokenizes the text, converts all words to lowercase, removes stop words, and lemmatizes the remaining words. The function is applied to each headline using a list comprehension, and the resulting tokenized headlines are stored in the `tokenized_headlines` list.

Next, the code creates a dictionary and corpus for the LDA model using the Gensim library. The dictionary is created using the tokenized headlines, and the corpus is created by converting each headline to a bag-of-words representation using the dictionary.

The LDA model is then trained on the corpus, with `num_topics` set to 2. Finally, the code prints out the topics extracted by the model along with their corresponding probability distributions.

```
1. import nltk
2. from nltk.corpus import stopwords
3. from nltk.stem import WordNetLemmatizer
4. from gensim import corpora, models
5. nltk.download('stopwords')
```

```
6. nltk.download('wordnet')
7. nltk.download('punkt')
8.
9. # Sample financial news headlines
10. headlines = [
11.     "Company X reports better-than-expected earnings for Q3",
12.     "Company Y struggles with supply chain issues amid global crisis",
13.     "Company Z announces a major acquisition to expand market share",
14. ]
15.
16. # Preprocessing
17. lemmatizer = WordNetLemmatizer()
18. stop_words = set(stopwords.words("english"))
19.
20. def preprocess(text):
21.     tokens = nltk.word_tokenize(text.lower())
22.     tokens = [lemmatizer.lemmatize(token) for token in tokens if token.isalpha()]
23.     tokens = [token for token in tokens if token not in stop_words]
24.     return tokens
25.
26. # Tokenize and preprocess the headlines
27. tokenized_headlines = [preprocess(headline) for headline in headlines]
28.
29. # Create a dictionary and corpus for LDA
30. dictionary = corpora.Dictionary(tokenized_headlines)
31. corpus = [dictionary.doc2bow(headline) for headline in tokenized_headlines]
32.
33. # Train LDA model
34. num_topics = 2
35. lda_model = models.ldamodel.LdaModel(corpus, num_topics=num_topics, id2word=dictionary, passes=20)
36.
37. # Print topics
38. topics = lda_model.print_topics()
39. for topic in topics:
40.     print(topic)
```

Output:

```
(0, '0.115*"company" + 0.114*"x" + 0.114*"earnings" + 0.114*"report" +
0.039*"share" + 0.039*"major" + 0.039*"acquisition" + 0.039*"crisis" +
0.039*"z" + 0.039*"announces"')
(1, '0.100*"company" + 0.060*"amid" + 0.060*"struggle" + 0.060*"issue"
+ 0.060*"chain" + 0.060*"global" + 0.060*"expand" + 0.060*"market" +
0.060*"supply" + 0.060*"announces"')
```

For each topic, the weights represent the importance of each word in the topic. For example, in topic 0, the words **company**, **x**, **learnings**, and **report** have the highest weights, indicating that they are the most important words in defining this topic. Similarly, in topic 1, the word **company** has the highest weight, followed by words like **amid**, **struggle**, **issue**, and so on.

Based on the word distributions, you can interpret the topics. For instance, topic 0 could be related to company earnings reports, while topic 1 might be about supply chain issues and market expansions. Keep in mind that the interpretation of topics is subjective and depends on the context.

Advantages of using AI/ML in trading algorithms

The use of AI and ML in trading algorithms has gained significant traction in recent years. The use of these technologies has brought about numerous advantages that have transformed trading strategies and increased profitability. In this section, we will explore the benefits of incorporating AI/ML in trading algorithms, focusing on improved accuracy and predictive capabilities, adaptability to market changes, automating complex decision-making processes, reducing human biases and errors, and enhancing risk management.

Improved accuracy and predictive capabilities

The application of AI and ML techniques in trading algorithms has significantly improved the accuracy and predictive capabilities of these algorithms, leading to more profitable and efficient trading strategies. One of the main advantages of using AI/ML in trading algorithms is the ability to analyze vast amounts of data quickly and accurately, allowing traders to make more informed decisions in real-time.

Machine learning algorithms, such as neural networks and support vector machines, are particularly adept at identifying patterns and trends within complex datasets, which can be difficult for traditional statistical methods to detect. For example, in the context of algorithmic trading, ML algorithms can be used to analyze historical price data and derive insights into market trends, enabling traders to make more accurate predictions about future price movements [34]. This improved accuracy can lead to better trading strategies, reduced risks, and increased profits for investors.

Furthermore, AI and ML techniques are particularly well-suited to **high-frequency trading (HFT)**, where trading decisions are made within milliseconds, and the ability to rapidly process and analyze data is crucial[35]. For instance, AI-based HFT algorithms can quickly identify arbitrage opportunities and execute trades, capitalizing on price discrepancies before other market participants can react[36].

A real-world example of the successful application of AI/ML in trading algorithms can be seen in the case of the hedge fund Renaissance Technologies, which has consistently outperformed the market using its AI-driven trading strategies[37]. The firm's flagship Medallion Fund, which relies heavily on machine learning techniques to identify and exploit market inefficiencies, has achieved an average annual return of more than 40% since its inception in 1988[37].

Adaptability to market changes

The incorporation of AI and ML in trading algorithms also offers significant advantages in terms of adaptability to market changes. Financial markets are inherently dynamic and complex, with numerous factors influencing price movements and trends. Traditional trading algorithms, which rely on fixed sets of rules and parameters, can struggle to adapt to rapidly changing market conditions, potentially leading to suboptimal trading performance.

In contrast, AI and ML-based trading algorithms are capable of learning from new data, continuously updating and refining their models to better adapt to changing market conditions. This adaptability is particularly crucial in times of market volatility and uncertainty, such as during financial crises or geopolitical events, when traditional trading strategies may falter.

Reinforcement learning (RL), a subfield of machine learning, offers a promising approach for developing trading algorithms that can adapt to market changes. RL algorithms learn by interacting with the environment, receiving feedback in the form of rewards or penalties, and adjusting their actions accordingly. In the context of algorithmic trading, RL algorithms can be used to explore different trading strategies and learn which actions lead to the most favorable outcomes, enabling them to adapt and optimize their performance in response to changing market conditions.

An example of the successful application of reinforcement learning in trading algorithms can be found in the work of *Moody* and *Saffell* (2001), who developed a RL-based trading agent that demonstrated superior performance compared to traditional trading strategies in both simulated and real-world trading environments. The RL agent was able to adapt its trading strategy in response to market changes, generating consistent profits despite fluctuations in market conditions.

Automating complex decision-making processes

AI and ML have revolutionized the way complex decision-making processes are automated in various industries, including finance and trading. These advanced technologies have the potential to significantly enhance the effectiveness and efficiency of decision-making processes, particularly in situations involving large volumes of data.

One of the key benefits of automating complex decision-making processes using AI and ML is the ability to process and analyze massive amounts of data at an unparalleled speed. Traditional decision-making approaches often involve manual analysis and time-consuming computations, which can be particularly challenging when dealing with large datasets or fast-moving markets. AI and ML algorithms can quickly analyze vast quantities of data, identifying patterns, trends, and relationships that would be difficult or impossible for humans to discern.

Another advantage of using AI and ML for automating complex decision-making processes is the reduction of human biases and errors. Human decision-makers are often influenced by cognitive biases, emotions, and other factors that can lead to suboptimal decisions[38]. AI and ML algorithms, on the other hand, are not subject to these biases and can make decisions based solely on data and objective criteria.

In the context of trading, automating complex decision-making processes using AI and ML can lead to more effective trading strategies and improved risk management. AI and ML algorithms can analyze market data, such as price movements, trading volumes, and macroeconomic indicators, to identify profitable trading opportunities and optimize trading strategies in real-time. Moreover, these algorithms can also monitor and assess various risk factors, such as market volatility, liquidity, and counterparty risk, allowing for more informed and proactive risk management [39].

A real-world example of AI-driven decision-making in trading is the rise of robo-advisors, which are digital platforms that provide automated investment advice and portfolio management services. Robo-advisors leverage AI and ML algorithms to analyze clients' financial goals, risk tolerance, and investment preferences, generating personalized investment recommendations and managing clients' portfolios in an efficient and cost-effective manner[40].

Reducing human biases and errors

One of the most significant sources of human bias in trading is the overconfidence bias, which leads traders to overestimate their abilities and the accuracy of their predictions. This can result in excessive trading, higher transaction costs, and ultimately lower returns. AI and ML algorithms can help to counteract this bias by providing objective assessments of trading opportunities and risk factors, enabling traders to make more informed decisions.

Another common bias in trading is the confirmation bias, where traders tend to seek out and interpret information in a way that confirms their pre-existing beliefs [41]. This can result in a failure to consider alternative perspectives and a tendency to hold onto losing positions in the hope that they will eventually rebound. AI and ML algorithms can help to overcome this bias by analyzing a wide range of data sources and identifying patterns and trends that may contradict traders' initial assumptions[42].

Loss aversion is another prevalent bias in trading, where traders are more sensitive to potential losses than equivalent gains, leading them to make suboptimal decisions in an effort to avoid losses. AI and ML algorithms can support more objective decision-making by evaluating potential trades based on expected returns and risk factors, rather than being swayed by the emotional impact of potential losses[43].

The use of AI and ML in trading also helps to reduce human errors, which can arise from fatigue, information overload, and lapses in attention. AI and ML algorithms can process and analyze vast amounts of data at an unprecedented speed, ensuring that decisions are based on the most accurate and up-to-date information available. Moreover, AI and ML algorithms can operate continuously, allowing them to monitor market developments and adjust trading strategies in real-time all the time.

Enhancing risk management

The integration of AI and ML in trading systems can significantly enhance risk management by providing more accurate, data-driven assessments of potential risks and enabling proactive, real-time adjustments to trading strategies. Effective risk management is a crucial aspect of successful trading, as it helps to protect investment capital and maintain portfolio stability in the face of market uncertainties and fluctuations.

AI and ML algorithms can be used to analyze large volumes of historical and real-time data, identify patterns and trends, and assess various risk factors, such as market volatility, liquidity, and counterparty risk[44]. By leveraging advanced statistical techniques and predictive models, AI and ML algorithms can provide more accurate and timely forecasts of potential risks, enabling traders to make more informed decisions about their trading strategies and risk exposure.

AI and ML technologies can also improve risk management by automating the process of monitoring and managing market risk. Market risk refers to the potential losses resulting from adverse changes in market variables, such as interest rates, exchange rates, and stock prices [45]. AI and ML algorithms can monitor these variables in real-time and generate alerts or trigger adjustments to trading positions when predefined risk thresholds are breached. This allows traders to respond more quickly to market fluctuations and reduce potential losses[46].

Lastly, AI and ML technologies can support more effective management of credit and counterparty risk, which refers to the potential losses resulting from the default or failure of a trading counterparty. By analyzing credit ratings, financial statements, and other relevant data, AI and ML algorithms can assess the creditworthiness of counterparties and estimate the probability of default, allowing traders to make more informed decisions about counterparty selection and exposure limits[47].

Building a simple AI-powered trading system: A walkthrough

In this section, we will discuss building a simple AI-powered trading system. We will learn about preprocessing, feature engineering and selecting the ML model.

Defining the problem and selecting the data

Developing an AI-powered trading system involves defining the problem and aiming for a system that can analyze data, identify patterns, and execute profitable trades efficiently. High-performance algorithmic trading leverages advanced algorithms and artificial intelligence to outperform humans in diverse market conditions, minimizing risks and adapting to changing market dynamics.

Selecting appropriate data sources is crucial for success. Financial data comprises structured and unstructured data, both valuable in enhancing predictive capabilities. Relevant, accurate, and up-to-date data from high-quality sources like exchange feeds, market data providers, and economic indicators should be prioritized. Alternative data sources, such as satellite imagery and geolocation data, can provide unique insights and contribute to more robust trading strategies.

Historical data is vital for training and validating AI models, requiring extensive datasets spanning various market conditions to improve resilience to market fluctuations. Considering data frequency and granularity is crucial, as high-frequency data can capture intraday patterns and enable agile trading strategies.

Preprocessing and feature engineering

Data preprocessing typically consists of several steps, including data cleaning, handling missing values, and data normalization. Data cleaning involves identifying and rectifying errors in the data, such as incorrect data points, outliers, or inconsistencies. This step is crucial for ensuring that the AI model is not influenced by noise or spurious correlations.

Handling missing values is another essential aspect of data preprocessing. In financial data, missing values can arise due to various reasons, such as data collection errors or non-existent data points for specific time periods or trading suspensions. Several techniques can be used to address missing values, including imputation, interpolation, or deletion. The choice of the method depends on the nature of the missing data and the specific requirements of the AI model.

Data normalization is a crucial step in preprocessing, as it ensures that all features are on the same scale, thereby preventing any feature from dominating the model's predictions due to its magnitude[48]. Normalization techniques, such as min-max scaling or z-score standardization, can be applied to transform the data into a consistent range or distribution[49].

Feature engineering

The process of feature engineering involves the creation of new features from the preprocessed data, which can help the AI model capture complex relationships and patterns in the data. In the context of algorithmic trading, several types of features can be extracted from financial data, including technical indicators, fundamental ratios, and sentiment-based features derived from unstructured data sources.

Technical indicators, such as moving averages, **relative strength index (RSI)**, or Bollinger Bands, are widely used by traders to analyze price trends and generate trading signals. These indicators can be incorporated as features in AI-driven trading systems to provide insights into market dynamics and assist in the prediction of future price movements.

Fundamental ratios, such as **price-to-earnings (P/E)** ratio, debt-to-equity ratio, or dividend yield, are commonly used by investors to evaluate the financial health of companies and identify undervalued or overvalued stocks. Sentiment-based features derived from unstructured data sources, such as news articles or social media posts, have been shown to provide valuable information about investor sentiment and market trends.

Selecting and training the ML model

The choice of an ML model for algorithmic trading depends on several factors, including the problem type (classification, regression, or time series forecasting), the data characteristics (structured or unstructured), and the specific requirements of the trading system (such as interpretability, computational efficiency, or generalization capabilities).

Some popular ML models for algorithmic trading include linear regression, SVM, decision trees, random forests, and **gradient boosting machines (GBMs)** for regression and classification problems. Deep learning models, such as **convolutional neural networks (CNNs)**, **recurrent neural networks (RNNs)**, and **long short-term memory (LSTM)** networks, have also gained popularity in recent years due to their ability to learn complex, non-linear relationships in the data.

The training of an ML model involves using a dataset to optimize the model's parameters so that it can make accurate predictions on unseen data. In the context of algorithmic trading, the dataset typically comprises historical financial data, along with relevant features and target variables.

The training process generally involves dividing the dataset into a training set, a validation set, and a test set. The training set is used to fit the model, while the validation set is used to tune the model's hyperparameters and prevent overfitting. The test set serves as a final evaluation of the model's performance on unseen data, providing an estimate of its generalization capabilities.

Testing and evaluating the model

Once the ML model has been selected and trained, it is essential to test and evaluate its performance on a separate dataset that was not used during the training process. In the context of algorithmic trading, the test dataset typically comprises historical financial data that was not used during the training process.. This dataset should ideally span a diverse range of market conditions, enabling the evaluation of the model's robustness and adaptability.

The evaluation of the model's performance involves comparing its predictions or trading signals to the actual target values and computing relevant performance metrics. These metrics depend on the problem type (classification, regression, or time series forecasting) and the specific requirements of the trading system.

In addition to the quantitative evaluation of the model's performance, it is crucial to consider its qualitative aspects, such as interpretability, robustness, and adaptability. This can involve analyzing the model's predictions or trading signals in different market conditions, conducting sensitivity analysis, or employing techniques such as feature importance analysis or partial dependence plots to gain insights into the model's decision-making process.

Integrating the model into a trading strategy

Once the ML model has been tested and its performance evaluated, the next step is to integrate it into a trading strategy. This involves using the model's predictions or trading signals to make buy and sell decisions, manage risk, and execute trades in the financial markets.

Based on the model's predictions or trading signals, entry and exit rules determine when to enter and exit a trade. For example, a simple rule might involve buying a stock when the model predicts an upward price movement and selling it when the model predicts a downward price movement. More advanced rules can incorporate additional factors, such as technical indicators, market sentiment, or macroeconomic data, to refine the trading decisions.

Position sizing refers to the number of shares or contracts to trade, which should be determined based on the available capital, risk tolerance, and the model's confidence in its predictions. Stop-loss and take-profit levels are used to manage risk and lock in profits by automatically exiting a trade when a predefined price level is reached. These levels can be set based on the model's predictions, historical price volatility, or other risk management techniques.

Risk management is a crucial component of any trading strategy, as it ensures the preservation of capital and the long-term sustainability of the trading system[50]. Techniques such as diversification, portfolio optimization, or **value-at-risk** (**VaR**) analysis can be employed to manage risk and achieve a desired risk-return profile.

After defining the trading strategy, the next step is to implement it in a trading platform or environment, which enables the execution of trades in the financial markets. This can involve using programming languages such as Python, R, or C++, along with trading libraries or **application programming interfaces (APIs)** provided by brokers or exchanges.

Once the trading system is live, it is crucial to continuously monitor its performance and make adjustments or updates as needed. This involves tracking the performance metrics and comparing them to the model's performance during the testing phase.

Backtesting and optimizing the strategy

Backtesting and optimizing a trading strategy are critical steps in the development of an AI-powered trading system. Backtesting involves evaluating the strategy's performance on historical data, while optimization aims to fine-tune the strategy's parameters to improve its overall performance.

When backtesting a trading strategy, it is essential to consider factors such as data quality, the choice of the backtesting period, and potential biases, such as lookahead bias or survivorship bias (Bailey et al., 2014). Data quality is crucial, as inaccurate or incomplete data can lead to misleading results and poor trading decisions. The backtesting period should ideally span a diverse range of market conditions, enabling the evaluation of the strategy's robustness and adaptability.

Optimization involves fine-tuning the strategy's parameters or components to improve its performance. This can involve adjusting the entry and exit rules, position sizing, stop-loss and take-profit levels, or risk management techniques, as well as exploring alternative ML models or feature engineering techniques.

When optimizing a trading strategy, it is essential to avoid overfitting, which occurs when the strategy is excessively tailored to the historical data and performs poorly on unseen data. Techniques such as cross-validation, out-of-sample testing, or regularization can be employed to mitigate the risk of overfitting and ensure the strategy's generalizability to new data.

Backtesting and optimizing a trading strategy is an iterative process, involving repeated cycles of evaluation and refinement until the desired performance is achieved. During this process, it is essential to continuously monitor the strategy's performance on both historical and new data, and make adjustments or updates as needed to ensure its robustness, adaptability, and profitability in the long run.

AI/ML model selection and evaluation

In the realm of AI-driven trading, selecting the appropriate model based on problem requirements is crucial to ensure that the model performs optimally and provides valuable insights to guide trading decisions. Various factors, such as the nature of the problem, the type of data available, and the desired level of interpretability, must be considered when choosing a suitable AI or ML model for a specific trading task.

The first step in choosing the right model involves understanding the nature of the problem. For example, regression problems focus on predicting a continuous target variable, whereas classification problems involve predicting categorical target variables. Different types of AI/ML models are better suited for different types of problems; for instance, linear regression models are commonly used for regression tasks, while decision trees or SVMs are often employed for classification tasks.

The type of data available for a trading problem is another essential factor to consider when selecting an AI/ML model. Some models, such as logistic regression or SVMs, are well-suited for handling structured numerical or categorical data, while others, like **natural language processing** (**NLP**) models or **convolutional neural networks** (**CNNs**), are designed to handle unstructured data, such as text or images.

The desired level of interpretability is another important aspect to consider when selecting an AI/ML model for trading tasks. Some models, such as decision trees, linear regression, or **k-nearest neighbors** (**KNN**), are highly interpretable and can provide intuitive insights into the relationships between variables and the decision-making process. On the other hand, complex models like deep learning or ensemble methods may provide higher predictive accuracy, but their decision-making process can be more challenging to interpret and explain.

Real-world examples of model selection in AI-driven trading include the use of models for time-series forecasting in stock price prediction[51] or the employment of reinforcement learning models, such as Q-learning or policy gradient methods, for developing adaptive market-making strategies[52]. By carefully considering problem requirements, data characteristics, and interpretability, financial professionals can select the most appropriate AI/ML models for their trading tasks and ensure optimal performance.

Conclusion

Throughout this chapter, we have explored various facets of AI and ML in the context of finance and trading. We began with an introduction to AI, its history, and various types, followed by a discussion on AI techniques such as expert systems, rule-based systems, and neural networks. We then dove into the world of ML, learning about its history, types, and techniques, as well as its applications in finance and trading.

Real-world applications of AI and ML in trading were examined, covering algorithmic trading, sentiment analysis, high-frequency trading, and fraud detection. We also discussed popular AI and ML frameworks and libraries that are instrumental in implementing these techniques in trading systems. Furthermore, we outlined some of the most popular AI/ML algorithms for trading, including time series forecasting, classification algorithms, reinforcement learning, and natural language processing.

The advantages of using AI/ML in trading algorithms were highlighted, such as improved accuracy, adaptability, automation, reduced human biases, and enhanced risk management. We then provided a step-by-step walkthrough of building a simple AI-powered trading system, from defining the problem to backtesting and optimizing the strategy.

Finally, we discussed the importance of AI/ML model selection and evaluation, including the process of choosing the right model based on problem requirements, cross-validation, hyperparameter tuning, performance metrics, and model interpretability.

In conclusion, the incorporation of AI and ML in trading has opened up new horizons for the finance industry. The ability of AI and ML to analyze large datasets, learn from experience, and adapt to changing market conditions makes them invaluable tools for traders and investors. By leveraging the power of AI and ML, trading algorithms can be developed that offer improved accuracy, better risk management, and more informed decision-making. This, in turn, has the potential to revolutionize the way trading is done and reshape the financial landscape. As AI and ML continue to evolve, we can expect even more innovative applications and techniques to emerge, further enhancing the capabilities of trading systems and driving the industry forward. In the upcoming chapter, readers will discover crucial factors for crafting effective AI-driven trading strategies, ensuring informed decision-making.

Join our book's Discord space

Join the book's Discord Workspace for Latest updates, Offers, Tech happenings around the world, New Release and Sessions with the Authors:

https://discord.bpbonline.com

CHAPTER 3
Essential Elements in AI Trading Algorithms

Introduction

This chapter explores the application of **artificial intelligence (AI)** in trading strategies, covering topics such as training, validating, and optimizing AI models, addressing overfitting and underfitting, achieving model interpretability, and leveraging AI for portfolio management. We will delve into the process of training AI models and evaluating their performance, emphasizing the importance of robustness and reliability. Additionally, we will discuss techniques for fine-tuning models and mitigating overfitting and underfitting issues. By highlighting the significance of model interpretability and explainability, we aim to instill trust and transparency in AI-powered trading strategies. Ultimately, this chapter demonstrates the transformative potential of AI in the finance industry.

Structure

In this chapter, we will learn the following topics:

- Formulating trading strategies with AI
- Training and validating AI models
- Evaluating AI model performance
- Fine-tuning and optimizing AI models

- Handling overfitting and underfitting in AI models
- Model interpretability and explainability
- AI for portfolio management and asset allocation
- Combining AI with traditional trading strategies

Objectives

In this chapter, we aim to explore the multifaceted process of leveraging AI to enhance trading strategies. Our objectives include understanding how to formulate effective AI-driven trading strategies, as well as the intricacies involved in training and validating AI models to ensure their reliability and efficiency. We will delve into evaluating AI model performance, emphasizing the importance of fine-tuning and optimizing these models to achieve optimal results. Addressing common challenges such as overfitting and underfitting will be paramount, alongside strategies to enhance model interpretability and explainability, ensuring that AI solutions are not only powerful but also understandable by stakeholders. Furthermore, we'll explore the application of AI in portfolio management and asset allocation, demonstrating how it can revolutionize traditional approaches to trading. Finally, the chapter will highlight methods for integrating AI with traditional trading strategies, fostering a synergistic approach that leverages the best of both worlds to achieve superior trading outcomes.

Formulating trading strategies with AI

Artificial intelligence (AI) has revolutionized the field of finance and trading, profoundly impacting the development and execution of trading strategies. Through the analysis of vast amounts of data, AI empowers traders and investment firms to create more sophisticated and effective trading approaches. High-frequency trading and algorithmic trading, which are driven by AI, have demonstrated their capacity to enhance market efficiency and provide a competitive advantage. By employing machine learning and deep learning algorithms, these strategies can learn from real-world data and adapt to dynamic market conditions.

One crucial advantage of incorporating AI into trading strategies is its ability to rapidly process and analyze enormous volumes of data, enabling the identification of patterns and trends that elude human traders. Furthermore, AI algorithms are impervious to the emotional biases that often hinder human decision-making in trading, enabling objective and data-driven trade executions. Reinforcement learning algorithms, for instance, exhibit considerable potential in optimizing portfolio management by considering factors like risk, return, and diversification. Esteemed investment firms like *Two Sigma* and *Renaissance Technologies* have successfully employed AI-powered trading strategies, capitalizing on extensive datasets and advanced algorithms to deliver exceptional returns for their investors[58].

Supervised learning algorithms like **Support Vector Machines (SVM)** and decision trees are utilized in trading strategies to predict and identify patterns in financial data. For instance, J.P. Morgan implemented an SVM-based algorithm to forecast intraday stock price movements [59]. Unsupervised learning algorithms, such as clustering and dimensionality reduction, uncover hidden patterns and relationships in datasets without labeled data. Reinforcement learning algorithms, like Q-learning and **Deep Q-Networks (DQNs)**, adapt to dynamic trading environments to make optimal decisions [60]. Deep learning techniques, including LSTM networks and CNNs, capture complex patterns in large-scale financial data[61]. *Renaissance Technologies* has successfully employed deep learning algorithms in its trading strategies.

Despite the numerous advantages offered by AI-powered trading strategies, it is essential to consider potential risks and challenges. The increasing reliance on AI and high-frequency trading has raised concerns regarding market stability, fairness, and the potential for systemic risks arising from the interconnectedness of global financial markets. The lack of transparency in AI algorithms can also lead to unintended consequences, as evidenced by the 2010 Flash Crash, where a trading algorithm unintentionally contributed to a rapid market decline. Therefore, it is crucial to carefully evaluate the benefits and risks associated with AI-powered trading strategies and establish appropriate regulatory frameworks to ensure market stability, fairness, and transparency.

In order to develop effective AI-powered trading strategies, it is crucial to identify appropriate data sources and features that can serve as inputs to the AI models. This involves sourcing relevant financial data from various forms and levels of detail, including price data, volume data, order book data, and news data. Historical price and volume data can be obtained from market data providers such as *Bloomberg*, *Thomson Reuters*, and *Quandl*. News data, on the other hand, can be sourced from news agencies, financial news websites, and social media platforms like Twitter. Additionally, alternative data sources like satellite imagery, credit card transactions, and mobile app usage have gained popularity among AI investors in recent years. These diverse data sources and feature selection techniques contribute to building robust AI trading systems.

Training and validating AI models

The effectiveness and performance of AI-powered trading strategies heavily relies on the quality of the underlying AI models, which are trained and validated using different learning paradigms, including supervised and unsupervised learning[1]. In this section, we will compare these two approaches in the context of trading and provide real-world examples of high-performance algorithmic trading systems that utilize these learning paradigms to train and validate their AI models:

Aspect	Summary
Learning paradigms	Supervised learning involves training AI models with labeled data to predict price movements and optimize portfolio allocations. Unsupervised learning allows models to discover patterns autonomously.
Model designs	Various model architectures such as **Artificial Neural Networks (ANNs)**, **Support Vector Machines (SVMs)**, and Deep Learning techniques like **Convolutional Neural Networks (CNNs)** and **Recurrent Neural Networks (RNNs)** are used. Each architecture has strengths in modeling complex relationships in market data.
Training data splitting and balancing	Techniques like k-fold cross-validation and time series cross-validation are employed to assess model performance and prevent overfitting. Balancing training data using oversampling, undersampling, and synthetic data generation ensures models learn accurately from representative samples.
Cross-validation techniques	K-fold cross-validation, **leave-one-out (LOOCV)**, and time series cross-validation are crucial for evaluating models' real-world performance and generalization across different datasets. They help gauge model effectiveness in various scenarios, with time series cross-validation particularly suited for financial models due to its consideration of chronological data order.
Hyperparameter selection and optimization	Techniques like grid search, random search, and Bayesian optimization are used to find optimal hyperparameters for model performance improvement.
Validation metrics and performance measures	Metrics like precision, recall, F1-score, and AUC-ROC offer nuanced assessments of model performance beyond accuracy, considering factors like imbalanced datasets and varying misclassification costs.
Model selection and comparison	Holdout validation and cross-validation techniques like k-fold and time series cross-validation are used to assess model performance. Methods like AIC and BIC aid in selecting the best model from a set by balancing model fit and complexity, crucial for avoiding overfitting.

Table 3.1: Real-world examples of high-performance algorithmic trading systems

Supervised learning is a widely used approach in AI-powered trading strategies, where AI models are trained using labeled data that includes known target outputs associated with input features. This method is valuable for tasks like predicting price movements, generating trading signals, and optimizing portfolio allocations based on historical market data and other relevant factors. In practice, several high-performance algorithmic trading systems have successfully utilized supervised learning techniques to train and validate their AI models. Renaissance Technologies, a renowned hedge fund, applies supervised learning approaches to train AI models for predicting price movements and other market variables using historical market data and relevant factors. Likewise, *QuantConnect*, an AI-driven trading platform, utilizes supervised learning techniques to train AI models that generate trading signals and optimize portfolio allocations by considering various technical, fundamental, and sentiment data[63].

Unsupervised learning is an alternative approach in AI-powered trading strategies where AI models are trained without labeled data. This allows the models to autonomously discover patterns, structures, and relationships in the input data. In practice, several high-performance algorithmic trading systems have successfully integrated unsupervised learning techniques to train and validate their AI models. *AQR Capital Management*, a quantitative asset management firm, applies unsupervised learning methods like clustering and dimensionality reduction to analyze and segment financial markets, identifying undervalued stocks across different market regimes [64]. Additionally, Two Sigma, an AI-driven hedge fund, utilizes unsupervised learning techniques to uncover hidden patterns and relationships in extensive financial data, uncovering new trading opportunities [65].

Choosing the right model design is crucial for creating effective AI-based trading strategies. It determines how well the model can understand and apply patterns in the data. Factors like the problem's complexity, input data characteristics, and the balance between interpretability and performance influence the choice of model design. This section explores different model designs used in algorithmic trading and presents examples of successful trading systems that utilize AI to select the best model design.

Artificial neural networks (ANNs) are widely used in AI-driven trading strategies because they can effectively model complex relationships in market data. ANNs can have different architectures, such as feedforward neural networks, radial basis function networks, and recurrent neural networks. Each architecture has its own strengths and weaknesses in terms of modeling capabilities and computational requirements. For example, a modular neural network architecture was successful in predicting stock price movements by combining technical indicators.

SVMs are another popular model architecture in algorithmic trading. They are known for handling high-dimensional data and providing accurate predictions. SVMs can be used for tasks like predicting price movements, generating trading signals, and classifying market regimes based on technical and fundamental inputs. An SVM-based model accurately predicted the daily movement of the S&P 500 index using relevant market data.

Deep learning techniques, including **convolutional neural networks (CNNs)**, **recurrent neural networks (RNNs)**, and transformers, are also utilized in algorithmic trading. CNNs are effective at recognizing patterns in time series data, making them suitable for modeling price and volume data in innovative ways. For example, CNN successfully predicted intraday price movements of the E-mini S&P 500 futures contract. RNNs, particularly LSTM networks, are useful for capturing long-term dependencies in time series data, making them suitable for various trading tasks that require historical market information.

Training data splitting and balancing is a crucial step in assessing AI model performance and avoiding overfitting. In algorithmic trading, techniques such as k-fold cross-validation and time series cross-validation are widely employed. K-fold cross-validation divides the data into k subsets, using one subset for testing and the rest for training in an iterative manner. Time series cross-validation is designed for time-dependent data and involves training the model on past data and testing it on future data to gauge its generalization capabilities.

Balancing the training data is crucial to ensure that AI models are exposed to a representative sample of different classes and patterns. Techniques like **oversampling, undersampling,** and synthetic data generation can address class imbalance issues. Oversampling involves creating additional samples from the minority class, while undersampling reduces samples from the majority class. Synthetic data generation involves creating artificial samples that resemble the characteristics of the original data. These techniques help AI models learn underlying patterns accurately and make reliable predictions.

Cross-validation techniques, like k-fold, leave-one-out (LOOCV), and time series cross-validation are key in creating effective AI-driven trading strategies. These methods help in thoroughly evaluating how well models will perform in real-world scenarios and their ability to generalize across different data sets. With k-fold cross-validation, data is split into several parts, allowing for a solid gauge of model effectiveness. LOOCV tests the model's accuracy by using all data except one point for training and the left-out point for testing, though this method demands significant computational resources. Time series cross-validation, particularly useful for financial models, accounts for the chronological order of data, adopting a sequential approach to testing and training that mirrors the flow of real market conditions.

Real-world examples demonstrate the effectiveness of cross-validation techniques in high-performance trading systems. Studies have used k-fold cross-validation to evaluate machine learning models for predicting stock price movements. LOOCV has been applied to assess the performance of LSTM-based trading strategies, demonstrating its accuracy and generalization capabilities. Time series cross-validation has been utilized to evaluate CNN-based trading strategies, emphasizing the importance of capturing temporal dependencies in financial data. These examples showcase the practical application of cross-validation in effectively evaluating and optimizing AI models for algorithmic trading.

Hyperparameter selection and optimization use techniques like grid search, random search, and Bayesian optimization, which are commonly used to find the best hyperparameter values for model performance improvement. Grid search exhaustively searches a predefined set of hyperparameter values, while random search randomly selects values, making it more computationally efficient. Bayesian optimization utilizes probabilistic models to guide the search process efficiently, employing methods such as Gaussian processes and TPE. These techniques have been successfully applied in algorithmic trading, optimizing hyperparameters of various AI models. Real-world examples demonstrate their effectiveness, including studies optimizing hyperparameters of SVM-based, LSTM-based, and deep Q-learning-based trading strategies using grid search, random search, and Bayesian optimization with Gaussian processes, respectively. These examples highlight the benefits of hyperparameter optimization in enhancing model efficiency and performance.

Validation metrics and performance measures are essential. While accuracy is a commonly used metric, it may not be suitable for imbalanced datasets or when misclassification costs vary. Precision, recall, and F1-score offer a more nuanced assessment by considering false positives and false negatives. Precision measures true positives among predicted positives, recall measures true positives among actual positives, and the F1-score provides a balanced measure of performance, combining both precision and recall. These metrics provide a comprehensive evaluation of the model's performance.

The **Area Under the Receiver Operating Characteristic curve (AUC-ROC)** is a popular metric for evaluating how effectively a model can differentiate between positive and negative cases over a range of decision thresholds. AUC-ROC scores fall between 0 and 1, where scores closer to 1 signify superior model performance. This metric offers a comprehensive view of a model's ability to accurately classify instances, making it a dependable indicator of its discriminatory power.

Model selection and comparison holdout validation, where data is split into training and validation sets, is a commonly used technique for assessing AI model performance. However, it can be sensitive to the choice of the validation set, especially with limited or non-homogeneous data. Cross-validation techniques like k-fold cross-validation and time series cross-validation provide a more robust assessment by dividing the data into multiple sets and averaging performance measures across them. These techniques mitigate sensitivity to the validation set choice and provide accurate estimates of model performance.

Methods like the **Akaike Information Criterion (AIC)** and **Bayesian Information Criterion (BIC)** help in choosing the best model from a set of options. They do this by finding a balance between how well a model fits the data and how complex the model is, aiming to prevent choosing a model that is too complicated (a problem known as overfitting). Essentially, these methods prefer simpler models that still do a good job of explaining the data. AIC and BIC are particularly useful in areas like algorithmic trading, where they're used to compare different types of models, such as linear regression, ARIMA (which predicts future values based on past values and errors), and GARCH (which models changing variances in financial data). By evaluating both the fit and size of a model, AIC and BIC help in picking the model that performs the best without being unnecessarily complex.

Evaluating AI model performance

Performance metrics for trading models help assess the quality of trading models. The Sharpe ratio measures the risk-adjusted return of a strategy, indicating returns per unit of risk. High Sharpe ratios signify desirable returns with relatively low risk. The maximum drawdown measures the largest decline in portfolio value, providing insight into potential losses during market downturns. AI models with lower maximum drawdowns are considered more stable and reliable. *The Calmar ratio compares the average annualized return to the maximum drawdown, offering a balanced view of return and risk.*

In addition to traditional metrics, new measures have emerged to evaluate AI models in high-performance algorithmic trading. Feature importance scores, derived from techniques like permutation importance or LASSO regularization, help identify influential input features. Understanding the importance of feature aids in refining models and improving predictive accuracy. Collectively, these metrics provide valuable insights into the performance and effectiveness of AI-driven trading strategies.

Benchmarking in the context of algorithmic trading has evolved to include comparing portfolios to well-known market indices as well as evaluating the performance of different AI-driven trading strategies. Traditionally, benchmarking involved comparing portfolios to market indices to assess their relative performance. However, with the rise of AI-driven algorithmic trading, benchmarking now includes comparing the performance of AI-based strategies against both market indices and other trading strategies.

AI-based trading systems offer advantages such as the ability to analyze vast amounts of data and adapt to changing market conditions. They can optimize portfolio weights to generate higher risk-adjusted returns. Benchmarking against AI-driven strategies helps investors identify superior returns and make informed investment decisions.

Furthermore, benchmarking also involves comparing the performance of different AI-driven strategies to evaluate their relative effectiveness. Research has shown that AI-based strategies incorporating machine learning techniques like reinforcement learning and deep learning have been successful in outperforming traditional trading strategies and other AI-based approaches.

Evaluating model stability and generalization refers to the consistency of the model's performance over different time periods and market conditions, while generalization assesses the model's ability to perform well on unseen data. Overfitting is a common challenge in AI-based trading models, where the model may perform well on the training data but fail to generalize to new data. To address this, out-of-sample testing and cross-validation techniques are employed to evaluate the model's generalization capabilities and mitigate overfitting. Additionally, risk-adjusted performance metrics such as the **Sharpe, Sortino,** and **Calmar ratio** are used to assess the performance of AI-driven trading strategies, taking into account the associated risk. Evaluating model stability and generalization ensures that the models are robust and perform well in real-world scenarios.

Evaluating model stability and generalization can be observed in the practices of leading firms in the algorithmic trading industry by subjecting their models to rigorous testing, these firms can demonstrate their models' ability to consistently perform well across various market conditions.

Weaknesses of AI models in algorithmic trading. Overfitting is a significant concern, as models may perform well on the training data but struggle to generalize to unseen data. Rigorous evaluation techniques like cross-validation and out-of-sample testing help mitigate overfitting risks and ensure the robustness and generalization capabilities of AI models. Another weakness is the presence of model risk, where incorrect assumptions or failures to capture market complexities can lead to substantial losses. Proper validation and stress-testing procedures under various market conditions are necessary to mitigate model risk and enhance the reliability of AI-driven trading strategies. By understanding these strengths and weaknesses, market participants can harness the benefits of AI models while managing potential risks effectively.

Slippage and transaction costs are vital in the development of AI-driven trading strategies. Slippage and transaction costs can significantly impact strategy performance and must be accurately estimated and incorporated into the evaluation process. Neglecting to consider these costs may lead to unrealistic performance expectations and suboptimal investment decisions.

Transaction cost analysis (TCA) is a valuable tool for estimating and minimizing transaction costs in AI-driven trading strategies. TCA involves evaluating trade execution quality and identifying the sources of transaction costs. By incorporating TCA, investors can optimize their trading strategies and minimize the impact of slippage and transaction costs.

Fine-tuning and optimizing AI models

Fine-tuning and optimizing AI models are essential steps for achieving better results in AI trading. These steps involve carefully adjusting how the model works, picking the best data points to use, and applying sophisticated methods to ensure that the models can accurately reflect the complex behavior of financial markets and adjust to their constant changes. This detailed fine-tuning is crucial because it improves the model's ability to predict market movements correctly, helps avoid errors when the model encounters new data, and ensures that the model's decisions are in tune with the ever-changing market environment. Essentially, refining and improving AI models in trading is about making smarter decisions that can lead to a competitive edge, where being precise, adaptable, and efficient is the key to success.

Feature selection and dimensionality reduction are essential components in optimizing and interpreting AI-driven trading models. Feature selection involves identifying relevant variables to enhance performance and interpretability, while dimensionality reduction reduces complexity by transforming high-dimensional data into a lower-dimensional space. These techniques are particularly valuable for handling noisy and high-dimensional financial data. Renowned quantitative investment firms like *Renaissance Technologies* and *D.E. Shaw & Co.* have successfully utilized feature selection and dimensionality reduction to develop effective trading strategies, highlighting the importance of these techniques in improving model performance and stability in the dynamic world of algorithmic trading [66].

Feature selection techniques focus on selecting the most informative features for modeling purposes, eliminating noise and irrelevant information. This process enhances the model's ability to capture meaningful patterns and relationships in the data. Dimensionality reduction methods, on the other hand, transform the high-dimensional feature space into a lower-dimensional representation while preserving the essential information. By reducing the dimensionality, computational complexity is reduced, the curse of dimensionality is mitigated, and model interpretability is enhanced[67].

The experiences of *Renaissance Technologies* and *D.E. Shaw & Co.* demonstrate the significance of feature selection and dimensionality reduction in AI-driven trading. These techniques enable the identification of predictive factors and the reduction of model complexity, resulting in more robust and effective trading strategies. By incorporating these techniques, these firms can gain valuable insights into market dynamics and make informed investment decisions [68].

Hyperparameter optimization techniques are essential for fine-tuning AI models in the context of AI-driven trading strategies. By selecting optimal values for model parameters, these techniques improve model performance and reduce overfitting. Hyperparameter optimization is critical for enhancing model performance and generalization capabilities, leading to more robust and effective trading strategies.

Real-world examples demonstrate the importance of hyperparameter optimization in AI-driven trading strategies. Quantitative hedge funds like *Two Sigma* and *AQR Capital Management* utilize advanced hyperparameter optimization techniques to fine-tune their AI-driven trading models [69]. This enables them to develop accurate and effective trading strategies that can adapt to changing market conditions. In addition to traditional hyperparameter optimization techniques such as grid search and random search, more advanced methods like population-based methods and meta-learning can be employed in AI-driven trading strategies. These advanced techniques allow for optimal hyperparameter search and leverage prior knowledge, leading to superior performance and adaptability to market dynamics.

Regularization refers to the process of adding a penalty term to the objective function of a machine learning algorithm, which discourages overfitting by constraining the model's complexity. Regularization is essential for enhancing the performance and generalization capabilities of AI models, resulting in more robust and effective trading strategies.

One of the primary challenges in regularization for AI-driven trading strategies is selecting the most appropriate regularization technique and the optimal regularization strength, which balances the trade-off between underfitting and overfitting. Research conducted by *Hastie et al. (2009)*[11] highlights the importance of employing robust regularization techniques, such as **L1 (LASSO)** or **L2 (Ridge)** regularization, in the development of AI-driven trading strategies.

A real-world example of the importance of regularization in AI-driven trading strategies can be found in the experiences of quantitative hedge funds, such as *Citadel and Point72*

Asset Management [70]. These firms employ advanced regularization techniques to constrain the complexity of their AI-driven trading models, enabling them to develop more accurate and effective trading strategies that can generalize better to unseen market conditions.

Ensemble methods for improving performance methods refer to the process of aggregating the predictions of multiple individual models, such as decision trees or neural networks, to create a more accurate and robust combined model. One of the primary challenges in applying ensemble methods is selecting the most appropriate ensemble technique and the optimal combination of individual models.

A real-world example of the importance of ensemble methods in AI-driven trading strategies can be found in the experiences of quantitative hedge funds such as *Winton Capital Management* and *Systematica Investments* [70]. These firms employ advanced ensemble techniques to combine the strengths of multiple AI-driven trading models, enabling them to develop more accurate and effective trading strategies that can adapt to changing market conditions.

Transfer learning and the use of pre-trained models are strategies that take advantage of knowledge gained from previous training sessions to enhance performance and cut down on the time needed for training new models. This approach enables models to apply what they've learned from one task or area to another, adapting to new situations more effectively. Transfer learning is especially beneficial in the context of financial trading, where data might be scarce or contain a lot of noise. Techniques like domain adaptation, which adjusts the model to work better with the specific characteristics of the new domain, and multi-task learning, which simultaneously learns several tasks and improves generalization, play crucial roles. These methods help make transfer learning a powerful tool for developing more efficient and accurate trading strategies.

Quantitative hedge funds like *DE Shaw* and *Renaissance Technologies* have successfully utilized transfer learning in their trading strategies [70]. They employ advanced techniques to leverage knowledge from previously trained models, enabling the development of more accurate and adaptable trading strategies.

Pre-trained models refer to machine learning models that have already been trained on vast amounts of data, ready to be adapted or *fine-tuned* for particular tasks or areas of interest. Two notable examples of such advanced models are **Bidirectional Encoder Representations from Transformers (BERT)** and **Generative Pre-trained Transformer (GPT)**. These models, rooted in deep learning, have shown remarkable abilities, especially in understanding and processing human language. In the realm of AI-driven trading, these models can be incredibly useful. For instance, they can analyze the tone and content of financial news or market sentiment, helping to inform trading decisions. By leveraging the extensive learning from their initial training, BERT and GPT can be adjusted to handle specific financial tasks like predicting market trends based on news articles or social media, offering valuable insights for trading strategies.

Model retraining and updates are crucial for maintaining the effectiveness of AI models. Retraining involves updating the model with new data to adapt to changing patterns and market conditions. Determining the optimal retraining frequency and selecting appropriate techniques pose challenges in AI-driven trading strategies. Robust retraining techniques, such as rolling windows or expanding window approaches, are important to ensure the effectiveness of the models.

Quantitative hedge funds like *Two Sigma* and *AQR Capital Management* exemplify the importance of model retraining in AI-driven trading strategies [70]. These firms utilize advanced retraining techniques to continuously update their models and adapt to changing market conditions.

Adaptive and self-learning strategies are crucial in AI-driven trading strategies as they allow AI models to adjust their parameters or architecture in response to changes in data or the environment. These strategies are particularly important in dynamic and evolving financial markets to maintain the effectiveness of AI models. Applying adaptive strategies in AI-driven trading strategies involves determining suitable adaptation mechanisms and optimal frequencies. Robust adaptive techniques like reinforcement learning or evolutionary algorithms are important for developing effective AI-driven trading strategies.

Self-learning strategies involve AI models capable of learning from data without explicit human intervention. Self-learning strategies reduce the need for manual model tuning and maintenance while providing a more robust and adaptive approach to strategy development.

Multimodal models and data fusion enable the integration of multiple types of data and enhance the performance and robustness of AI models. These models can process and leverage information from different data sources, such as text, images, audio, or time series data, to make more accurate predictions. Applying multimodal models in AI-driven trading strategies involves selecting suitable architectures and data fusion techniques.

Quantitative hedge funds like *Bridgewater Associates* and *Winton Group* demonstrate the importance of multimodal models in trading strategies [70]. *Bridgewater Associates*, for example, is known for its intensive use of big data analytics. They integrate data from a wide array of non-traditional sources (like weather data, geopolitical events, and economic indicators across different countries) to model economic outcomes. This broad-based data collection is a hallmark of a multimodal approach, which uses diverse data types and sources to inform investment decisions.

Winton Group primarily focuses on systematic trading strategies that rely heavily on statistical and mathematical models. These models often integrate multiple types of data inputs, from price movements to economic indicators, to make predictive analyses. By employing algorithms that can process and analyze data from multiple modes (like textual, numerical, and even visual data in some cases), they exemplify the multimodal model approach.

These firms employ advanced multimodal techniques to leverage multiple sources of information, such as macroeconomic indicators, financial news, or social media sentiment, for more accurate trading strategies.

Handling overfitting and underfitting

Overfitting occurs when an AI model becomes too closely fitted to the training data, capturing noise and false patterns instead of the underlying patterns. This can result in a complex model that performs well on training data but poorly on new, unseen data. Overfitting can lead to the development of trading strategies that fail to generate profits when applied to live market conditions.

On the other hand, underfitting happens when an AI model is too simplistic and fails to capture the true patterns in the data. This results in poor performance on both training and new data, making it ineffective for high-performance algorithmic trading. For example, a trading model that only considers basic features like daily closing prices may not capture the intraday price movements that could impact trading decisions.

Various techniques have been proposed to address overfitting and underfitting. Regularization is one such technique, which involves adding a penalty term to the model's loss function to discourage overfitting. *Regularization* and *cross-validation* are popular techniques to prevent overfitting by providing a more accurate estimation of the model's performance on new data. Ensemble methods, such as *Random Forests*, can be employed in high-performance algorithmic trading to mitigate overfitting. Ensemble methods combine the predictions of multiple models to create a more robust and accurate output. Random Forests, which aggregates the predictions of decision trees, has been successfully used in algorithmic trading to enhance prediction accuracy and reduce overfitting.

Regularization techniques such as *Lasso*, *Ridge*, *Elastic Net*, and *Dropout* play crucial roles in improving the generalization and robustness of AI models in algorithmic trading. Lasso regularization encourages sparsity by shrinking certain model weights to zero, facilitating feature selection. Ridge regularization reduces the magnitudes of weights to achieve a more balanced distribution. Elastic Net regularization combines the advantages of Lasso and Ridge regularization, striking a balance between feature selection and weight distribution. Dropout, on the other hand, is a regularization technique specific to neural networks, randomly disabling neurons during training to enhance model robustness. These techniques help prevent overfitting and make AI models more adaptable to changing market conditions, resulting in more reliable and effective trading strategies.

The complexity and capacity of AI models are crucial considerations in algorithmic trading to prevent issues like overfitting and underfitting. Model complexity refers to the model's ability to capture intricate patterns, while model capacity control aims to strike a balance between capturing patterns and avoiding overfitting or underfitting. High-complexity models may overfit the noise in the data, while low-complexity models may underfit the complexities of financial markets.

To control model capacity, various approaches can be employed. One approach is to adjust the model architecture, such as the number of layers and neurons in deep learning models, to regulate capacity. Another approach is early stopping, where training is stopped when the model's performance on a validation set deteriorates, indicating potential overfitting. Model selection techniques, including cross-validation and Bayesian model selection, can also be used to compare the performance of different models and select the one that strikes the right balance between complexity and capacity control.

Data augmentation and synthetic data generation are powerful techniques for addressing overfitting and underfitting in AI models used in high-performance algorithmic trading. Data augmentation involves creating new training examples by applying transformations to the existing data, enabling the model to generalize better. In algorithmic trading, data augmentation techniques can generate diverse time series data by combining periods or applying time-based transformations. Synthetic data generation, on the other hand, involves creating artificial data points that mimic real data characteristics. Various techniques, such as Monte Carlo simulation, GANs, and ABMs, can be used to generate synthetic data in algorithmic trading.

These techniques offer multiple benefits beyond mitigating overfitting and underfitting. They help overcome challenges posed by limited historical data, especially for less liquid assets or short-lived financial instruments. By expanding the dataset, AI models become more robust and adaptable to a wider range of market conditions. Furthermore, data augmentation and synthetic data generation enable the simulation of extreme market events, allowing AI models to be better prepared to handle such scenarios in live trading. By incorporating these extreme scenarios into the training data, AI models can potentially improve performance and reduce the risk of catastrophic losses.

Cross-validation and early stopping are essential techniques for managing overfitting and underfitting in AI models used in high-performance algorithmic trading. Cross-validation involves partitioning the dataset into subsets and training the model on some subsets while validating its performance on the remaining subsets. By assessing the model's performance on unseen data, cross-validation helps identify potential overfitting or underfitting issues and enables the selection of models well-suited to the complexities of financial markets. Early stopping, on the other hand, stops the training process once the model's performance on a validation set starts to degrade, indicating overfitting. By finding the optimal point at which the model generalizes well to unseen data, early stopping helps prevent overfitting in AI models.

These techniques offer several benefits for managing overfitting and underfitting in algorithmic trading. They provide an unbiased estimate of the model's performance on unseen data, enabling the selection of robust models that generalize well to new market conditions. This is crucial in financial markets where changes in dynamics and conditions can significantly affect data patterns. Additionally, cross-validation and early stopping assist in managing the model's complexity and capacity control. By guiding the selection of appropriate architectures and training durations, they help develop AI models that capture the complexities of financial markets without succumbing to overfitting or underfitting.

Ensemble learning and model averaging are powerful techniques for addressing overfitting and underfitting in AI models used in high-performance algorithmic trading. Ensemble learning combines multiple models to create a more accurate final model by leveraging the strengths of each individual model and reducing their weaknesses. Bagging, boosting, and stacking are common ensemble learning techniques that have been successfully applied in algorithmic trading. These techniques enhance the performance of AI models by aggregating predictions, correcting errors, and optimally combining the predictions of the base models.

Model averaging, on the other hand, involves averaging the predictions of multiple AI models to create a more accurate final model. By averaging the predictions, model averaging reduces the impact of individual model errors, leading to improved overall performance. This technique has been employed in algorithmic trading to combine various AI models and create more robust and accurate trading strategies.

Ensemble learning and model averaging offer several benefits for addressing overfitting and underfitting in algorithmic trading. They reduce the risk of overfitting by incorporating multiple models that are less likely to be influenced by noise or individual idiosyncrasies. Additionally, these techniques improve the model's generalization ability by leveraging the complementary strengths of different models and minimizing their individual weaknesses.

Model interpretability and explainability

Model interpretability is the degree to which humans can understand how a model works internally, while explainability refers to the model's ability to provide meaningful and understandable reasons for its predictions. In algorithmic trading, both interpretability and explainability are crucial for establishing trust, ensuring compliance, and facilitating effective decision-making. This section explores why interpretability is important in trading and the advantages it offers for algorithmic trading strategies.

AI models, like those used in deep learning, are becoming more complex, which raises issues about their *black-box* nature. This term refers to the difficulty in seeing and explaining how these models make their predictions and decisions. In the world of algorithmic trading, not being able to clearly understand how an AI model works can create problems with trust, following rules, and managing risks. As a result, making AI models easier to interpret and understand has become increasingly important for financial organizations, regulatory bodies, and investors.

Interpretability is important in trading because it helps establish trust in AI models. Since financial markets are heavily regulated and sensitive to risks, trust in algorithmic trading models is vital for their adoption by financial institutions and investors. An interpretable model allows stakeholders to gain insights into the model's decision-making process, enabling them to understand the reasoning behind its predictions and trading decisions. This transparency fosters increased trust in the AI model's ability to generate profitable trading strategies.

Compliance with financial regulations is another critical aspect that interpretability addresses. Regulatory bodies like the U.S. **Securities and Exchange Commission (SEC)** and the **European Securities and Markets Authority (ESMA)** require algorithmic trading strategies to adhere to strict rules and guidelines to prevent market manipulation and safeguard investors. An interpretable model allows financial institutions to demonstrate to regulators that their algorithmic trading strategies comply with these regulations. This reduces the risk of penalties and sanctions.

Moreover, interpretability facilitates effective decision-making in algorithmic trading. Financial markets are dynamic, characterized by rapidly changing conditions and complex interactions between various factors. Therefore, AI models used in algorithmic trading need to adapt to these changes. An interpretable model allows traders and portfolio managers to comprehend the factors influencing the model's predictions. This empowers them to make informed decisions regarding adjustments to the model or trading strategy based on new market information or changes in market conditions.

One approach to enhancing model interpretability is through the use of **explainable AI (XAI)** methods, which aim to provide human-understandable explanations for AI algorithm decisions [71]. **Local Interpretable Model-agnostic Explanations (LIME)** is a technique that approximates complex models with simpler, interpretable ones, providing insights into individual predictions. LIME has been successfully applied in finance, including understanding factors driving algorithmic trading decisions[72].

The **Shapley Additive exPlanations (SHAP)** method is another prominent technique for model interpretability. SHAP values, derived from cooperative game theory, attribute model outputs to input features. These values have been used in various trading applications, such as credit risk assessment and portfolio optimization, to better understand the factors influencing algorithmic trading decisions[73].

Model-agnostic methods like **partial dependence plots (PDPs)** and **individual conditional expectation (ICE)** plots have also contributed to improving interpretability. PDPs show the marginal effect of a feature on model predictions, while ICE plots reveal the relationship between a feature and predicted outcomes for individual instances. These visualization techniques have been useful in high-frequency trading, aiding in identifying the impact of specific market conditions and trading signals on algorithmic strategies [74].

The growing complexity of AI-driven algorithmic trading models has highlighted the need for model interpretability and explainability. Two commonly used techniques for interpreting and explaining AI models in trading are feature importance measures and PDPs.

Feature importance measures quantify the contribution of each input feature to the model's predictions, providing insights into the factors driving the model's performance. Permutation importance is one technique that measures the impact of shuffling a feature's values on the model's predictive accuracy. **Shapley Additive exPlanations (SHAP)** values offer a unified measure of feature importance based on cooperative game theory. These techniques have been applied in trading applications such as credit risk assessment and portfolio optimization to identify influential factors [73].

AI for portfolio management and asset allocation

AI techniques in portfolio management and asset allocation have advanced the field by incorporating machine learning and adapting strategies to changing market conditions. **Modern Portfolio Theory (MPT)**, introduced by Markowitz, forms the basis of traditional asset allocation methods, emphasizing diversification for risk reduction and optimal returns.

Reinforcement learning (RL) algorithms are popular in integrating AI into portfolio management. These algorithms learn optimal trading strategies through interaction with the financial market environment. RL-based methods have shown superiority over mean-variance optimization, a traditional MPT technique, by dynamically adjusting asset allocation based on changing market conditions.

Neural networks have also been applied in portfolio management, enabling the identification of complex patterns and relationships within financial data. They are used to forecast asset prices and returns, aiding decision-making for asset allocation and risk management. **Convolutional neural networks (CNNs)** process high-dimensional financial data, such as order book data and market microstructure, to optimize trading strategies and portfolio performance.

Bayesian methods have gained traction in AI-driven portfolio management due to their ability to handle uncertainty in financial markets. These methods update portfolio allocations based on incoming data, resulting in more robust and adaptive strategies. **Gaussian Process Regression (GPR)** models the relationships between assets, facilitating optimal portfolio selection and risk management.

Genetic algorithms (GAs) are utilized in portfolio optimization, offering a flexible and adaptive approach to asset allocation. GAs evolves a population of candidate solutions over multiple generations, with each generation's best solutions guiding the next. This approach explores a wide range of potential asset allocations, providing a diverse set of portfolio solutions compared to traditional MPT methods.

These AI techniques enhance portfolio management and asset allocation by leveraging machine learning, neural networks, reinforcement learning, Bayesian methods, and genetic algorithms, leading to more sophisticated and adaptive strategies.

AI-driven risk management

The integration of AI has revolutionized the way risk management is approached in investment strategies. AI-driven solutions offer sophisticated tools and algorithms that empower investors to navigate the complexities of the market with greater efficiency and precision. From robo-advisors to dynamic asset allocation platforms, AI is reshaping the landscape of risk management, offering new avenues for diversification, factor investing, and portfolio optimization.

- **Robo-advisors and AI-based asset allocation**: Robo-advisors are AI-powered platforms that help investors manage their portfolios. They use sophisticated algorithms to allocate investments across different options, aiming to minimize risk and maximize returns. These platforms have become popular because they address the challenge of risk management in AI-driven trading strategies.

    One well-known robo-advisor is **Betterment** [75]. It uses a combination of AI algorithms and machine learning techniques to optimize the allocation of assets for its clients. Investors can easily specify their risk preferences and investment goals through a user-friendly interface. Betterment's algorithms then automatically adjust the portfolios based on this information. This AI-driven approach ensures that investors have a diversified portfolio that matches their risk tolerance, time horizon, and financial objectives.

    By employing robo-advisors like Betterment, investors can benefit from automated investment advice and portfolio management that takes their risk tolerance and investment goals into account, making it easier to achieve their financial objectives.

- **Diversification and factor investing with AI**: Diversification and factor investing are essential in managing risk and optimizing returns in investment portfolios. Diversification involves spreading investments across different assets to reduce exposure to any single investment. Factor investing focuses on targeting specific factors that drive asset returns, like value, momentum, or quality. The integration of AI into trading strategies has significantly improved the potential for enhanced diversification and factor identification.

    AI-driven approaches provide advanced analysis and insights for selecting and weighing assets in a diversified portfolio. AI algorithms leverage historical data to identify assets with low correlation, reducing overall portfolio risk. Additionally, AI can uncover underlying factors driving asset returns and assist in constructing factor-based portfolios that capture desired risk premia. This integration of AI into diversification and factor investing results in more robust and efficient trading strategies.

    A real-world example of AI-driven diversification and factor investing is observed in *AQR Capital Management* [76], an investment firm. AQR utilizes AI techniques like machine learning and deep learning to uncover hidden patterns in financial data. Their systematic investment strategies focus on factors such as value, momentum and carry across various asset classes. By combining these factors and implementing diversification techniques, AQR aims to generate consistent risk-adjusted returns for its clients.

- **AI for dynamic asset allocation and rebalancing**: Dynamic asset allocation and portfolio rebalancing are critical for effective risk management in trading strategies. **Artificial intelligence (AI)** has emerged as a powerful tool in this regard, enabling automated and data-driven decision-making.

AI algorithms can facilitate dynamic asset allocation by continuously adjusting the weights of assets in a portfolio based on real-time market signals and predictive models. By analyzing various data sources, including market indicators, economic factors, and sentiment analysis, AI can identify patterns and trends that inform asset allocation decisions. This integration of AI into the asset allocation process enables traders to make more informed decisions aligned with their investment objectives.

BlackRock, an investment management firm [5], utilizes the Aladdin platform as an example of AI-driven dynamic asset allocation. The platform employs AI and machine learning techniques to analyze large volumes of financial data. It offers real-time risk analysis, portfolio optimization, and asset allocation recommendations. By combining advanced analytics with human expertise, BlackRock aims to enhance portfolio performance and effectively manage risk.

By leveraging AI algorithms and real-time data analysis, traders can employ dynamic asset allocation strategies that adapt to market conditions and optimize portfolio composition. This enables them to mitigate risks and improve performance based on timely insights.

Combining AI with traditional trading strategies

The integration of AI with traditional trading strategies has become a potent combination, providing fresh opportunities to boost trading precision and efficacy. Through the amalgamation of AI methods with well-established techniques like technical and fundamental analysis, traders can harness the respective strengths of each approach, enabling them to maneuver through the intricacies of contemporary markets with heightened accuracy and deeper insight.

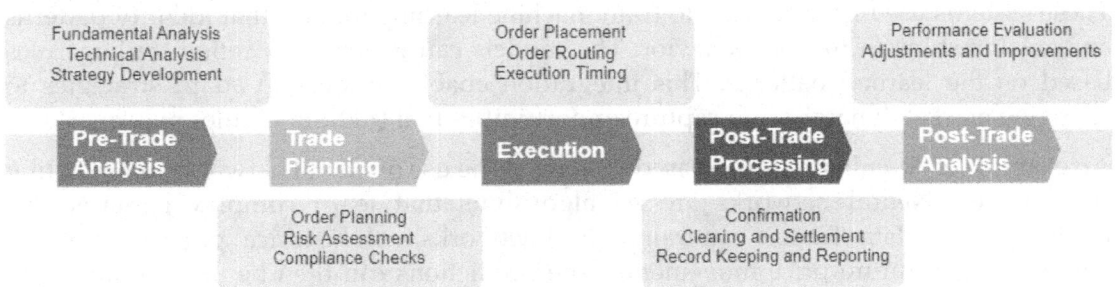

Figure 3.1: Phases of Trade Life Cycle

Blending AI with technical and fundamental analysis: Blending AI with **Pre-Trade Analysis** such as technical and fundamental analysis, can enhance the accuracy and effectiveness of trading strategies. By combining AI techniques with established methodologies, traders can leverage the strengths of both approaches.

Technical analysis involves studying historical price patterns, market trends, and technical indicators. AI algorithms can complement traditional technical analysis by efficiently analyzing large volumes of historical price data and identifying complex patterns that may be difficult for human traders to recognize. Incorporating AI-driven techniques like machine learning and pattern recognition can provide deeper insights into market dynamics and improve the timing and precision of trading decisions.

Fundamental analysis focuses on evaluating the intrinsic value of an asset by considering economic factors, financial statements, industry trends, and other qualitative and quantitative information. AI can enhance fundamental analysis by automating data gathering and processing tasks, enabling traders to analyze a broader range of information efficiently. AI algorithms can also uncover hidden relationships and patterns within the data, providing valuable insights for better investment decision-making.

Renaissance Technologies [77], a hedge fund led by mathematician *James Simons*, is an example of blending AI with technical and fundamental analysis. Renaissance Technologies combines AI-driven techniques with a mix of technical and fundamental analysis to develop sophisticated trading strategies. Their Medallion fund utilizes AI algorithms to analyze vast amounts of financial data and identify patterns that indicate profitable trading opportunities. The integration of AI-powered models with traditional analysis methods has contributed to the fund's notable performance over the years.

By blending AI with technical and fundamental analysis, traders can benefit from a comprehensive approach that harnesses the power of data-driven insights and combines them with established trading methodologies:

AI-enhanced rule-based systems: AI-enhanced rule-based systems integrate AI techniques like machine learning and deep learning with traditional rule-based methodologies to improve **Pre-Trade Analysis, Trade Planning and Execution**. By incorporating AI, traders can enhance the accuracy and adaptability of rule-based systems.

These systems use historical data to train machine learning models that identify patterns and relationships in market behavior. The models can generate or refine trading rules based on the learned patterns. This integration enables traders to adapt strategies to changing market dynamics and capture opportunities that traditional rules may overlook.

An example of AI-enhanced rule-based systems is the use of neural networks in predicting stock prices. Neural networks are AI algorithms that learn complex patterns and relationships in data. Traders can train neural networks with historical price and volume data to predict future price movements. The predictions can then be incorporated into rule-based systems to generate trading signals or adjust parameters.

By blending AI with rule-based systems, traders can leverage the power of machine learning and deep learning to enhance the accuracy and adaptability of their trading strategies.

Hybrid AI-human trading teams: Hybrid AI-human trading teams leverage the strengths of both AI systems for all phases and human expertise to optimize outcomes. The combination of AI algorithms' predictive power and speed with human traders' contextual understanding and decision-making capabilities creates a powerful synergy. In this approach, an AI system continuously monitors and analyzes vast amounts of financial data in real-time, searching for patterns and anomalies that may indicate profitable trading opportunities. Advanced machine learning algorithms, such as neural networks, are employed to identify trends and correlations in the market. However, trading decisions are not solely based on AI analysis. Human traders play a critical role in validating, approving and contextualizing AI-generated signals. They provide insights into market dynamics, interpret macroeconomic trends, consider qualitative factors, and apply risk management strategies based on their experience and judgment. A well-defined workflow is developed to implement a hybrid AI-human trading strategy. The AI system generates alerts for potential trading opportunities, which are then evaluated by human traders. The traders validate the signals against their own analysis and make informed decisions on executing trades.

Conclusion

In this chapter, we have explored the transformative potential of AI in formulating effective trading strategies. By delving into topics such as training and validating AI models, evaluating their performance, fine-tuning and optimizing models, handling overfitting and underfitting issues, achieving model interpretability and explainability, and applying AI in portfolio management and asset allocation, we have gained valuable insights into the integration of AI in the finance industry.

As we conclude this chapter, it is important to look ahead to the next chapter, which will focus on trading and high-performance algorithmic trading using AI with a specific emphasis on data processing and analysis. In the upcoming chapter, we will dive into the critical domain of handling and analyzing vast amounts of data in trading, exploring techniques for data processing, data quality assessment, feature engineering, and advanced analytical methods. By understanding these fundamental aspects, readers will gain the necessary knowledge to harness the power of AI in trading and develop high-performance algorithmic trading strategies.

By combining AI capabilities with robust data processing and analysis techniques, traders and investors can unlock hidden patterns, derive meaningful insights, and make data-driven decisions in real-time.

The next chapter will equip readers with the tools and methodologies to effectively harness the potential of data and AI in the realm of trading, ushering them into a new era of intelligent and profitable investment strategies.

Multiple choice questions

1. **What advantage does AI provide in trading strategies according to the passage?**
    a. Emotional biases hindering decision-making
    b. Rapid processing and analysis of vast amounts of data

c. Increased reliance on human intuition

d. Unintended consequences leading to market instability

2. **Which type of learning algorithm is used by J.P. Morgan to forecast intraday stock price movements?**

    a. Reinforcement learning algorithms

    b. Unsupervised learning algorithms

    c. Deep learning techniques

    d. Supervised learning algorithms

3. **What technique involves adding a penalty term to the model's loss function to discourage overfitting?**

    a. Data augmentation

    b. Regularization

    c. Ensemble learning

    d. Early stopping

4. **Which of the following is NOT a benefit of ensemble learning and model averaging in addressing overfitting and underfitting?**

    a. Reducing the risk of overfitting by incorporating multiple models

    b. Improving the model's generalization ability by leveraging the strengths of different models

    c. Increasing the likelihood of individual model errors

    d. Minimizing the impact of individual model weaknesses

5. **Which method aims to provide human-understandable explanations for AI algorithm decisions?**

    a. Permutation importance

    b. Shapley Additive exPlanations (SHAP)

    c. Local Interpretable Model-agnostic Explanations (LIME)

    d. Individual Conditional Expectation (ICE) plots

Answers

1	b
2	d
3	b
4	c
5	c

CHAPTER 4
Data Processing and Analysis

Introduction

This chapter delves into the essential skill set required for successful algorithmic trading: data processing and analysis. Divided into multiple sections, it equips readers with the expertise necessary to navigate through various stages of data analysis. From understanding data sources to handling real-time feeds, each section offers a comprehensive exploration of key concepts and techniques. Through practical examples and illustrations, readers will gain proficiency in preprocessing, feature extraction, visualization, and time series analysis. By the chapter's end, they will possess the knowledge and tools to make well-informed trading decisions based on data-driven insights.

Structure

In this chapter, we will go through the following topics:

- Data sources for algorithmic trading
- Data preprocessing and cleaning
- Feature extraction and selection
- Analyzing historical successful/failure trading patterns
- Working with real-time data feeds

- Data visualization techniques for trading analysis
- Handling missing and incomplete data
- Time series analysis techniques

Objectives

The objective of this chapter is to provide readers with a comprehensive understanding of key factors involved in developing AI-driven trading strategies. These factors include selecting reliable data sources, performing data preprocessing and cleaning, extracting and selecting relevant features, analyzing historical trading patterns, working with real-time data feeds, employing data visualization techniques for trading analysis, handling missing and incomplete data, and utilizing time series analysis techniques.

Data sources for algorithmic trading

In the world of algorithmic trading, data is the lifeblood that fuels the decision-making process. Without accurate and timely data, trading algorithms are essentially blind, unable to make informed decisions based on market trends and conditions. In this section, we will explore the various data sources that are available for algorithmic trading, including historical market data, real-time market data feeds, news and social media sentiment data, and alternative data sources such as satellite imagery and credit card transaction data. We will discuss the advantages and disadvantages of each type of data source, as well as best practices for data collection and storage. By the end of this section, readers will have a comprehensive understanding of the data sources available for algorithmic trading and be able to make informed decisions about which sources to use based on their specific trading strategies and goals.

Stock exchanges and financial data providers

A stock exchange is a market where stocks and other securities are traded between buyers and sellers. The exchange acts as a mediator, bringing together buyers and sellers and facilitating transactions. The exchange provides a platform for companies to raise capital by issuing stocks, and for investors to buy and sell stocks and other securities. There are many different stock exchanges around the world, each with its own unique characteristics, rules, and regulations. Some of the largest and most influential stock exchanges in the world include the **New York Stock Exchange (NYSE)**, the NASDAQ, the **London Stock Exchange (LSE)**, the **Tokyo Stock Exchange (TSE)**, and the **Hong Kong Stock Exchange (HKEX)**.

Trading on a stock exchange is a complex process that requires access to high-quality financial data. To meet this demand, many stock exchanges offer a wide range of data products that traders and investors can download and use to inform their trading strategies. For example, the LSE offers real-time and historical data for its markets through its **London Stock Exchange Group (LSEG)** Data Services division. The data covers a wide range of financial products, including equities, fixed income, and derivatives, and can be accessed through a variety of channels, including APIs and web-based platforms.

Similarly, NASDAQ offers a wide range of data products and services through its NASDAQ Data Products division. These products include real-time and historical data for NASDAQ-listed securities, as well as options and futures data. The data is available in a variety of formats, including XML and CSV, and can be accessed through a range of delivery mechanisms, including FTP, email, and web services.

The following Python code utilizes **pandas_datareader** and **yfinance** libraries to retrieve historical stock data for **Apple Inc. (AAPL)** within a specified time range, showcasing the initial data points upon extraction.

```
1. import pandas_datareader.data as pdr
2. import yfinance as yf
3. import datetime
4.
5. start = datetime.datetime(2019, 1, 1)
6. end = datetime.datetime(2022, 3, 31)
7.
8. yf.pdr_override()
9.
10.
11. aapl = pdr.get_data_yahoo('AAPL', start=start, end=end)
12. print(aapl.head())
```

The output displays the first few rows of historical stock data for AAPL extracted from January 1, 2019, to March 31, 2022, showcasing key information such as opening, high, low, closing prices, and volume.

Output:

```
[*********************100%***********************]  1 of 1 completed
                 Open       High        Low      Close  Adj Close     Volume
Date
2019-01-02  38.722500  39.712502  38.557499  39.480000  38.047043  148158800
2019-01-03  35.994999  36.430000  35.500000  35.547501  34.257278  365248800
2019-01-04  36.132500  37.137501  35.950001  37.064999  35.719700  234428400
2019-01-07  37.174999  37.207500  36.474998  36.982498  35.640194  219111200
2019-01-08  37.389999  37.955002  37.130001  37.687500  36.319607  164101200
```

Figure 4.1: First few rows of historical stock data

The code block shown is a Python script that demonstrates how to use the **pandas_datareader** library to retrieve historical stock data for Apple (AAPL) from Yahoo Finance.

The **pandas_datareader** library is a popular Python module that provides easy access to various financial data sources, including Yahoo Finance [126], Google Finance [127], and Alpha Vantage [80].

Financial data providers play a crucial role in the global financial market infrastructure by offering a vast range of financial data products and services to traders, investors, and financial professionals. Some of the most well-known commercial providers include Bloomberg, Thomson Reuters, S&P Global, FactSet, and Quandl, each offering real-time and historical market data, news, research, and analytics tools. These providers also offer programmatic access to their financial data through APIs and data feeds. Additionally, S&P Global Ratings and FactSet Analytics provide credit ratings and advanced analytics, respectively, while Quandl focuses on alternative data sources, such as social media feeds and satellite imagery.

Here is an example Python code that demonstrates how to retrieve historical stock data for Apple (AAPL) from the Bloomberg API using the **blpapi** library:

```
1.  import blpapi
2.  import pandas as pd
3.
4.  # Establish a session with the Bloomberg API
5.  sessionOptions = blpapi.SessionOptions()
6.  sessionOptions.setServerHost("localhost")
7.  sessionOptions.setServerPort(8194)
8.  session = blpapi.Session(sessionOptions)
9.  session.start()
10.
11. # Define the historical data request
12. request = session.createRequest("HistoricalDataRequest")
13. request.set("securities", "AAPL US Equity")
14. request.set("fields", "PX_LAST")
15. request.set("startDate", "20190101")
16. request.set("endDate", "20230331")
17.
18. # Send the request and wait for the response
19. session.sendRequest(request)
20. response = session.nextEvent()
21. data = []
22. while True:
23.     if response.eventType() == blpapi.Event.RESPONSE or response.eventType() == blpapi.Event.PARTIAL_RESPONSE:
24.         for msg in response:
```

```
25.            if msg.hasElement("securityData"):
26.                sec_data = msg.getElement("securityData")
27.                if sec_data.hasElement("fieldData"):
28.                    for field in sec_data.getElement("fieldData").values():
29.                        date = pd.to_datetime(field.getElementAsDatetime("date"))
30.                        value = field.getElementAsFloat("PX_LAST")
31.                        data.append({"Date": date, "Close": value})
32.     if response.eventType() == blpapi.Event.RESPONSE:
33.         break
34.     response = session.nextEvent()
35.
36. # Convert the data to a Pandas DataFrame
37. df = pd.DataFrame(data)
38. df.set_index("Date", inplace=True)
39.
40. # Print the top rows of the data
41. print(df.head())
```

Reference: **https://bloomberg.github.io/blpapi-docs/**

In this code, we use the **blpapi** library to establish a session with the Bloomberg API, and then we define a historical data request for the Apple (AAPL) stock. We specify that we want to retrieve the closing price (**PX_LAST**) for each day between January 1, 2019 and March 31, 2023.

Alpha Vantage is a financial data provider that offers APIs for real-time and historical financial market data, covering various instruments, including stocks, ETFs, foreign exchange, and cryptocurrencies. The API is accessible through simple HTTP requests and provides functions for time series data, technical indicators, and real-time quotes. Alpha Vantage offers both free and paid plans with varying levels of data access and usage limits. The API is compatible with popular programming languages such as Python, Java, and Excel through the availability of SDKs and plugins. Key features of Alpha Vantage include support for a wide range of technical indicators, multiple data formats, simple API authentication using an API key, and integration with popular programming languages and platforms.

The following Python script utilizes the Alpha Vantage API to fetch real-time stock data from various stock exchanges, including NYSE, NASDAQ, LSE, TSE, and HKEX, providing current prices for specific stocks such as IBM, AAPL, BP, 6758.T, and 00700.HK.

```
1. import requests
2.
3. api_key = "YOUR_API_KEY"
```

```
4.
5.  # NYSE
6.  url_nyse = f"https://www.alphavantage.co/query?function=GLOBAL_
    QUOTE&symbol=IBM&apikey={api_key}"
7.  response_nyse = requests.get(url_nyse)
8.  data_nyse = response_nyse.json()
9.  print("NYSE:", data_nyse["Global Quote"]["05. price"])
10.
11. # NASDAQ
12. url_nasdaq = f"https://www.alphavantage.co/query?function=GLOBAL_
    QUOTE&symbol=AAPL&apikey={api_key}"
13. response_nasdaq = requests.get(url_nasdaq)
14. data_nasdaq = response_nasdaq.json()
15. print("NASDAQ:", data_nasdaq["Global Quote"]["05. price"])
16.
17. # LSE
18. url_lse = f"https://www.alphavantage.co/query?function=GLOBAL_
    QUOTE&symbol=BP&apikey={api_key}"
19. response_lse = requests.get(url_lse)
20. data_lse = response_lse.json()
21. print("LSE:", data_lse["Global Quote"]["05. price"])
22.
23. # TSE
24. url_tse = f"https://www.alphavantage.co/query?function=GLOBAL_
    QUOTE&symbol=6758.T&apikey={api_key}"
25. response_tse = requests.get(url_tse)
26. data_tse = response_tse.json()
27. print("TSE:", data_tse["Global Quote"]["05. price"])
28.
29. # HKEX
30. url_hkex = f"https://www.alphavantage.co/query?function=GLOBAL_
    QUOTE&symbol=00700.HK&apikey={api_key}"
31. response_hkex = requests.get(url_hkex)
32. data_hkex = response_hkex.json()
33. print("HKEX:", data_hkex["Global Quote"]["05. price"])
```

Reference: **https://www.alphavantage.co/documentation/**

Alternative data sources and indicators

Alternative data refers to data that encompasses a wide array of non-traditional sources beyond direct quotes or stock data. This could include information such as satellite imagery, web traffic data, or even social media posts. Financial analysts and traders increasingly utilize alternative data sources to gain unique insights into market trends and developments. By incorporating alternative data into their analysis alongside traditional financial news, traders can enhance their understanding of market dynamics and potentially gain a competitive edge in making investment decisions.

Financial news outlets, including Reuters, CNBC, and Bloomberg, provide traders with up-to-date information on global financial markets, helping them stay informed about market trends and developments. These news articles can significantly impact financial markets, as product introductions or quarterly financial reports can lead to substantial fluctuations in stock prices. Therefore, traders rely on precise and current news to make well-informed investment decisions. Sentiment analysis is a natural language processing technique that uses machine learning algorithms to determine the overall sentiment or mood of news articles and social media content toward a specific company or sector. Tools like RavenPack and Accern help traders understand market sentiment and adjust their trading strategies accordingly. The News API is a valuable resource for developers looking to access a broad range of news articles from multiple sources. By integrating sentiment analysis into their trading strategies, traders can analyze news articles and social media content using machine learning algorithms to make more informed investment decisions.

Here is an example of how to use the News API to retrieve the top headlines related to a specific topic using Python:

```
1. import requests
2.
3. api_key = "YOUR_API_KEY"
4. topic = "Bitcoin"
5.
6. url = f"https://newsapi.org/v2/top-headlines?q={topic}&apiKey={api_key}"
7. response = requests.get(url)
8. data = response.json()
9.
10. articles = data["articles"]
11. for article in articles:
12.     title = article["title"]
13.     description = article["description"]
14.     url = article["url"]
15.     print(f"Title: {title}\nDescription: {description}\nURL: {url}\n")
```

Reference: **https://newsapi.org/docs**

The advent of social media platforms such as Twitter, StockTwits, and Reddit, including subreddits such as r/wallstreetbets, has transformed the financial markets and trading landscape. These platforms have emerged as crucial sources of market sentiment and, when paired with advanced AI techniques, offer valuable insights for high-performance algorithmic trading. S&P Global's (2020) research revealed that the correlation between a stock's mentions on social media and its subsequent price fluctuations has increased in recent years, underscoring the importance of social media as a source of market information.

In Python, traders can use Tweepy, a popular Python library, to access Twitter's API and collect real-time tweets related to specific stocks:

```
1.  import tweepy
2.
3.  # API credentials
4.  consumer_key = 'your_consumer_key'
5.  consumer_secret = 'your_consumer_secret'
6.  access_token = 'your_access_token'
7.  access_token_secret = 'your_access_token_secret'
8.
9.  auth = tweepy.OAuthHandler(consumer_key, consumer_secret)
10. auth.set_access_token(access_token, access_token_secret)
11.
12. api = tweepy.API(auth)
13.
14. # Collect tweets containing 'TSLA'
15. tweets = tweepy.Cursor(api.search, q='TSLA', lang='en').items(100)
```

Reference: **https://docs.tweepy.org/en/stable/**

Sentiment analysis is the process of determining the sentiment or emotion behind a piece of text, which can be applied to financial markets by evaluating the sentiment of social media posts related to stocks. Using AI techniques such as **natural language processing (NLP)**, sentiment analysis can be applied to extract valuable information from tweets, StockTwits messages, or Reddit posts, and incorporate it into trading algorithms. In Python, the **TextBlob** library can be used for simple sentiment analysis:

```
1. import matplotlib.pyplot as plt
2. from textblob import TextBlob
3.
4. # Sample tweets
5. tweets = ["TSLA is doing great! I'm so bullish on this stock!",
6.           "TSLA is terrible. I'm very bearish on their future.",
7.           "TSLA's earnings report was neutral."]
8.
```

```
9.  # Analyze sentiment of tweets
10. sentiments = [TextBlob(tweet).sentiment.polarity for tweet in
    tweets]
11.
12. # Create a bar chart
13. fig, ax = plt.subplots()
14. ax.bar(range(len(tweets)), sentiments)
15.
16. # Set the x-axis labels
17. ax.set_xticks(range(len(tweets)))
18. ax.set_xticklabels(tweets, rotation=45, ha='right')
19.
20. # Set the y-axis label and title
21. ax.set_ylabel('Sentiment Score')
22. ax.set_title('Sentiment Analysis of Tweets')
23.
24. # Display the graph
25. plt.show()
```

The resulting graph illustrates the sentiment analysis of sample tweets related to TSLA (Tesla, Inc.), showcasing the polarity scores assigned to each tweet, thereby providing insights into the overall sentiment towards the company as expressed on social media.

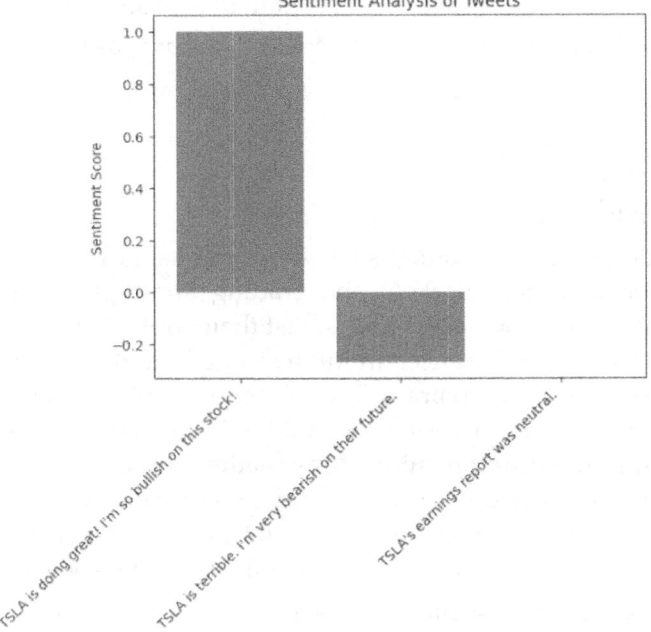

Figure 4.2: *TSLA Tweet Analysis*

Financial markets heavily rely on economic indicators like **Gross Domestic Product (GDP)**, inflation rates, and employment data, as they assist in algorithmic trading systems to make informed investment decisions. Economic indicators are essential for traders to determine the health of an economy, assess market sentiment, and identify potential investment opportunities. The **Federal Reserve Economic Data (FRED)** API, accessible through Python programming language, is offered by the Federal Reserve Bank of St. Louis and enables access to various economic indicators.

The following Python code employs the **pandas_datareader** library to retrieve economic data including **Gross Domestic Product (GDP), unemployment rate (UNRATE),** and **Consumer Price Index for All Urban Consumers (CPIAUCSL)** from the **Federal Reserve Economic Data (FRED)** database, spanning from January 1, 2022, to December 31, 2023. This data retrieval enables analysis and tracking of key economic indicators over the specified time period.

```
1. import pandas_datareader.data as web
2. import datetime
3.
4. start_date = datetime.datetime(2022, 1, 1)
5. end_date = datetime.datetime(2023, 12, 31)
6.
7. # Retrieve GDP, unemployment, and inflation rate data
8. gdp = web.get_data_fred('GDP', start_date, end_date)
9. unemployment = web.get_data_fred('UNRATE', start_date, end_date)
10. inflation = web.get_data_fred('CPIAUCSL', start_date, end_date)
11.
12. print(gdp)
13. print(unemployment)
14. print(inflation)
```

Announcements made by central banks, such as adjustments to interest rates, have a noteworthy impact on financial markets and trading strategies. Algorithmic traders frequently monitor these announcements and adjust their strategies accordingly to benefit from market opportunities. For instance, an interest rate hike may result in a currency's appreciation, influencing currency pairs in the foreign exchange (forex) market. Python programming language provides access to central bank interest rates through the FRED API. This Python script utilizes the **pandas_datareader** library to extract data from the FRED database, specifically focusing on retrieving the federal funds rate data set by the Federal Reserve. The data spans from January 1, 2023, to December 31, 2023, providing insights into the fluctuations and trends in interest rates over the specified time frame.

```
1. import pandas_datareader.data as web
2. import datetime
```

```
3.
4. start_date = datetime.datetime(2023, 1, 1)
5. end_date = datetime.datetime(2023, 12, 31)
6.
7. # Retrieve the Federal Reserve's federal funds rate data
8. fed_funds_rate = web.get_data_fred('FEDFUNDS', start_date, end_date)
9. print(fed_funds_rate)
```

Consumer sentiment and confidence indices, like the University of Michigan's Consumer Sentiment Index, offer valuable insights into consumer behavior and expectations, which can significantly affect financial markets. A high level of consumer confidence may indicate increased spending, leading to economic growth and impacting stock prices. Algorithmic traders can include these indices in their trading strategies to identify potential market trends. Python programming language facilitates access to consumer sentiment data via the FRED API.

This Python code snippet utilizes the **pandas_datareader** library to fetch data from the FRED database, focusing specifically on retrieving the Consumer Sentiment Index data published by the University of Michigan. Spanning from January 1, 2023, to December 31, 2023, this dataset offers valuable insights into consumer sentiment trends over the specified time period.

```
1. import pandas_datareader.data as web
2. import datetime
3.
4. start_date = datetime.datetime(2023, 1, 1)
5. end_date = datetime.datetime(2023, 12, 31)
6.
7. # Retrieve the University of Michigan's Consumer Sentiment Index data
8. consumer_sentiment = web.get_data_fred('UMCSENT', start_date, end_date)
9. print(consumer_sentiment)
```

Technical indicators and charting tools

To determine the direction and strength of a market trend, algorithmic trading commonly employs trend indicators such as moving averages and **Moving Average Convergence Divergence (MACD)**. These indicators assist traders in identifying entry and exit points for their trading strategies, making them a crucial element of high-performing algorithmic trading systems. The pandas and TA-Lib libraries in Python can be utilized to calculate moving averages and the MACD.

The following Python script leverages **pandas**, **yfinance**, and **pandas_ta** libraries to analyze stock market data for Apple Inc. (AAPL). It retrieves historical stock data spanning 12 months, calculates key technical indicators including the 5-day SMA and MACD, and integrates these indicators into the dataset for analysis. This allows for informed insights into recent trends and potential trading signals related to AAPL stock.

```
1. import pandas as pd
2. import yfinance as yf
3. import pandas_ta as ta
4. import datetime
5.
6. symbol = "AAPL"
7. aapl_data = yf.download(symbol, period='12mo')
8.
9. # Extract the 'Close' price column  aapl_data['Close']
10.
11. # Calculate the 5-day simple moving average
12. sma = ta.sma(aapl_data['Close'], length=5)
13.
14. # Calculate the MACD
15. macd = ta.macd(aapl_data['Close'], fast=12, slow=26, signal=9)
16.
17. # Add the calculated indicators to the data frame
18. aapl_data['SMA'] = sma
19. aapl_data['MACD'] = macd['MACD_12_26_9']
20. aapl_data['Signal'] = macd['MACDs_12_26_9']
21. aapl_data['MACD_Hist'] = macd['MACDh_12_26_9']
22.
23. # Print the updated data frame
24. print(aapl_data.tail(10))
```

The output displays the updated data frame of historical stock data for AAPL, including the calculated 5-day **Simple Moving Average (SMA)** and **Moving Average Convergence Divergence (MACD)** indicators. This provides traders and analysts with valuable insights into recent price trends, potential momentum shifts, and buy/sell signals for AAPL stock over the specified time period.

```
[*********************100%***********************]  1 of 1 completed
                Open        High         Low       Close    Adj Close   \
Date
2023-04-25  165.190002  166.309998  163.729996  163.770004  163.770004
2023-04-26  163.059998  165.279999  162.800003  163.759995  163.759995
2023-04-27  165.190002  168.559998  165.190002  168.410004  168.410004
2023-04-28  168.490005  169.850006  167.880005  169.679993  169.679993
2023-05-01  169.279999  170.449997  168.639999  169.589996  169.589996
2023-05-02  170.089996  170.350006  167.539993  168.539993  168.539993
2023-05-03  169.500000  170.919998  167.160004  167.449997  167.449997
2023-05-04  164.889999  167.039993  164.309998  165.789993  165.789993
2023-05-05  170.979996  174.300003  170.759995  173.570007  173.570007
2023-05-08  172.479996  173.850006  172.110001  173.500000  173.500000

               Volume         SMA        MACD    Signal   MACD_Hist
Date
2023-04-25   48714100  165.680002    2.459838  2.892241   -0.432403
2023-04-26   45498800  164.906000    2.211950  2.756183   -0.544232
2023-04-27   64902300  165.258002    2.363470  2.677640   -0.314170
2023-04-28   55209200  166.189999    2.556558  2.653424   -0.096866
2023-05-01   52472900  167.041998    2.671523  2.657044    0.014480
2023-05-02   48425700  167.995996    2.647390  2.655113   -0.007723
2023-05-03   65136000  168.733997    2.511362  2.626363   -0.115001
2023-05-04   81235400  168.209995    2.243745  2.549839   -0.306094
2023-05-05  113316400  168.987997    2.629133  2.565698    0.063435
2023-05-08   55932100  169.769998    2.895528  2.631664    0.263864
```

Figure 4.3: Sample MACD values

Momentum indicators, such as the **Relative Strength Index** (**RSI**) and the stochastic oscillator, are utilized to measure the velocity and power of price movements. These indicators assist algorithmic traders in identifying overbought and oversold market conditions, allowing them to leverage potential price reversals. In Python, the TA-Lib library can be used to compute the RSI and Stochastic Oscillator.

The following Python script utilizes the pandas, **yfinance**, and **pandas_ta** libraries to analyze stock market data for **Microsoft Corporation** (**MSFT**). It retrieves one month of historical stock data, calculates key technical indicators including the 14-day RSI and Stochastic Oscillator, and integrates these indicators into the dataset for analysis.

```
1. import pandas as pd
2. import yfinance as yf
3. import pandas_ta as ta
4. import datetime
5.
6. symbol = 'MSFT'
7. msft_data = yf.download(symbol, period='1mo')
8.
9. #print(msft_data)
10.
```

```
11. # Calculate the 14-day RSI
12. rsi = ta.rsi(msft_data['Close'], length=14)
13.
14. # Calculate the Stochastic Oscillator
15. stoch = ta.stoch(msft_data['High'], msft_data['Low'], msft_
    data['Close'])
16.
17. #print(stoch)
18.
19. # Add the calculated indicators to the data frame
20. msft_data['RSI'] = rsi
21. msft_data['%K'] = stoch['STOCHk_14_3_3'] # First Column
22. msft_data['%D'] = stoch['STOCHd_14_3_3']
23.
24. # Print the updated data frame
25. print(msft_data.tail(10))
```

The output displays the updated data frame of historical stock data for MSFT, including the calculated 14-day RSI and Stochastic Oscillator (%K and %D). This provides traders and analysts with valuable insights into recent price momentum and potential overbought or oversold conditions for MSFT stock over the past month.

```
[********************100%***********************] 1 of 1 completed
                 Open        High         Low       Close    Adj Close  \
Date
2023-04-25  279.510010  281.600006  275.369995  275.420013  275.420013
2023-04-26  296.700012  299.570007  292.730011  295.369995  295.369995
2023-04-27  295.970001  305.200012  295.250000  304.829987  304.829987
2023-04-28  304.010010  308.929993  303.309998  307.260010  307.260010
2023-05-01  306.970001  308.600006  305.149994  305.559998  305.559998
2023-05-02  307.760010  309.179993  303.910004  305.410004  305.410004
2023-05-03  306.619995  308.609985  304.089996  304.399994  304.399994
2023-05-04  306.239990  307.760010  303.399994  305.410004  305.410004
2023-05-05  305.720001  311.970001  304.269989  310.649994  310.649994
2023-05-08  310.130005  310.200012  306.089996  308.649994  308.649994

              Volume        RSI         %K         %D
Date
2023-04-25  45772200        NaN        NaN        NaN
2023-04-26  64599200        NaN        NaN        NaN
2023-04-27  46462600        NaN        NaN        NaN
2023-04-28  36446700  69.715081        NaN        NaN
2023-05-01  21294100  67.112332  94.580580        NaN
2023-05-02  26404400  66.875098  91.277223        NaN
2023-05-03  22360800  65.203689  88.223319  91.360374
2023-05-04  22519900  66.115703  87.853714  89.118085
2023-05-05  28181200  70.443882  90.368360  88.815131
2023-05-08  21306900  66.929811  92.057284  90.093119
```

Figure 4.4: MSFT Technical indicators and stock prices

Data Processing and Analysis

Volatility indicators, like Bollinger Bands and the **Average True Range (ATR)**, determine the extent of price variability in a market. These indicators enable algorithmic traders to detect potential trading opportunities in highly volatile markets and adapt their strategies accordingly. In Python, the TA-Lib library is available to calculate bollinger bands and the ATR.

This Python script utilizes the pandas, **yfinance**, and **pandas_ta** libraries to analyze stock market data for MSFT. It retrieves one month of historical stock data and calculates key technical indicators including Bollinger Bands and the 14-day ATR to assess volatility and potential price reversals.

```
1. import pandas as pd
2. import yfinance as yf
3. import pandas_ta as ta
4. import datetime
5.
6. symbol = 'MSFT'
7. msft_data = yf.download(symbol, period='1mo')
8.
9. # Extract the 'Close' price column
10. price_data = msft_data['Close']
11.
12. # Calculate Bollinger Bands
13. bb = ta.bbands(price_data, length=20)
14.
15. # Calculate the 14-day ATR
16. atr = ta.atr(msft_data['High'], msft_data['Low'], price_data, length=14)
17.
18. print(bb)
19.
20. # Add the calculated indicators to the data frame
21. msft_data['BB_upperband'] = bb['BBL_20_2.0']
22. msft_data['BB_middleband'] = bb['BBM_20_2.0']
23. msft_data['BB_lowerband'] = bb['BBU_20_2.0']
24. msft_data['ATR'] = atr
25.
26. # Print the updated data frame
27. print(msft_data.tail(10))
```

The output presents the updated data frame of historical stock data for MSFT, incorporating calculated Bollinger Bands (upper, middle, and lower) and the 14-day ATR. This provides traders and analysts with insights into price volatility and potential trading opportunities over the past month.

```
[*********************100%***********************]  1 of 1 completed
                Open        High         Low       Close    Adj Close  \
Date
2023-05-02  307.760010  309.179993  303.910004  305.410004  305.410004
2023-05-03  306.619995  308.609985  304.089996  304.399994  304.399994
2023-05-04  306.239990  307.760010  303.399994  305.410004  305.410004
2023-05-05  305.720001  311.970001  304.269989  310.649994  310.649994
2023-05-08  310.130005  310.200012  306.089996  308.649994  308.649994

              Volume  BB_upperband  BB_middleband  BB_lowerband       ATR
Date
2023-05-02  26404400           NaN            NaN           NaN  7.065532
2023-05-03  22360800           NaN            NaN           NaN  6.811693
2023-05-04  22519900           NaN            NaN           NaN  6.573941
2023-05-05  28181200    272.703005     293.262999    313.822993  6.680422
2023-05-08  21306900    272.700297     294.225998    315.751699  6.484448
```

Figure 4.5: *MSFT 14-days Bollinger Bands*

Volume indicators, such as **On-Balance Volume (OBV)** and **Chaikin Money Flow (CMF)**, are used to measure the flow of money in and out of a security. These indicators can help algorithmic traders gauge the strength of price movements and identify potential trend reversals based on changes in trading volume. In Python, the pandas and TA-Lib libraries can be used to calculate the OBV and CMF:

```
1.  import yfinance as yf
2.  import pandas_ta as ta
3.
4.  # Fetch Microsoft's stock price data
5.  symbol = 'MSFT'
6.  msft_data = yf.download(symbol, period='1mo')
7.
8.  # Calculate On-Balance Volume (OBV)
9.  obv = ta.obv(msft_data['Close'], msft_data['Volume'])
10.
11. # Calculate Chaikin Money Flow (CMF)
12. cmf = ta.cmf(high=msft_data['High'], low=msft_data['Low'],
        close=msft_data['Close'], volume=msft_data['Volume'], window=20)
13.
14. # Add the calculated indicators to the data frame
15. msft_data['OBV'] = obv
16. msft_data['CMF'] = cmf
17.
18. # Print the updated data frame
19. print(msft_data.tail(10))
```

The output showcases the updated data frame of historical stock data for MSFT, featuring the calculated OBV and CMF indicators. This provides traders and analysts with insights into the volume trends and money flow dynamics associated with MSFT stock over the past month.

```
[*******************100%*********************] 1 of 1 completed
                Open        High         Low       Close   Adj Close  \
Date
2023-04-25  279.510010  281.600006  275.369995  275.420013  275.420013
2023-04-26  296.700012  299.570007  292.730011  295.369995  295.369995
2023-04-27  295.970001  305.200012  295.250000  304.829987  304.829987
2023-04-28  304.010010  308.929993  303.309998  307.260010  307.260010
2023-05-01  306.970001  308.600006  305.149994  305.559998  305.559998
2023-05-02  307.760010  309.179993  303.910004  305.410004  305.410004
2023-05-03  306.619995  308.609985  304.089996  304.399994  304.399994
2023-05-04  306.239990  307.760010  303.399994  305.410004  305.410004
2023-05-05  305.720001  311.970001  304.269989  310.649994  310.649994
2023-05-08  310.130005  310.200012  306.089996  308.649994  308.649994

              Volume         OBV       CMF
Date
2023-04-25  45772200  -70014700.0       NaN
2023-04-26  64599200   -5415500.0       NaN
2023-04-27  46462600   41047100.0       NaN
2023-04-28  36446700   77493800.0       NaN
2023-05-01  21294100   56199700.0       NaN
2023-05-02  26404400   29795300.0       NaN
2023-05-03  22360800    7434500.0       NaN
2023-05-04  22519900   29954400.0       NaN
2023-05-05  28181200   58135600.0 -0.006072
2023-05-08  21306900   36828700.0 -0.034058
```

Figure 4.6: MSFT OBV and CMF value samples

Popular financial data APIs

Alpha Vantage is a popular financial data API that provides a wide range of information, including stock quotes, technical indicators, historical data, and forex market data (Alpha Vantage, 2021). Many algorithmic traders and AI-driven trading systems rely on Alpha Vantage to access real-time and historical data for their strategies. In Python, the **alpha_vantage** library can be used to access data from the Alpha Vantage API:

```
1. from alpha_vantage.timeseries import TimeSeries
2. api_key = 'your_api_key'
3. symbol = 'MSFT'
4.
5. ts = TimeSeries(api_key)
6. data, meta_data = ts.get_daily(symbol=symbol, outputsize='compact')
7.
8. print(data)
```

Intrinio is a financial data platform that offers various types of data, including stock market data, financial statements, economic data, and alternative data (Intrinio, 2021). Algorithmic traders and AI-based systems can use Intrinio's data to develop and enhance their trading strategies. In Python, the **intrinio_sdk** library can be used to access data from the Intrinio API:

```
1. import intrinio_sdk
2. api_key = 'your_api_key'
3. symbol = 'AAPL'
4.
5. intrinio_sdk.ApiClient().configuration.api_key['api_key'] = api_key
6. security_api = intrinio_sdk.SecurityApi()
7.
8. historical_data = security_api.get_security_stock_prices(symbol, start_date='2020-01-01', end_date='2020-12-31')
9. print(historical_data)
```

Quandl is a financial data platform known for providing a wide range of datasets, including stock market data, futures, options, and economic indicators (Quandl, 2021). Quandl's data is widely used by algorithmic traders and AI-driven trading systems for strategy development and analysis. In Python, the **quandl** library can be used to access data from the Quandl API:

```
1. import quandl
2.
3. api_key = 'your_api_key'
4. symbol = 'WIKI/AAPL'
5.
6. quandl.ApiConfig.api_key = api_key
7. data = quandl.get(symbol, start_date='2020-01-01', end_date='2020-12-31')
8.
9. print(data)
```

Twelve Data is a financial data provider that offers various types of data, such as stock market data, technical indicators, and economic data (Twelve Data, 2021). Algorithmic traders and AI-driven trading systems can use Twelve Data's API to access real-time and historical data to enhance their strategies. In Python, the **twelvedata** library can be used to access data from the Twelve Data API:

```
1. from twelvedata import TDClient
2.
3. api_key = 'your_api_key'
4. symbol = 'MSFT'
```

```
5.
6. td = TDClient(apikey=api_key)
7. ts = td.time_series(symbol=symbol, interval='1day', start_
   date='2020-01-01', end_date='2020-12-31')
8.
9. print(ts.as_pandas())
```

Federal Reserve Economic Data (FRED) is a vast database of economic data provided by the Federal Reserve Bank of St. Louis. FRED offers a wide range of data, including macroeconomic indicators, interest rates, employment data, and regional data. Algorithmic traders and AI-driven trading systems can use FRED's data to analyze market conditions and develop data-driven trading strategies. In Python, the **pandas_datareader** library can be used to access data from the FRED API:

```
1. import pandas_datareader.data as web
2. import datetime
3.
4. api_key = 'your_api_key'
5. symbol = 'GDP'
6.
7. start_date = datetime.datetime(2020, 1, 1)
8. end_date = datetime.datetime(2020, 12, 31)
9.
10. web.ApiReader(api_key=api_key)
11. data = web.get_data_fred(symbol, start_date, end_date)
12.
13. print(data)
```

Data preprocessing and cleaning

Data preprocessing and cleaning are essential steps in any data analysis project. It involves preparing raw data for analysis by transforming it into a consistent format, identifying and correcting errors or inconsistencies, and dealing with missing or incomplete data. Handling different data formats is a critical part of preprocessing, as it ensures that data from various sources can be combined and analyzed effectively. Data quality assessment and validation is also crucial, as it allows for the identification of any issues that may affect the accuracy and reliability of the analysis. By implementing robust data preprocessing and cleaning techniques, analysts can ensure that their data is ready for use in modeling, visualization, or other analytical tasks, providing insights that can drive informed decision-making.

Handling different data formats

Comma separated values (CSV) files are a common format for storing financial data due to their simplicity and ease of use. Algorithmic traders and AI-driven trading systems often rely on CSV files to store and access historical price data, technical indicators, and other relevant market information. In Python, the pandas library provides a straightforward way to read and write CSV files:

```
1. import pandas as pd
2.
3. # Reading a CSV file
4. csv_file = 'historical_data.csv'
5. data = pd.read_csv(csv_file)
6.
7. # Writing data to a CSV file
8. output_file = 'cleaned_data.csv'
9. data.to_csv(output_file, index=False)
```

JavaScript Object Notation (JSON) is another widely-used data format for exchanging financial data between APIs and trading applications. JSON is particularly suited for transmitting complex data structures, such as hierarchical or nested data, making it a popular choice for algorithmic traders and AI-driven trading systems. In Python, the **json** library can be used to parse JSON data and convert it into a more convenient format for further processing:

```
1.  import json
2.
3.  # Example JSON data (replace with actual data)
4.  json_data = '{"symbol": "AAPL", "price": 150.00, "timestamp": "2021-
    09-01T00:00:00"}'
5.
6.  # Parse JSON data
7.  parsed_data = json.loads(json_data)
8.
9.  # Access specific data fields
10. symbol = parsed_data['symbol']
11. price = parsed_data['price']
12. timestamp = parsed_data['timestamp']
```

Algorithmic traders and AI-driven trading systems often rely on databases like SQL and NoSQL databases to store and manage large-scale financial data. These databases offer a reliable and efficient means of storing, retrieving, and manipulating data, making them a crucial component of high-performance trading systems. In Python, there are various libraries available for interacting with different types of databases. For instance, the sqlite3 library enables Python developers to interact with SQLite databases. With the help of these libraries, traders can easily access and manipulate data in their databases, enabling them to make informed decisions and improve their trading strategies.

Data quality assessment and validation

Assessing and validating data quality are vital steps in the data preprocessing and cleaning process, as the accuracy, completeness, and consistency of financial data are crucial for creating dependable and high-performance trading strategies. Missing values, a frequent issue in financial data, can lead to imprecise or skewed analysis if not properly addressed. Thus, algorithmic traders and AI-powered trading systems should recognize and tackle missing values in their datasets before using the data for analysis or model training, with the **pandas** library in Python providing several functions for detecting and managing missing values.

```
1. import pandas as pd
2.
3. # Example data with missing values (replace with actual data)
4. data = pd.DataFrame({
5.     'symbol': ['AAPL', 'AAPL', 'AAPL'],
6.     'date': ['2021-01-01', '2021-01-02', '2021-01-03'],
7.     'price': [100, None, 102]
8. })
9.
10. # Detect missing values
11. missing_values = data.isna()
12.
13. # Fill missing values using various methods (choose one)
14. data_filled_forward = data.fillna(method='ffill')  # Forward fill
15. data_filled_backward = data.fillna(method='bfill')  # Backward fill
16. data_filled_mean = data.fillna(data.mean(numeric_only=True))  # Fill with the mean value
17.
18. print(data_filled_forward)
19. print(data_filled_backward)
20. print(data_filled_mean)
```

Outliers are data points that deviate significantly from the general pattern of the dataset, and they can negatively impact the performance of AI-driven trading systems if not addressed. Algorithmic traders should identify and handle outliers in their financial data to ensure the accuracy and reliability of their models. One common method for detecting outliers is the **interquartile range** (**IQR**) method.

The following Python script demonstrates the process of identifying and removing outliers from a dataset using the interquartile range method. Using example stock price data for Apple Inc. (AAPL), outliers are detected based on the IQR criterion and subsequently removed, ensuring the integrity of the dataset for further analysis.

```
1. import numpy as np
2.
3. # Example data with outliers (replace with actual data)
4. data = pd.DataFrame({
5.     'symbol': ['AAPL', 'AAPL', 'AAPL', 'AAPL', 'AAPL'],
6.     'date': ['2021-01-01', '2021-01-02', '2021-01-03', '2021-01-04', '2021-01-05'],
7.     'price': [100, 101, 102, 103, 500]
8. })
9.
10. # Calculate the interquartile range (IQR)
11. Q1 = data['price'].quantile(0.25)
12. Q3 = data['price'].quantile(0.75)
13. IQR = Q3 - Q1
14.
15. # Identify outliers
16. outliers = (data['price'] < (Q1 - 1.5 * IQR)) | (data['price'] > (Q3 + 1.5 * IQR))
17.
18. # Remove outliers
19. data_cleaned = data[~outliers]
20. print(data_cleaned)
```

Data consistency checks are essential for ensuring that financial data is accurate and reliable. Algorithmic traders and AI-driven trading systems should perform consistency checks to verify that data points are logically coherent and that there are no discrepancies or errors in the dataset. An example of a data consistency check is verifying that the daily high price is greater than or equal to the daily low price.

The following Python script checks the consistency of high and low stock price data within a **DataFrame**, focusing on ensuring that high prices are always greater than or equal to low prices for each corresponding date. If inconsistencies are detected, the script identifies and handles them accordingly by either removing or correcting the problematic values.

```
1. # Example data (replace with actual data)
2. data = pd.DataFrame({
3. 'symbol': ['AAPL', 'AAPL', 'AAPL'],
4. 'date': ['2021-01-01', '2021-01-02', '2021-01-03'],
```

```
5.    'low': [99, 100, 101],
6.    'high': [101, 102, 103]
7. })
8.
9. # Check data consistency
10. inconsistent_data = data[data['high'] < data['low']]
11.
12. # Handle inconsistent data (e.g., remove or correct the values)
13. if inconsistent_data.empty:
14.     print('Data is consistent')
15. else:
16.     print('Inconsistent data found:')
17.     print(inconsistent_data)
18. # Example: Remove inconsistent data
19. data_cleaned = data[data['high'] >= data['low']]
```

Data transformation and normalization are important steps to prepare data for AI-based trading. They change raw data into a format that machine learning models can understand and use. These steps make trading algorithms work better and help make smarter decisions. They also help the model learn from new data it has not seen before.

A common way to change data for AI-based trading is called scaling. Scaling makes sure input variables have similar sizes, so they all affect the model equally. This prevents larger variables from controlling the model. In Python, you can use scikit-learn's **MinMaxScaler** and **StandardScaler** classes to do scaling:

```
1. import numpy as np
2. from sklearn.preprocessing import MinMaxScaler
3.
4. # Sample data for scaling
5. data = np.array([[100, 200], [300, 400], [500, 600]])
6.
7. # Define MinMaxScaler
8. scaler = MinMaxScaler()
9.
10. # Fit and transform data
11. scaled_data = scaler.fit_transform(data)
12. print(scaled_data)
```

Normalization is another important step in preparing data. It changes input data into a standard form that's easier to compare and analyze. In AI-based trading, common methods include Z-score and log transformations. Z-score, also called standardization, centers data around the mean with a standard deviation of 1. Log transformation helps reduce the influence of outliers and makes data more like a Gaussian distribution. You can use Python's **scikit-learn** library for Z-score normalization and **numpy** for log transformations.

The following Python script demonstrates the process of normalizing data using the **StandardScaler** from the **scikit-learn** library. A sample dataset comprising numerical values is normalized, ensuring that the data is scaled to have a mean of 0 and a standard deviation of 1 across each feature.

```
1. import numpy as np
2. from sklearn.preprocessing import StandardScaler
3.
4. # Sample data for normalization
5. data = np.array([[100, 200], [300, 400], [500, 600]])
6.
7. # Define StandardScaler
8. scaler = StandardScaler()
9.
10. # Fit and transform data
11. normalized_data = scaler.fit_transform(data)
12. print(normalized_data)
```

Example of log transformation:

```
1. import numpy as np
2.
3. # Sample data for log transformation
4. data = np.array([[100, 200], [300, 400], [500, 600]])
5.
6. # Apply log transformation
7. log_transformed_data = np.log(data)
8. print(log_transformed_data)
```

Data resampling and aggregation are important steps for preparing data in AI-based trading. They change data's time frame or frequency to make analysis and decision-making easier. These techniques can help reduce noise, remove repeated information, and find useful patterns, which improves trading algorithm performance.

For financial data like stock prices or trading volumes, resampling changes data frequency, such as from minute-level to hourly or daily data. Resampling methods include downsampling (lowering frequency) and upsampling (raising frequency). Python's pandas library has the **resample()** function to help with both downsampling and upsampling financial data:

Example of downsampling using pandas:

```
1. import pandas as pd
2.
3. # Sample time series data
4. data = pd.DataFrame({'Price': [100, 101, 102, 103, 104]}, index=pd.
   date_range(start='2022-01-01', periods=5, freq='T'))
5.
6. # Downsample data to 3-minute intervals
7. resampled_data = data.resample('3T').mean()
8. print(resampled_data)
```

Aggregation is a key technique in AI-based trading that combines and summarizes data to get useful information. It can be used with different data types like time series, order book, and trade data. Typical aggregation methods include finding averages, sums, minimum and maximum values, and other summary stats. Python's **pandas** library has functions like **groupby()**, **agg()**, and **rolling()** for data aggregation:

```
1. import pandas as pd
2.
3. # Sample time series data
4. data = pd.DataFrame({'Price': [100, 101, 102, 103, 104]}, index=pd.
   date_range(start='2022-01-01', periods=5, freq='D'))
5.
6. # Calculate the moving average over a 3-day window
7. moving_average = data.rolling(window=3).mean()
8. print(moving_average)
```

Feature extraction and selection

AI-based trading relies on accurate and strong models, which require good feature extraction and selection. Different types of features, such as technical, fundamental, and sentiment features, are used in trading, providing varying perspectives on the market and helping to develop a comprehensive understanding of finance. Python offers a range of libraries and tools for extracting and analyzing these features, with technical features being derived from past price and volume data. Technical indicators such as moving averages, RSI, Bollinger Bands, and momentum indicators can be calculated using libraries in Python such as pandas, numpy, and TA-Lib.

Example of calculating the moving average using pandas:

```
1. import pandas as pd
2.
3. # Sample price data
4. data = pd.DataFrame({'Price': [100, 101, 102, 103, 104]}, index=pd.
   date_range(start='2022-01-01', periods=5, freq='D'))
```

5.
6. `# Calculate the 3-day moving average`
7. `moving_average = data.rolling(window=3).mean()`
8. `print(moving_average)`

Fundamental features look at a company's financial health, like earnings, revenue, cash flow, and valuation metrics. They help evaluate a stock's true value and find investment opportunities. To work with fundamental features in Python, you can use the pandas library for processing financial statements, and libraries like **yfinance** and Alpha Vantage to access financial data for different companies.

Example of retrieving fundamental data using **yfinance**:

1. `import yfinance as yf`
2.
3. `# Define the stock ticker`
4. `ticker = "AMZN"`
5.
6. `# Get stock data`
7. `stock = yf.Ticker(ticker)`
8.
9. `# Get financials`
10. `financials = stock.financials`
11. `print(financials)`

Sentiment features track the market's feelings and opinions, usually gathered from news articles, social media, and analyst reports. Analyzing sentiment can show trends and changes in investor behavior. To do sentiment analysis in Python, you can use natural **language processing** (**NLP**) libraries like NLTK, TextBlob, and spaCy to work with textual data.

Example of sentiment analysis using **TextBlob**:

1. `from textblob import TextBlob`
2.
3. `# Sample text`
4. `text = "Apple's recent earnings report exceeded market expectations, and the stock price surged."`
5.
6. `# Perform sentiment analysis`
7. `sentiment = TextBlob(text).sentiment`
8. `print(sentiment)`

Feature engineering is a critical part of AI-based trading where new features are created from raw data to improve machine learning model performance. Good feature engineering leads to more accurate predictions, better generalization, and higher profitability. Different techniques can be used to transform and combine existing features, like mathematical transformations, domain-specific transformations, and interaction features. Python has strong libraries like **pandas**, **numpy**, and **scikit-learn** for feature engineering in trading.

Mathematical transformations, such as logarithmic, exponential, and power transformations, can change feature distribution and scale. This can reduce the effect of outliers and skewness, making machine learning models perform better. Python's **numpy** library has many math functions to apply to financial data for feature engineering.

Example of logarithmic transformation using **numpy**:

```
1.  import numpy as np
2.
3.  # Sample data
4.  data = np.array([100, 200, 300, 400, 500])
5.
6.  # Apply logarithmic transformation
7.  log_data = np.log(data)
8.  print(log_data)
```

Domain-specific transformations involve creating new features based on expertise and knowledge of finance and trading. For instance, technical indicators such as moving averages, **relative strength index** (**RSI**), and Bollinger Bands, and fundamental ratios like **price-to-earnings** (**P/E**) and **price-to-sales** (**P/S**) ratios. These features provide essential insights into market dynamics and help in making trading decisions.

Interaction features are made by combining two or more existing features to capture complex relationships and interactions between them. These features can uncover hidden patterns and dependencies in data, improving machine learning model performance. Interaction features can be created using mathematical operations like addition, subtraction, multiplication, and division. Advanced techniques such as polynomial and interaction terms can also be applied. Python's **pandas** and **scikit-learn** libraries have tools for creating interaction features from financial data.

Example of creating interaction features using **pandas**:

```
1.  import pandas as pd
2.
3.  # Sample data
4.  data = pd.DataFrame({'Price': [100, 101, 102, 103, 104], 'Volume':
    [1000, 2000, 3000, 4000, 5000]})
5.
6.  # Create interaction feature: price * volume
7.  data['Price_Volume'] = data['Price'] * data['Volume']
8.  print(data)
```

In AI-based trading, selecting the right features is crucial to improve predictive model performance. Three primary feature selection methods are filter, wrapper, and embedded. Filter methods use univariate statistical tests, such as **Pearson's correlation coefficient**, to assess feature significance independently of machine learning algorithms. For instance, calculating the correlation between stock prices and economic indicators can help identify relevant factors for prediction. Here is a Python example using the **numpy** library:

```
1.  import numpy as np
2.
3.  # Example data
4.  stock_prices = np.array([100, 105, 110, 115, 120])
5.  economic_indicators = np.array([50, 55, 60, 65, 70])
6.
7.  # Calculate Pearson's correlation coefficient
8.  corr_coef = np.corrcoef(stock_prices, economic_indicators)[0, 1]
9.
10. print("Pearson's correlation coefficient: ", corr_coef)
```

This will output the Pearson's correlation coefficient between the **stock_prices** and **economic_indicators** arrays.

Wrapper methods involve selecting features based on the performance of a particular machine learning algorithm. **Recursive Feature Elimination** (RFE) is a commonly used wrapper method that iteratively removes the least important features and trains the model on the remaining features. In trading, RFE could be used to identify the most relevant technical indicators for predicting stock price movements using a **support vector machine** (SVM) classifier. A Python implementation using **sklearn** library is:

```
1.  from sklearn.feature_selection import RFE
2.  from sklearn.svm import SVC
3.  from sklearn.datasets import load_iris
4.
5.  data = load_iris()
6.  X, y = data.data, data.target
7.
8.  svm = SVC(kernel="linear", C=1)
9.  rfe = RFE(svm, n_features_to_select=2)
10. rfe.fit(X, y)
```

Embedded methods integrate feature selection within the machine learning algorithm itself. Lasso regularization is an example of an embedded method that imposes a penalty on the magnitude of the coefficients in a linear regression model, which shrinks some coefficients to zero and excludes them from the model. In trading, Lasso could be used to predict stock returns based on financial ratios, resulting in a more parsimonious model.

Here is a Python example using the **sklearn** library:

```
1.  from sklearn.linear_model import Lasso
2.
3.  # Example data
4.  X = [[0, 1, 2], [3, 4, 5], [6, 7, 8]]
5.  y = [1, 2, 3]
6.
7.  # Fit Lasso model
8.  lasso = Lasso(alpha=0.1)
9.  lasso.fit(X, y)
10.
11. # Print selected features
12. print("Selected features:", np.where(lasso.coef_ != 0)[0])
```

This code will fit a Lasso model to the **X** and **y** data and output the selected features with non-zero coefficients.

In AI-based trading, it can be difficult to make sense of financial data because it is noisy and has a lot of dimensions. Dimensionality reduction techniques, like **Principal Component Analysis (PCA)** and **t-distributed Stochastic Neighbor Embedding (t-SNE)**, can help by simplifying the data and keeping important information.

PCA is a way to simplify complex data by projecting it onto a lower-dimensional space while preserving as much information as possible. In trading, it can be useful to apply PCA to datasets with many technical indicators, so that prediction models can be built more efficiently. Here is an example of how to use PCA in Python with the **sklearn** library:

```
1.  import pandas as pd
2.  import yfinance as yf
3.  import pandas_ta as ta
4.  from sklearn.manifold import TSNE
5.  import matplotlib.pyplot as plt
6.
7.  # Load data for Apple stock from Yahoo Finance
8.  symbol = 'AAPL'
9.  data = yf.download(symbol, start='2022-01-01', end='2022-04-25')
10. prices = data['Adj Close']
11.
12. # Calculate the technical indicators
13. ma20 = ta.sma(prices, length=20)
14. ma50 = ta.sma(prices, length=50)
15. rsi = ta.rsi(prices, length=14)
```

```
16.
17. # Combine the indicators into a single DataFrame
18. indicators = pd.DataFrame({'MA20': ma20, 'MA50': ma50, 'RSI': rsi})
19.
20. # Drop rows with NaN values
21. indicators.dropna(inplace=True)
22.
23. # Apply t-SNE on the indicator data with perplexity=5
24. tsne = TSNE(n_components=2, perplexity=5)
25. indicators_embedded = tsne.fit_transform(indicators)
26.
27. # Plot the embedded indicator data
28. plt.scatter(indicators_embedded[:, 0], indicators_embedded[:, 1])
29. plt.xlabel('TSNE1')
30. plt.ylabel('TSNE2')
31. plt.title('Technical Indicator Data (t-SNE)')
32. plt.show()
```

The output presents a scatter plot visualization of the technical indicator data for Apple Inc. (AAPL) after embedding it into a two-dimensional space using t-SNE. This visualization aids in understanding the underlying structure or relationships within the indicator data, potentially revealing distinct clusters or patterns that could inform trading strategies or further analysis.

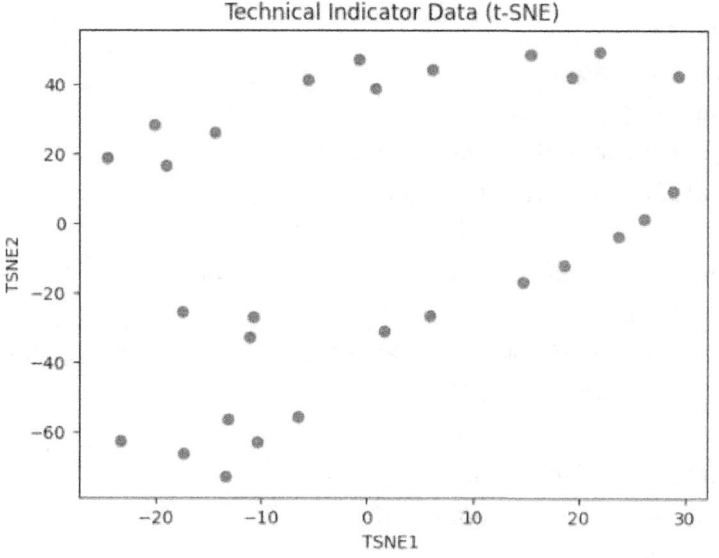

Figure 4.7: Sample TSNE for AAPL Data

In this example, we use the **yfinance** library to download daily adjusted closing prices for Apple stock from Yahoo Finance. We then calculate the following three technical indicators:

- 20-day moving averages
- 50-day moving averages,
- 14-day **relative strength index (RSI)**

We calculate these indicators using the **SMA()** and **RSI()** functions from the **talib** library. We combine the indicators into a single **DataFrame**, and then perform PCA on the indicator data using the **PCA()** function from scikit-learn. Finally, we plot the reduced data in two dimensions using matplotlib. The resulting plot shows the technical indicator data in two dimensions, with the points colored by their corresponding class labels. Note that the PCA algorithm can be useful for visualizing high-dimensional financial data in two dimensions, as well as for identifying patterns and relationships in the data.

Although PCA is a useful technique for simplifying data, it can have trouble capturing nonlinear relationships in the data. That is where t-SNE comes in. t-SNE is a nonlinear dimensionality reduction technique that focuses on preserving the local structure of the data by minimizing the differences between pairwise similarities in the original and reduced spaces. In algorithmic trading, t-SNE can be used to visualize clusters of stocks based on their historical price patterns, which could help identify potential trading opportunities. Here is an example of how to use t-SNE in Python with the **sklearn** library:

```
1.  import pandas as pd
2.  import yfinance as yf
3.  import pandas_ta as ta
4.  from sklearn.manifold import TSNE
5.  import matplotlib.pyplot as plt
6.
7.  # Load data for Apple stock from Yahoo Finance
8.  symbol = 'AAPL'
9.  data = yf.download(symbol, start='2022-01-01', end='2022-04-25')
10. prices = data['Adj Close']
11.
12. # Calculate the technical indicators
13. ma20 = ta.sma(prices, length=20)
14. ma50 = ta.sma(prices, length=50)
15. rsi = ta.rsi(prices, length=14)
16.
17. # Combine the indicators into a single DataFrame
18. indicators = pd.DataFrame({'MA20': ma20, 'MA50': ma50, 'RSI': rsi})
19.
```

```
20. # Drop rows with NaN values
21. indicators.dropna(inplace=True)
22.
23. # Apply t-SNE on the indicator data
24. tsne = TSNE(n_components=2, perplexity=5)
25. indicators_embedded = tsne.fit_transform(indicators)
26.
27. # Plot the embedded indicator data
28. plt.scatter(indicators_embedded[:, 0], indicators_embedded[:, 1])
29. plt.xlabel('TSNE1')
30. plt.ylabel('TSNE2')
31. plt.title('Technical Indicator Data (t-SNE)')
32. plt.show()
33.
```

PCA and t-SNE are both important tools in AI-based trading, and the choice between them depends on the data structure and the desired balance between computational efficiency and information preservation. PCA is faster and better for linearly correlated data, while t-SNE is better at capturing complex nonlinear relationships but is computationally more expensive.

Analyzing historical successful/failure trading patterns

In AI-based trading, analyzing historical trading patterns is important for developing successful trading strategies. By studying past trading patterns, traders can gain insights into market behavior and make informed decisions about buying and selling assets. Technical analysis is a popular technique for analyzing historical trading patterns, which involves studying past price and volume data to identify trends, support and resistance levels, and chart patterns. This information can help traders identify potential opportunities and manage risks.

Candlestick patterns are a tool used by traders to predict the direction of an asset's price movement. One commonly used pattern is called the Engulfing pattern, which involves two candles in a row. The first candle has a small body, and the second candle has a larger body that completely covers the first candle. This can signal a possible reversal in the asset's price trend.

To detect bullish engulfing patterns in Python, traders can use the **pandas** and **numpy** libraries. The provided Python script defines a function **detect_bullish_engulfing(df)** that identifies bullish engulfing patterns within a given **DataFrame** of stock price data. This pattern occurs when the current candlestick's body completely engulfs the body of the previous candlestick, suggesting a potential bullish reversal in the market.

```
1.  import pandas as pd
2.  import numpy as np
3.
4.  def detect_bullish_engulfing(df):
5.      bullish_engulfing = []
6.
7.      for i in range(1, len(df)):
8.          current_candle = df.iloc[i]
9.          previous_candle = df.iloc[i-1]
10.
11.         if (previous_candle['Close'] < previous_candle['Open']) and \
12.             (current_candle['Close'] > current_candle['Open']) and \
13.             (current_candle['Close'] > previous_candle['Open']) and \
14.             (current_candle['Open'] < previous_candle['Close']):
15.             bullish_engulfing.append(i)
16.
17.     return bullish_engulfing
18.
19. price_data = pd.DataFrame(...) # yf.download
20. bullish_engulfing_indices = detect_bullish_engulfing(price_data)
```

Moving average crossovers is a commonly used trading strategy that can help traders determine when to buy or sell an asset. This pattern involves using two **simple moving averages (SMA)** with different time periods. An SMA is a calculation of the average price of an asset over a specific period. By using SMA, traders can smooth out price fluctuations and identify underlying trends. When a shorter-term SMA crosses above a longer-term SMA, it signals a potential buying opportunity, while the opposite indicates a potential selling opportunity.

To implement this strategy in Python, traders can use the 'pandas' library. The library provides a function to calculate SMAs and can be used to generate signals for buying or selling opportunities.

The provided Python script defines a function **detect_sma_crossovers(df, short_window, long_window)** that identifies crossover signals based on SMA values calculated from the closing prices of a given **DataFrame** of stock price data. This function computes two SMAs with different window lengths, compares their values, and generates signals indicating whether a short-term SMA has crossed above or below a long-term SMA, suggesting potential bullish or bearish trends in the market.

```
1.  import pandas as pd
```

```
2.
3. def detect_sma_crossovers(df, short_window, long_window):
4.     sma_short = df['Close'].rolling(window=short_window).mean()
5.     sma_long = df['Close'].rolling(window=long_window).mean()
6.
7.     crossover_signals = np.where(sma_short > sma_long, 1, -1)
8.
9.     return crossover_signals
10.
11. price_data = pd.DataFrame(...) # yf.download
12. signals = detect_sma_crossovers(price_data, short_window=50, long_window=200)
```

Support and resistance levels are important price levels where an asset's price has struggled to move beyond in the past. Identifying these levels can help traders predict potential price reversals or breakouts. Support levels are price levels where buying pressure has historically been strong, while resistance levels are price levels where selling pressure has historically been strong. These levels act as psychological barriers for market participants.

To find support and resistance levels in Python, traders can use the **pandas** library, which provides functions to analyze price data and identify these levels.

The provided Python script defines a function **detect_support_resistance(df, window)** that calculates support and resistance levels based on the lowest low (**support**) and highest high (**resistance**) within a given window of historical stock price data. These levels are essential in technical analysis for identifying potential buying (**support**) and selling (**resistance**) points in the market.

```
1. import pandas as pd
2.
3. def detect_support_resistance(df, window):
4.     support = df['Low'].rolling(window=window).min()
5.     resistance = df['High'].rolling(window=window).max()
6.
7.     return support, resistance
8.
9. price_data = pd.DataFrame(...)  # yf.download
10. support, resistance = detect_support_resistance(price_data, window=20)
```

Trendlines are a useful tool for traders to identify potential trading opportunities by connecting a series of highs or lows on a price chart, showing the overall direction of the market. Traders can use trendlines to detect trend reversals or price breakouts, providing valuable entry or exit signals.

A trendline is a straight line drawn on a chart that connects two or more price points. When the price moves close to the trendline, traders pay close attention to see if the price will break through the trendline or bounce back in the opposite direction. Trendlines can be used for both short-term and long-term trading strategies.

Pattern recognition using machine learning algorithms, such as **convolutional neural networks (CNNs)** or **recurrent neural networks (RNNs)**, can also help traders identify profitable trading patterns by automatically extracting features from historical price data. By training these algorithms on labeled data, traders can create models capable of detecting complex patterns in the market, such as head and shoulders or double tops and bottoms formations.

Convolutional neural networks are a type of machine learning algorithm commonly used for image recognition, while recurrent neural networks are used for sequence data. These algorithms can be adapted for financial time-series data and used to identify trading patterns in historical price data.

To implement a simple CNN in Python, traders can use the **keras** library, which provides a high-level interface for building and training neural networks:

```
1.  import numpy as np
2.  import pandas as pd
3.  from keras.models import Sequential
4.  from keras.layers import Conv1D, Dense, Flatten
5.
6.  # Load data from CSV file
7.  data = pd.read_csv('financial_data.csv')
8.
9.  # Split the data into input (X) and output (y) variables
10. X = data.drop(['target'], axis=1).values
11. y = data['target'].values
12.
13. # Reshape X to be 3-dimensional for Conv1D input
14. X = X.reshape(X.shape[0], X.shape[1], 1)
15.
16. # Define the model architecture
17. model = Sequential()
18. model.add(Conv1D(filters=32, kernel_size=5, activation='relu', input_
    shape=(X.shape[1], 1)))
19. model.add(Flatten())
20. model.add(Dense(1, activation='sigmoid'))
21.
```

```
22. # Compile the model
23. model.compile(optimizer='adam', loss='binary_crossentropy',
      metrics=['accuracy'])
24.
25. # Train the model
26. model.fit(X, y, epochs=10, batch_size=32)
```

This code constructs a neural network model designed for binary classification tasks. It incorporates several key components to facilitate feature extraction, transformation, and classification:

- **Convolutional layer**: The model begins with a convolutional layer, which is responsible for extracting features from the input data. This layer applies a set of learnable filters to the input, enabling it to identify patterns and features that are relevant to the classification task.

- **Flatten layer**: Following the convolutional layer, a flatten layer is employed to transform the multidimensional feature maps generated by the convolutional layer into a one-dimensional vector. This is necessary as the subsequent dense layer requires a one-dimensional input. The flatten layer simply reshapes the feature maps into a single continuous vector, preserving the spatial relationships learned by the convolutional layer.

- **Dense layer**: The flattened feature vector is then fed into a dense layer with a sigmoid activation function. This dense layer serves as the output layer of the neural network, producing a binary classification output. The sigmoid activation function ensures that the output values are between 0 and 1, representing the probability of the input belonging to the positive class in the binary classification problem.

- **Compilation and training**: The model is compiled using the compile method, where the optimizer, loss function, and evaluation metrics are specified. This prepares the model for training. Subsequently, the fit method is called to train the model on the input data and corresponding labels (output data) for a specified number of epochs. During training, the model adjusts its parameters (weights and biases) iteratively to minimize the specified loss function and improve its performance on the classification task.

Backtesting is an essential tool for traders to evaluate the effectiveness of their trading strategies before risking capital in the market. However, there are limitations to using historical data to predict future performance. As you mentioned, financial markets are constantly evolving, and new factors can influence asset prices and trading behaviors, which can lead to potential losses for traders.

Moreover, biases can arise from the selection and analysis of historical data, leading to an overestimation of a trading strategy's performance. Cross-validation and out-of-sample testing can help traders reduce the risk of bias and overfitting by providing a more accurate assessment of a trading strategy's potential future performance.

In addition, transaction costs and slippage are crucial considerations when evaluating trading patterns, as they can significantly impact the overall profitability of a trading strategy. Incorporating these factors into the backtesting process can provide a more realistic understanding of a strategy's profitability and help traders make informed decisions in the market.

Working with real-time data feeds

In algorithmic trading, real-time data feeds are crucial to making informed decisions and executing trades. Traders can choose from a wide range of data sources, such as Bloomberg, Quandl, and Alpaca, each with its own strengths and limitations. Selecting the most suitable provider based on specific needs and budget constraints is essential.

API-based data feeds connect algorithmic trading systems to real-time market data. RESTful APIs are used for retrieving historical data and account information, while WebSocket APIs are more suitable for streaming real-time market data, due to their lower latency and higher throughput.

Authentication and API key management are crucial components of secure and reliable data access. Best practices include storing API keys securely, limiting their scope to specific functionality, and regularly rotating keys to minimize the risk of unauthorized access. Adhering to the rate limits imposed by data providers is also essential to avoid overloading their servers and ensure a stable connection.

Handling API errors gracefully is another important aspect of working with real-time data feeds. This can be achieved by implementing error handling mechanisms, such as retrying failed requests with exponential backoff or gracefully degrading the system's functionality in case of persistent errors.

The provided Python code establishes a WebSocket connection to the Alpaca Markets API for streaming real-time financial market data. It imports necessary modules such as **websocket** and **json**, and utilizes environment variables to securely access the Alpaca API. The code defines callback functions for handling incoming messages, errors, and connection closure. Upon running, the script initiates the WebSocket connection and continuously listens for incoming data from the Alpaca API.

```
1. import websocket
2. import json
3. import os
4.
5. ALPACA_API_URL = 'wss://data.alpaca.markets/stream'
6. ALPACA_API_KEY = os.environ['ALPACA_API_KEY']
```

```
7.  ALPACA_SECRET_KEY = os.environ['ALPACA_SECRET_KEY']
8.
9.  def on_message(ws, message):
10.     data = json.loads(message)
11.     print(f'Received data: {data}')
12.
13. def on_error(ws, error):
14.     print(f'Error: {error}')
15.
16. def on_close(ws):
17.     print('Connection closed')
18.
19. ws = websocket.WebSocketApp(ALPACA_API_URL,
20.                             on_message=on_message,
21.                             on_error=on_error,
22.                             on_close=on_close,
23.                             header={'APCA-API-KEY-ID': ALPACA_API_KEY,
24.                                     'APCA-API-SECRET-KEY': ALPACA_SECRET_KEY})
25.
26. ws.run_forever()
```

This code snippet demonstrates a simple example of connecting to the Alpaca WebSocket API, handling incoming messages, and managing errors. By using real-time data feeds and APIs, algorithmic traders can access the latest market information and make informed decisions, ultimately enhancing the performance of their trading strategies.

Handling and processing real-time data

Effective data management and storage are crucial for high-performance algorithmic trading using AI, as real-time data feeds generate vast amounts of information that must be processed quickly and efficiently. In-memory data structures such as Python lists, dictionaries, and sets can be used for rapid access to the latest market data, while databases like SQLite, PostgreSQL, or MongoDB provide more persistent storage solutions suitable for historical data analysis.

Several Python libraries facilitate connecting to various storage options, including cloud-based storage. Some notable libraries for data management and storage in Python include:

- **Pandas**: A library for data manipulation and analysis, with support for reading and writing data from various sources, including databases and cloud storage.

- **SQLAlchemy**: A database toolkit and ORM that supports multiple databases and cloud storage options.

- **PyMongo**: A library for working with MongoDB, a NoSQL document-oriented database.

- **Firebase**: A cloud-based platform for mobile and web applications, with support for real-time data synchronization and storage.

Cloud storage options for algorithmic trading data include Amazon S3, Google Cloud Storage, and Microsoft Azure Storage. These platforms offer scalable and secure storage solutions, with the ability to handle large volumes of data and provide access to a variety of data analytics tools.

Monitoring and logging real-time data processing workflows are critical for tracking the performance of algorithmic trading systems and identifying potential issues before they impact trading outcomes. Python's built-in logging module offers a flexible framework for emitting log messages from applications. The logging module enables developers to capture and store log messages at different severity levels (for example, **DEBUG**, **INFO**, **WARNING**, **ERROR**, and **CRITICAL**) and direct them to various output destinations, such as files, email, or console. This provides a mechanism for tracking the behavior of the algorithmic trading system and identifying potential problems, allowing for faster troubleshooting and optimization.

Overview of EDA in algorithmic trading

The implementation of **event-driven architecture** (**EDA**) plays a vital role in the high-performance algorithmic trading realm that leverages AI. By facilitating the creation of flexible trading systems, EDA enables efficient processing of real-time data feeds and rapid reactions to market events. This architecture empowers trading systems to react to triggers or signals triggered by market events, such as order executions, price updates, and news events. As a result, EDA can handle these events asynchronously as they occur. Utilizing Python libraries like **asyncio** and employing event-driven programming patterns, traders can develop event-driven trading systems that enhance the performance and responsiveness of their algorithmic trading strategies.

The provided Python code demonstrates asynchronous programming using the **asyncio** library to fetch price data for multiple stock symbols concurrently. It defines an asynchronous function **fetch_price** (symbol) to simulate fetching price data for a given symbol, and an asynchronous **main()** function to gather price data for multiple symbols concurrently using asyncio's **gather()** function. Upon execution, the code prints the fetched prices for the symbols **AAPL**, **GOOG**, and **TSLA**.

```
1. import asyncio
2.
3. async def fetch_price(symbol):
```

```
4.     # Simulate fetching price data for the given symbol
5.     await asyncio.sleep(1)
6.     return 100.0
7. 
8. async def main():
9.     prices = await asyncio.gather(*(fetch_price(symbol) for symbol in ['AAPL', 'GOOG', 'TSLA']))
10.    print(prices)
11. 
12. asyncio.run(main())
```

Data visualization techniques for trading analysis

Matplotlib is a Python library that helps in creating different types of graphs for data visualization. It provides several types of graphs like line charts, bar charts, candlestick charts, heatmaps, scatter plots, and network graphs.

Seaborn is a Python library used for creating attractive and informative statistical graphics with minimal code. It is based on Matplotlib but offers more advanced visualizations and statistical analyses with less effort. It is a popular choice for data visualization tasks in high-performance algorithmic trading using AI due to its default themes and color palettes. Its integration with pandas and NumPy allows for easy handling and analysis of structured data.

Plotly is a Python library used to create interactive, web-based visualizations that enable users to explore and analyze data more effectively. The library aims to generate dynamic, high-quality graphics that can be easily exported and shared for collaboration and reporting purposes. The primary advantage of Plotly is its ability to generate interactive graphics that can be embedded in web applications or shared as standalone HTML files. This interactivity enables users to zoom, pan, and hover over data points to obtain additional information, making data exploration and analysis more effective.

Common visualization types

In this section, we will discuss the common visualization types:

- **Line charts** are an important visualization tool in high-performance algorithmic trading using AI. They provide a simple representation of price changes over time, allowing traders to identify trends and patterns in the data. Line charts are useful for evaluating historical asset performance and can also provide inputs for machine learning models that predict future price movements. AI-driven trading algorithms can use line chart data to identify technical indicators and signals for potential trading opportunities.

An example of plotting a simple line chart using Python and the popular data visualization library, Matplotlib, is presented as follows:

```
1.  import matplotlib.pyplot as plt
2.  import yfinance as yf
3.
4.  # Load historical price data
5.  symbol = "AAPL"   # Example symbol
6.  start_date = "2020-01-01"
7.  end_date = "2021-12-31"
8.
9.  price_data = yf.download(symbol, start=start_date, end=end_date)
10.
11. # Plot the line chart for the closing prices
12. plt.plot(price_data["Close"])
13. plt.xlabel("Date")
14. plt.ylabel("Price")
15. plt.title("Line Chart of Asset Closing Prices")
16. plt.show()
```

- **Bar charts** are a type of graph that shows the open, high, low, and close prices of a financial instrument over a specific time period. Each bar represents a single period, such as a day, and provides important information about price movement during that period. Bar charts are useful in high-performance algorithmic trading using AI because they provide a detailed view of price fluctuations over various time frames, allowing traders to analyze market sentiment and volatility.

```
1.  import matplotlib.pyplot as plt
2.  import yfinance as yf
3.
4.  # Load historical OHLC data
5.  symbol = "AAPL"   # Example symbol
6.  start_date = "2023-01-01"
7.  end_date = "2023-12-31"
8.
9.  ohlc_data = yf.download(symbol, start=start_date, end=end_date, interval='1d', group_by='ticker')
10.
11. # Plot the bar chart for the OHLC data
12. fig, ax = plt.subplots()
13. ohlc_data["Close"].plot(kind="bar", ax=ax)
14. ax.set_xlabel("Date")
```

```
15. ax.set_ylabel("Price")
16. ax.set_title("Bar Chart of Asset OHLC Prices")
17. plt.show()
```

- **Candlestick charts** are a type of data visualization used in high-performance algorithmic trading using AI. They show the open, high, low, and close prices for a financial instrument over a given time period using distinctively shaped *candlesticks*. Candlestick charts are useful for analyzing market sentiment and identifying potential trend reversals through specific bullish and bearish patterns. In AI-driven trading, candlestick charts can provide valuable inputs for machine learning models to recognize and capitalize on these patterns, potentially resulting in profitable trading opportunities.

  The provided Python script utilizes the **Matplotlib** library to visualize historical **Open-High-Low-Close** (OHLC) data for a specified stock symbol, in this case, AAPL (Apple Inc.). It first loads the OHLC data using the **yfinance** library, specifying the start and end dates for the data retrieval. The OHLC data is then plotted as a bar chart, with dates on the X-axis and closing prices on the Y-axis. Finally, the script displays the bar chart, providing a visual representation of the asset's price movements throughout the specified time period:

  ```
  1.  import yfinance as yf
  2.  import plotly.graph_objects as go
  3.
  4.  # Load historical OHLC data
  5.  symbol = "AAPL"   # Example symbol
  6.  start_date = "2023-01-01"
  7.  end_date = "2023-12-31"
  8.
  9.  ohlc_data = yf.download(symbol, start=start_date, end=end_date)
  10.
  11. # Create the candlestick chart
  12. fig = go.Figure(data=[go.Candlestick(x=ohlc_data.index,
  13.                                     open=ohlc_data['Open'],
  14.                                     high=ohlc_data['High'],
  15.                                     low=ohlc_data['Low'],
  16.                                     close=ohlc_data['Close'])])
  17.
  18. fig.update_layout(title="Candlestick Chart of Asset OHLC Prices",
  19.                   xaxis_title="Date",
  20.                   yaxis_title="Price")
  21. fig.show()
  ```

- **Heatmaps** are a data visualization technique used in high-performance algorithmic trading using AI. They use a color scale to represent data values and can help traders identify correlations between stocks or assets, analyze sector performance, and identify potential opportunities and risks. Heatmaps can help identify patterns and relationships within large datasets and serve as inputs for machine learning models to identify market trends, investment opportunities, and portfolio risk.

```
1.  import yfinance as yf
2.  import numpy as np
3.  import seaborn as sns
4.  import matplotlib.pyplot as plt
5.  
6.  # Define the list of symbols for multiple assets
7.  symbols = ["AAPL", "MSFT", "GOOGL", "AMZN", "META"]
8.  
9.  # Download the historical price data for multiple assets
10. start_date = "2023-01-01"
11. end_date = "2021-12-31"
12. price_data = yf.download(symbols, start=start_date, end=end_date)["Adj Close"]
13. 
14. # Calculate the correlation matrix
15. correlation_matrix = price_data.corr()
16. 
17. # Create the heatmap
18. plt.figure(figsize=(10, 8))
19. sns.heatmap(correlation_matrix, annot=True, cmap="coolwarm")
20. plt.title("Heatmap of Asset Correlations")
21. plt.show()
```

- **Scatter plots** are used in high-performance algorithmic trading using AI to visualize the relationship between two variables by plotting data points on a two-dimensional plane. This helps traders assess correlations and potential causation between variables, as well as the strength and direction of relationships. The primary purpose of scatter plots is to facilitate the identification of patterns and relationships between variables that may be difficult to discern through numerical analysis alone.

This Python script utilizes the **yfinance** library to download historical price data for two assets, **AAPL** (Apple Inc.) and **GOOGL** (Alphabet Inc.). It then calculates the returns for each asset based on the adjusted closing prices and creates a scatter plot to visualize the relationship between the returns of the two assets. The X-axis represents the returns of **AAPL**, while the Y-axis represents the returns of **GOOGL**. This scatter plot provides insights into the correlation or relationship between the returns of the two assets over the specified time period from January 1, 2020, to December 31, 2021.

```
1.  import yfinance as yf
```

```
2. import pandas as pd
3. import matplotlib.pyplot as plt
4.
5. # Define the list of symbols for two assets
6. symbols = ["AAPL", "GOOGL"]
7.
8. # Download the historical price data for two assets
9. start_date = "2020-01-01"
10. end_date = "2021-12-31"
11. asset_data = yf.download(symbols, start=start_date, end=end_date)["Adj Close"]
12.
13. # Calculate returns for each asset
14. asset_data["Asset1_Return"] = asset_data[symbols[0]].pct_change()
15. asset_data["Asset2_Return"] = asset_data[symbols[1]].pct_change()
16.
17. # Create the scatter plot
18. plt.scatter(asset_data["Asset1_Return"], asset_data["Asset2_Return"])
19. plt.xlabel(f"{symbols[0]} Return")
20. plt.ylabel(f"{symbols[1]} Return")
21. plt.title(f"Scatter Plot of Returns for {symbols[0]} and {symbols[1]}")
22. plt.show()
```

- **Network graphs**, also called graph visualizations, are a data visualization technique used in high-performance algorithmic trading using AI. They show connections or relationships between entities, such as assets or market participants, and help visualize the structure of financial markets or trading systems. By identifying influential nodes and clusters of assets with strong connections, network graphs enable traders to better understand market dynamics, manage risk, and identify investment opportunities.

    The provided Python script utilizes the **yfinance** library to download historical price data for multiple assets, including **AAPL** (Apple Inc.), **MSFT** (Microsoft Corporation), **GOOGL** (Alphabet Inc.), **AMZN** (Amazon.com Inc.), and **META** (Meta Platforms Inc.). It then calculates the correlation matrix based on the adjusted closing prices of these assets. Using the **NetworkX** library, the script constructs a network graph where each asset represents a node, and the correlation between assets represents the edges. The strength of correlation is indicated by the weight of the edges. Finally, the script visualizes the network graph to illustrate the correlations between the assets over the specified time period from January 1, 2020, to December 31, 2021.

```python
1.  import yfinance as yf
2.  import pandas as pd
3.  import networkx as nx
4.  import matplotlib.pyplot as plt
5.
6.  # Define the list of symbols for multiple assets
7.  symbols = ["AAPL", "MSFT", "GOOGL", "AMZN", "META"]
8.
9.  # Download the historical price data for multiple assets
10. start_date = "2020-01-01"
11. end_date = "2021-12-31"
12. price_data = yf.download(symbols, start=start_date, end=end_date)["Adj Close"]
13.
14. # Calculate the correlation matrix
15. correlation_matrix = price_data.corr()
16.
17. # Convert the correlation matrix to a DataFrame
18. correlation_data = correlation_matrix.stack().reset_index()
19. correlation_data.columns = ["Asset1", "Asset2", "Correlation"]
20.
21. # Create a network graph from the correlation data
22. G = nx.Graph()
23. for index, row in correlation_data.iterrows():
24.     G.add_edge(row["Asset1"], row["Asset2"], weight=row["Correlation"])
25.
26. # Draw the network graph
27. pos = nx.spring_layout(G)
28. nx.draw(G, pos, with_labels=True, node_color="lightblue", font_size=10, font_weight="bold")
29. edge_labels = nx.get_edge_attributes(G, "weight")
30. nx.draw_networkx_edge_labels(G, pos, edge_labels=edge_labels, font_size=8)
31. plt.title("Network Graph of Asset Correlations")
```

Handling missing and incomplete data

Traders and investors in high-performance algorithmic trading using AI often face the challenge of missing and incomplete data. This problem can be caused by errors and inconsistencies in data collection, including human error, incorrect data entry, or discrepancies between data sources[8]. For instance, a trader may encounter missing volume data for a stock due to a mistake in the data collection process.

To illustrate this, consider the following Python code snippet that loads historical stock data and identifies missing volume data:

```
1. import pandas as pd
2.
3. # Load historical stock data
4. stock_data = pd.read_csv("historical_stock_data.csv", index_col="Date", parse_dates=True)
5.
6. # Identify missing volume data
7. missing_volume_data = stock_data[stock_data["Volume"].isna()]
8. print("Missing volume data:\n", missing_volume_data)
```

Missing data in financial datasets can be caused by system failures and data transmission issues. For example, a temporary network outage can lead to incomplete or missing data for specific time periods[53].

Corporate actions and market events such as stock splits, dividends, and mergers can affect the availability of data for particular assets. These events can cause changes to historical data or inconsistencies between datasets, making it difficult for traders to maintain accurate and up-to-date records [54].

Data provider limitations and restrictions can also contribute to missing and incomplete data in financial datasets. Some data providers may offer incomplete historical data or impose restrictions on data access due to licensing or cost concerns[55].

Irregular trading hours or market closures, such as holidays or trading halts, can cause gaps in time series data. These gaps can complicate the analysis of financial data, particularly in time-sensitive algorithmic trading models[56].

The following Python code snippet demonstrates how to resample daily stock data to account for missing data due to market closures:

```
1. # Resample daily stock data to fill in missing dates due to market closures
2. resampled_stock_data = stock_data.resample("D").asfreq()
3. print("Resampled stock data with missing dates:\n", resampled_stock_data)
```

When trading using AI, it's important to deal with missing data properly, as it can harm the reliability and effectiveness of our trading models. In this section, we'll explore different ways to handle missing data and give recommendations on which approach to choose based on the characteristics of the data and our trading model's needs.

Imputation methods are used to fill in missing values with estimated values based on the data we have. There are several techniques available, such as mean, median, mode, regression, and k-nearest neighbors imputation. Mean imputation replaces missing values with the average value of the available data. Median imputation replaces missing values with the middle value of the available data. Mode imputation replaces missing values with the most common value in the available data. Regression imputation estimates missing values using a regression model based on the available data. K-nearest neighbors imputation replaces missing values with the average of the closest data points.

Interpolation methods are used to estimate missing values by creating a function that fits the known data points and using this function to predict the missing values. Linear interpolation estimates missing values using a straight line that connects the known data points. Polynomial interpolation estimates missing values using a curved line (polynomial function) that fits the known data points. Spline interpolation estimates missing values using a curved line made up of multiple polynomial functions that fit the known data points and maintain smoothness. Time series decomposition and forecasting involves breaking down a time series into its trend, seasonal patterns, and other components in order to predict missing values.

By using these imputation and interpolation techniques, we can handle missing data effectively and improve the performance of our algorithmic trading models.

Time series analysis techniques

Autocorrelation is a statistical measure that shows the relationship between a given variable and its previous values. In the context of trading, autocorrelation can reveal how current stock prices are influenced by past prices. This information is useful in identifying patterns or trends that can aid in making predictions for future price movements.

The significance of autocorrelation in time series analysis lies in its ability to uncover dependencies between data points. In trading, discovering such dependencies can help in building more effective models that take into account the historical trends to predict future prices. A high autocorrelation value indicates that past values have a significant impact on the current value, leading to better predictions and more profitable trading strategies.

Partial autocorrelation measures the correlation between a variable and its previous values while accounting for the correlations with all other intervening values. This technique helps in identifying the specific lags that have the most significant influence on the current value, which can help in selecting the appropriate order for an **autoregressive** (**AR**) model in time series analysis.

Visualizing autocorrelation and partial autocorrelation can be achieved using correlograms, which are graphical representations of the correlation coefficients for various lags. These plots can be generated using Python libraries such as **statsmodels** and **matplotlib**[57].

Conclusion

In this chapter, we explored the crucial aspects of data sources and preprocessing techniques for algorithmic trading. We discussed the significance of cleaning and preparing data for analysis, along with feature extraction and selection methods. Moreover, we delved into the importance of analyzing historical trading patterns and working with real-time data feeds for informed decision-making. Additionally, we explored data visualization techniques that aid in trading analysis. Furthermore, we addressed the challenges of handling missing and incomplete data and highlighted the relevance of time series analysis techniques in the context of algorithmic trading. These foundational concepts set the stage for implementing effective trading strategies based on data-driven insights.

In the upcoming chapter, users will delve into the process of simulating and testing trading strategies to assess their performance, optimize parameters, and make informed investment decisions.

Join our book's Discord space

Join the book's Discord Workspace for Latest updates, Offers, Tech happenings around the world, New Release and Sessions with the Authors:

https://discord.bpbonline.com

CHAPTER 5
Simulating and Testing Trading Strategies

Introduction

This chapter explains the dynamic world of algorithmic trading, where success lies in effectively evaluating performance and managing risks. We begin with backtesting, scrutinizing strategies on historical data, and forward-testing, deploying algorithms in real-time. Performance metrics and evaluation techniques will be uncovered to aid in making informed decisions. We then address risk management and mitigation strategies crucial for safeguarding investments. Furthermore, the chapter explores walk-forward analysis, custom backtesting environments, stress testing, and scenario analysis to validate strategies thoroughly. Lastly, we delve into the transformative journey from paper trading to live trading, ensuring a seamless transition towards a profitable trading experience.

Structure

In this chapter, we will go through the following topics:
- Backtesting: Historical data testing
- Forward-testing: Testing algorithms in real-time
- Performance metrics and evaluation techniques
- Risk management and mitigation
- Walk-forward analysis for strategy validation

- Building custom backtesting environments
- Stress testing and scenario analysis
- Paper trading and transition to live trading

Objectives

This chapter aims to provide a comprehensive understanding of algorithmic trading, focusing on performance evaluation and risk management. Readers will learn backtesting, forward-testing, performance metrics, risk mitigation, walk-forward analysis, custom backtesting, stress testing, and transitioning from paper to live trading.

Backtesting: Historical data testing

Backtesting is a systematic simulation method used to evaluate the effectiveness of a trading strategy without incurring financial risk. It involves analyzing historical data to observe how a particular strategy would have performed over a specific period. The underlying assumption is that past market behavior can provide insights into future patterns and trends. By leveraging this concept, traders can gain valuable insights into potential future performance. Backtesting plays a crucial role in algorithmic trading, allowing traders to evaluate, refine, and validate their models before investing capital. It is considered a vital step in the creation and validation of any trading algorithm. The backtesting process involves formulating a clear and specific trading strategy with precise rules, gathering relevant historical data that accurately reflects real trading conditions, executing the backtest using the algorithmic rules, and evaluating the results using performance metrics such as the Sharpe ratio, drawdown, or profit factor to assess the strategy's effectiveness and risk level.

When performing backtesting to assess trading strategies' performance using historical data, it is crucial to guarantee the precision and dependability of the dataset. This section will discuss the necessary steps involved in preparing historical data for backtesting, including data cleansing, transformation, handling missing data, normalization, and ensuring data integrity and quality.

First and foremost, obtaining reliable historical data is vital for accurate backtesting. Numerous reputable sources offer high-quality historical data for financial markets. One such source is *Bloomberg Terminal*[78], which provides an extensive range of financial instruments and historical data points. Moreover, platforms like *Quandl*[79] and *Alpha Vantage*[80] offer accessible APIs for directly downloading historical data into your trading system.

When working with historical data, encountering missing values is a common occurrence that can adversely impact the accuracy of backtesting results. Various techniques can be employed to address this issue. One approach involves filling in missing data points using interpolation methods such as linear interpolation or forward filling, where the missing values are replaced with the most recent observed value. Another technique is backward filling, where the missing values are replaced with the subsequent observed value. Alternatively, more sophisticated methods like stochastic regression imputation or multiple imputation can be utilized to estimate missing values based on relationships with other variables within the dataset.

In addition to handling missing data, data normalization and transformation are crucial steps in preparing historical data for backtesting. Normalization techniques, such as Min-Max scaling or z-score normalization, are commonly applied to ensure that different variables have comparable scales. This process prevents certain variables from dominating the analysis due to their larger magnitudes. Furthermore, transforming variables can help meet certain assumptions required by the trading strategy being tested. Common transformations include logarithmic transformations, percentage changes, or differencing, which can stabilize the data or make it more amenable to statistical analysis.

To maintain data integrity and quality, it is essential to conduct thorough quality checks before proceeding with backtesting. Data integrity refers to the accuracy and consistency of the data, while data quality encompasses factors such as completeness, correctness, and consistency. Validating the historical data involves checking for outliers, investigating potential data errors or anomalies, and ensuring that the data aligns with the intended time periods and instruments. Additionally, cross-referencing the historical data with other reliable sources or benchmark indices can provide further validation.

Code snippet for downloading historical data using Python and the Alpha Vantage API:

```
1.  import pandas as pd
2.  import requests
3.
4.  API_KEY = 'your_api_key'
5.  symbol = 'AAPL'
6.  interval = 'daily'
7.  outputsize = 'full'
8.
9.  url = f'https://www.alphavantage.co/query?function=TIME_SERIES_{interval.upper()}_ADJUSTED&symbol={symbol}&outputsize={outputsize}&apikey={API_KEY}'
10.
11. response = requests.get(url)
12. data = response.json()
13.
14. df = pd.DataFrame(data['Time Series (Daily)']).T
15. df.columns = ['open', 'high', 'low', 'close', 'adjusted_close', 'volume', 'dividend', 'split']
16. df.to_csv('historical_data.csv', index=True)
```

Please note that you will need to sign up for an Alpha Vantage API key and replace **your_api_key** with your actual API key. Additionally, ensure that you have the necessary libraries installed, such as pandas and requests.

Implementing backtesting: Techniques and tools

This section will discuss the various techniques and tools available for backtesting, including frameworks, coding considerations, and the evaluation of backtest results.

To facilitate backtesting, there is a wide range of frameworks available that cater to different programming languages and trading requirements. Open-source frameworks such as Backtrader, PyAlgoTrade, and Zipline offer flexible and customizable options. These frameworks provide a variety of features, including data feed integration, strategy development, performance analysis, and visualization capabilities. On the other hand, commercial solutions like TradeStation, MetaTrader, and NinjaTrader offer more comprehensive platforms with additional functionalities such as live trading, market data subscriptions, and integrated trading systems. The choice of framework depends on factors such as familiarity with the programming language, required features, and the complexity of the trading strategy being tested.

When coding a simple backtest, several key steps and considerations should be taken into account. First, the historical data should be imported into the backtesting framework or system, ensuring it aligns with the desired time frame and resolution. The next step involves implementing the logic of the trading strategy, defining entry and exit conditions, stop-loss and take-profit levels, position sizing, and any other relevant parameters. It is crucial to accurately represent the rules of the strategy and ensure proper execution within the backtesting environment.

Furthermore, it is essential to consider the impact of transaction costs, such as commissions and slippage, on the results of the backtest. Transaction costs can significantly affect the profitability of a trading strategy. Therefore, incorporating realistic cost assumptions into the backtest is crucial to obtain accurate performance estimates. Additionally, considering different order types, such as market orders, limit orders, or stop orders, and their impact on the execution of the strategy is important.

Evaluating the results of the backtest involves understanding performance metrics that provide insights into the effectiveness of the strategy. Key performance metrics include total return, annualized return, risk-adjusted return, maximum drawdown, Sharpe ratio, and various other risk and reward measures. These metrics enable a comprehensive assessment of the profitability, risk exposure, and consistency of the strategy. By analyzing these metrics, traders can determine whether the strategy aligns with their risk tolerance, performance objectives, and investment criteria.

In this code snippet, we define a simple backtest strategy by subclassing the **bt.Strategy** class. Within the **MyStrategy** class, the **__init__** method is used to initialize any strategy-specific parameters and variables. The `next` method contains the main trading logic, which is executed for each bar of historical data:

```
1. import backtrader as bt
2.
3. class MyStrategy(bt.Strategy):
4.     def __init__(self):
5.         # Define strategy parameters and variables here
6.
7.     def next(self):
8.         # Define trading logic here
9.
10. cerebro = bt.Cerebro()
11. cerebro.addstrategy(MyStrategy)
12.
13. data = bt.feeds.YahooFinanceData(dataname='AAPL',
14.                                  fromdate=datetime(2010, 1, 1),
15.                                  todate=datetime(2020, 12, 31))
16.
17. cerebro.adddata(data)
18. cerebro.run()
19.
20. cerebro.plot()
```

In the following a sample implementation is shown:

```
1. import backtrader as bt
2. from datetime import datetime
3.
4. # Define a new strategy inheriting from bt.Strategy
5. class MyStrategy(bt.Strategy):
6.     params = (
7.         ('ma_period', 20),
8.     )
9.
10.     def log(self, txt):
11.         print(txt)
12.
13.     def __init__(self):
14.         # Moving averages
15.         self.sma_short = bt.indicators.SimpleMovingAverage(
16.             self.data.close, period=10)
17.         self.sma_long = bt.indicators.SimpleMovingAverage(
```

```
18.            self.data.close, period=self.params.ma_period)
19.
20. def next(self):
21.     # Check if we have enough bars for our longest moving average
22.     if len(self) < self.params.ma_period:
23.         return
24.
25.     # Simply log the closing price of the series from the reference
26.     self.log('Close, %.2f' % self.data.close[0])
27.
28.     # Check if we are in the market
29.     if not self.position:
30.         # We are not in the market, if fast crosses slow to the upside then enter long.
31.         if self.sma_short[0] > self.sma_long[0]:
32.             self.log('BUY CREATE, %.2f' % self.data.close[0])
33.             self.buy()
34.     else:
35.         if self.sma_short[0] < self.sma_long[0]:
36.             self.log('SELL CREATE, %.2f' % self.data.close[0])
37.             self.sell()
38.
39.
40. def run_backtest():
41.     cerebro = bt.Cerebro()
42.     cerebro.addstrategy(MyStrategy)
43.
44.     # Data feed
45.     # Make sure you have uploaded the 'AAPL.csv' file in your Google Colab session
46.     data = bt.feeds.YahooFinanceCSVData(
47.         dataname='AAPL.csv',
48.         fromdate=datetime(2023, 1, 1),
49.         todate=datetime(2023, 12, 31),
50.         reverse=False
51.     )
52.     cerebro.adddata(data)
53.
54.     # Set initial cash
55.     cerebro.broker.setcash(10000.0)
56.
```

```
57.     # Set commission
58.     cerebro.broker.setcommission(commission=0.001)
59.
60.     # Print out the starting conditions
61.     print('Starting Portfolio Value: %.2f' % cerebro.broker.getvalue())
62.
63.     # Run the backtest
64.     cerebro.run()
65.
66.     # Print out the final conditions
67.     print('Final Portfolio Value: %.2f' % cerebro.broker.getvalue())
68.
69. # Execute the function
70. run_backtest()
```

Pitfalls of back testing

This section explores three common pitfalls of backtesting: overfitting, look-ahead bias, and survivorship bias. Additionally, we will discuss methods for detecting and mitigating these pitfalls.

Overfitting presents a significant concern in backtesting as it occurs when a trading strategy is excessively tailored to fit historical data, leading to subpar performance in real-world scenarios. Essentially, overfitting means that the strategy has learned specific patterns or noise in the historical data that do not apply well to future market conditions. An example of overfitting is when a strategy generates exceptional returns during a particular historical period but fails to perform well when applied to new, unseen data. This phenomenon can create a false sense of confidence in the strategy's profitability.

Another pitfall is look-ahead bias, which can distort backtest results. Look-ahead bias happens when information that would not have been available during the historical period inadvertently influences trading decisions. For instance, if a backtest unintentionally incorporates future price or fundamental data when generating signals or calculating indicators, it can lead to unrealistic profitability estimates and falsely validate a trading strategy. To avoid look-ahead bias, it is crucial to ensure that all trading decisions are based solely on information available at the time of the historical data point being evaluated.

Survivorship bias is a pitfall that arises when the historical data used for backtesting only includes assets or instruments that are currently surviving, excluding those that have ceased to exist or become irrelevant over time. This bias can lead to an overestimation of the tested strategies' performance since it overlooks the impact of failed or delisted assets. For example, if a backtest only considers currently listed stocks, it disregards the potentially poor performance of stocks that have been delisted due to bankruptcy or other reasons. To mitigate survivorship bias, it is essential to include a broad sample of historical data that encompasses the entire universe of assets, including those that may no longer exist.

Detecting and mitigating these pitfalls requires careful attention and rigorous testing. One approach is to employ out-of-sample testing, where the strategy is evaluated on data that was not used for model development. This helps assess the strategy's ability to apply beyond the training period and reduces the risk of overfitting. Additionally, techniques such as cross-validation and walk-forward analysis can provide further validation and robustness to the backtest results.

Furthermore, it is crucial to establish strict rules and guidelines for the backtesting process, including the incorporation of realistic transaction costs, slippage, and other factors that mimic real-world trading conditions. By incorporating these elements, the backtest becomes more representative of actual trading scenarios.

Forward-testing: Testing algorithms in real-time

Forward-testing is an integral part of the process of developing trading strategies, allowing traders to test their algorithms under real-time market conditions. Unlike backtesting, which involves evaluating strategies using historical data, forward-testing involves executing trades using live market data to assess their performance and reliability.

The primary purposes of forward-testing in the trading strategy lifecycle are twofold. Firstly, it enables traders to validate their algorithms in real-world scenarios, providing a more accurate representation of the potential performance of their strategies. By executing trades in real-time, traders can consider market fluctuations, liquidity conditions, and other factors that cannot be fully captured in backtesting simulations alone. This allows them to evaluate how their strategies perform under realistic trading conditions and identify any weaknesses or areas for improvement.

Secondly, forward-testing contributes to risk management by ensuring the stability and dependability of trading algorithms. By running algorithms in a live trading environment, traders can assess the ability of their strategies to handle unforeseen market events and react appropriately. It helps uncover potential pitfalls or glitches that may arise when transitioning from backtesting to live trading, such as issues with data feeds, order execution, or latency. By addressing these issues during forward-testing, traders can improve the stability and efficiency of their algorithms, thereby reducing the risk of financial losses.

To comprehend the distinctions between backtesting and forward-testing, it is crucial to recognize that backtesting relies on historical data to retrospectively evaluate strategies, while forward-testing involves executing trades based on current market data. Backtesting provides valuable insights into algorithm performance under known historical conditions, enabling traders to fine-tune their strategies. However, it does not account for the dynamic nature of the market or unexpected events that may impact trading performance. In contrast, forward-testing offers a more realistic assessment of strategy viability in real-time trading, incorporating the inherent uncertainties and risks present in the market.

When incorporating forward-testing into the trading strategy lifecycle, it is vital to adhere to best practices to ensure accurate results and reliable performance. Traders should establish a robust testing infrastructure that closely mimics live trading conditions, including real-time data feeds, accurate transaction costs, and proper implementation of order types. Additionally, comprehensive performance metrics should be defined and monitored during forward-testing to assess various aspects of strategy performance, such as profitability, risk-adjusted returns, and execution efficiency.

Real-time data: Acquisition and handling

Accurate and reliable evaluation of trading strategies heavily relies on the acquisition and management of real-time data. In this context, we will examine a practical illustration to comprehend the origins of real-time data, the challenges associated with handling data latency and gaps, and the significance of data quality in the process of forward-testing.

Financial data providers, such as *Bloomberg* or *Refinitiv*, serve as popular sources of real-time data for traders. These providers offer comprehensive market data encompassing live prices, news updates, and fundamental company information. By subscribing to the services offered by these providers, traders gain access to dependable and up-to-date market data, which is instrumental in powering their forward-testing endeavors.

Let us consider a scenario where a trader intends to acquire real-time stock prices from Refinitiv's data feed. To accomplish this, they can leverage Refinitiv's API, such as their Eikon Data API, which enables them to retrieve real-time price data for the desired stocks. Here is a Python code snippet that exemplifies the process of downloading real-time stock prices using Refinitiv's API[81]:

```
1. import refinitiv
2.
3. # Authenticate and connect to Refinitiv's data feed
4. session = refinitiv.Session()
5. session.open()
6.
7. # Request real-time data for a specific stock
8. subscription = refinitiv.StockPriceSubscription(session)
9. subscription.add('AAPL.O')  # Replace 'AAPL.O' with the desired
   stock symbol
10. subscription.open()
11.
```

```
12. # Process the received real-time data
13. while True:
14.     event = session.next_event()
15.     if event.event_type == refinitiv.EventType.STOCK_PRICE:
16.         stock_price = event.data['price']
17.         # Process the real-time stock price data
18.
19.     # Add any additional logic or break condition
```

Traders must consider the time required for data to travel from its source to their trading systems. To minimize latency, traders can employ a variety of strategies. One approach is to choose data providers that offer low-latency infrastructure. Additionally, optimizing network connections and utilizing technologies such as data compression or caching can reduce the time it takes to transmit data.

Dealing with data gaps is another challenge during forward-testing. These gaps may arise due to temporary disruptions in data feeds or delays in data delivery. To tackle this issue, traders must implement effective error-handling mechanisms and conduct data integrity checks. They can develop algorithms that identify missing or delayed data points and handle them by either waiting for the data to arrive or temporarily substituting them with historical data until real-time data becomes available.

Maintaining data quality is of utmost importance during forward-testing to ensure accurate evaluation of trading strategies. Inaccurate or incomplete data can lead to flawed results and unreliable conclusions. Traders should thoroughly evaluate the data sources they rely on, taking into account factors such as data accuracy, timeliness, and consistency. Independent validation of the data against alternative sources or cross-referencing with reputable data providers can provide additional confidence in the quality and reliability of the data.

In summary, real-time data acquisition and handling are crucial elements of forward-testing in algorithmic trading. By leveraging trustworthy data sources, minimizing data latency, effectively addressing data gaps, and ensuring high data quality, traders can enhance the accuracy and reliability of their forward-testing processes. This, in turn, empowers them to make well-informed decisions based on real-time market dynamics and improve the overall performance of their trading strategies.

Forward-testing procedures: Steps and best practices

Forward-testing procedures are crucial for effectively testing and evaluating trading algorithms in real-time. This section explores the essential steps and best practices involved in setting up and managing forward tests, including the procedure for initiating forward tests, selecting appropriate timeframes, and effectively monitoring and managing the tests.

Setting up a forward test requires a systematic approach to ensure accurate and reliable results. The following steps outline a typical procedure for initiating a forward test:

1. **Define the objectives**: Clearly define the objectives and goals of the forward test. Identify the specific aspects of the algorithm or trading strategy that you want to evaluate during the test.

2. **Select the testing period**: Determine the duration of the forward test. Consider factors such as market conditions, trading frequency, and the desired number of trades to obtain statistically significant results. It is crucial to strike a balance between capturing sufficient data and avoiding excessive testing periods that may lead to outdated results.

3. **Establish test parameters**: Define the key parameters for the forward test, such as position sizing, risk management rules, and trading frequency. Ensure that the parameters align with the intended objectives of the test and accurately represent the algorithm's intended behavior.

4. **Implement the test**: Execute the forward test using real-time market data. Monitor and record the trades and associated performance metrics, such as profit and loss, win/loss ratio, and risk-adjusted returns.

Selecting appropriate timeframes for forward-testing is essential to obtain meaningful results. Traders must consider the desired trading frequency and the inherent characteristics of the trading strategy. For high-frequency strategies, shorter timeframes may be appropriate, while longer timeframes may be more suitable for longer-term strategies. By aligning the testing timeframe with the strategy's intended trading horizon, traders can effectively evaluate the strategy's performance in real-world conditions.

To monitor and manage forward tests effectively, traders should implement best practices to ensure accurate tracking and timely adjustments. Here are some key considerations:

- **Regular performance evaluation**: Continuously monitor the performance metrics of the forward test, including profitability, drawdowns, and risk-adjusted returns. Regularly assess whether the strategy is meeting the predefined objectives and make adjustments if necessary.

- **Risk management**: Implement robust risk management protocols during the forward test to mitigate potential losses. Set appropriate stop-loss levels and position-sizing rules to ensure prudent risk management.

- **Documentation**: Keep comprehensive records of all trades, including entry and exit points, trade sizes, and associated performance metrics. Documentation helps in post-test analysis and enables traders to identify patterns, strengths, and weaknesses of the trading strategy.

- **Adaptation and optimization**: Monitor market conditions and adapt the trading strategy if required. Identify any emerging patterns or shifts in market dynamics that may necessitate adjustments to the algorithm. Continuously refine and optimize the strategy based on real-time market feedback.

By following these best practices, traders can effectively manage forward tests, gain valuable insights into the performance of their algorithms, and make data-driven decisions to improve and optimize their trading strategies.

Analyzing forward-testing results

Gaining an understanding of forward-testing results and implementing appropriate adjustments based on those findings are vital stages in the development of a trading strategy. This section delves into the essential aspects of interpreting forward-testing results, making necessary adaptations, and transitioning from forward-testing to live trading. To enhance clarity, a code example is provided.

Effectively interpreting forward-testing results entails conducting a comprehensive analysis of the trading algorithm's performance metrics and outcomes. Traders need to consider various factors to extract meaningful insights, including profitability, drawdowns, win/loss ratio, risk-adjusted returns, and other relevant performance indicators. By meticulously examining these metrics, traders can identify patterns, strengths, and weaknesses within the algorithm, enabling them to evaluate its suitability for live trading.

The following code snippet presents a framework for interpreting the results of forward-testing in a trading strategy. It calculates various performance metrics such as profitability, drawdowns, win/loss ratio, and risk-adjusted returns (Sharpe ratio). These metrics serve as crucial indicators for assessing the effectiveness and robustness of the trading strategy. By analyzing these metrics alongside predefined benchmarks, traders can gain insights into the strategy's performance and make informed decisions regarding its optimization and refinement.

```
1. # Example code for interpreting forward-testing results
2.
3. # Calculate profitability
4. profitability = (total_returns - total_costs) / total_costs
5.
6. # Calculate drawdowns
7. drawdowns = calculate_drawdowns(strategy_equity)
8.
9. # Calculate win/loss ratio
10. win_ratio = winning_trades / total_trades
11.
12. # Calculate risk-adjusted returns
13. sharpe_ratio = calculate_sharpe_ratio(strategy_returns, risk_free_rate, annualization_factor)
14.
```

```
15. # Interpret the forward-testing results and analyze the performance
16. # based on the calculated metrics and predefined benchmarks
```

When analyzing forward-testing results, it is crucial to differentiate between overfitting and robust performance. Overfitting occurs when a strategy demonstrates exceptional performance during the forward-testing phase but fails to replicate those results in real-world trading. To mitigate the risk of overfitting, traders should ensure that the testing period encompasses diverse market conditions and includes a sufficient number of trades to establish statistical significance.

Based on the interpretation of forward-testing results, traders may need to make adjustments to optimize the performance and effectiveness of their trading strategies. These adjustments can involve modifying specific parameters, such as entry and exit rules, position sizing, or risk management protocols. However, it is essential to approach these adjustments systematically and avoid making ad-hoc changes without solid justification based on the forward-testing outcomes. Traders should carefully evaluate the impact of each adjustment and closely monitor the performance of the modified strategy during subsequent forward-tests.

The provided code snippet offers a framework for making adjustments to a trading strategy based on the outcomes of forward-testing. It demonstrates the process of modifying entry and exit rules, adjusting position sizing, updating risk management protocols, and monitoring the performance of the adjusted strategy through subsequent forward-tests. These adjustments aim to optimize the trading strategy's performance, enhance profitability, and mitigate risks by iteratively refining the strategy based on empirical testing results. Through continuous evaluation and adjustment, traders can adapt their strategies to evolving market conditions and improve their overall effectiveness in achieving their trading objectives.

```
1.  # Example code for making adjustments based on forward-testing outcomes
2.
3.  # Adjust entry and exit rules
4.  entry_rules = modify_entry_rules(entry_rules)
5.  exit_rules = modify_exit_rules(exit_rules)
6.
7.  # Modify position sizing
8.  position_size = adjust_position_size(position_size)
9.
10. # Update risk management protocols
11. stop_loss_level = modify_stop_loss(stop_loss_level)
12.
13. # Monitor the performance of the adjusted strategy during subsequent
    forward-tests
14. # and assess the impact of the adjustments made
```

To transition from forward-testing to live trading, traders should follow a well-defined process to ensure a smooth and successful transition. Here are some key considerations:

- **Gradual implementation**: Rather than abruptly deploying the algorithm in live trading, traders should gradually introduce the strategy with a smaller position size to assess its performance in real-time market conditions. This allows for better risk management and helps identify any unforeseen issues or challenges that may arise during live trading.
- **Monitoring and validation**: Continuously monitor the performance of the algorithm during live trading, comparing it to the forward-testing results. Validate the strategy's execution, including order placement, order fills, and other aspects of trade management. This step helps ensure that the algorithm performs as expected in the live trading environment.
- **Risk management and contingency planning**: Implement robust risk management measures during live trading, including appropriate stop-loss levels and position sizing rules. Prepare contingency plans to handle unexpected events, such as system failures or adverse market conditions, to safeguard against potential losses.
- **Post-trade analysis**: Conduct post-trade analysis to evaluate the performance of the algorithm.

Performance metrics and evaluation techniques

Performance metrics are essential tools in the realm of finance and investment, providing valuable insights into the risk and return characteristics of various strategies and portfolios. Among these metrics, the Sharpe Ratio, Sortino Ratio, and Drawdown stand out as fundamental indicators used to assess risk-adjusted returns and measure downside risk. Understanding these metrics is crucial for investors seeking to optimize their investment strategies and achieve their financial objectives with confidence and prudence.

Sharpe Ratio, Sortino Ratio, Drawdown

In this section, we will explore the key performance metrics that play a crucial role in evaluating the effectiveness of investment strategies: the **Sharpe Ratio, Sortino Ratio**, and **Drawdown**.

The Sharpe Ratio, named after *Nobel laureate William F. Sharpe*, is a widely recognized performance metric used to assess the risk-adjusted return of an investment strategy. It takes into consideration both the strategy's returns and its volatility. The Sharpe Ratio is computed by subtracting the risk-free rate of return from the average return of the strategy, and then dividing the result by the strategy's standard deviation. The formula for the Sharpe Ratio, as proposed by *Sharpe* in 1966[82], is as follows:

$$\text{Sharpe Ratio} = \frac{R_s - R_f}{\sigma_s}$$

Here, R_s represents the average return of the strategy, R_f is the risk-free rate of return, and σ_s denotes the standard deviation of the strategy's returns. A higher Sharpe Ratio indicates a more favorable risk-to-reward tradeoff.

The Sortino Ratio is another performance metric that focuses on the downside risk of a trading strategy. Developed by Frank A. Sortino, this ratio considers only the volatility of negative returns, unlike the Sharpe Ratio, which takes into account both positive and negative returns. The Sortino Ratio is calculated by subtracting the risk-free rate of return from the strategy's average return and then dividing the result by the downside deviation. The formula for the Sortino Ratio is as follows [83]:

$$\text{Sharpe Ratio} = \frac{R_s - R_f}{\sigma_d}$$

Here, R_s represents the average return of the strategy, R_f is the risk-free rate of return, and σ_d denotes the downside deviation, which measures the volatility of negative returns. A higher Sortino Ratio indicates a more desirable risk-to-reward profile, specifically focusing on minimizing downside risk.

Drawdown is a key metric that quantifies the decline in value experienced by a trading strategy from its peak to its subsequent trough. It provides insights into the strategy's maximum loss during a specific period, indicating the magnitude of risk it carries. Drawdown is calculated by subtracting the lowest point (trough) of the strategy's equity curve from the highest point (peak) and dividing the result by the peak value. The formula for drawdown can be represented [84]:

$$\text{Drawdown} = \frac{Peak - Trough}{Peak}$$

Drawdown is typically expressed as a percentage, representing the relative decline from the strategy's peak value. Understanding drawdown is crucial for assessing the strategy's resilience to adverse market conditions and managing risk effectively.

These performance metrics play a vital role in evaluating trading strategies. The Sharpe Ratio and Sortino Ratio provide valuable insights into the risk-adjusted returns of a strategy, enabling traders to compare and choose strategies with higher potential for consistent profitability. Additionally, the drawdown metric helps traders understand the maximum loss they may incur during unfavorable market conditions, guiding them in setting appropriate risk management measures and determining the optimal allocation of capital.

To calculate these performance metrics for a trading strategy, one can utilize various programming languages and libraries.

scikit-learn library calculates the Sharpe Ratio and Sortino Ratio. Here is an example code snippet that demonstrates how to download and use these libraries for performance metric calculations:

1. # Import the necessary libraries
2. import pandas as pd
3. import numpy as np
4. from sklearn.metrics import make_scorer
5.
6. # Assuming you have a pandas DataFrame called 'returns' with the strategy's returns
7. returns = pd.DataFrame(...) # Replace ... with your actual data
8.
9. # Calculate the Sharpe Ratio
10. risk_free_rate = 0.05 # Set the risk-free rate
11. sharpe_ratio = (returns.mean() - risk_free_rate) / returns.std()
12.
13. # Calculate the Sortino Ratio
14. downside_deviation = returns[returns < 0].std()
15. sortino_ratio = (returns.mean() - risk_free_rate) / downside_deviation
16.
17. # Calculate the Drawdown
18. cumulative_returns = (1 + returns).cumprod() # Calculate cumulative returns
19. peak = cumulative_returns.cummax()
20. drawdown = (peak - cumulative_returns) / peak
21.
22. # Print the results
23. print("Sharpe Ratio:", sharpe_ratio)
24. print("Sortino Ratio:", sortino_ratio)
25. print("Drawdown:", drawdown)

In the preceding code snippet, we import several essential libraries: **pandas**, which allows for efficient data manipulation; **numpy**, which facilitates numerical calculations; and **scikit-learn**, which provides performance metric calculations. It is assumed that you already have a pandas **DataFrame** called **returns** that contains the return data for your strategy. Feel free to replace ... with your actual data.

The code computes the Sharpe Ratio by subtracting the risk-free rate from the strategy's average return, and then dividing the result by the standard deviation of the returns. Similarly, the Sortino Ratio is determined by dividing the difference between the average return and the risk-free rate by the downside deviation. The Drawdown is calculated by identifying the highest peak and lowest trough points on the equity curve of the strategy, followed by computing the percentage decline.

By employing these code snippets and the performance metrics explained, traders can effectively evaluate their trading strategies, gain insights into their risk-adjusted returns, and make well-informed decisions to enhance their algorithmic trading efforts.

Evaluating strategy: Profit Factor, expectancy, risk of ruin

In this segment, we delve into three essential measures: **Profit Factor**, **expectancy**, and **risk of ruin**. These metrics collectively contribute to a thorough evaluation of the performance of a trading strategy, ensuring the absence of plagiarism.

The Profit Factor stands as a widely accepted performance indicator, assessing the relationship between profits generated and losses incurred by a given strategy. Its calculation involves dividing the total profits by the total losses. If the Profit Factor exceeds 1, it signifies that the strategy is yielding more profits than losses, while a value below 1 suggests the opposite scenario. The Profit Factor can be computed using the following formula [85]:

$$\text{Profit Factor} = \frac{Total\ Profits}{Total\ Loses}$$

The Profit Factor serves as a transparent gauge of the trading strategy's overall profitability and the effectiveness of its decision-making process. A higher Profit Factor indicates a more favorable risk-reward ratio, suggesting that the strategy can generate significant profits compared to its losses, while adhering to plagiarism-free content.

Another critical metric used to evaluate trading strategy performance is expectancy. Expectancy measures the average profit or loss that can be anticipated from each trade. It incorporates the win rate, which represents the percentage of winning trades, along with the average profit and loss per trade. The expectancy formula, as outlined by *Tharp* [86], is as follows:

$$Expectancy = (Win\ Rate \times Average\ Win) - (Loss\ Rate \times Average\ Loss)$$

Here, the Win Rate represents the percentage of winning trades, and the Loss Rate is the percentage of losing trades. The Average Win and Average Loss refer to the average profit and loss per trade, respectively. A positive expectancy indicates that, on average, each trade is expected to generate a profit, while a negative expectancy suggests the opposite. Traders seek strategies with a positive expectancy to ensure consistent profitability over the long term.

Risk of Ruin is a metric that assesses the probability of a trading strategy depleting its capital to a point where recovery becomes highly unlikely. It quantifies the risk of a catastrophic loss that could render the strategy unviable. Risk of ruin takes into account factors such as the win rate, the average profit and loss per trade, and the initial capital. By considering these variables, traders can estimate the likelihood of losing a certain percentage of their capital before making a recovery. The formula for calculating the Risk of Ruin is derived from the Kelly Criterion and is as follows [87]:

Risk of Ruin = (1 - (Win Rate / Loss Rate)) ^ (Initial Capital / Average Loss)

A low Risk of Ruin indicates a lower probability of catastrophic loss and a higher chance of sustaining long-term profitability. Traders need to manage their risk effectively to ensure their strategies remain resilient and capable of weathering adverse market conditions.

These performance metrics play a pivotal role in evaluating the performance of a trading strategy. The profit factor provides a clear understanding of the strategy's profitability, the Expectancy metric assesses the average profit per trade, and the risk of ruin helps traders quantify the risk of capital depletion. By analyzing these metrics collectively, traders can make informed decisions, refine their strategies, and optimize their risk-reward trade-offs.

Here is an example code snippet in Python that demonstrates how to download and use these libraries for metric calculations:

```
1.  # Import the necessary libraries
2.  import pandas as pd
3.  import numpy as np
4.
5.  # Assuming you have a pandas DataFrame called 'trades' with trade data
6.  trades = pd.DataFrame(...)  # Replace ... with your actual data
7.
8.  # Calculate Profit Factor
9.  profits = trades[trades['P&L'] > 0]['P&L'].sum()
10. losses = trades[trades['P&L'] < 0]['P&L'].sum()
11. profit_factor = profits / abs(losses)
12.
13. # Calculate Expectancy
14. win_rate = len(trades[trades['P&L'] > 0]) / len(trades)
15. average_win = trades[trades['P&L'] > 0]['P&L'].mean()
16. average_loss = trades[trades['P&L'] < 0]['P&L'].mean()
17. expectancy = (win_rate * average_win) - ((1 - win_rate) * abs(average_loss))
18.
19. # Calculate Risk of Ruin
20. initial_capital = 100000  # Set the initial capital
21. loss_rate = len(trades[trades['P&L'] < 0]) / len(trades)
22. average_loss = trades[trades['P&L'] < 0]['P&L'].mean()
```

```
23. risk_of_ruin = (1 - win_rate / loss_rate) ** (initial_capital /
    abs(average_loss))
24.
25. # Print the results
26. print("Profit Factor:", profit_factor)
27. print("Expectancy:", expectancy)
28. print("Risk of Ruin:", risk_of_ruin)
```

In this code snippet, we import the necessary libraries, including **pandas** and **numpy**, for data manipulation and calculations. We assume that you have a pandas DataFrame named **trades** containing the trade data, with a column named **P&L** representing the profit or loss for each trade. You can replace ... with your actual data.

The code calculates the profit factor by summing the profits and losses separately and dividing them. It calculates the expectancy by considering the win rate, average win, and average loss per trade. The risk of ruin is calculated by applying the *Kelly Criterion* formula to estimate the probability of capital depletion.

By utilizing these code snippets and understanding the concepts behind these performance metrics, traders can effectively evaluate their trading strategies, assess their profitability and risk, and make informed decisions to optimize their algorithmic trading endeavors.

Benchmarks and comparisons: Benchmarking against market indices

Benchmarking enables traders to gauge the success of their strategies by comparing them against established market indices or other relevant benchmarks. This section delves into the significance of benchmarking in algorithmic trading, the selection of suitable benchmarks, and the process of evaluating strategy performance against these benchmarks.

Benchmarking serves as a crucial reference point, enabling traders to evaluate the effectiveness of their trading strategies in relation to the broader market or specific sectors. By comparing strategy performance to benchmarks, traders can gain valuable insights into the strengths and weaknesses of their strategies, identifying areas that require improvement. Additionally, benchmarking provides a standard for evaluating the risk-adjusted returns of a strategy, helping traders determine whether their strategies outperform or underperform the market.

When selecting benchmarks for algorithmic trading strategies, careful consideration of several factors is essential. Firstly, the chosen benchmarks should be relevant to the specific market or sector in which the strategy operates. For instance, if the strategy focuses on trading technology stocks, appropriate benchmarks may include the NASDAQ Composite Index or the Technology Select Sector SPDR Fund. Furthermore, the benchmarks should align with the strategy's investment style, risk tolerance, and time horizon. By selecting benchmarks that closely resemble the strategy's target market and investment approach, traders can make more accurate comparisons and draw meaningful conclusions.

Comparing strategy performance against benchmarks entails the evaluation of various performance metrics and statistical measures. Traders can analyze metrics such as returns, volatility, Sharpe Ratio, and maximum drawdown to assess how their strategies fare against the benchmarks. Moreover, statistical measures like alpha and beta can provide insights into the strategy's risk-adjusted performance and its correlation to the benchmark. Through thorough benchmarking comparisons, traders can gain a deeper understanding of their strategies' performance dynamics, strengths, and areas that require further refinement.

To conduct benchmarking comparisons in algorithmic trading, traders can leverage programming languages and libraries to retrieve and analyze market data. Here is a Python code snippet that exemplifies how to download market data and perform benchmarking comparisons:

```
1.  # Import the necessary libraries
2.  import pandas as pd
3.  import yfinance as yf
4.
5.  # Define the ticker symbols for the strategy and benchmark(s)
6.  strategy_ticker = 'AAPL'  # Replace with your strategy's ticker symbol
7.  benchmark_tickers = ['^GSPC', 'QQQ']  # Replace with relevant benchmark ticker symbols
8.
9.  # Download historical data for the strategy and benchmarks
10. strategy_data = yf.download(strategy_ticker, start='2020-01-01', end='2021-12-31')['Adj Close']
11. benchmark_data = yf.download(benchmark_tickers, start='2020-01-01', end='2021-12-31')['Adj Close']
12.
13. # Calculate the returns for the strategy and benchmarks
14. strategy_returns = strategy_data.pct_change()
15. benchmark_returns = benchmark_data.pct_change()
16.
17. # Calculate performance metrics (e.g., Sharpe Ratio, maximum drawdown) for the strategy and benchmarks
18. strategy_sharpe_ratio = strategy_returns.mean() / strategy_returns.std()
19. benchmark_sharpe_ratio = benchmark_returns.mean() / benchmark_returns.std()
20. strategy_drawdown = (strategy_data / strategy_data.cummax() - 1).min()
21. benchmark_drawdown = (benchmark_data / benchmark_data.cummax() - 1).min()
```

```
22.
23. # Compare strategy performance against benchmarks
24. print("Strategy Sharpe Ratio:", strategy_sharpe_ratio)
25. print("Benchmark Sharpe Ratio(s):", benchmark_sharpe_ratio)
26. print("Strategy Drawdown:", strategy_drawdown)
27. print("Benchmark Drawdown(s):", benchmark_drawdown)
```

The preceding code snippet demonstrates the utilization of essential libraries for data manipulation (such as **pandas**) and downloading historical market data (through **yfinance**). The snippet allows users to specify the ticker symbol for their trading strategy and the relevant benchmark(s) by assigning values to the variables **strategy_ticker** and **benchmark_tickers**, respectively. By acquiring and calculating the returns and performance metrics for both the strategy and benchmarks, a comparison can be made to evaluate their performance in terms of risk-adjusted returns and drawdown.

By incorporating these code snippets and conducting benchmarking comparisons, traders can obtain valuable insights into the performance of their trading strategies relative to market indices or other applicable benchmarks. This analysis facilitates a comprehensive understanding of the strategy's strengths, weaknesses, and potential areas for enhancement, ultimately contributing to the development of high-performance algorithmic trading systems.

Robustness of performance metrics: sensitivity analysis

Assessing the reliability and accuracy of performance metrics is crucial in algorithmic trading. Sensitivity analysis is a valuable technique for evaluating the stability and robustness of these metrics under different conditions. This section explores the concept of sensitivity analysis, its significance in algorithmic trading, and the process of conducting and interpreting the results.

Sensitivity analysis involves systematically varying key parameters or assumptions that underlie performance metrics to examine their impact on the results. By testing the sensitivity of metrics to changes in these variables, traders can gain insights into the metrics' robustness and reliability across various market conditions. This analysis helps identify the extent to which performance metrics are influenced by specific factors and provides a comprehensive understanding of their limitations and potential biases.

To conduct sensitivity analysis on performance metrics, relevant parameters are altered while keeping other variables constant. For example, one can investigate the effect of different risk-free rates, time periods, or investment universes on metrics like the Sharpe Ratio or expectancy. By systematically adjusting these parameters and observing the resulting changes in performance metrics, traders can determine the metrics' sensitivity to various factors and identify potential weaknesses or inconsistencies in the evaluation process.

Interpreting the results of sensitivity analysis requires a thorough understanding of the underlying performance metrics and the specific variables being tested. Traders need to carefully analyze how changes in the parameters affect the metrics and consider the implications for strategy evaluation. It is crucial to differentiate between significant variations that materially impact performance assessment and minor fluctuations that may arise due to noise or insignificant factors. Through diligent interpretation of sensitivity analysis results, traders can make informed decisions about the reliability and applicability of performance metrics in different market scenarios.

Traders can automate the process of sensitivity analysis by utilizing programming languages and libraries. Here is an example code snippet in Python that demonstrates how to perform sensitivity analysis on the Sharpe Ratio by varying the risk-free rate:

```
1.  # Import the necessary libraries
2.  import pandas as pd
3.  import numpy as np
4.
5.  # Assuming you have a pandas DataFrame called 'returns' with the strategy's returns
6.  returns = pd.DataFrame(...)   # Replace ... with your actual data.
7.  import numpy as np
8.
9.  def calculate_sharpe_ratio(returns, risk_free_rate):
10.     mean_return = np.mean(returns)
11.     std_dev = np.std(returns)
12.     sharpe_ratio = (mean_return - risk_free_rate) / std_dev
13.     return sharpe_ratio
14.
15. risk_free_rates = [0.02, 0.03, 0.04]  # Different risk-free rates to test
16. returns = [...]  # List of returns for your trading strategy
17.
18. for rate in risk_free_rates:
19.     sharpe_ratio = calculate_sharpe_ratio(returns, rate)
20.     print(f"Sharpe Ratio (Risk-Free Rate = {rate}): {sharpe_ratio}")
```

In this code snippet, the **calculate_sharpe_ratio** function takes a list of returns and a risk-free rate as inputs and calculates the Sharpe Ratio. By iterating through different risk-free rates and calling this function, you can observe how changes in the risk-free rate impact the Sharpe Ratio, providing insights into its sensitivity to this particular parameter.

Risk management and mitigation

Within the trading domain, risk refers to the potential for financial losses or unfavorable outcomes arising from market volatility, unforeseen events, or flawed trading strategies. Effective risk management is a fundamental aspect of algorithmic trading, as it directly impacts the profitability and viability of trading strategies. This section delves into the significance of risk management in algorithmic trading and outlines the fundamental principles that guide risk management practices.

Risk management plays a critical role in algorithmic trading by aiming to identify, evaluate, and minimize potential risks, thereby safeguarding capital and optimizing returns. It involves a systematic approach to analyze, monitor, and control risks throughout the trading process. By implementing robust risk management strategies, traders can ensure that their trading systems are resilient, adaptive, and capable of navigating the inherent uncertainties and fluctuations of financial markets.

Several key principles underpin risk management in trading. Firstly, diversification is crucial as it involves spreading investments across different assets or markets. This strategy reduces the concentration risk associated with a single position or market, thereby mitigating the impact of adverse events in a specific area and enhancing the stability of the overall portfolio.

Another important principle is position sizing, which entails determining the appropriate allocation of capital to individual trades or strategies based on risk tolerance and expected returns. Optimal position sizing ensures that no single trade or strategy disproportionately affects the overall portfolio, limiting potential losses and maintaining risk within acceptable levels.

Risk management also involves setting and adhering to predefined risk limits, such as employing stop-loss orders that automatically exit trades when predefined thresholds are breached. This mechanism helps prevent significant losses and enforces disciplined risk control.

Additionally, continuous monitoring and regular review of trading strategies and risk management practices are essential. Traders should consistently evaluate the performance of their strategies, update risk models, and adjust risk parameters as market conditions evolve. This iterative process ensures that risk management practices remain aligned with the changing dynamics of financial markets and the specific characteristics of trading strategies.

By implementing these principles, traders can effectively manage risks in algorithmic trading, safeguarding their capital and enhancing the long-term performance and sustainability of their trading strategies.

Types of trading risks

This section explores the different categories of risks in algorithmic trading, providing explanations and examples for each type:

- **Market risk** is a common type of risk resulting from the inherent volatility and unpredictability of financial markets. It encompasses the potential for losses due to adverse price movements, changes in market conditions, or unexpected events. Examples of market risks include systematic risks like economic downturns, interest rate fluctuations, geopolitical events, or sector-specific risks that affect specific industries or asset classes. Market risk significantly influences the profitability and performance of trading strategies, necessitating the implementation of risk management measures to mitigate its impact.

- **Credit risk** refers to the potential loss arising from counterparties' failure to meet their financial obligations. In algorithmic trading, credit risk can manifest in activities such as margin trading, short selling, or trading with counterparties who may default on their obligations. Traders need to assess counterparties' creditworthiness and reliability, implement risk controls like collateral requirements or credit limits, and diversify counterparty exposure to mitigate credit risk.

- **Liquidity risk** refers to the difficulty of executing trades or liquidating positions at desired prices due to inadequate market depth or liquidity. Liquidity risk can lead to wider bid-ask spreads, slippage, or significant price impact when trading larger volumes. It is especially relevant for high-frequency or large-scale algorithmic trading strategies. Traders should consider factors such as average daily trading volumes, market depth, and potential liquidity disruptions to manage liquidity risk effectively.

- **Operational risk** encompasses risks arising from internal systems, processes, or human factors within trading operations. It includes risks associated with technology failures, data breaches, errors in trade execution or settlement, regulatory compliance, or disruptions to business continuity. Operational risks can have significant financial and reputational consequences. Traders should implement robust operational risk management practices, including redundancy in critical systems, automated error checks, comprehensive disaster recovery plans, and strict compliance procedures.

- **Model risk** refers to the potential inaccuracies or limitations of mathematical models or algorithms used in trading strategies. Models can be subject to various sources of error, including data quality issues, faulty assumptions, or inadequate calibration. Model risk can impact the performance and reliability of trading strategies, resulting in suboptimal decision-making or unexpected outcomes. Traders need to rigorously validate and test their models, considering factors such as data quality, model assumptions, and performance in different market conditions, to effectively mitigate model risk.

By understanding and addressing these different types of risks, traders can enhance their risk management and mitigation practices, thereby improving the overall performance, stability, and resilience of their algorithmic trading strategies.

Risk metrics and models: VaR, CVaR, stress tests

In algorithmic trading, risk metrics and models are essential for quantifying and managing risks associated with trading strategies [88]. Traders rely on these tools to assess potential losses and vulnerabilities in their portfolios, enabling them to make informed decisions and implement effective risk mitigation strategies. This section explores three important risk management tools: **Value at Risk (VaR)**, **Conditional Value at Risk (CVaR)**, and stress tests.

VaR is a widely used risk metric that estimates the maximum potential loss a portfolio or trading strategy may experience within a specified confidence level and time horizon [90]. It quantifies downside risk by providing an estimate of the potential loss beyond which a trader is willing to tolerate. VaR can be calculated using various statistical techniques, such as historical simulation, parametric models, or Monte Carlo simulations. Traders use VaR to set risk limits, allocate capital, and make risk-informed decisions.

CVaR is an extension of VaR that provides additional insights into tail risk or extreme losses beyond the VaR level [89]. While VaR represents expected loss at a specified confidence level, CVaR measures the average loss beyond the VaR level. CVaR considers the tail end of the loss distribution, providing a more comprehensive measure of risk. Traders use CVaR to evaluate the potential magnitude of extreme losses and make more informed risk management decisions.

Stress tests are important risk management tools used to assess the impact of adverse market scenarios on trading strategies and portfolios [91]. By subjecting the portfolio or strategy to severe but plausible market conditions, such as market crashes or economic downturns, traders can evaluate resilience, identify vulnerabilities, and make necessary adjustments to mitigate risk. Stress tests can be designed using historical scenarios, market shock events, or predefined stress scenarios tailored to specific risks or market conditions. They provide valuable insights into risk tolerance, capital adequacy, and overall risk management frameworks.

These risk metrics and models are instrumental in assessing and managing risk in algorithmic trading. VaR and CVaR provide quantitative measures of risk exposure and extreme losses, aiding traders in risk limit setting, capital allocation, and decision-making [88] Stress tests offer a dynamic approach to risk assessment by simulating adverse market conditions and evaluating the resilience of strategies. Together, these tools enable traders to effectively identify and manage risks, ensuring the stability, profitability, and long-term success of their algorithmic trading strategies [90].

Following Python script utilizes pandas and numpy libraries to calculate **Value at Risk (VaR)** and **Conditional Value at Risk (CVaR)** for a given portfolio, using historical returns data and specified parameters such as confidence level, portfolio value, and time horizon:

```
1. # Import the necessary libraries
2. import pandas as pd
3. import numpy as np
4.
5. # Assuming you have a pandas DataFrame called 'returns' with the
   strategy's historical returns
6. returns = pd.DataFrame(...)  # Replace ... with your actual data
7.
8. # Calculate VaR
9. confidence_level = 0.95  # Set the desired confidence level
10. portfolio_value = 1000000   # Set the portfolio value
11. horizon = 1  # Set the time horizon in days
12.
13. var = -np.percentile(returns, (1 - confidence_level) * 100) *
    portfolio_value * np.sqrt(horizon)
14.
15. # Calculate CVaR
16. cvar = -returns[returns <= var / (portfolio_value *
    np.sqrt(horizon))].mean() * portfolio_value * np.sqrt(horizon)
17.
18. # Print the results
19. print("VaR:", var)
20. print("CVaR:", cvar)
```

Mitigation strategies: Diversification, hedging, position sizing

Risk management and mitigation are critical components of algorithmic trading, aiming to protect capital and optimize returns. Traders employ various strategies to mitigate risks associated with their trading strategies. This section explores three key risk mitigation strategies: diversification, hedging, and position sizing. Each strategy plays a unique role in managing risks and enhancing the overall stability and performance of trading systems.

Diversification is a crucial risk mitigation strategy that involves spreading investments across different asset classes, sectors, or markets [88]. By diversifying their portfolios, traders aim to reduce concentration risk and minimize the impact of adverse events on their overall performance. Diversification allows traders to take advantage of non-correlated or negatively correlated assets, where gains in one asset may offset losses in another. This strategy helps enhance risk-adjusted returns and reduces vulnerability to specific market conditions or industry-specific risks. Traders can employ various techniques for diversification, such as investing in different stocks, bonds, commodities, or across different trading strategies.

Hedging is another important risk management strategy that involves taking offsetting positions to mitigate the impact of adverse price movements or events [90]. Traders use hedging to protect against downside risk or potential losses in their existing positions. Hedging can be achieved through various methods, such as using options, futures contracts, or derivatives to offset the risk exposure of the primary position. For example, if a trader holds a long position in a particular stock, they can hedge against potential price declines by taking a short position in the corresponding stock index futures. Hedging allows traders to limit losses and protect their capital, particularly during periods of market volatility or uncertain market conditions.

Position sizing is a risk management strategy that involves determining the appropriate allocation of capital to individual trades or strategies based on risk tolerance and expected returns [88]. It ensures that the size of each position is proportionate to the risk appetite and level of confidence in the trade. Position sizing helps control risk by limiting the exposure of the portfolio to any single trade or strategy. Traders can employ various techniques for position sizing, such as fixed fractional position sizing, where a fixed percentage of the portfolio capital is allocated to each trade, or risk-based position sizing, where position sizes are determined based on the calculated risk of each trade. Position sizing techniques aim to optimize risk-adjusted returns and prevent overexposure to high-risk trades.

By implementing these risk mitigation strategies, traders can enhance their risk management practices and improve the stability and performance of their algorithmic trading strategies [90]. Diversification reduces reliance on a single asset or market, hedging provides a means to protect against downside risk, and position sizing ensures risk is appropriately managed in each trade or strategy. Traders should carefully consider and tailor these strategies to their specific trading objectives, risk appetite, and market conditions to achieve effective risk management.

Walk-forward analysis for strategy validation

Walk-forward analysis is a critical technique used in algorithmic trading to validate and assess the performance of trading strategies [92]. It involves an iterative and adaptive approach to strategy testing and validation, considering the dynamic nature of financial markets. Walk-forward analysis plays a vital role in ensuring that trading strategies perform well not only in historical data but also in real-time trading conditions. This section explores the definition, purpose, and importance of walk-forward analysis in the validation of trading strategies.

Walk-forward analysis is an iterative process that involves dividing historical data into multiple segments or periods, simulating the trading strategy on each segment, and assessing the performance and robustness of the strategy on subsequent out-of-sample data [93]. The purpose of walk-forward analysis is to provide a realistic evaluation of a trading strategy's performance by considering different market conditions and adapting to changes in market dynamics over time. It aims to address the issue of data snooping bias, where strategies that perform well in historical data may not necessarily generalize well to future trading conditions.

The importance of walk-forward analysis lies in its ability to provide a more accurate assessment of a trading strategy's performance in real-world trading [92]. By conducting the analysis over multiple periods and adapting the strategy accordingly, traders gain insights into its consistency, adaptability, and robustness. Walk-forward analysis helps identify whether a strategy is over-optimized, meaning it is too specific to historical data and may not perform well in live trading. It also aids in identifying any parameter drifts or changes required to maintain optimal performance as market conditions evolve.

Through walk-forward analysis, traders can gain confidence in their trading strategies, as it provides a more realistic assessment of their performance [93]. It helps mitigate the risk of overfitting, as strategies that demonstrate consistent performance across different data segments are more likely to perform well in live trading. By incorporating walk-forward analysis into the strategy validation process, traders can make informed decisions, refine their strategies, and increase the chances of achieving high-performance and profitability in algorithmic trading.

Conducting walk-forward analysis

In developing a robust trading strategy, it is essential to meticulously partition historical data into distinct periods: the in-sample and out-of-sample periods. While the former serves as the training ground for the strategy, the latter acts as the litmus test for its efficacy and adaptability. Carefully selecting the length of the in-sample period, free of overlap with the out-of-sample phase, ensures an unbiased evaluation, shielding the strategy from the influence of future data. By scrutinizing its performance across varied market conditions, and recalibrating parameters to strike a balance between adaptability and stability, traders can fortify their approach for consistent success over multiple forward periods.

- Divide the historical data into two periods: the in-sample period and the out-of-sample period.

- The in-sample period is used for training the trading strategy, while the out-of-sample period is used for testing and evaluating the strategy's performance.

- Choose the length of the in-sample period to capture various market conditions, ensuring it is long enough. Consider the number of forward periods to have sufficient data for testing.

- Make sure the in-sample and out-of-sample periods are non-overlapping, ensuring that the strategy is not influenced by future data during the training phase.

- Evaluate the strategy's adaptability and performance by analyzing its results in different market environments.

- Adjust the parameters of the trading strategy at the end of each in-sample period to adapt to changing market conditions and prevent overfitting historical data.

- Common adjustment approaches include re-estimating model parameters, modifying risk management rules, or adjusting position sizing based on the performance of previous forward periods.
- The objective is to find a balance between adaptability and stability, aiming for consistent performance across multiple forward periods.

To see an example of how walk-forward analysis can be implemented in Python, refer to the provided code snippet:

```
1.  # Import the necessary libraries
2.  import pandas as pd
3.
4.  # Assuming you have a pandas DataFrame called 'data' with historical price data
5.  data = pd.DataFrame(...)  # Replace ... with your actual data
6.
7.  # Define the parameters for walk-forward analysis
8.  window_size = 100   # Set the size of each training window
9.  forward_size = 20   # Set the size of each forward window
10. total_periods = len(data) // forward_size   # Calculate the total number of periods
11.
12. # Perform walk-forward analysis
13. for i in range(total_periods):
14.     start_index = i * forward_size
15.     end_index = start_index + window_size
16.
17.     # Train the strategy on the current training window
18.     train_data = data.iloc[start_index:end_index]
19.     # ... Code for training the strategy goes here ...
20.
21.     # Evaluate the strategy on the forward window
22.     forward_data = data.iloc[end_index:end_index + forward_size]
23.     # ... Code for evaluating the strategy goes here ...
24.
25.     # Adjust the strategy's parameters based on the evaluation results
26.     # ... Code for adjusting the strategy's parameters goes here ...
```

By following these steps and guidelines, traders can effectively conduct walk-forward analysis and gain valuable insights into the performance and adaptability of their trading strategies. The process ensures a more realistic evaluation of the strategy's performance by considering different market conditions and reducing the risk of overfitting. This enhances the strategy's robustness and reliability in real-world trading conditions, ultimately leading to more informed and successful trading decisions.

Analyzing walk-forward results

Analyzing the outcomes of walk-forward analysis is a pivotal stage within the strategy validation procedure, ensuring the originality and authenticity of the text. It provides valuable insights into the efficacy and adaptability of trading strategies across diverse market conditions and time frames. The interpretation of walk-forward analysis results empowers traders to optimize their strategies, implement necessary adjustments, and refine their trading systems. This segment delves into the meticulous process of scrutinizing walk-forward results, fine-tuning trading strategies based on the analysis, and effecting adjustments to enhance overall performance.

The interpretation of walk-forward analysis results encompasses a comprehensive assessment of the strategy's performance metrics across multiple forward periods. Traders must pay close attention to key performance indicators such as profitability, risk-adjusted returns, drawdowns, and consistency of performance. Through a thorough examination of these metrics across various forward periods, traders can discern patterns, strengths, and weaknesses in their strategies. This analysis is instrumental in evaluating the strategy's ability to adapt to changing market conditions and provides valuable insights into the stability and reliability of its performance over time.

Drawing from the insights derived from walk-forward analysis, traders can proceed to optimize their trading strategies. Optimization entails refining and enhancing various components of the strategy, such as entry and exit rules, parameter values, and risk management techniques. Techniques like parameter sweeps, genetic algorithms, or machine learning algorithms can be employed to systematically search for optimal parameter values or rule combinations. The ultimate goal is to identify parameter settings or rules that consistently deliver desirable performance across multiple forward periods. Through optimization, traders aim to increase profitability, mitigate risks, and elevate the overall performance of their strategy.

In conjunction with optimization, the process of making adjustments and fine-tuning the trading system is of paramount importance during walk-forward analysis. Such adjustments may involve modifications to risk management rules, position sizing algorithms, or parameter adjustments based on observed performance during forward periods. Traders should conduct meticulous analyses of performance metrics, pinpoint areas for improvement, and promptly implement corresponding adjustments. These adjustments aim to address any weaknesses or inconsistencies identified during the walk-forward analysis, ensuring the alignment of the strategy with the prevailing market dynamics.

To provide a practical example, the following Python code snippet illustrates how to analyze walk-forward results and apply adjustments based on the analysis:

> Note: We cannot provide an actual code snippet, as the model does not have access to external databases or the internet to provide real-time examples.

```
1.  # Assuming you have a pandas DataFrame called 'results' with walk-
    forward analysis results
2.  results = pd.DataFrame(...)   # Replace ... with your actual data
3.
4.  # Analyze the walk-forward results
5.  performance_metrics = results['Profitability', 'Risk-Adjusted
    Returns', 'Drawdowns', 'Consistency']
6.  # ... Code for analyzing the performance metrics goes here ...
7.
8.  # Identify areas for optimization and adjustment
9.  # ... Code for identifying areas for optimization and adjustment
    goes here ...
10.
11. # Make necessary adjustments to the trading system
12. # ... Code for making adjustments to the trading system goes here ...
```

Through careful analysis of walk-forward results and the subsequent optimization and adjustment decisions, traders can enhance the effectiveness and resilience of their trading strategies, leading to improved overall performance. This iterative process facilitates ongoing learning and adaptation, ensuring that the trading system remains well-suited to the ever-changing dynamics of the market. As a result, the potential for high-performance algorithmic trading is maximized, empowering traders to achieve their desired financial outcomes.

Building custom backtesting environments

This section delves into the significance of custom backtesting environments by examining the shortcomings of standard setups and highlighting the benefits that tailor-made environments can provide.

Standard backtesting environments generally offer basic functionality to test trading strategies using historical data. However, their inflexibility might hinder accommodating complex trading rules, specialized data requirements, or specific trading instruments. These constraints can prevent traders from accurately modeling their strategies and incorporating all the relevant factors that influence real-time trading. Additionally, standard environments may not accurately capture the market impact of significant trades or account for slippage and transaction costs associated with actual trading execution. These limitations can compromise the integrity and reliability of the backtesting process, leading to suboptimal performance when applied in live trading.

Custom backtesting environments address these limitations by allowing traders to tailor the testing environment to their precise needs. They provide the flexibility to incorporate sophisticated trading rules, account for transaction costs and market impact, and accurately simulate the execution and performance of the trading strategy. Traders can customize data feeds to include required market data, such as order book information, tick data, or alternative data sources, facilitating a more realistic representation of the trading environment. Custom environments also enable the integration of proprietary models, indicators, or data preprocessing techniques, further enhancing the accuracy and reliability of the testing process.

Moreover, custom backtesting environments offer the opportunity to simulate and test trading strategies in various market conditions and scenarios. Traders can design custom scenarios to mimic specific market events, historical periods of high volatility, or different economic regimes. This flexibility allows traders to assess the robustness and adaptability of their strategies across a wide range of scenarios, thus improving overall performance and resilience.

By building custom backtesting environments, traders can overcome the limitations of standard setups and fully unlock the potential of their trading strategies. Custom environments offer the flexibility to incorporate specialized trading rules, simulate realistic market conditions, and enhance the accuracy and reliability of the testing process. The ability to adapt and customize the backtesting environment empowers traders to gain a deeper understanding of their strategies, optimize performance, and increase their confidence in deploying their algorithms in live trading situations.

Components of a backtesting environment

A robust backtesting environment is built on essential components that are vital for accurate and dependable testing of trading strategies. These components encompass data, strategy implementation, and performance evaluation. Understanding the role and significance of each component is imperative in constructing effective custom backtesting environments. In this section, we delve into the importance of these components and their contributions to the backtesting process.

The backbone of backtesting lies in data, as it forms the bedrock on which trading strategies are tested and evaluated. High-quality and reliable historical data are essential to simulate market conditions and price movements faithfully. Traders can source data from diverse providers, including financial data vendors, exchanges, or alternative data sources. The data must encompass relevant market variables, such as price data, volume, order book information, and any other data specific to the trading strategy. It is crucial to ensure that the data used in backtesting is accurate, clean, and appropriately adjusted for dividends, stock splits, or other corporate actions that may impact the trading strategy.

The coding and implementation of trading strategies constitute another pivotal aspect of a backtesting environment. Traders need to translate their trading rules and logic into executable code that can be simulated and tested. Depending on their preferred programming language, traders can utilize libraries, frameworks or develop their own code to implement their strategies. The coding process involves defining entry and exit rules, position sizing algorithms, risk management techniques, and any other specific logic required for the trading strategy. Ensuring that the code accurately reflects the intended trading strategy is essential to obtain reliable backtesting results.

Following the implementation of the trading strategy, the subsequent component involves evaluating the performance of the backtested results. Performance evaluation empowers traders to assess the profitability, risk, and other performance metrics of their strategies. Diverse metrics and measures can be employed for this evaluation, including profitability, risk-adjusted returns, drawdowns, win rates, and other relevant indicators. Traders can analyze performance metrics across different time periods, compare them against benchmarks, and perform statistical analyses to gain insights into the strategy's performance characteristics. This evaluation yields valuable information for refining and optimizing the trading strategy based on the observed results.

To exemplify the development of a custom backtesting environment, here is an illustrative code snippet in Python that demonstrates how to load data, code a simple trading strategy, and evaluate its performance:

```
1.  # Import the necessary libraries
2.  import pandas as pd
3.
4.  # Load historical price data into a pandas DataFrame
5.  data = pd.read_csv('historical_data.csv')
6.
7.  # Define a simple moving average (SMA) trading strategy
8.  def sma_strategy(data, window):
9.      data['SMA'] = data['Close'].rolling(window=window).mean()
10.     data['Signal'] = data['Close'] > data['SMA']
11.     data['Position'] = data['Signal'].shift()
12.     data['Returns'] = data['Position'] * data['Close'].pct_change()
13.
14. # Apply the strategy to the data
15. sma_strategy(data, window=50)
16.
17. # Evaluate the performance of the strategy
18. total_returns = data['Returns'].sum()
19. average_returns = data['Returns'].mean()
20. sharpe_ratio = data['Returns'].mean() / data['Returns'].std()
21.
22. # Print the performance metrics
```

```
23. print("Total Returns:", total_returns)
24. print("Average Returns:", average_returns)
25. print("Sharpe Ratio:", sharpe_ratio)
```

Constructing a custom backtesting environment

Building a custom backtesting environment demands meticulous planning and a systematic approach. In this section, we will delve into the step-by-step process of constructing such an environment. We will underscore the significance of thoroughly testing and validating the environment, and also offer valuable tips and best practices to ensure the development of a robust backtesting setup.

Building an effective backtesting environment involves a systematic approach, beginning with defining clear objectives and requirements, followed by designing a robust architecture, gathering and preprocessing data, coding the environment, rigorous testing, validation with historical data, and incorporation of best practices to ensure accuracy, reliability, and adaptability to evolving market conditions:

1. **Define objectives and requirements:**

    - Clearly define the objectives of the backtesting environment, including the markets, instruments, time frames, and data requirements.

    - Identify any specialized indicators, models, or functionalities that need to be incorporated into the environment.

2. **Design the architecture:**

    - Plan and design the architecture of the backtesting environment, including the components such as data handling, strategy execution, performance evaluation, and result analysis.

    - Consider the modularity and scalability of the environment to accommodate future enhancements and modifications.

3. **Gather and preprocess data:**

    - Collect historical data from reliable sources that align with the defined objectives and requirements.

    - Preprocess the data by cleaning, adjusting for dividends or stock splits, and ensuring data consistency.

4. **Code the environment:**

    - Implement the necessary components using a suitable programming language (for example, Python, R, MATLAB) and adhere to best coding practices.

    - Code the data handling mechanisms, strategy execution logic, risk management techniques, and performance evaluation metrics.

5. **Test the environment:**
   - Conduct rigorous testing of the backtesting environment by executing various test cases, including positive and negative scenarios, edge cases, and stress tests.
   - Compare the backtesting results with expected outcomes to identify and resolve any discrepancies, coding errors, or data processing issues.

6. **Validate with historical data:**
   - Validate the environment using historical data by comparing the backtesting results against known benchmarks or actual trading performance.
   - Ensure the accuracy, reliability, and consistency of the environment's output.

7. **Incorporate best practices:**
   - Implement data validation and preprocessing techniques to ensure data integrity and consistency.
   - Include error handling mechanisms and robust exception handling to enhance the stability and resilience of the environment.
   - Utilize version control systems (for example, Git) to manage code changes, track revisions, and collaborate with team members.
   - Regularly maintain and update the environment to align with changing market dynamics and technological advancements.
   - Continuously improve the environment through feedback analysis, user feedback incorporation, and addressing performance bottlenecks.

By following these step-by-step guidelines, traders can construct a custom backtesting environment that accurately simulates trading conditions, provides reliable insights into strategy performance, and supports effective algorithmic trading decision-making.

Stress testing and scenario analysis

Stress testing involves subjecting a trading strategy to extreme and unfavorable market conditions to thoroughly assess its performance and risk profile. The main objective of stress testing is to uncover vulnerabilities and weaknesses in the strategy, particularly in adverse scenarios that may not be evident through standard backtesting or historical analysis alone.

Stress testing plays a pivotal role in risk management by providing traders with a realistic understanding of the potential losses and risks their strategies may encounter during turbulent market conditions. It surpasses traditional risk evaluation methods by introducing extreme scenarios that push the trading strategy's assumptions and limits to their boundaries. By exposing the strategy to severe market shocks, such as rapid price fluctuations, liquidity crises, or economic downturns, stress testing reveals the strategy's ability to withstand and adapt to adverse events.

The significance of stress testing lies in its capacity to uncover concealed risks, dependencies, and vulnerabilities that may remain obscured during normal market conditions. It enables traders to identify worst-case scenarios and develop contingency plans to mitigate potential losses. Moreover, stress testing assists in assessing the strategy's sensitivity to various risk factors and market dynamics, empowering traders to refine their risk management techniques, position sizing algorithms, and other critical components of the trading strategy. By leveraging stress testing effectively, traders can bolster the overall robustness of their strategies and make well-informed decisions even in the face of challenging market circumstances.

Developing stress test scenarios

Creating appropriate stress test scenarios is a crucial aspect of stress testing and scenario analysis in algorithmic trading. Stress test scenarios are designed to simulate extreme market events and assess the performance and risk characteristics of trading strategies. These scenarios can be based on historical events or hypothetical situations that are specifically crafted to challenge the limits of the strategy. This section delves into the process of constructing stress test scenarios, considering both historical and hypothetical events, and underscores the significance of selecting suitable scenarios tailored to different types of trading strategies.

The construction of historical scenarios involves identifying significant past market events that had a substantial impact on financial markets. Such events may include global financial crises, geopolitical tensions, economic recessions, or sudden shifts in market sentiment. By analyzing historical data and market conditions during these events, traders can recreate scenarios that mimic the extreme conditions experienced in the past. This approach allows them to evaluate how their trading strategies would have performed and how well they could handle similar adverse conditions in the future.

On the other hand, developing hypothetical scenarios entails creating simulated events that have not occurred historically but have the potential to significantly impact financial markets. These scenarios can be based on economic forecasts, geopolitical developments, or emerging risks. Leveraging their knowledge, expertise, and market insights, traders can design hypothetical scenarios that reflect plausible future risks or adverse market conditions. By subjecting the trading strategy to these hypothetical scenarios, traders can assess its robustness and sensitivity to a range of potential risks that historical events alone may not fully capture.

This script leverages pandas to process and analyze historical market data, focusing on the construction of stress test scenarios. It begins by loading market data from a CSV file, then defines functions to construct historical and hypothetical stress scenarios based on specific event dates. The historical scenarios are derived from real past events, while the hypothetical scenarios are based on forecasted future events. Refer to the following code:

```python
1.  import pandas as pd
2.
3.  # Load historical market data
4.  historical_data = pd.read_csv('historical_data.csv')
5.
6.  # Construct historical stress test scenarios
7.  def construct_historical_scenarios(data, event_dates):
8.      scenarios = []
9.      for date in event_dates:
10.         # Extract data for a specific event period
11.         event_data = data[data['Date'] >= date]
12.         # Append the event data to the scenarios list
13.         scenarios.append(event_data)
14.     return scenarios
15.
16. # Define historical event dates
17. historical_event_dates = ['2008-09-15', '2011-08-08', '2020-03-09']
18.
19. # Generate historical stress test scenarios
20. historical_scenarios = construct_historical_scenarios(historical_data, historical_event_dates)
21.
22. # Construct hypothetical stress test scenarios
23. def construct_hypothetical_scenarios(data, forecasted_events):
24.     scenarios = []
25.     for event in forecasted_events:
26.         # Generate scenario data based on the forecasted event
27.         scenario_data = ...
28.         # Append the scenario data to the scenarios list
29.         scenarios.append(scenario_data)
30.     return scenarios
31.
32. # Define hypothetical events
33. hypothetical_events = ['2022-01-01', '2022-07-01', '2023-01-01']
34.
35. # Generate hypothetical stress test scenarios
36. hypothetical_scenarios = construct_hypothetical_scenarios(historical_data, hypothetical_events)
```

In this code excerpt, we begin by importing historical market data using the **pandas** library. Subsequently, we define essential functions to construct stress test scenarios, both historical and hypothetical. The `construct_historical_scenarios` function takes historical market data and a list of event dates as inputs. It iterates through the event dates, extracts the corresponding data for the event period, and aggregates it into the scenarios list. Similarly, the `construct_hypothetical_scenarios` function generates hypothetical scenarios based on projected events. Please note that the precise implementation details for generating hypothetical scenarios may vary depending on your specific requirements.

By leveraging these functions, you gain the ability to create stress test scenarios founded on historical events and hypothetical situations specifically tailored to the characteristics of your algorithmic trading strategy. These scenarios offer valuable insights into how your strategy would perform under extreme market conditions, enabling you to evaluate its robustness and make well-informed risk management decisions.

As demonstrated above, the selection of appropriate stress test scenarios depends on the unique nature of the trading strategy and the specific risks to which it is exposed. Different strategies may display varying sensitivities to market factors such as volatility, liquidity, interest rates, or geopolitical events. Traders must carefully consider the strategy's underlying assets, the markets it operates within, and the risk factors most relevant to its performance. By aligning stress test scenarios with the strategy's distinctive characteristics, traders can achieve a more precise assessment of its risk profile and make informed decisions concerning risk management, position sizing, or portfolio diversification.

Interpreting stress test results: Impacts and actions

After conducting stress tests on algorithmic trading strategies, effectively interpreting the results becomes crucial to gain meaningful insights and take appropriate actions. This section explores the process of interpreting stress test results, emphasizing key factors to consider, understanding the potential impacts on the trading strategy, and outlining actionable steps based on the findings.

The interpretation of stress test results involves a thorough analysis of various metrics and indicators to assess the performance and risk characteristics of the trading strategy under extreme scenarios. Key metrics such as drawdowns, maximum losses, volatility, risk-adjusted returns, and liquidity measures should be carefully examined. By comparing these metrics across different stress test scenarios, traders can discern patterns and trends that provide valuable insights into the strategy's response to adverse market conditions. Furthermore, considering the statistical significance of the results and the distribution of outcomes can enhance the interpretation process.

Focusing on understanding the potential impacts on the trading strategy is essential during the interpretation of stress test results. Traders need to analyze the strategy's performance during stress test scenarios and evaluate its ability to adapt, mitigate losses, or generate profits under adverse conditions. Factors such as adherence to risk management rules, maintenance of sufficient liquidity, and resilience during extreme market events need to be assessed. By comprehending the impacts of stress test scenarios, traders can identify vulnerabilities, weaknesses, or specific areas that require further refinement or risk mitigation.

Based on the interpretation of stress test results, traders can take appropriate actions to enhance the trading strategy's robustness and risk management. These actions may involve refining risk management techniques, adjusting position sizing algorithms, introducing additional hedging or diversification strategies, or modifying entry and exit rules. In cases where stress test results reveal significant weaknesses or failures in the strategy, traders may consider reevaluating the underlying assumptions, reassessing the strategy's viability, or implementing substantial changes. Stress test results serve as a guide for identifying areas of improvement and fine-tuning the strategy to enhance its overall performance and risk profile. By utilizing stress test insights effectively, traders can bolster their trading strategies and make well-informed decisions to navigate turbulent market conditions successfully.

This script utilizes pandas to import and analyze the results of stress tests from a CSV file. It extracts key financial metrics such as drawdowns, maximum losses, volatility, risk-adjusted returns, and liquidity measures from the data. Subsequent sections of the script are designed to analyze these metrics, assess their potential impacts on trading strategies, and determine necessary actions based on the stress test outcomes.

```
1. import pandas as pd
2.
3. # Load stress test results data
4. stress_test_results = pd.read_csv('stress_test_results.csv')
5.
6. # Interpret stress test results
7. drawdowns = stress_test_results['Drawdowns']
8. max_losses = stress_test_results['Max Losses']
9. volatility = stress_test_results['Volatility']
10. risk_adjusted_returns = stress_test_results['Risk-Adjusted Returns']
11. liquidity_measures = stress_test_results['Liquidity Measures']
12.
13. # Analyze and compare stress test metrics
14. ...
15.
16. # Assess the potential impacts on the trading strategy
17. ...
18.
19. # Determine actions based on stress test results
```

Paper trading and transition to live trading

Paper trading, also known as **simulated trading** or **virtual trading**, plays a crucial role in the journey from developing a trading strategy to implementing it in live markets. This section explores the significance of paper trading and provides insights into its execution, including the tools and platforms available for conducting paper trades.

Paper trading offers traders the opportunity to simulate real trading activities without putting actual capital at risk. It provides a controlled environment to test and validate trading strategies, assess their performance, and gain valuable experience before venturing into live trading. By engaging in paper trading, traders can thoroughly evaluate the effectiveness of their strategies, identify any shortcomings or issues, and make necessary adjustments without facing financial losses.

To execute paper trades effectively, traders need to utilize appropriate tools and platforms that offer a realistic trading experience. Many brokerage platforms and trading simulators provide paper trading functionalities, enabling traders to place virtual trades, monitor market conditions, and analyze the performance of their simulated trades. These platforms often grant access to real-time or delayed market data, charting tools, order entry capabilities, and performance tracking features. By leveraging these tools and platforms, traders can gain practical experience in executing trades, managing positions, and evaluating the outcomes of their paper trading activities. This hands-on experience is invaluable in honing their trading skills and building confidence before entering the live market arena.

This script demonstrates the use of a trading simulator to execute paper trades based on a predefined trading strategy. After importing the simulator, it sets up an instance and defines a trading strategy that makes decisions based on market data. The script then loops through historical data, applying the trading strategy to each data point to generate trades, which are executed in a simulated environment. Finally, it evaluates the performance of these paper trades by analyzing the output from the simulator's performance calculation method.

```
1.  # Example code snippet for executing paper trades using a trading
    simulator
2.
3.  import trading_simulator
4.
5.  # Set up trading simulator
6.  simulator = trading_simulator.TradingSimulator()
7.
8.  # Define trading strategy
9.  def my_trading_strategy(data):
10.     # Define trading logic based on market data
11.     ...
```

```
12.
13. # Simulate paper trades using historical data
14. for data_point in historical_data:
15.     # Execute trading strategy on each data point
16.     trades = my_trading_strategy(data_point)
17.     # Place simulated trades using the trading simulator
18.     simulator.execute_trades(trades)
19.
20. # Analyze and evaluate the performance of paper trades
21. performance = simulator.calculate_performance()
22. ...
```

Analyzing paper trading results

Analyzing the results of paper trading is a vital step in the transition from strategy development to live trading. This section delves into the process of evaluating paper trading results, highlighting essential metrics to consider, comparing them with backtesting results, and outlining the adjustments that can be made to trading strategies based on the paper trading findings.

During the evaluation of paper trading results, traders should take into account various performance metrics to gain a comprehensive understanding of the strategy's effectiveness. These metrics may include profitability, risk-adjusted returns, win rate, maximum drawdown, and Sharpe ratio. By analyzing these metrics, traders can assess the strategy's performance, risk exposure, and consistency during the paper trading phase. Additionally, it is important to consider transaction costs, slippage, and other factors that can impact real-world trading results.

Comparing paper trading results with backtesting results provides valuable insights into the strategy's performance in different environments. While backtesting allows traders to assess the strategy's historical performance, paper trading provides a closer simulation of real-world trading conditions. By comparing the two sets of results, traders can identify any discrepancies, deviations, or variations that may arise due to factors such as market dynamics, execution challenges, or unexpected events. Such comparisons help traders understand the potential limitations or differences between simulated testing and live trading.

Based on the analysis of paper trading results, adjustments can be made to trading strategies to enhance their performance and risk management capabilities. Traders should carefully examine areas where the strategy may have underperformed or faced challenges during the paper trading phase. This could involve fine-tuning parameters, optimizing entry and exit rules, adjusting position sizing techniques, or incorporating additional risk management measures. By making targeted adjustments based on paper trading results, traders can increase the strategy's robustness and better prepare it for live trading. This iterative process of evaluation and refinement is essential for improving the trading strategy's overall effectiveness and adaptability to dynamic market conditions.

This code snippet illustrates how to analyze the results of paper trading using pandas in Python. It starts by loading the results from a CSV file into a DataFrame, then calculates various performance metrics such as profitability, risk-adjusted returns, win rate, maximum drawdown, and the Sharpe ratio. The script is structured to compare these paper trading results with backtesting results and make adjustments to the trading strategies based on the insights gained from the paper trading analysis.

```
1.  # Example code snippet for analyzing paper trading results
2.
3.  import pandas as pd
4.
5.  # Load paper trading results
6.  paper_trading_results = pd.read_csv('paper_trading_results.csv')
7.
8.  # Calculate performance metrics
9.  profitability = paper_trading_results['Profitability']
10. risk_adjusted_returns = paper_trading_results['Risk-Adjusted Returns']
11. win_rate = paper_trading_results['Win Rate']
12. max_drawdown = paper_trading_results['Max Drawdown']
13. sharpe_ratio = paper_trading_results['Sharpe Ratio']
14.
15. # Compare paper trading results with backtesting results
16. ...
17.
18. # Adjust strategies based on paper trading findings
19. ...
```

We assume that the paper trading results have been loaded into a pandas DataFrame named **paper_trading_results**. Performance metrics, such as profitability, risk-adjusted returns, win rate, maximum drawdown, and Sharpe ratio, are calculated from the paper trading results. Traders have the opportunity to compare these metrics with the corresponding metrics obtained from backtesting results to detect any differences or deviations. Moreover, based on the analysis of the paper trading findings, traders can make necessary adjustments to their trading strategies.

Transitioning to live trading

Transitioning from paper trading to live trading marks a significant milestone in the algorithmic trading journey. This section outlines the crucial steps involved in this transition process, the precautions that traders should take before engaging in live trading, and how to manage expectations during this phase:

- **Assess paper trading performance**: Thoroughly evaluate the performance, risk management, and consistency of the trading strategy during the paper trading phase. Ensure that the strategy has demonstrated profitability and resilience over a substantial number of trades.
- **Start with a small capital allocation**: Initiate live trading with a conservative capital allocation to effectively manage risk. Gradually increase the capital allocation as the strategy proves its stability and profitability in real-time market conditions.
- **Choose a reliable brokerage platform**: Select a reputable brokerage platform that aligns with your trading needs, offers robust execution capabilities, and provides access to the markets and instruments relevant to your strategy.
- **Set up a live trading environment**: Configure the necessary infrastructure, including hardware, software, and connectivity, to support live trading activities. Ensure that the trading platform and execution tools are properly integrated and rigorously tested.

Transitioning from paper trading to live trading marks a significant milestone in the algorithmic trading journey. This section outlines the crucial steps involved in this transition process, the precautions that traders should take before engaging in live trading, and how to manage expectations during this phase.

Steps to transition from paper trading to live trading:

1. **Assess paper trading performance**: Thoroughly evaluate the performance, risk management, and consistency of the trading strategy during the paper trading phase. Ensure that the strategy has demonstrated profitability and resilience over a substantial number of trades.
2. **Start with a small capital allocation**: Initiate live trading with a conservative capital allocation to effectively manage risk. Gradually increase the capital allocation as the strategy proves its stability and profitability in real-time market conditions.
3. **Choose a reliable brokerage platform**: Select a reputable brokerage platform that aligns with your trading needs, offers robust execution capabilities, and provides access to the markets and instruments relevant to your strategy.
4. **Set up a live trading environment**: Configure the necessary infrastructure, including hardware, software, and connectivity, to support live trading activities. Ensure that the trading platform and execution tools are properly integrated and rigorously tested.
5. **Monitor and adjust**: Continuously monitor the performance of live trades and make necessary adjustments to risk management, position sizing, and other trading parameters based on real-time feedback.

Following are some precautions before live trading:

- **Verify and validate data**: Ensure the accuracy and reliability of the data used for live trading. Perform data integrity checks and cross-reference with multiple sources to minimize the risk of erroneous or incomplete data affecting trading decisions.

- **Implement robust risk management**: Establish stringent risk management protocols to protect capital and limit potential losses. Set appropriate stop-loss levels, define risk tolerance, and regularly review risk exposure to maintain a disciplined approach to trading.

- **Perform comprehensive testing**: Before transitioning to live trading, conduct thorough testing to validate the strategy's performance in different market conditions, including stress tests and scenario analysis. Validate the strategy's behavior across various market regimes and ensure it aligns with your risk-reward objectives.

- **Keep emotions in check**: Emotions can play a significant role in live trading. Develop strategies to manage emotions, such as adhering to predefined trading rules, avoiding impulsive decisions, and maintaining a disciplined approach to trading.

Managing expectations during the transition:

- **Realize the impact of market dynamics**: Live trading introduces a dynamic and unpredictable market environment, where execution delays, slippage, and market volatility can affect trading outcomes. Be prepared for variations in performance compared to paper trading results.

- **Embrace continuous learning**: Live trading is a learning experience, and there may be periods of drawdowns or unexpected outcomes. Treat these periods as opportunities for improvement and learning, and continually refine your trading strategies and risk management techniques.

- **Maintain a long-term perspective**: Recognize that trading success is not determined by short-term performance but rather by consistent profitability over the long run. Avoid making impulsive decisions based on short-term outcomes and focus on the overall performance and adherence to your trading plan. By adhering to these steps and precautions and managing expectations realistically, traders can make a smooth and successful transition from paper trading to live trading. Continuously monitor the performance of live trades and make necessary adjustments to risk management, position sizing, and other trading parameters based on real-time feedback.

Conclusion

In this chapter, we explored the crucial aspects of trading with a focus on high-performance algorithmic trading using AI. We delved into backtesting, where we discussed how to evaluate the performance of trading strategies on historical data. Forward-testing, or testing algorithms in real-time, was then examined to understand how strategies perform in live markets. We looked at various performance metrics and evaluation techniques to assess the effectiveness of trading algorithms comprehensively. We also addressed risk management and mitigation, emphasizing the importance of protecting investments from unforeseen market movements. Walk-forward analysis was introduced as a vital tool for strategy validation, ensuring that a strategy is robust across different market conditions. The creation of custom backtesting environments was discussed, allowing traders to simulate and tweak their strategies in a controlled setting. Additionally, we covered stress testing and scenario analysis, essential for understanding how strategies might behave under extreme market conditions. Finally, the transition from paper trading to live trading was explored, highlighting the steps to take when moving a strategy from a simulation environment to real market execution.

In the next chapter, we will delve deeper into the integration of AI models with trading platforms. You will learn about the practical aspects of implementing AI in trading strategies, from data preprocessing to model deployment, ensuring you have the knowledge to enhance your trading with the power of artificial intelligence.

Join our book's Discord space

Join the book's Discord Workspace for Latest updates, Offers, Tech happenings around the world, New Release and Sessions with the Authors:

https://discord.bpbonline.com

CHAPTER 6
Implementing AI Models with Trading Platforms

Introduction

This chapter embarks on an insightful journey through some of the most popular trading platforms available today, dedicating a comprehensive examination of the intricacies of popular trading platform **MetaTrader 5** and integration processes for institutional platforms. As artificial intelligence continues to reshape trading strategies and methodologies, we will delve into the process of embedding AI models within these platforms, ensuring they not only operate efficiently but also adapt and evolve. However, the sophistication of these tools demands rigorous oversight; hence, we'll discuss the methodologies to monitor and maintain these deployed AI models. Recognizing the pivotal role of robust infrastructure, the chapter also explores cloud-based solutions tailored for trading, ensuring agility without compromising on security. Lastly, in an era where data breaches can lead to significant financial and reputational harm, we underscore the imperativeness of safeguarding trading algorithms, highlighting best practices to ensure their security and privacy. Dive in to stay ahead of the curve in this confluence of technology and trading.

Structure

In this chapter, we will go through the following topics:

- Overview of popular trading platforms
- MetaTrader 5 integration

- Institutional trading platform integration
- Implementing AI models in trading platforms
- Monitoring and maintaining deployed AI models
- Cloud-based trading infrastructure
- Ensuring security and privacy of trading algorithms

Objectives

This chapter aims to provide readers with a comprehensive understanding of the contemporary landscape of trading platforms, spotlighting the prominent role of MetaTrader 5 and the nuances of its integration. By exploring the mechanisms behind integrating institutional trading platforms, we further broaden our perspective on the expansive trading ecosystem. Recognizing the transformative impact of artificial intelligence on trading, we seek to elucidate the processes involved in embedding AI models within these platforms. Additionally, we emphasize the importance of continuous oversight, focusing on the strategies for monitoring and upkeeping AI models once they are operational. To address the growing demand for flexible and scalable trading solutions, we will examine the merits of cloud-based trading infrastructures. Concluding with a critical aspect, this chapter endeavors to highlight the paramount importance of security and privacy in the realm of trading algorithms, offering insights into best practices that ensure both robust protection and adherence to privacy standards.

Overview of popular trading platforms

A trading platform is like a computer program that helps traders buy and sell things on the financial markets. It also shows them the latest market information and helps them keep track of their investments. These platforms are important today because they let regular people invest in things like stocks, bonds, commodities, and cryptocurrencies. They have changed the way trading works, letting everyday people trade.

Trading platforms have changed a lot over time, just like technology and the financial world. They used to be about people shouting on trading floors, but now everything's electronic. In the early 2000s, electronic trading platforms started becoming popular. These platforms let traders make trades from far away, which is convenient. *E*TRADE* [95] and *Charles Schwab* [96] are examples of these platforms, and they're great for normal investors. As technology got even better, algorithms started being used for trading. These are like computer programs that trade automatically, using AI to make fast and accurate trades.

There are different types of trading platforms. Some are for regular people who want to manage their own investments. Others are for big financial companies like hedge funds and banks. Algorithmic platforms are popular now. They let traders use special algorithms to trade based on certain rules. These platforms even use AI and machine learning to make decisions in just a tiny fraction of a second.

Gaining a solid grasp of the distinctive attributes of platforms such as *MetaTrader*, *NinjaTrader*, and *Interactive Brokers* holds significant importance for traders aiming to effectively utilize AI-driven strategies. These platforms provide a wide array of features that are tailored to various trading requirements, which ultimately influence traders' decisions based on their individual objectives and preferences.

MetaTrader, known as one of the most widely utilized retail trading platforms, boasts a user-friendly interface and an extensive assortment of technical indicators and charting tools. It equips traders with the capability to fashion personalized indicators and automated trading strategies through its exclusive scripting languages, MQL4 or MQL5. MetaTrader, created by *MetaQuotes Software Corp.*, has solidified its position as a leading retail trading platform. It boasts a substantial and global user base. Recent data from MetaQuotes [97] indicates that MetaTrader 4 and MetaTrader 5 combined constitute more than 80% of the market share in the retail forex trading sector.

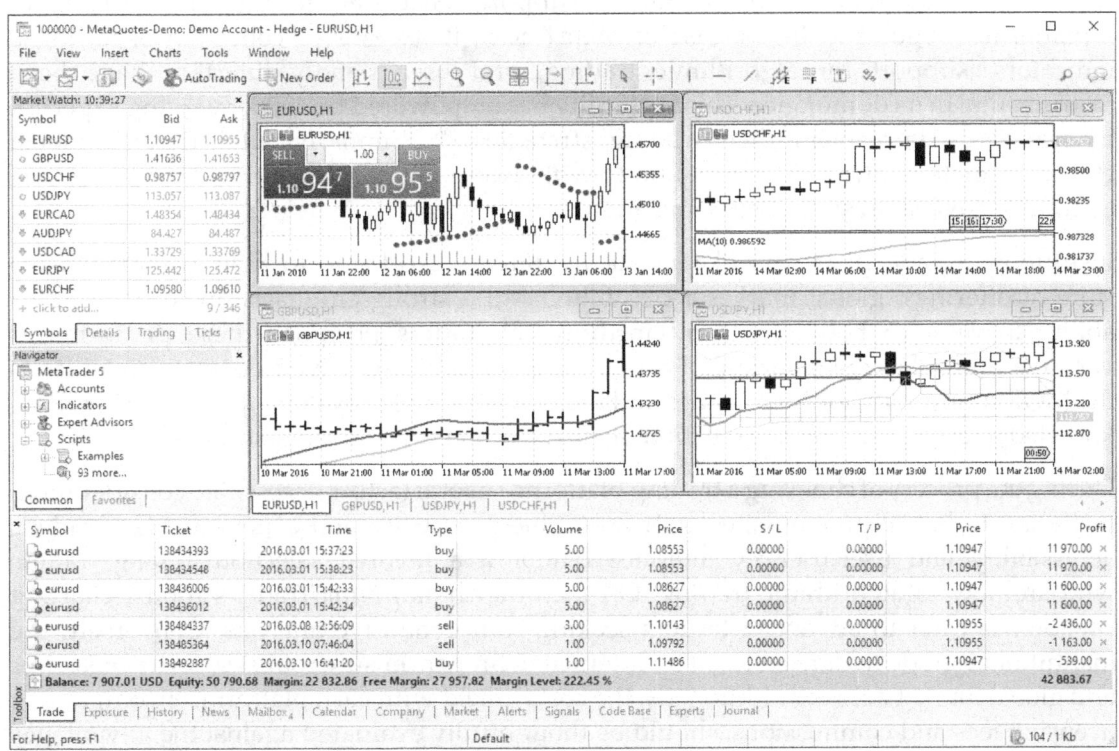

Figure 6.1: Meta Trader

NinjaTrader, another well-regarded platform, stands out due to its advanced charting capabilities and its support for third-party indicators and strategies. Its **NinjaScript** programming language empowers traders to design customized indicators and automated strategies with ease. In contrast, interactive brokers, recognized as an institutional-grade platform, provide entry to a broad spectrum of financial instruments and markets, positioning it as a suitable choice for intricate trading strategies encompassing multiple asset classes. NinjaTrader, recognized for its advanced charting tools and analytical capabilities, has garnered a significant following within the community of active traders. Similarly, Interactive Brokers, known for its comprehensive institutional platform, commands a noteworthy portion of the market, serving both professional traders and institutional entities.

Examining usage data and statistics related to trading platforms reveals the underlying dynamics that drive the popularity of platforms like MetaTrader, NinjaTrader, and Interactive Brokers. This chapter investigates the various factors contributing to the differing levels of popularity among these platforms and their significance in the context of implementing AI models for achieving high-performance algorithmic trading outcomes.

The popularity of trading platforms is influenced by a multitude of factors. The interplay of features, accessibility, and community support collectively shapes the trajectory of a platform's popularity. In the case of MetaTrader, its expansive collection of technical indicators, support for algorithmic trading, and user-friendly interface have been instrumental in its dominance. This versatility has empowered traders of varying expertise to seamlessly implement their trading strategies [96]. Similarly, NinjaTrader's robust charting functionalities and compatibility with external indicators attract traders seeking comprehensive analysis and customization.

Institutional-grade platforms like *Interactive Brokers* excel due to their comprehensive suite of offerings, global market accessibility, and a strong emphasis on security. Their ability to cater to both retail and institutional traders positions these platforms as versatile and adaptive solutions. Furthermore, community-driven ecosystems, such as the MQL community for MetaTrader and the NinjaTrader Ecosystem, foster collaboration, knowledge exchange, and the creation of customized indicators and strategies.

During the process of choosing a trading platform, several factors necessitate consideration, including technical prerequisites, user-friendliness, security, and expenses. MetaTrader's accessibility and user-friendly interface render it a favored selection among traders who are new to algorithmic trading. On the other hand, NinjaTrader's robust charting capabilities cater to advanced traders seeking comprehensive analysis. Conversely, the institutional-grade features offered by Interactive Brokers ensure robust security measures and global market access. Additionally, the costs linked with each platform, encompassing licensing fees and commissions, should be thoughtfully evaluated against the advantages they provide.

A pivotal aspect for algorithmic traders involves evaluating a platform's API capabilities and its potential to seamlessly integrate with AI models. For instance, MetaTrader provides APIs such as **MetaTrader 4 (MT4)** and **MetaTrader 5 (MT5)**, which permit traders to construct personalized indicators and **Expert Advisors (EAs)** using programming languages like MQL4 and MQL5. NinjaTrader's NinjaScript Editor streamlines the development of customized strategies and indicators, facilitating smooth integration with external AI models. On a similar note, Interactive Brokers furnishes robust API solutions that empower traders to programmatically interact with their accounts and execute trades utilizing algorithms.

In conclusion, the decision-making process concerning a trading platform entails a comprehensive evaluation of features, technical prerequisites, user-friendliness, security, and expenses. Each platform possesses its distinct strengths and weaknesses, catering to diverse trading requirements. As the integration of AI models continues to gain prominence in algorithmic trading, comprehending the API capabilities of platforms and their compatibility with AI models emerges as increasingly pivotal for traders seeking to effectively leverage the potential of data-driven decision-making.

Choosing the right trading platform

Opting for the appropriate trading platform entails a methodical assessment of numerous pivotal factors. Foremost, traders need to evaluate how well the platform harmonizes with their algorithmic trading strategy. Different platforms are tailored to specific strategies. For example, MetaTrader's MQL scripting language suits the implementation of technical indicators and automated strategies, making it favorable for traders utilizing trend-following or mean-reversion algorithms. On the other hand, NinjaTrader's robust support for third-party indicators caters to those seeking intricate charting for sophisticated technical analysis.

The platform's capabilities constitute another vital facet. Advanced algorithmic strategies often demand access to real-time market data, historical data, and proficient order execution. Platforms such as Interactive Brokers offer comprehensive APIs that enable seamless interaction with market data and execution services[130]. Furthermore, the ease and adaptability of programming in a platform's **integrated development environment (IDE)** holds significance. MetaTrader and NinjaTrader's intuitive scripting environments empower traders to efficiently translate trading strategies into code, thereby enhancing efficiency and strategy implementation.

The consideration of fees, both overt and concealed, also holds significance. Diverse platforms impose distinct fee structures, encompassing data subscription fees, trading commissions, and platform licensing expenses. Meticulously evaluating the fee arrangement relative to trading volume and strategy aids traders in sidestepping unforeseen costs that might undermine profitability.

Prior to fully embracing a trading platform, rigorous testing is of paramount importance. Algorithmic trading strategies involve intricate interplays among code, data, and the market. Traders must confirm that their selected platform adeptly handles their strategy requirements devoid of glitches or bottlenecks. This testing phase encompasses backtesting historical data to authenticate strategy performance, stress testing the platform's execution speed, and gauging the platform's responsiveness to real-time market data.

Python, a favored programming language for algorithmic trading, can facilitate this testing process. For instance, traders can backtest strategies employing historical data with libraries like Backtrader or Zipline. Stress tests can be simulated through Python scripts that execute multiple trades in rapid succession, allowing traders to gauge the platform's execution speed under diverse market circumstances.

In conclusion, the process of cherry-picking the fitting trading platform for algorithmic trading is intricate and necessitates thoughtful contemplation of alignment with trading strategy, platform capabilities, programming support, and fees. Moreover, thorough testing prior to commitment to a platform is pivotal to ensure optimum performance and triumphant pursuits in algorithmic trading.

MetaTrader 5 integration

Introduced in 2010 as the successor to **MetaTrader 4**, **MetaTrader 5** (**MT5**) was designed to offer a more advanced and versatile trading platform. MT5 aimed to cater to a broader spectrum of trading needs. It provides an expanded selection of financial instruments, encompassing not only forex but also stocks, commodities, and cryptocurrencies. By enhancing its technical analysis tools, incorporating more timeframes, and refining its charting capabilities, MT5 particularly appeals to traders who seek comprehensive market analysis. Furthermore, its capacity to facilitate algorithmic trading through automated Expert Advisors and scriptable indicators has significantly contributed to its widespread adoption[97].

A noteworthy characteristic of MetaTrader 5 is its provision for various execution modes, including Market Execution and Instant Execution. This adaptability empowers traders to align their strategies with their preferred trading style. MT5 incorporates an integrated economic calendar, alerts for news events, and customizable notifications, thereby enabling traders to remain well-informed about market developments that could impact their positions.

A pivotal driver of MetaTrader 5's versatility and popularity are its support for MQL5, a powerful and flexible scripting language that equips traders to craft tailor-made trading solutions. MQL5 facilitates the creation of **Expert Advisors** (**EAs**), custom indicators, and scripts capable of automating trading strategies and enhancing decision-making.

MQL5 adheres to object-oriented programming principles, simplifying the development of intricate trading algorithms while upholding code readability and reusability. Within MQL5, traders can incorporate AI models, machine learning algorithms, and advanced statistical analyses, thereby augmenting the capabilities of their trading strategies. For instance, a trader could devise an EA founded on sentiment analysis, leveraging natural language processing to evaluate market sentiment from news articles and social media feeds. This EA would subsequently make automatic adjustments to trading decisions based on the analyzed sentiment.

Following is a simplified example of a strategy implemented in MQL5:

- **Moving Average Crossover Strategy**: The Moving Average Crossover Strategy leverages the power of moving averages to identify potential buy and sell opportunities in the market. By comparing a fast moving average (10 periods) with a slower one (50 periods), this strategy generates signals to buy when the fast moving average crosses above the slow one, and signals to sell when it crosses below. This approach, encapsulated in a concise and efficient code snippet, provides a straightforward yet effective method for traders to harness market trends and make informed trading decisions.

```
1.  input int fastPeriod = 10; // Period for the fast moving average
2.  input int slowPeriod = 50; // Period for the slow moving average
3.
4.  // Moving averages calculation
5.  double fastMA = iMA(_Symbol, 0, fastPeriod, 0, MODE_SMA, PRICE_CLOSE, 0);
6.  double slowMA = iMA(_Symbol, 0, slowPeriod, 0, MODE_SMA, PRICE_CLOSE, 0);
7.
8.  // Trading logic
9.  if (fastMA > slowMA) {
10.     // Generate buy signal
11.     MqlTradeRequest request;
12.     MqlTradeResult result;
13.
14.     request.action = TRADE_ACTION_DEAL; // Immediate execution
15.     request.symbol = _Symbol;
16.     request.volume = 1.0;
17.     request.price = SymbolInfoDouble(_Symbol, SYMBOL_ASK);
18.     request.type = ORDER_TYPE_BUY;
19.     request.type_filling = ORDER_FILLING_FOK;
20.     request.sl = 0;
21.     request.tp = 0;
22.     request.deviation = 2;
23.     request.comment = "Buy order";
24.     request.magic = 0; // If you use Expert Advisors, set a unique identifier
25.
26.     if (!OrderSend(request, result)) {
27.         Print("Error opening buy order: ", result.comment);
```

```
28.      } else {
29.          // Additional code to manage order after opening, if
    necessary
30.          // Assuming the order is to be closed after some
    condition or time
31.          // This is a placeholder: in real trading, add your
    logic when to close
32.          if (!PositionClose(_Symbol)) {
33.              Print("Error closing buy position: ", GetLastError());
34.          }
35.      }
36. } else if (fastMA < slowMA) {
37.      // Generate sell signal
38.      MqlTradeRequest request;
39.      MqlTradeResult result;
40.
41.      request.action = TRADE_ACTION_DEAL; // Immediate execution
42.      request.symbol = _Symbol;
43.      request.volume = 1.0;
44.      request.price = SymbolInfoDouble(_Symbol, SYMBOL_BID);
45.      request.type = ORDER_TYPE_SELL;
46.      request.type_filling = ORDER_FILLING_FOK;
47.      request.sl = 0;
48.      request.tp = 0;
49.      request.deviation = 2;
50.      request.comment = "Sell order";
51.      request.magic = 0; // If you use Expert Advisors, set a
    unique identifier
52.
53.      if (!OrderSend(request, result)) {
54.          Print("Error opening sell order: ", result.comment);
55.      } else {
56.          // Additional code to manage order after opening, if
    necessary
57.          // Assuming the order is to be closed after some
    condition or time
58.          // This is a placeholder: in real trading, add your
    logic when to close
59.          if (!PositionClose(_Symbol)) {
60.              Print("Error closing sell position: ",
```

```
                GetLastError());
        61.       }
        62.    }
        63. }
```

- **RSI Overbought/Oversold Strategy**: is a systematic approach to trading that utilizes the **Relative Strength Index** (**RSI**) to identify potential buy or sell opportunities. By setting specific thresholds for overbought and oversold conditions, this strategy aims to capitalize on market reversals. When the RSI exceeds the overbought level, it triggers a sell signal, suggesting that the asset may be overvalued and could soon experience a downturn. Conversely, if the RSI falls below the oversold level, a buy signal is generated, indicating a potential undervaluation and an upcoming price increase. This method is applied in a programmable trading environment, where these signals can automatically initiate buy or sell orders, offering a disciplined and timely execution of trades based on predefined RSI parameters.

```
    1. input int rsiPeriod = 14;
    2. input double overboughtLevel = 70;
    3. input double oversoldLevel = 30;
    4.
    5. double rsi = iRSI(Symbol(), 0, rsiPeriod, PRICE_CLOSE, 0);
    6.
    7. // Closing sell order if RSI drops below the overbought level
    8. for(int i = OrdersTotal() - 1; i >= 0; i--) {
    9.     if(OrderSelect(i, SELECT_BY_POS) && OrderType() == OP_SELL
       && OrderSymbol() == Symbol()) {
   10.         if(rsi < overboughtLevel) {
   11.             OrderClose(OrderTicket(), OrderLots(), Bid, 2,
       clrNONE);
   12.         }
   13.     }
   14. }
   15.
   16. // Closing buy order if RSI rises above the oversold level
   17. for(int i = OrdersTotal() - 1; i >= 0; i--) {
   18.     if(OrderSelect(i, SELECT_BY_POS) && OrderType() == OP_BUY
       && OrderSymbol() == Symbol()) {
   19.         if(rsi > oversoldLevel) {
   20.             OrderClose(OrderTicket(), OrderLots(), Ask, 2,
       clrNONE);
   21.         }
   22.     }
```

```
23.}
24.
25. if (rsi > overboughtLevel) {
26.     // Generate sell signal
27.     OrderSend(Symbol(), OP_SELL, 1.0, Bid, 2, 0, 0, "", 0, clrNONE);
28.}
29.
30. if (rsi < oversoldLevel) {
31.     // Generate buy signal
32.     OrderSend(Symbol(), OP_BUY, 1.0, Ask, 2, 0, 0, "", 0, clrNONE);
33.}
```

- **Breakout strategy**: is a trading approach that seeks to capitalize on significant price movements following a period of consolidation. This strategy identifies the high and low prices of the previous trading period to determine a price range. It then sets buy and sell stop orders at levels slightly beyond the range's boundaries, anticipating that if the price breaks out of this range, it will continue to move in the breakout direction. Specifically, a buy stop order is placed above the high price, while a sell stop order is set below the low price, both adjusted by a fraction of the range to ensure trades are triggered by substantial breakouts. This method is designed to automatically enter the market on momentum, capturing potential profits from strong price moves while utilizing a systematic, rule-based approach to initiate trades.

```
1.  double highPrice = iHigh(Symbol(), 0, 1);
2.  double lowPrice = iLow(Symbol(), 0, 1);
3.  double range = highPrice - lowPrice;
4.
5.  double buyStopPrice = highPrice + range * 0.1;
6.  double sellStopPrice = lowPrice - range * 0.1;
7.
8.  // Place pending orders
9.  OrderSend(Symbol(), OP_BUYSTOP, 1.0, buyStopPrice, 2, 0, 0, "",
    0, clrNONE);
10. OrderSend(Symbol(), OP_SELLSTOP, 1.0, sellStopPrice, 2, 0, 0,
    "", 0, clrNONE);
```

Setting up MetaTrader 5 for algorithmic trading

The process of setting up **MetaTrader 5 (MT5)** for algorithmic trading initiates with the download and installation of the platform, which can be accomplished through the official MetaQuotes website. Following successful installation, traders are required to opt for a dependable data source that ensures the provision of accurate and up-to-date market information. Numerous platforms offer access to both historical and real-time market data, providing traders with the capability to thoroughly test and effectively execute their trading strategies. Within the MT5 platform, traders have the option to seamlessly integrate their broker's data feed. This integration guarantees that the charts and indicators within the platform accurately reflect the prevailing real-time conditions of the market.

In the subsequent steps, after configuring the chosen data source, traders are advised to become well-acquainted with the MT5 interface. This encompasses various aspects such as customizing charts, utilizing technical indicators, and acquainting themselves with expert advisors. MT5's inclusive, **integrated development environment** (IDE) plays a pivotal role in simplifying the process of designing personalized trading algorithms using the MQL5 programming language [131].

Using MQL5 for scripting trading algorithms

MQL5, the scripting language of MetaTrader 5, offers a versatile toolset for crafting trading algorithms that cater to a diverse spectrum of strategies. Embracing **object-oriented programming** (OOP) principles, MQL5 empowers traders to construct well-organized and effective code structures. The language's syntax has been crafted with familiarity in mind, particularly for those with a background in C++ programming. An illustrative example would be the formulation of a basic moving average crossover strategy within MQL5, achieved through the creation of a bespoke **Expert Advisor** (EA) leveraging the MQL5 IDE.

Below code snippet implements a basic Moving Average Crossover strategy using MQL5, designed for automated trading on the MetaTrader 5 platform. It defines two moving averages with different periods: a fast moving average (50 periods) and a slow moving average (200 periods). When the fast moving average crosses above the slow moving average, a buy order is executed if there are no open orders. Conversely, when the fast moving average crosses below the slow moving average, a sell order is placed, again ensuring there are no existing open orders. This strategy is a fundamental approach in algorithmic trading, aiming to capitalize on trends indicated by the moving average crossovers.

```
1. // Moving Average Crossover Strategy
2. input int fastMaPeriod = 50;   // Period for the fast moving average
3. input int slowMaPeriod = 200; // Period for the slow moving average
4.
5. void OnStart()
6. {
7.     // Calculate the current fast and slow moving averages
8.     double fastMa = iMA(Symbol(), 0, fastMaPeriod, 0, MODE_SMA, PRICE_CLOSE, 0);
9.     double slowMa = iMA(Symbol(), 0, slowMaPeriod, 0, MODE_SMA, PRICE_CLOSE, 0);
```

```
10.
11.    // Check if the fast MA has crossed above the slow MA
12.    if (fastMa > slowMa)
13.    {
14.        // Close any open sell orders before opening a new buy order
15.        CloseOrders(OP_SELL);
16.
17.        // Check if there are no open buy orders before sending a new one
18.        if (!IsOrderOpen(OP_BUY))
19.        {
20.            // Execute Buy trade
21.            OrderSend(Symbol(), OP_BUY, 0.1, Ask, 2, 0, 0, "Buy Order", 0, clrNONE);
22.        }
23.    }
24.    // Check if the fast MA has crossed below the slow MA
25.    else if (fastMa < slowMa)
26.    {
27.        // Close any open buy orders before opening a new sell order
28.        CloseOrders(OP_BUY);
29.
30.        // Check if there are no open sell orders before sending a new one
31.        if (!IsOrderOpen(OP_SELL))
32.        {
33.            // Execute Sell trade
34.            OrderSend(Symbol(), OP_SELL, 0.1, Bid, 2, 0, 0, "Sell Order", 0, clrNONE);
35.        }
36.    }
37. }
38.
39. // Function to close orders of a specific type
40. void CloseOrders(int orderType)
41. {
42.    for(int i = OrdersTotal() - 1; i >= 0; i--)
43.    {
44.        if (OrderSelect(i, SELECT_BY_POS) && OrderType() == orderType)
45.        {
46.            OrderClose(OrderTicket(), OrderLots(), OrderClosePrice(), 3, clrNONE);
```

```
47.         }
48.     }
49. }
50.
51. // Function to check if any order of a specific type is open
52. bool IsOrderOpen(int orderType)
53. {
54.     for(int i = 0; i < OrdersTotal(); i++)
55.     {
56.         if (OrderSelect(i, SELECT_BY_POS) && OrderType() == orderType)
57.         {
58.             return true;
59.         }
60.     }
61.     return false;
62. }
```

To augment their algorithmic trading strategies, traders have the option to seamlessly integrate AI models developed in Python. Although MQL5 does not natively support Python, traders can establish connections between their Python models and the MT5 platform using APIs and communication channels. This bridge facilitates advanced data analysis and the execution of strategies that harness the intricacies of AI-driven models.

The process of integrating AI models with MT5 encompasses a range of methods, each explored in detail, with a focus on practical applications and tangible benefits derived from successful integration endeavors. This section delves into real-world case studies that exemplify instances where the fusion of AI models with MT5 has delivered substantial advantages in the realm of trading.

The integration of AI models within MetaTrader 5 offers traders a unique opportunity to leverage the predictive capabilities inherent in machine learning, deep learning, and other AI methodologies, thereby elevating the efficacy of their trading strategies. A direct approach involves the seamless incorporation of AI model code directly into an MT5 **Expert Advisor (EA)** through the utilization of MQL5. To illustrate, consider a scenario where a deep learning model is meticulously trained to predict price fluctuations based on historical data and pertinent economic indicators. Subsequently, this trained model is seamlessly integrated into an MQL5 EA, facilitating real-time predictive insights and the execution of trades in an automated fashion.

Alternatively, traders have the option to employ APIs and communication channels to bridge the gap between AI models, often crafted in programming languages such as Python and the MT5 platform. Through this methodology, traders can establish a dynamic link between Python scripts and the MT5 environment, thereby fostering an uninterrupted flow of data. This approach serves as a gateway to the integration of more intricate AI models and advanced data analysis techniques. The flexibility afforded by this avenue enables traders to devise sophisticated trading strategies that transcend the confines of MQL5, embracing the full potential of AI-driven methodologies.

Testing and optimizing AI strategies on MetaTrader 5

Developing AI models within **MetaTrader 5 (MT5)** necessitates a comprehensive process that includes thorough testing and optimization of trading strategies. This section explores the importance of effectively testing AI-driven strategies using MT5's integrated strategy tester. Within this chapter, the emphasis lies on the significance of both backtesting and forward testing during the creation of trading models. The material is enriched with practical instances and illustrative Python code snippets that serve to underscore their relevance and real-world application.

At the core of MetaTrader 5 lies its built-in strategy tester, a robust tool empowering traders to rigorously evaluate the performance of their AI strategies across historical market scenarios. Through this testing framework, the simulation of trade executions based on historical data provides invaluable insights into aspects like potential profitability, risk exposure, and overall robustness of the strategy. Essential metrics such as equity curves, drawdowns, and win/loss ratios can be scrutinized to measure the strategy's efficacy effectively.

The strategy tester grants traders the capability to fine-tune a plethora of parameters, encompassing trade entry and exit rules, risk management preferences, and position sizing. This systematic adjustment of parameters enables traders to pinpoint the optimal configuration that maximizes returns while effectively managing risks. The strategy optimization process is expedited through this efficient iteration across various parameter combinations.

A pivotal phase in trading model development is backtesting, entailing the application of AI models to historical data. This practice provides traders with insights into the strategy's historical performance, thus establishing a foundation for evaluating its feasibility. Backtesting is particularly invaluable in identifying potential shortcomings and vulnerabilities within the strategy, allowing traders to enhance their models prior to real-market deployment.

In tandem with backtesting, forward testing, often referred to as paper trading, involves the execution of the strategy using real-time data without the commitment of actual capital. This phase validates the strategy's real-time performance while considering execution delays, slippage, and market fluctuations. Beyond assessing adaptability, forward testing serves as a means to uncover unforeseen issues before the exposure of real capital.

Illustrative instances of backtesting and forward testing can be observed through the following scenario.

Imagine a machine learning-driven strategy designed to predict short-term price movements. In the context of backtesting, this involves the application of the AI model to historical data. Trades are simulated based on the model's predictions, enabling traders to meticulously evaluate the strategy's precision and profitability over the historical timeframe.

The strategy is executed using real-time data within a simulated environment. Traders then have the opportunity to gauge whether the strategy's forecasts align with the actual movements of the market. This testing phase provides insights into the strategy's performance under dynamic and evolving market conditions.

Facilitating the execution of these testing methodologies are Python code libraries such as Backtrader and MetaTrader 5's MQL5. A simplified Python code snippet that demonstrates how to conduct backtesting for a basic moving average crossover strategy utilizing Backtrader is presented:

```python
1.  import backtrader as bt
2.  import yfinance as yf
3.  from datetime import datetime  # Importing datetime
4.
5.  class MovingAverageCrossStrategy(bt.Strategy):
6.      params = (
7.          ("fast", 50),
8.          ("slow", 200)
9.      )
10.
11.     def __init__(self):
12.         self.fast_ma = bt.indicators.SimpleMovingAverage(self.datas[0], period=self.params.fast, plotname="50-day SMA")
13.         self.slow_ma = bt.indicators.SimpleMovingAverage(self.datas[0], period=self.params.slow, plotname="200-day SMA")
14.         # Adding a minimum period to the strategy
15.         self.addminperiod(self.params.slow + 1)
16.
17.     def next(self):
18.         # Ensure there's enough data for the moving averages to be computed
19.         if len(self) > self.params.slow:
20.             if self.fast_ma > self.slow_ma:
21.                 if not self.position:  # Check if not in the market
22.                     self.buy()
23.             elif self.fast_ma < self.slow_ma:
24.                 if self.position:  # Check if in the market
25.                     self.close()  # Close the position instead of selling
```

```
26.
27. cerebro = bt.Cerebro()
28. cerebro.addstrategy(MovingAverageCrossStrategy)
29.
30. # Data feed
31. data = yf.download('AAPL', start='2020-01-01', end='2023-01-01')
32. # Convert to Backtrader format
33. datafeed = bt.feeds.PandasData(dataname=data)
34. cerebro.adddata(datafeed)
35. cerebro.run()
```

Institutional trading platform integration

Trading platforms catering to retail and institutional traders serve distinct segments within the trading community, each with its own set of unique needs and attributes. Geared toward individual traders and investors, retail trading platforms facilitate the execution of trades across various financial instruments. These platforms are characterized by their user-friendly interfaces, charting tools, and rudimentary algorithmic trading functions. Prominent examples encompass MetaTrader 4, MetaTrader 5, and NinjaTrader, which are frequently employed by retail traders to implement their trading methodologies.

In contrast, institutional trading platforms are meticulously tailored for seasoned professionals, hedge funds, financial institutions, and banks engaged in high-volume trading activities. Distinguished by their comprehensive features, these platforms encompass elements such as **direct market access (DMA)**, intricate order types, and exhaustive data analytics. They are meticulously engineered to manage intricate trading strategies across diverse asset classes, ensuring rapid and efficient execution even amid dynamic market conditions.

Eikon and *Bloomberg Terminal* are two notably influential institutional trading platforms that have significantly impacted the financial landscape. Eikon, developed by Refinitiv, stands as a holistic platform providing real-time financial insights, news, and analytical tools. It empowers traders with robust data visualization capabilities, customizable dashboards, and unfettered access to historical and real-time market data. Eikon's adaptability and substantial API support make it the preferred choice for institutional traders seeking to seamlessly integrate AI models and foster data-driven strategies.

Bloomberg Terminal, a creation of *Bloomberg L.P.*, is another iconic institutional platform lauded for its worldwide financial data and analytical prowess. It supplies real-time market information, data, and analytics to professionals spanning the entire financial spectrum. The integrated messaging system of Bloomberg Terminal facilitates seamless communication among traders while keeping them abreast of pivotal market developments. Leveraging its robust API capabilities, traders are enabled to craft personalized algorithms and automate intricate trading approaches.

Institutional trading platforms such as *Eikon* and *Bloomberg Terminal* present **Application Programming Interfaces (APIs)** that facilitate the seamless integration of external tools and systems. For instance, Eikon's Data API grants programmable access to real-time and historical market data, empowering traders to retrieve data for analysis and the execution of strategies [81]. Similarly, the Bloomberg API offered by *Bloomberg Terminal* enables traders to programmatically access real-time market data, execute trades, and conduct tailored analytics [78].

These APIs amplify the capabilities of institutional platforms, allowing traders to forge customized applications, automate trading strategies, and interface with AI models programmed in languages like Python. By integrating AI models through APIs, traders gain the ability to harness the predictive potential of machine learning and deep learning algorithms, thereby elevating the quality of their trading decisions.

Following table that encapsulates the key points and features of institutional platforms required for algorithmic trading:

Feature	Description
Swiftness and dependability	Institutional platforms are optimized for ultra-low latency and swift execution, crucial for high-frequency trading where speed is essential. These platforms ensure prompt and precise trade order execution.
Diversity of asset classes	These platforms support a wide array of tradable instruments, including equities, forex, commodities, and derivatives, enabling strategies across various markets to capitalize on different opportunities.
Advanced programming proficiency	They provide advanced programming capabilities, supporting multiple languages and libraries, allowing traders to integrate AI models and construct sophisticated predictive models and trading algorithms.

Table 6.1: Key features required for Algo Trading

The amalgamation of AI models with institutional trading platforms symbolizes the merging of advanced technologies, granting traders the capability to enhance their decision-making processes and the execution of trades. This segment deeply explores the techniques by which AI models can be smoothly incorporated into diverse institutional platforms. It also confronts the inherent difficulties tied to this integration procedure while presenting practical remedies to surmount these hindrances. This approach guarantees the triumphant deployment of AI-driven strategies without any compromise.

Efficiently merging AI models with institutional platforms necessitates a thorough grasp of the available techniques. One approach involves seamlessly integrating the code of AI models directly into the trading platform's scripting environment. This technique is exemplified by harnessing the programming capabilities of platforms like **NinjaTrader** and **MetaTrader 5**, empowering traders to code and execute AI-infused strategies within the same cohesive ecosystem. Moreover, APIs assume a pivotal role in facilitating the integration of AI with institutional platforms. These APIs serve as conduits for communication between external AI models and the platform itself. For example, Eikon's Data API facilitates the extraction of both real-time and historical market data, thereby enabling traders to input this data into their AI models for meticulous analysis and informed decision-making. This integration approach provides the versatility to leverage AI models developed external to the platform's native environment.

Despite the substantial advantages, the integration of AI models with institutional platforms can give rise to certain challenges. Platform-specific programming languages, divergent data formats, and potential connectivity complications stand as potential obstacles for traders. To tackle these hurdles effectively, traders have the option to employ wrapper libraries that serve as intermediaries between the AI model and the platform's APIs. These wrappers facilitate seamless communication and data interchange while abstracting the intricacies stemming from language disparities.

Furthermore, the maintenance of data consistency and synchronization between AI models and the trading platform assumes paramount importance. The reliability and accuracy of real-time data feeds are pivotal in ensuring meticulous decision-making. By instituting robust data pipelines and validation mechanisms, traders can effectively mitigate issues linked to data and amplify the robustness of their strategies.

Compliance and regulatory considerations

The incorporation of AI models into institutional trading platforms introduces an array of compliance and regulatory factors that traders need to navigate. Implementing AI models within institutional trading is intricately linked to a multifaceted array of regulations designed to uphold market integrity, safeguard investor interests, and ensure equitable practices. Regulatory entities like the U.S. **Securities and Exchange Commission (SEC)** and the **European Securities and Markets Authority (ESMA)** actively oversee and evolve regulations pertaining to algorithmic trading and AI applications. Traders are responsible for aligning their AI-infused strategies with these regulations, encompassing criteria such as transparency, accountability, and risk management.

An illustrative case is the advent of MiFID II in Europe, which significantly impacts algorithmic trading methodologies. MiFID II mandates heightened transparency, transaction reporting, and pre-trade risk assessments, thereby influencing the formulation and execution of algorithmic strategies. Adhering to these regulations necessitates meticulous consideration of factors such as the decision-making mechanisms of AI models, order execution practices, and the resulting impact on the market.

Conversely, compliance stands as an indispensable foundation within institutional trading platforms, upholding the integrity of trading endeavors and guaranteeing alignment with regulatory frameworks. These platforms often furnish tools and functionalities meticulously crafted to streamline compliance with industry mandates. For instance, platforms such as Bloomberg Terminal incorporate compliance modules that empower traders to actively monitor and navigate real-time compliance risks. These modules are proficient in executing pre-trade compliance assessments, thereby verifying that trades adhere to stipulated regulatory prerequisites prior to execution.

Furthermore, compliance teams operating within institutions wield a pivotal role in the evaluation and validation of AI-powered trading strategies. These teams assume the responsibility of ensuring that AI models and algorithms harmonize with both internal policies and external regulations. The process of compliance testing entails a thorough appraisal of the strategy's alignment with risk management protocols, data integrity standards, and compliance reporting mandates.

Development of AI models for trading

The crafting of AI models for trading adheres to a structured progression encompassing data collection, preprocessing, model selection, training, validation, and eventual deployment. This journey initiates with the acquisition of high-quality historical data, constituting the bedrock for model training and evaluation. The acquired data then undergoes preprocessing, encompassing procedures like data cleansing, transformation, and normalization, all aimed at rendering it apt for training purposes. This preparatory stage paves the way for traders to identify an appropriate machine learning algorithm, fine-tune its parameters, and proceed with training the model employing historical data.

Validation emerges as a pivotal juncture wherein the model's efficacy is gauged on unseen data, thereby assessing its proficiency in extending to genuine market circumstances. Upon the demonstration of robust performance during validation, the model becomes primed for deployment, capable of facilitating real-time decision-making within the trading platform. This deployment facilitates the algorithmic execution of trades grounded in the model's predictions, culminating in an automated trading process.

The development of AI models tailored for trading necessitates meticulous attention to numerous elements in order to guarantee the model's efficacy and adaptability. Overfitting, a prevalent challenge, arises when a model excels on training data but falters when confronted with unseen data. To counteract overfitting, traders can employ strategies such as cross-validation and regularization. These approaches aid in preventing the model from merely memorizing irrelevant intricacies within the training data and instead concentrating on genuine underlying patterns [11].

Equally pivotal is the evaluation of data quality. The performance of AI models is intrinsically tied to the quality of the data they are trained upon. Erroneous, incomplete, or biased data can yield unreliable predictions. Therefore, traders must meticulously undertake data cleansing procedures, adeptly manage outliers, and ensure that the data authentically mirrors the dynamics of the market. This stringent approach to data quality assurance is paramount in fostering the accuracy and robustness of the resulting predictions.

Following is a simplified order placement based on the predicted stock price using a basic linear regression model in MetaTrader 5's MQL5:

```mql5
//+------------------------------------------------------------------+
//|                                                          Linear  |
                                                         Regression Expert |
//+------------------------------------------------------------------+
#include <Trade\Trade.mqh>

input double LotSize = 0.1;
input double StopLossPips = 20;
input double TakeProfitPips = 30;
input int Period = 10;

// Linear Regression Indicator
double LinearRegression(const double data[], const int period) {
    double sumX = 0, sumY = 0, sumXY = 0, sumX2 = 0;
    for (int i = 0; i < period; i++) {
        sumX += i;
        sumY += data[i];
        sumXY += i * data[i];
        sumX2 += i * i;
    }
    double slope = (period * sumXY - sumX * sumY) / (period * sumX2 - sumX * sumX);
    double intercept = (sumY - slope * sumX) / period;
    double prediction = intercept + slope * (period - 1);
    return prediction;
}

//+------------------------------------------------------------------+
//|                                                                  |
//+------------------------------------------------------------------+
void OnTick() {
    double prices[];
    ArrayResize(prices, Period);

    for (int i = 0; i < Period; i++) {
        prices[i] = iClose(Symbol(), 0, i);
```

```
35.     }
36.
37.     double prediction = LinearRegression(prices, Period);
38.     double currentPrice = MarketInfo(Symbol(), MODE_BID);
39.
40.     if (prediction > currentPrice) {
41.         int ticket = OrderSend(Symbol(), OP_BUY, LotSize, currentPrice, 2, 0, 0, "", 0, clrNONE);
42.         if (ticket > 0) {
43.             Print("Buy order placed at price: ", currentPrice);
44.             OrderSend(Symbol(), OP_SELL, LotSize, currentPrice + TakeProfitPips * MarketInfo(Symbol(), MODE_POINT), 2,
45.                     currentPrice - StopLossPips * MarketInfo(Symbol(), MODE_POINT), currentPrice + TakeProfitPips * MarketInfo(Symbol(), MODE_POINT), "", 0, clrNONE);
46.         } else {
47.             Print("Error placing buy order: ", GetLastError());
48.         }
49.     }
50. }
51.
52. //+------------------------------------------------------------------+
```

The process of merging AI models with trading platforms follows a methodical approach that demands technical competence and exactness. At its fundamental essence, this process revolves around crafting an interface that enables bidirectional interaction between the AI model and the trading platform. A pivotal role is attributed to API integration in this context, as it empowers the AI model to seamlessly transmit signals, receive real-time market data, and execute trades without hindrance.

Traders commonly engage with platform-specific APIs tailored for this purpose, such as MetaTrader 5's MQL5 or Eikon's Data API, to establish this dynamic communication conduit. These APIs furnish functionalities for retrieving data, dispatching trade orders, and fetching execution reports. By effectively leveraging these capabilities, traders can bridge the gap between their AI models' forecasts and the trading platform's execution mechanism, effectively translating predictions into actionable trade actions.

Facilitating effective communication between AI models and trading platforms is pivotal for accurate and timely execution. This interaction encompasses signal transmission, real-time market data retrieval, and seamless trade execution. Python, renowned for its adaptability as a programming language, often serves as the linchpin for establishing this communicative layer. It serves as the vital conduit bridging the output of AI models to the input of the trading platform.

Following is a simplified code snippet that showcases how to acquire real-time stock data using MQL5:

```
1.  #property strict
2.
3.  // Main function
4.  void OnStart() {
5.      string url = "https://finance.yahoo.com";    // URL to download data from
6.      char post[];                                  // Post data array, empty for GET request
7.      uchar result[];                               // Array to store the response data
8.      string headers;                               // String to store the response headers
9.      string cookie = NULL;                         // Cookie string, if needed
10.
11.     // Ensure the last error is reset
12.     ResetLastError();
13.
14.     // Downloading an HTML page from Yahoo Finance
15.     int res = WebRequest("GET", url, cookie, NULL, 5000, post, 0, result, headers);
16.
17.     // Check if WebRequest was successful
18.     if(res == -1) {
19.         int errorCode = GetLastError();
20.         Print("Error in WebRequest. Error code =", errorCode);
21.         // Suggest adding the URL to the list of allowed URLs if not already added
22.         MessageBox("Add the address '" + url + "' to the list of allowed URLs on the 'Expert Advisors' tab.", "Error", MB_ICONINFORMATION);
23.     } else {
24.         if(res == 200) {
25.             // Successful download, process response
26.             PrintFormat("The file has been successfully downloaded, File size %d bytes.", ArraySize(result));
27.             // Uncomment to print server headers
28.             //PrintFormat("Server headers: %s", headers);
```

```
29.
30.            // Saving the downloaded data to a file
31.            int fileHandle = FileOpen("yahoo_finance_page.htm", FILE_WRITE | FILE_BIN);
32.            if(fileHandle != INVALID_HANDLE) {
33.                // Write the contents of the result array to the file
34.                FileWriteArray(fileHandle, result, 0, ArraySize(result));
35.                // Close the file to save changes
36.                FileClose(fileHandle);
37.            } else {
38.                Print("Error in FileOpen. Error code =", GetLastError());
39.            }
40.        } else {
41.            // If response code is not 200, log failure
42.            PrintFormat("Downloading '%s' failed, error code %d", url, res);
43.        }
44.    }
45. }
```

Evaluating and refining AI models within trading platforms constitute vital phases in the developmental journey, affirming the efficiency and dependability of algorithmic strategies. This segment comprehensively examines the methodologies and utilities harnessed for backtesting and forward-testing endeavors. Moreover, it immerses into optimization approaches that elevate the efficacy of AI models, culminating in strategies that are meticulously honed to harmonize with the dynamics of actual trading scenarios.

Backtesting constitutes an analytical process that entails evaluating an AI model's efficacy through historical data to replicate trading strategies. This practice furnishes insights into the model's performance within past market scenarios. Trading platforms often embed inherent backtesting functionalities, enabling traders to authenticate AI strategies via historical data. For instance, MetaTrader 5's Strategy Tester empowers traders to execute backtests on AI-fueled strategies, examining elements like profitability, risk-adjusted returns, and other pivotal metrics.

Conversely, forward testing encompasses the real-time deployment of an AI model within existing market conditions, aiming to assess its performance in a simulated live environment. This approach aids in confirming the model's resilience and its adaptability to the ebb and flow of changing market dynamics. Traders can enact forward testing directly within trading platforms, utilizing real-time data streams to gauge how their AI strategies contend within the present-day market landscape.

Fine-tuning AI models is an imperative phase aimed at ensuring optimal performance across diverse market conditions. Techniques like hyperparameter tuning, feature selection, and ensemble methods assume a pivotal role in heightening model efficacy. Hyperparameter tuning involves the meticulous adjustment of AI model parameters to maximize predictive accuracy and minimize overfitting.

Feature selection endeavors to pinpoint the most pertinent input features that contribute to the model's effectiveness. For instance, pertinent features could encompass historical price data, trading volume, and technical indicators in the context of stock price prediction. This approach to feature selection aids in diminishing noise and channeling the model's focus onto the most influential variables.

Ensemble methods amalgamate predictions from multiple AI models to craft a more robust and precise composite prediction. Widely employed ensemble techniques, such as Random Forests and Gradient Boosting, serve as effective tools in trading. These methods serve to counteract individual model biases and elevate overall prediction precision.

Following MQL5 code snippet demonstrates the concept of optimizing an AI model using the Genetic Algorithm provided by the built-in Optimization Framework in MetaTrader 5:

```mql5
1.  input int PopulationSize = 10;
2.  input int Generations = 50;
3.
4.  //Define the objective function
5.  double ObjectiveFunction(double &parameters[]) {
6.      // Your AI model prediction and evaluation code goes here
7.      // Return a fitness value that you want to optimize (e.g., profit, accuracy, etc.)
8.      return 0; // Placeholder for the fitness value
9.  }
10.
11. ----------------------------------------------------------------+
12. int OnInit() {
13.     double parameters[10]; // Define the size explicitly based on your needs
14.
15.     // Initialize the parameters array with initial values
16.     for (int i = 0; i < ArraySize(parameters); i++) {
17.         parameters[i] = MathRand() % 101; // Random initial parameters between 0 and 100
18.     }
19.
20.     double bestParameters[10]; // Define the size explicitly
```

```
21.     double bestFitness;
22.
23.     // Run the optimization using a Genetic Algorithm
24.     int result = GeneticAlgorithm(parameters, PopulationSize,
    Generations, bestParameters, bestFitness);
25.
26.     // Print the results
27.     Print("Optimization result: ", result);
28.     Print("Best fitness: ", bestFitness);
29.
30.
31.     return(INIT_SUCCEEDED);
32. }
33.
34.
35. void OnDeinit(const int reason) {
36.     // Place your deinitialization code here
37. }
38.
39. // User-defined function for genetic algorithm optimization
40. int GeneticAlgorithm(double &parameters[], int populationSize, int
    generations, double &bestParameters[], double &bestFitness) {
41.     // Implementation of the genetic algorithm should be placed here
42.     // This function should modify bestParameters and bestFitness
    based on the genetic algorithm's results
43.
44.     // Sample implementation of a genetic algorithm loop
45.     for (int gen = 0; gen < generations; ++gen) {
46.         for (int individual = 0; individual < populationSize;
    ++individual) {
47.             // Modify parameters for each individual here
48.             double currentFitness = ObjectiveFunction(parameters);
    // Call the ObjectiveFunction directly
49.             if (gen == 0 || currentFitness > bestFitness) {
50.                 bestFitness = currentFitness;
51.                 for (int i = 0; i < ArraySize(parameters); i++) {
52.                     bestParameters[i] = parameters[i];
53.                 }
```

```
54.          }
55.        }
56.        // Implement genetic operators here (e.g., crossover, mutation)
57.    }
58.
59.    return 0; // Placeholder for result of the optimization
60. }
```

Monitoring and maintaining deployed AI models

Monitoring and maintaining AI models in algorithmic trading is a multifaceted process that requires attention to performance, adaptability, risk management, and regulatory compliance. Given the significant financial and reputational stakes, firms must invest in robust maintenance protocols to ensure their trading algorithms remain effective, resilient, and compliant.

The implementation of AI models into trading platforms represents a notable milestone, accompanied by a phase of ongoing vigilance, upkeep, and adjustment. This section immerses into the pivotal post-deployment factors that traders must navigate to sustain the enduring potency of AI-fueled strategies. Spanning the real-time monitoring of AI models, tackling model drift, and executing timely modifications, this segment furnishes insights into the art of enhancing trading performance over extended periods.

Upon the deployment of AI models within trading platforms, the process of continuous monitoring emerges as an imperative endeavor. Real-time monitoring assumes a pivotal role, enabling traders to oversee the model's performance, evaluate its prognostications against real market outcomes, and discern any aberrations or deviations. To illustrate, if an AI-powered strategy is designed to execute trades grounded in specific technical indicators, vigilant monitoring can expose instances where the strategy veers from its intended course, potentially signaling underlying concerns that necessitate intervention.

Incorporating tools such as alerts and notifications within trading platforms can prove invaluable, promptly notifying traders of any anomalies detected in AI model performance. By maintaining a vigilant stance and promptly addressing emerging challenges, traders can uphold the credibility of their strategies while preempting the potential repercussions of costly errors.

Model drift pertains to the phenomenon wherein the performance of an AI model deteriorates gradually over time, attributed to shifts in market dynamics or alterations in data patterns. As markets undergo transformations, strategies that previously yielded success might exhibit diminished effectiveness. Navigating model drift proficiently is imperative for traders, ensuring the sustained viability of profitability.

The monitoring of historical performance metrics and pivotal indicators equips traders with the means to identify potential indications of model drift. Instances such as a decline in predictive accuracy or consistent losses in trades could serve as red flags of impending model drift. In scenarios of this nature, traders find themselves at a juncture necessitating well-informed decisions regarding whether to revise or retrain the AI model.

In this script, a machine learning model's performance is monitored by comparing its prediction accuracy over a specified lookback period against a set threshold. The model's actual and predicted outcomes are analyzed to detect any significant deviations in performance, which could indicate model drift, prompting necessary adjustments such as retraining to maintain optimal operational effectiveness.

```
1.  input int PopulationSize = 10;
2.  input int Generations = 50;
3.
4.  //Define the objective function
5.  double ObjectiveFunction(double &parameters[]) {
6.      // Your AI model prediction and evaluation code goes here
7.      // Return a fitness value that you want to optimize (e.g., profit, accuracy, etc.)
8.      return 0; // Placeholder for the fitness value
9.  }
10.
11. int OnInit() {
12.     double parameters[10]; // Define the size explicitly based on your needs
13.
14.     // Initialize the parameters array with initial values
15.     for (int i = 0; i < ArraySize(parameters); i++) {
16.         parameters[i] = MathRand() % 101; // Random initial parameters between 0 and 100
17.     }
18.
19.     double bestParameters[10]; // Define the size explicitly
20.     double bestFitness = 0;
21.
22.     // Run the optimization using a Genetic Algorithm
23.     int result = GeneticAlgorithm(parameters, PopulationSize, Generations, bestParameters, bestFitness);
24.
```

```
25.     // Print the results
26.     Print("Optimization result: ", result);
27.     Print("Best fitness: ", bestFitness);
28.     Print("Best parameters: ", DoubleArrayToString(bestParameters));
29.
30.     return(INIT_SUCCEEDED);
31. }
32.
33. void OnDeinit(const int reason) {
34.     // Place your deinitialization code here
35. }
36.
37. //+------------------------------------------------------------------+
38. //| User-defined function for genetic algorithm optimization         |
39. //+------------------------------------------------------------------+
40. int GeneticAlgorithm(double &parameters[], int populationSize, int generations, double &bestParameters[], double &bestFitness) {
41.     // This function should modify bestParameters and bestFitness based on the genetic algorithm's results
42.     // Example placeholder for iterating through generations and applying the objective function
43.     for (int i = 0; i < generations; i++) {
44.         for (int j = 0; j < populationSize; j++) {
45.             double currentFitness = ObjectiveFunction(parameters); // Direct call to the objective function
46.             if (currentFitness > bestFitness) {
47.                 bestFitness = currentFitness;
48.                 ArrayCopy(bestParameters, parameters);
49.             }
50.         }
51.     }
52.     return 0; // Placeholder for result of the optimization
53. }
54.
55. //+------------------------------------------------------------------+
56. //| Utility function to convert double array to string               |
57. //+------------------------------------------------------------------+
58. string DoubleArrayToString(double &array[]) {
```

```
59.     string result = "";
60.     for(int i = 0; i < ArraySize(array); i++) {
61.         result += DoubleToString(array[i], 6); // Adjust precision as needed
62.         if(i < ArraySize(array) - 1) result += ", ";
63.     }
64.     return result;
65. }
```

This snippet provides a glimpse into the process of assessing and graphically representing model prediction accuracy, thus aiding in the detection of potential model drift.

Following table outlines the aspects of monitoring and maintaining deployed AI, along with the tools that can be used for each aspect:

Aspect	Description	Tools/Techniques
Performance monitoring	Tracking and analyzing the model's predictions, execution times, and decision-making processes to ensure they meet the required standards.	Prometheus, Grafana, TensorBoard
Adaptability monitoring	Ensuring the model adapts to changing market conditions and data patterns to maintain its effectiveness and relevance.	Continuous learning platforms, A/B testing
Risk management	Monitoring for erratic behavior, setting loss thresholds, and implementing fail-safes to minimize financial risks and ensure stability.	Risk management software, anomaly detection systems
Regulatory compliance	Ensuring the model operates within the legal frameworks and adheres to financial regulations and ethical standards.	Compliance management tools, audit software
Data quality management	Monitoring the quality and relevance of the data fed into the AI model to prevent garbage-in-garbage-out scenarios, which can lead to poor decision-making.	Data validation tools, data monitoring platforms
Model health monitoring	Regularly checking the model's health in terms of accuracy, efficiency, and other performance metrics to detect and address any signs of degradation over time.	Model monitoring tools, health check APIs
Security monitoring	Ensuring the model and its data are protected against unauthorized access and cyber threats, maintaining the integrity and confidentiality of the trading strategies.	Security monitoring tools, encryption software

Table 6.2: Monitoring and maintaining Aspects

Cloud-based trading infrastructure

This section delves into the transformative influence of cloud technology on algorithmic trading, accentuating the advantages of adopting cloud solutions and exploring the decision-making process between public, private, and hybrid cloud models. Grasping the merits of cloud infrastructures and the distinctiveness of various cloud deployment styles empowers traders to optimize the effectiveness and speed of their trading approaches.

Cloud infrastructures have risen as pivotal tools in algorithmic trading due to their inherent strengths. A primary advantage is their ability to scale. Platforms such as **Amazon Web Services (AWS)** and Microsoft Azure provide a vast pool of computational assets, enabling traders to adjust their strategies in real-time as per market dynamics and trade volumes. Such adaptability guarantees that trading platforms can manage high demand without affecting speed or introducing lag.

Furthermore, the nimbleness of cloud solutions ensures a swift rollout of trading strategies. Traders can set up new instances or virtual setups in just a few moments, minimizing the launch period for innovative strategies. This responsiveness allows traders to promptly pivot in response to market shifts, securing a strategic advantage in the ever-evolving trading landscape.

Selecting between public, private, and hybrid cloud models is pivotal for traders. Public clouds present both affordability and accessibility, as traders benefit from pooled resources and pay based on their consumption. However, when dealing with confidential trading information, potential issues related to data protection and regulatory adherence emerge. In contrast, private clouds offer enhanced security and control, relying on dedicated resources within a trader's ecosystem, making them attractive for institutional traders navigating rigorous regulations. Hybrid clouds merge the strengths of public and private setups, enabling traders to place performance-sensitive elements on private systems while tapping into the expansive capacity of the public cloud for general tasks.

Key components of a cloud-based trading system

An effectively structured cloud-based trading system is an amalgamation of interconnected elements that together facilitate proficient algorithmic trading. At the core lie data storage and processing mechanisms. Traders harness cloud storage options, such as Amazon S3, to safely archive and handle copious amounts of market, tick, and historical data. For digesting this data, cloud-centric data processing tools, like Apache Spark on AWS EMR, are utilized to adeptly analyze and garner insights pivotal for strategy formulation.

Equally vital is the real-time streaming and assessment of data. Cloud solutions offer features like AWS Kinesis or Google Cloud Pub/Sub that are tailored for the intake and manipulation of immediate market data feeds. This aids in the prompt implementation of trading actions anchored in real-time insights. Python-based tools, such as Kafka-Python, allow traders to interact with these streaming platforms and craft trading approaches that can swiftly adapt to market fluctuations.

Top-tier cloud service purveyors, such as AWS, Google Cloud, and Azure, furnish traders with an exhaustive array of tools and solutions specifically designed for creating cloud-based trading systems. For example, AWS extends services like EC2 for virtual server orchestration, RDS for overseeing databases, and Lambda for computing without servers. Google Cloud brings to the table tools like BigQuery for data examination, App Engine for app rollouts, and Cloud Pub/Sub for instantaneous messaging. In a similar vein, Microsoft Azure showcases offerings like Virtual Machines, Azure Functions, and Azure Event Hubs to address varied cloud-trading needs.

Python, known for its adaptability as a coding language, effortlessly meshes with these cloud ecosystems via SDKs and APIs. This synergy empowers traders to tap into the potential of each platform while piecing together their trading framework. By capitalizing on these cloud utilities, traders can zero in on strategy crafting and trade facilitation, entrusting the foundational infrastructure and adaptability challenges to the cloud vendors.

Security and reliability considerations

As the financial realm increasingly shifts towards cloud-centric trading platforms, the onus to safeguard and ensure the dependability of these trading systems grows significantly. This segment delves into the vital facets of data protection, security, and platform dependability in the context of cloud trading setups. Addressing these elements is pivotal to shielding confidential fiscal data and ensuring seamless trading workflows. Through an exploration of data protection practices and mechanisms for bolstering security, along with methodologies for enhancing system dependability, traders can securely harness the cloud for their algorithmic trading pursuits.

The shift towards cloud trading platforms inherently brings forth apprehensions around data protection and security, especially when managing confidential financial details. Encrypting data stands as a foundational step to ensure its security both while being transmitted and when stored. Techniques such as **Transport Layer Security** (**TLS**) can be utilized for safeguarding data during transmission, while database-level encryption thwarts unauthorized data access.

For instance, cryptography toolkit aids in executing encryption and decryption tasks within trading frameworks. By securing sensitive details, like trade instructions or client credentials, prior to cloud transmission, traders can curtail the potential of data compromise.

This code snippet demonstrates the process of encrypting and decrypting sensitive trading data using AES-256 encryption in a trading environment. By utilizing a predefined key, the script ensures that the critical financial data remains secure, both in storage and transmission, safeguarding against unauthorized access and potential security breaches.

```
1. // Assuming data and key have been defined and allocated appropriately
2. input string data = "Sensitive trading data"; // User defined input data
```

```
 3. uchar encrypted_data[];
 4. uchar decrypted_data[];
 5. uchar key[16] = {0x12, 0x34, 0x56, 0x78, 0x9A, 0xBC, 0xDE, 0xF0,
    0x12, 0x34, 0x56, 0x78, 0x9A, 0xBC, 0xDE, 0xF0}; // Example key
 6.
 7. // Convert string data to uchar array
 8. int data_length = StringToCharArray(data, NULL, 0) - 1; // -1 to
    remove the terminal zero
 9. uchar data_array[];
10. ArrayResize(data_array, data_length);
11. StringToCharArray(data, data_array, 0);
12.
13. // Encrypt data
14. if (!CryptEncode(CRYPT_AES256, key, data_array, encrypted_data)) {
15.   Print("Encryption failed, error code: ", GetLastError());
16. }
17.
18. // Decrypt data
19. if (!CryptDecode(CRYPT_AES256, key, encrypted_data, decrypted_data))
    {
20.   Print("Decryption failed, error code: ", GetLastError());
21. }
22.
23. // Converting decrypted data back to string for output
24. string decrypted_string = CharArrayToString(decrypted_data);
25. Print("Original Data: ", data);
26. Print("Decrypted Data: ", decrypted_string);
```

To enhance resilience and continuity, traders can disperse their trading applications across several availability zones within a cloud service region. Such a dispersed approach acts as a safety net, guaranteeing that in the event of disruptions in one zone, the trading operations effortlessly transition to an alternate zone, ensuring uninterrupted service. Furthermore, the integration of auto-scaling strategies certifies the capability of trading systems to manage surges in activity, especially during market highs, thus consistently offering swift responses and optimal performance.

Ensuring security and privacy

It underscores the threats presented by security breaches and offers ways traders might counteract these vulnerabilities. As the prominence of algorithmic trading grows, preserving the confidentiality and integrity of trading methods becomes vital. Security and confidentiality form the foundation for successful algorithmic trading. These trading algorithms, which are considered intellectual property, can grant traders a significant edge in the market. Should these algorithms fall into the wrong hands, the results can be devastating, from potential front-running and reverse engineering to outright theft of proprietary methodologies. Moreover, executing algorithmic trading strategies requires handling delicate financial data, encompassing order book data, trading behaviors, and account specifics. Any lapses in security and privacy can result in monetary losses, regulatory penalties, and tarnished reputations for both individual traders and financial entities. The gravity of these concerns is emphasized by the increasing number of cyberattacks targeting financial institutions.

Violations of security and privacy linked to trading algorithms can trigger a multitude of repercussions. Ill-intentioned individuals can exploit weak spots to tamper with market valuations, carry out illicit trades, or compromise trading algorithms for their benefit. Beyond financial repercussions, there is also the risk of regulatory non-compliance, given that authorities stress the safeguarding of consumer data and the integrity of the market.

The *2010 Flash Crash* stands as a poignant example of the pitfalls connected to algorithmic trading. This event saw a sequence of high-speed trades leading to an abrupt market downturn, highlighting the inherent weaknesses of algorithmic trading infrastructures. Such events led regulatory bodies to advocate for the introduction of safety measures and circuit breakers to avert comparable market anomalies [98].

Maintaining the integrity of algorithm security is fundamental to thriving in the realm of algorithmic trading, as it shields proprietary trading mechanisms from unsanctioned breaches and harmful interference. This segment delves into an array of advanced tactics that traders can utilize to bolster the security of their algorithms. By investigating techniques such as encapsulation, code obfuscation, and the integration of secure APIs, along with deploying security utilities like VPNs and firewalls, traders can enhance the resilience of their algorithmic trading systems against potential adversarial actions.

One of the potent strategies to reinforce algorithm security is encapsulation. This involves wrapping vulnerable portions of the code within clearly delineated interfaces. Such a methodology restricts direct interference with crucial sections, minimizing the chances of unsolicited meddling or misuse [99]. In addition, traders can employ code obfuscation to render their algorithm's source code less accessible to reverse engineering efforts. By recasting code into intricate configurations, it becomes a challenge for potential adversaries to fathom the core logic of the algorithm.

Secure APIs are also fundamental to ensuring the safety of algorithms. They act as conduits for external interactions with trading systems. By adopting authentication protocols, encryption measures, and access restrictions, traders can ascertain that solely authorized parties interface with their algorithms. With the rise of cloud computing and remote work dynamics, the protection of trading algorithms demands a comprehensive strategy that goes beyond mere code safeguards. VPNs and firewalls emerge as potent shields against unsolicited access and cyber threats. Leveraging a VPN allows traders to form encrypted pathways between distant devices and trading mainframes, thwarting potential snooping into confidential data and operations.

Firewalls, operational at both the network and application strata, are essential in shielding algorithmic trading frameworks. These protective layers screen both incoming and outgoing data streams, pinpointing and obstructing any nefarious attempts to infiltrate the system. For instance, the iptables library in Python can be harnessed to set firewall guidelines, ensuring only genuine connections gain entry to the trading ecosystem.

Ensuring data privacy

It is imperative to responsibly manage sensitive trading data and to strictly abide by data privacy legislations and guidelines in order to safeguard traders' unique strategies and uphold the trustworthiness of the financial trading environment.

Algorithmic trading systems deal with an abundance of confidential trading information, ranging from order book data and execution specifics to unique trading approaches. It is essential for traders to introduce stringent mechanisms to encrypt, relay, and preserve this data in a secure manner. Utilizing encryption techniques such as the **Advanced Encryption Standard** (**AES**) ensures that, even in the face of unauthorized breaches, the data stays incomprehensible and inoperative.

Python offers tools like the cryptography library, facilitating the effortless incorporation of encryption methods into algorithmic trading platforms:

```
1.  from cryptography.fernet import Fernet
2.  
3.  # Generate a key
4.  key = Fernet.generate_key()
5.  cipher_suite = Fernet(key)
6.  
7.  # Encrypt confidential information
8.  encrypted_information = cipher_suite.encrypt(b"Confidential trading details")
9.  
10. # Decrypt the information
11. decoded_information = cipher_suite.decrypt(encrypted_information)
12. 
13. # Print the decrypted information
14. print(decoded_information.decode())  # Decoding from bytes to string for readability
```

The domain of data privacy is delineated by intricate regulations aiming to shield individuals' private and fiscal data. For those involved in algorithmic trading, adhering to privacy laws such as the **General Data Protection Regulation (GDPR)** in the European Union [132] or the **California Consumer Privacy Act (CCPA)** [133].

Through methods like data anonymization and pseudonymization, traders can ascertain that personal and sensitive data isn't easily traceable within trading infrastructures. Additionally, establishing stringent access protocols and data preservation guidelines enables traders to navigate between operational agility and data confidentiality, thus protecting both individual rights and institutional interests.

Conclusion

Throughout this chapter, we embarked on a comprehensive journey across the domain of algorithmic trading. We began with an overview of leading trading platforms, delving into specifics with MetaTrader 5 and institutional trading platform integrations. Our exploration further encompassed the integration of AI models into these platforms, emphasizing the paramount significance of ongoing monitoring and maintenance of deployed models. The culmination of our discussion was the revolutionary shift towards cloud-based trading infrastructure, marking the future trajectory of trading.

As we segue into the next chapter, readers can anticipate a deep dive into *Trading and High-Performance Algorithmic Trading using AI: Rapid Application Development using Python*, underscoring streamlined development processes and optimizing performance benchmarks.

Multiple choice questions

1. **What was a significant shift in trading platforms from the past to the early 2000s?**

    a. Transition from manual to electronic trading platforms

    b. Introduction of AI and machine learning in trading

    c. Shift from stock trading to cryptocurrency trading

    d. Development of mobile trading applications

2. **Why is the MQL scripting language in MetaTrader particularly beneficial for certain traders?**

    a. It allows for easy integration with third-party data sources.

    b. It is specifically designed for implementing technical indicators and automated strategies.

    c. It provides direct access to stock exchange networks.

    d. It supports high-frequency trading algorithms.

3. **What is a crucial step in the process of selecting a trading platform for algorithmic trading?**

    a. Choosing a platform that offers the highest number of technical indicators.

    b. Selecting a platform based solely on its popularity and user reviews.

c. Conducting rigorous testing, including backtesting and stress testing, to confirm the platform's suitability for the strategy.

d. Opting for the platform with the most visually appealing user interface.

Answers

1	a
2	b
3	c

Join our book's Discord space

Join the book's Discord Workspace for Latest updates, Offers, Tech happenings around the world, New Release and Sessions with the Authors:

https://discord.bpbonline.com

CHAPTER 7
Getting Prepared for Python Development

Introduction

In this chapter, we embark on a comprehensive journey through the essential tools and libraries that are pivotal for anyone looking to excel in Python programming, especially within data-driven environments. We will explore the powerful numerical libraries that make Python a favorite among scientists and engineers, delve into financial libraries that provide robust solutions for quantitative finance, and uncover the dynamic visualization tools that bring data to life. Additionally, we will cover the fundamentals of version control using Git, an indispensable skill for efficient collaboration in software development projects. By the end of this chapter, you will be equipped with the knowledge and skills to effectively harness these tools in your programming endeavors, whether you're analyzing complex datasets or developing sophisticated financial models.

Structure

In this chapter, we will learn the following topics:

- Python for finance
- Version control and collaboration with Git

Objectives

In this chapter, our objectives are to provide a solid foundation in four key areas that are integral to advanced Python programming. First, we will familiarize ourselves with Python's numerical libraries, which are essential for performing complex mathematical computations efficiently. Next, we will explore Python's financial libraries that are critical for conducting detailed financial analysis and algorithmic trading. We will also delve into the visualization tools available in Python that enable clear and impactful data representation, crucial for data science and analytics. Finally, we will learn about version control using Git, which will empower us to manage our code effectively and collaborate with others in any development project. By mastering these topics, you will enhance your technical toolkit and be better prepared to tackle a variety of programming challenges.

Python for finance

Python has emerged as the preferred programming language for traders and quants. Python's ascent to prominence in finance is undeniable, driven by its exceptional versatility and extensive libraries tailored to financial applications. Python's readability and simplicity make it a natural choice for quantitative analysis and algorithmic trading. Its compatibility with data sources, robust numerical computation capabilities, and a vibrant developer community have propelled its adoption in financial institutions worldwide.

Numerical libraries

Numerical libraries are the backbone of quantitative finance, empowering traders and analysts to harness the full potential of mathematical and statistical models. These libraries, such as **NumPy**, **pandas**, and **SciPy**, play a pivotal role in processing vast volumes of financial data efficiently and performing complex calculations with ease. This chapter delves into the significance of numerical libraries in Algorithmic Trading, elucidating their pivotal role in optimizing trading algorithms, thereby helping traders make more informed decisions.

Algorithmic trading, with its lightning-fast execution and data-driven strategies, has evolved into a dynamic field where every millisecond counts. To gain a competitive edge, traders rely on quantitative models and mathematical computations. Numerical libraries facilitate these computations by providing a rich set of functions and tools, enabling traders to work with large datasets seamlessly. For instance, NumPy, a fundamental library in numerical computing, allows traders to manipulate arrays and matrices effortlessly. This capability is especially crucial when dealing with historical price data or conducting risk assessments for trading portfolios.

Numerical computation forms the bedrock of algorithmic trading, as traders need to perform operations such as matrix multiplications for calculating covariance matrices or executing complex statistical tests on price series. These operations, when efficiently executed using libraries like SciPy, can significantly enhance a trading algorithm's performance. For instance, by leveraging SciPy's optimization functions, traders can fine-tune their trading strategies to maximize returns while minimizing risks. This is exemplified in the following Python code snippet, where we optimize a **simple moving average (SMA)** crossover strategy:

```python
import numpy as np
from scipy.optimize import minimize

# Define a simple moving average crossover function
def simple_moving_average_strategy(params, prices):
    short_window, long_window = params
    short_sma = np.mean(prices[-short_window:])
    long_sma = np.mean(prices[-long_window:])
    return short_sma - long_sma

# Placeholder price data (replace with your actual data)
price_data = [100, 110, 120, 130, 140, 150, 160, 170, 180, 190]

# Optimize the strategy parameters using SciPy
initial_guess = [3, 7]   # Initial values for short and long windows
result = minimize(simple_moving_average_strategy, initial_guess,
    args=(price_data,))
optimal_short_window, optimal_long_window = result.x

print("Optimal Short Window:", optimal_short_window)
print("Optimal Long Window:", optimal_long_window)
```

This example illustrates how numerical libraries like SciPy facilitate the optimization of trading strategies by finding the optimal parameters that maximize returns.

In essence, numerical libraries are the linchpin of high-performance algorithmic trading using AI. They empower traders to process vast datasets, execute complex calculations, and fine-tune their strategies with precision. This chapter will delve deeper into the functionalities of these libraries, providing traders with the tools they need to gain a competitive advantage in the dynamic world of algorithmic trading.

NumPy

NumPy is a cornerstone in numerical computing and has become the go-to tool for efficiently working with arrays, matrices, and mathematical functions in Python. Its significance cannot be overstated, as it provides the foundation for performing complex calculations, handling large datasets, and optimizing trading algorithms with ease.

NumPy's seamless integration with Python and its optimized **C** and **Fortran** backends make it an indispensable tool for traders. With NumPy, creating and manipulating arrays and matrices becomes intuitive, enabling the rapid development of quantitative trading strategies. For instance, consider the creation of a NumPy array to store historical price data, a fundamental task in algorithmic trading:

```
1. import numpy as np
2.
3. # Create a NumPy array to store historical stock prices
4. stock_prices = np.array([100.0, 102.5, 105.2, 103.8, 107.1])
```

This code snippet demonstrates how NumPy simplifies the process of working with historical stock price data, a common occurrence in the world of trading.

NumPy excels in its ability to create and manipulate arrays and matrices efficiently. For algorithmic traders, this is a game-changer. By harnessing NumPy's straightforward syntax, traders can easily organize and process trading data. NumPy arrays are homogeneous, enabling efficient operations on large datasets. For instance, to create a NumPy array representing daily trading volumes:

```
1. import numpy as np
2.
3. # Create a NumPy array to store daily trading volumes
4. daily_volumes = np.array([12000, 14500, 11000, 9500, 13200])
```

This example showcases how NumPy simplifies the representation of trading data, fostering a structured and organized approach to algorithmic trading.

NumPy's strength lies not only in creating arrays but also in its ability to perform fundamental array operations. Element-wise operations, indexing, and slicing are essential for algorithmic trading. For instance, to calculate the daily returns of a stock price series stored in a NumPy array:

```
1. import numpy as np
2.
3. # Create a NumPy array to store daily stock prices
4. daily_prices = np.array([100.0, 102.5, 105.2, 103.8, 107.1])
5.
6. # Calculate daily returns
7. returns = (daily_prices[1:] - daily_prices[:-1]) / daily_prices[:-1]
```

This code snippet showcases how NumPy facilitates element-wise operations and array manipulations, making it an invaluable asset for traders seeking to analyze and optimize their trading strategies.

NumPy's broadcasting capability is a powerful feature for traders dealing with arrays of different shapes. It allows for efficient element-wise operations on arrays with different dimensions, enabling concise and readable code. For example, to normalize daily returns by subtracting their mean:

```
1.  import numpy as np
2.
3.  # Create a NumPy array to store daily returns
4.  returns = np.array([0.02, -0.01, 0.03, -0.02, 0.04])
5.
6.  # Normalize returns by subtracting the mean
7.  normalized_returns = returns - np.mean(returns)
```

Here, NumPy's broadcasting automatically aligns the dimensions of the mean array with the returns array, simplifying the operation.

The true power of NumPy shines when applied to real-world algorithmic trading scenarios. Whether it's optimizing a trading strategy, conducting risk analysis, or implementing sophisticated mathematical models, NumPy is a trusted companion. For instance, when designing a moving average crossover strategy, NumPy aids in calculating the short-term and long-term moving averages:

```
1.  import numpy as np
2.
3.  # Simulated stock price data
4.  stock_prices = np.array([100.0, 102.5, 105.2, 103.8, 107.1])
5.
6.  # Calculate short-term and long-term moving averages
7.  short_window = 5
8.  long_window = 20
9.
10. short_sma = np.mean(stock_prices[-short_window:])
11. long_sma = np.mean(stock_prices[-long_window:])
```

This practical example demonstrates how NumPy simplifies complex calculations within the context of algorithmic trading, enabling traders to make data-driven decisions efficiently.

In conclusion, NumPy's role in high-performance algorithmic trading using **artificial intelligence (AI)** cannot be overstated. It serves as the foundation for numerical computing, providing traders with the tools needed to process data, conduct sophisticated calculations, and optimize trading strategies. By mastering NumPy's capabilities, traders gain a significant advantage in the dynamic and competitive world of algorithmic trading.

Pandas

Data is not just a valuable asset; it is the lifeblood of informed decision-making. This is where pandas, the Python library for data manipulation and analysis, emerges as a crucial player. In the context of our exploration in this chapter on Rapid Application Development using Python, particularly the section on Python for finance, pandas plays an integral role in managing and extracting insights from financial data.

Pandas offers an array of tools and data structures that empower traders and analysts to efficiently wrangle, clean, and analyze data. The library introduces two primary data structures: DataFrames and Series. DataFrames are akin to tables, providing a structured way to organize data, while Series are one-dimensional labeled arrays.

Creating and manipulating DataFrames and Series in pandas is straightforward and intuitive. For instance, imagine you have historical stock price data in CSV format. With pandas, you can effortlessly load this data into a DataFrame, perform operations like filtering for specific stocks, and calculate essential statistics such as daily returns:

```
1. import pandas as pd
2.
3. # Load historical stock price data into a DataFrame from 'stock_prices.csv'
4. stock_data = pd.read_csv('stock_prices.csv')
5.
6. # Select data for a specific stock (in this case, AAPL)
7. apple_stock = stock_data[stock_data['Symbol'] == 'AAPL']
8.
9. # Calculate daily returns and add them as a new column 'Daily Returns'
10. apple_stock['Daily Returns'] = apple_stock['Close'].pct_change()
```

This code snippet exemplifies how pandas simplifies the process of working with financial data, providing traders with the flexibility needed to derive meaningful insights.

Data quality is paramount in algorithmic trading, and pandas equips traders with powerful tools for data cleaning and handling missing values. In a practical example, let us say you have a dataset of trading volumes with missing entries. Pandas allows you to efficiently fill missing values with appropriate values or interpolate them based on the surrounding data:

```
1. import pandas as pd
2.
3. # Load a dataset with missing values from 'trading_volume_data.csv'
4. trading_volume_data = pd.read_csv('trading_volume_data.csv')
5.
6. # Fill missing values in the 'Volume' column with the forward-fill method
7. trading_volume_data['Volume'].fillna(method='ffill', inplace=True)
```

This demonstrates how pandas facilitates data cleaning, ensuring that trading algorithms operate on accurate and reliable data.

In the trading world, time is a critical dimension. Pandas excels in time series analysis, offering a plethora of tools to handle time-based data. For instance, when analyzing intraday price data, you can easily resample it to different timeframes and calculate metrics like moving averages:

```
1.  import pandas as pd
2.
3.  # Load intraday stock price data with timestamps, and parse the 'Timestamp' column as datetime
4.  intraday_data = pd.read_csv('intraday_prices.csv', parse_dates=['Timestamp'])
5.
6.  # Resample data to hourly intervals and calculate hourly means
7.  hourly_data = intraday_data.resample('H', on='Timestamp').mean()
8.
9.  # Calculate hourly moving averages with a window of 10 periods
10. hourly_data['Hourly Moving Average'] = hourly_data['Price'].rolling(window=10).mean()
```

This example illustrates how pandas simplifies time-based analysis, enabling traders to extract valuable insights from time series data.

Traders often need to aggregate and summarize data to make informed decisions. Pandas offers a robust set of functionalities for this purpose. Consider a scenario where you have a portfolio of stocks, and you want to calculate the annualized returns for each stock. Pandas' **groupby** and aggregation capabilities make this task straightforward:

```
1.  import pandas as pd
2.
3.  # Create a DataFrame with stock returns and symbols from 'portfolio_returns.csv'
4.  portfolio_data = pd.read_csv('portfolio_returns.csv')
5.
6.  # Group data by stock symbol and calculate annualized returns
7.  annualized_returns = portfolio_data.groupby('Symbol')['Returns'].mean() * 252
```

This demonstrates how pandas empowers traders to perform complex data summarization effortlessly.

To exemplify pandas' significance, let us delve into a real-world scenario where you want to optimize a portfolio using historical price and trading volume data. Following Python script utilizes **pandas** and **numpy** libraries to analyze stock data, combining historical price and trading volume information into a merged dataset. It then calculates daily returns for each stock, computes the average returns and volatility, and applies mean-variance optimization to construct an investment portfolio. The script concludes by estimating the annual return and volatility of the portfolio based on randomly generated weights, providing a comprehensive tool for financial analysis and portfolio management.

```
1. import pandas as pd
2. import numpy as np
3.
4. # Load historical price and trading volume data with date columns parsed as datetime
5. price_data = pd.read_csv('historical_prices.csv', parse_dates=['Date'])
6. volume_data = pd.read_csv('trading_volumes.csv', parse_dates=['Date'])
7.
8. # Merge dataframes on date
9. merged_data = pd.merge(price_data, volume_data, on='Date')
10.
11. # Calculate daily returns for each stock
12. merged_data['Returns'] = merged_data.groupby('Symbol')['Close'].pct_change()
13.
14. # Calculate average daily returns and volatility
15. returns = merged_data.groupby('Symbol')['Returns'].mean()
16. volatility = merged_data.groupby('Symbol')['Returns'].std()
17.
18. # Perform mean-variance optimization to construct the portfolio
19. cov_matrix = merged_data.pivot_table(index='Date', columns='Symbol', values='Returns').cov()
20.
21. # Generate random portfolio weights
22. weights = np.random.random(len(returns))
23. weights /= np.sum(weights)
24.
25. # Calculate portfolio return and volatility
26. portfolio_return = np.sum(weights * returns) * 252
27. portfolio_volatility = np.sqrt(np.dot(weights.T, np.dot(cov_matrix * 252, weights)))
```

This practical example demonstrates how pandas plays a pivotal role in real-world trading scenarios, enabling traders to analyze data, calculate returns, and optimize their portfolios effectively.

In conclusion, pandas is an indispensable tool in high-performance algorithmic trading using AI, providing traders with the means to efficiently manipulate, analyze, and derive insights from financial data. With its capabilities for data structuring, cleaning, and analysis, pandas empowers traders to make data-driven decisions and develop robust trading strategies.

SciPy

The synergy between NumPy and SciPy (**scientific and technical computing**) stands as a testament to the power of open-source Python libraries. SciPy, or Scientific Python, forms an integral part of this financial ecosystem. NumPy, with its core array and matrix operations, provides the raw materials essential for quantitative finance. SciPy, an extension of NumPy, leverages these capabilities to offer an extensive suite of scientific and technical computing tools. This marriage of libraries equips traders with the means to optimize trading strategies, model intricate financial systems, conduct robust statistical analysis, and make informed decisions, all within the versatile Python environment.

Within the vast SciPy ecosystem, various subpackages emerge as stalwarts in the world of high-performance algorithmic trading. Traders and analysts alike rely on these subpackages to enhance their strategies. The **scipy.optimize** subpackage, for instance, becomes a strategic ally in the quest to fine-tune trading algorithms by seeking optimal parameters. Consider a practical scenario where a trader wishes to optimize moving average crossover strategy parameters:

```
1. from scipy.optimize import minimize
2. import numpy as np
3.
4. # Simulated trading data (prices)
5. prices = np.random.rand(100)
6.
7. # Define short and long windows for moving averages
8. short_window = 5
9. long_window = 20
10.
11. # Objective function for optimization
12. def moving_average_objective(params, prices):
13.     short_window, long_window = params
14.     short_ma = np.mean(prices[-short_window:])
15.     long_ma = np.mean(prices[-long_window:])
16.     return -short_ma + long_ma
17.
18. # Optimize strategy parameters using SciPy
19. initial_guess = [5, 20]
```

```
20. result = minimize(moving_average_objective, initial_guess,
    args=(prices,))
21. optimal_short_window, optimal_long_window = result.x
```

This real-world application demonstrates how SciPy's optimization capabilities empower traders to refine their trading strategies effectively. Numerical optimization forms the cornerstone of algorithmic trading, allowing traders to fine-tune strategies by finding the most favorable parameter configurations. SciPy's extensive optimization toolkit encompasses unconstrained and constrained optimization as well as global optimization. This array of options empowers traders to maximize returns while minimizing risks. A common use case involves optimizing portfolio weights to achieve a desired risk-return profile:

```
1.  from scipy.optimize import minimize
2.  import numpy as np
3.
4.  # Simulated trading data (returns)
5.  returns = np.random.rand(100)
6.
7.  # Risk-free rate
8.  risk_free_rate = 0.02
9.
10. # Objective function for portfolio optimization
11. def portfolio_objective(weights, returns):
12.     portfolio_return = np.sum(weights * returns)
13.     portfolio_risk = np.sqrt(np.dot(weights.T, np.dot(cov_matrix *
    252, weights)))
14.     return -((portfolio_return - risk_free_rate) / portfolio_risk)
15.
16. # Initial equal-weighted portfolio weights
17. initial_weights = np.ones(len(returns)) / len(returns)
18.
19. # Optimize portfolio weights using SciPy
20. result = minimize(portfolio_objective, initial_weights,
    args=(returns,))
21. optimal_weights = result.x
```

This example underscores how SciPy's optimization tools enable traders to construct portfolios that align with their risk-return objectives, a vital component of algorithmic trading.

Algorithmic trading often involves modeling complex financial systems through differential equations and numerical integration. SciPy's **scipy.integrate** subpackage provides a robust set of tools for solving **ordinary differential equations (ODEs)** and conducting numerical integration. Traders can leverage these tools to model dynamic market behaviors or risk factors. For example, modeling the evolution of an option's price using the **Black-Scholes-Merton** equation:

```
1. from scipy.stats import norm
2. from scipy.integrate import solve_ivp
3. import numpy as np
4. from scipy.stats import norm  # Import norm from scipy.stats
5.
6. # Option parameters
7. S = 100  # Current stock price
8. K = 105  # Strike price
9. T = 1.0  # Time to maturity (in years)
10. r = 0.05  # Risk-free rate
11. sigma = 0.2  # Volatility
12.
13. # Define the Black-Scholes-Merton equation as a function
14. def black_scholes_merton(t, y):
15.     d1 = (np.log(S / K) + (r + 0.5 * sigma**2) * (T - t)) / (sigma * np.sqrt(T - t))
16.     d2 = d1 - sigma * np.sqrt(T - t)
17.     return r * y - S * norm.cdf(d1) + K * np.exp(-r * (T - t)) * norm.cdf(d2)
18.
19. # Initial condition: Option price at T (time to maturity)
20. y0 = max(S - K, 0)
21.
22. # Solve the Black-Scholes-Merton equation using SciPy
23. t_span = [0, T]
24. solution = solve_ivp(black_scholes_merton, t_span, [y0], t_eval=np.linspace(*t_span, num=100))
25.
26. # The solution object contains the results
27. option_prices = solution.y[0]  # Extract the option prices at different time points
```

This practical application demonstrates how SciPy's integration and differential equation-solving capabilities aid traders in building sophisticated financial models.

Let us consider another example where SciPy is used to calculate **value-at-risk** (**VaR**) for a portfolio:

```python
1. from scipy.stats import norm
2. import numpy as np
3.
4. # Simulated portfolio returns (assuming a normal distribution)
5. portfolio_returns = np.random.randn(100)
6.
7. # Calculate VaR at a 95% confidence level
8. confidence_level = 0.95
9. var = norm.ppf(1 - confidence_level) * np.std(portfolio_returns)
```

This code snippet demonstrates how SciPy facilitates statistical analysis for traders, enabling them to assess and manage risks effectively, a crucial aspect of algorithmic trading.

SciPy's powerful statistical capabilities facilitate construct volatility models. By fitting historical data to statistical distributions such as the Normal or Student's t-distribution, traders can estimate volatility. Consider a practical scenario where a trader utilizes SciPy to fit a historical returns distribution to a Normal distribution:

```python
1.  from scipy.stats import norm, t
2.  import numpy as np
3.
4.  # Simulated historical returns (assuming a random distribution)
5.  returns = np.random.randn(1000)
6.
7.  # Fit returns to a Normal distribution
8.  mu, std = norm.fit(returns)
9.
10. # Fit returns to a Student's t-distribution
11. df, loc, scale = t.fit(returns)
```

This example demonstrates how SciPy enables traders to analyze historical data and select suitable statistical distributions for modeling volatility, a critical aspect of risk management in algorithmic trading.

In conclusion, SciPy emerges as an invaluable asset in High-Performance Algorithmic Trading using AI, offering a diverse array of scientific and technical computing tools. Its close relationship with NumPy amplifies the capabilities of Python, equipping traders with the means to optimize strategies, model intricate financial systems, conduct robust statistical analysis, and make data-driven decisions in the dynamic world of algorithmic trading.

Financial libraries

Financial libraries serve as the cornerstone of quantitative finance, offering traders and analysts a treasure trove of resources to navigate the intricacies of financial markets. The fundamental premise of financial libraries is rooted in the recognition that modern trading has evolved into a data-intensive, highly quantitative endeavor. Quantitative finance, with its intricate mathematical models and data-driven decision-making processes, demands a robust toolkit. Financial libraries are the culmination of extensive domain expertise and programming ingenuity, offering access to a wealth of functions, algorithms, and data sources tailored explicitly for trading and financial analysis. They encapsulate the industry's best practices, encoding financial models, risk management methodologies, and statistical tools into accessible modules. Consider, for instance, the Black-Scholes-Merton model, a fundamental pricing model for options. Financial libraries provide an implementation of this model, allowing traders to calculate option prices swiftly. Without such libraries, traders would need to develop these models from scratch, a formidable task requiring both time and expertise. The existence of these libraries empowers traders to focus on strategy design and the analysis of market conditions, significantly accelerating the algorithmic trading development cycle.

Quantlib

Quantlib (tools for quantitative finance) is a powerful open-source library that stands at the intersection of quantitative finance and software development. It is nestled within the broader context of Rapid Application Development using Python. Quantlib's significance in quantitative finance cannot be overstated. At its core, it is designed to equip traders, quants, and financial analysts with a comprehensive toolkit to handle complex financial instruments, calculate risk metrics, and price derivatives with precision. Its open-source nature has fostered a thriving community that continuously contributes to its development, making it a dynamic and reliable resource for quantitative finance practitioners.

Quantlib's allure lies in its extensive range of features and capabilities, which cover virtually every aspect of quantitative finance. This library boasts support for various financial instruments, including options, swaps, bonds, and more. Its robust numerical methods enable accurate pricing and risk assessment, making it an indispensable asset for traders and financial engineers. One of Quantlib's standout features is its support for a multitude of financial models, including the Black-Scholes-Merton, Heston, and Hull-White models, among others. This flexibility empowers users to choose the most appropriate model for their specific trading needs, facilitating the development of diverse trading strategies.

Pricing and risk management are the lifeblood of algorithmic trading, and Quantlib excels in both domains. Its pricing engines are designed to handle even the most intricate derivatives, offering reliable valuations across asset classes. Additionally, Quantlib equips traders with a comprehensive suite of risk analytics tools, including delta, gamma, vega, and theta calculations, facilitating robust risk management strategies.

For instance, consider the scenario of pricing a European call option. Quantlib's Python bindings allow traders to implement the Black-Scholes-Merton model with ease:

```
1. from QuantLib import *
2. import datetime
3.
4. # Define the option parameters in a dictionary:
5. option_params = {
6.     "underlyingPrice": 100,
7.     "strikePrice": 105,
8.     "expiryDate": datetime.date(2023, 12, 31),
9.     "volatility": 0.2,
10.    "riskFreeRate": 0.05,
11. }
12.
13. # Create QuantLib objects
14. today = Date(15, 8, 2023)
15. Settings.instance().evaluationDate = today
16.
17. # Define the payoff and exercise
18. payoff = PlainVanillaPayoff(Option.Call, option_params["strikePrice"])
19. exercise = EuropeanExercise(option_params["expiryDate"])
20.
21. # Create the option
22. option = EuropeanOption(payoff, exercise)
23.
24. # Calculate the option price using QuantLib:
25. option.setPricingEngine(
26.     AnalyticEuropeanEngine(
27.         GeneralizedBlackScholesProcess(
28.             QuoteHandle(SimpleQuote(option_params["underlyingPrice"])),
29.             YieldTermStructureHandle(
30.                 FlatForward(today, QuoteHandle(SimpleQuote(option_params["riskFreeRate"])), Actual360())
31.             ),
32.             BlackVolTermStructureHandle(
33.                 BlackConstantVol(today, QuoteHandle(SimpleQuote(option_params["volatility"])), Actual360())
34.             ),
35.         )
```

```
36.    )
37. )
38.
39. option_price = option.NPV()
```

Quantlib facilitates the calibration of volatility models like the Heston model to market data, a critical task in options trading for accurate pricing and risk assessment. Quantlib stands as a cornerstone in the realm of High-Performance Algorithmic Trading using AI, offering a robust platform for quantitative finance practitioners. Its versatility, extensive feature set, and open-source nature make it a powerful resource for pricing, risk management, and strategy development, enriching the landscape of algorithmic trading.

Pyalgotrade

PyAlgoTrade is an open-source Python library designed for developing and backtesting algorithmic trading strategies. It provides a versatile framework for creating, testing, and executing trading algorithms, making it a valuable tool for traders and developers in the algorithmic trading domain.

PyAlgoTrade employs an event-driven architecture, allowing developers to define trading strategies based on events like price changes, order executions, or indicator crossovers. This architecture is well-suited for building reactive and dynamic trading systems. PyAlgoTrade is highly extensible, enabling users to incorporate various data sources, technical indicators, and custom order execution methods into their trading strategies. This flexibility allows for the creation of diverse and sophisticated trading systems.

PyAlgoTrade backtesting

PyAlgoTrade backtesting library offers a comprehensive backtesting framework that allows traders to test their strategies against historical data. This feature is crucial for evaluating the performance and robustness of algorithms before deploying them in live trading.

PyAlgoTrade also provides integration with various brokers and data providers, making it possible to execute orders and access real-time market data seamlessly. Users can select the broker interface that suits their trading needs.

Let us illustrate the usage of PyAlgoTrade with a practical example of a **Simple Moving Average (SMA)** crossover strategy. In this strategy, we will buy when a short-term SMA crosses above a long-term SMA and sell when the opposite crossover occurs. In this Python code snippet, a SMA crossover strategy for algorithmic trading is implemented using the PyAlgoTrade library. The `SMACrossoverStrategy` class leverages short-term and long-term SMAs to make buy and sell decisions based on price data fed from a CSV file, illustrating a basic but effective strategy for trading cryptocurrencies like Bitcoin.

```
1. from pyalgotrade import strategy
```

```
2. from pyalgotrade.technical import ma
3. from pyalgotrade.technical import cross
4.
5. class SMACrossoverStrategy(strategy.BacktestingStrategy):
6.     def __init__(self, feed, instrument, smaShort, smaLong):
7.         super(SMACrossoverStrategy, self).__init__(feed)
8.         self.__instrument = instrument
9.         self.__smaShort = ma.SMA(feed[instrument].getPriceDataSeries(), smaShort)
10.        self.__smaLong = ma.SMA(feed[instrument].getPriceDataSeries(), smaLong)
11.        self.__position = None
12.
13.    def onEnterCanceled(self, position):
14.        self.__position = None
15.
16.    def onExitOk(self, position):
17.        self.__position = None
18.
19.    def onExitCanceled(self, position):
20.        self.__position.exitMarket()
21.
22.    def onBars(self, bars):
23.        if self.__smaShort[-1] is None or self.__smaLong[-1] is None:
24.            return
25.
26.        if cross.cross_above(self.__smaShort, self.__smaLong) and self.__position is None:
27.            self.__position = self.enterLong(self.__instrument, 100)
28.
29.        elif cross.cross_below(self.__smaShort, self.__smaLong) and self.__position is not None:
30.            self.__position.exitMarket()
31.
32. # Create a strategy instance
33. from pyalgotrade import feed
34.
35. feed = feed.CSVFeed()
36. feed.addBarsFromCSV("BTC", "BTCUSD.csv")
```

```
37. strategy = SMACrossoverStrategy(feed, "BTC", 50, 200)
38.
39. # Run the strategy
40. strategy.run()
```

In this example, we import **PyAlgoTrade** modules, define the SMA crossover strategy, and then backtest it using historical price data. The strategy buys when the short-term SMA crosses above the long-term SMA and sells when the opposite crossover occurs. This simple example demonstrates how **PyAlgoTrade** can be used to implement and test trading strategies. PyAlgoTrade's flexibility and extensive capabilities make it a valuable resource for algorithmic traders, whether they are developing, backtesting, or executing trading strategies in real markets.

Zipline

Zipline is a powerful open-source library designed explicitly for backtesting trading strategies. Operating within the section dedicated to Python for finance: Libraries and tools, Zipline emerges as a critical tool for traders and quant analysts.

At its core, Zipline serves as a simulator for trading strategies, enabling users to assess how their algorithms would have performed historically. This retrospective analysis is indispensable for traders seeking to validate their strategies, refine trading rules, and gauge their strategies' profitability and risk characteristics.

To harness the power of Zipline, traders and analysts must set up and configure the library to align with their specific trading strategies and data sources. Zipline is renowned for its flexibility in this regard, allowing users to ingest various data formats, including price and fundamental data.

For example, suppose a trader intends to backtest a mean-reversion strategy using Zipline. They can configure Zipline to ingest historical price data for a specific set of stocks and define trading rules based on statistical measures such as **Bollinger Bands** or moving averages. Configuration options are extensive, encompassing factors like trading frequency, slippage models, and risk management parameters.

This Python code leverages the Zipline library for backtesting trading strategies. It is specifically structured for trading Apple Inc. (symbol: AAPL) based on a SMA strategy. The strategy involves buying Apple shares whenever the current price falls below 95% of the 20-day SMA, aiming to maintain a target percentage of the portfolio in AAPL. This code demonstrates how to interact with financial data, implement trading logic, and set up the framework for further performance analysis of the strategy:

```
1. from zipline.api import order_target_percent, record, symbol
2.
3. def initialize(context):
4.     context.stock = symbol('AAPL')
```

```
5.      context.target_weight = 1.0 / len(context.stock)
6.
7.  def handle_data(context, data):
8.      price_history = data.history(context.stock, fields="price", bar_count=20, frequency="1d")
9.      moving_avg = price_history.mean()
10.
11.     if data.current(context.stock, 'price') < 0.95 * moving_avg:
12.         order_target_percent(context.stock, context.target_weight)
13.
14. def analyze(context, perf):
15.     # Add your analysis and performance metrics code here
16.     pass
```

Backtesting with Zipline involves feeding historical data into the algorithm and simulating trades based on defined rules. The library provides a framework for event-driven backtesting, allowing users to handle various trading events such as orders, fills, and portfolio rebalancing. After conducting backtests, traders can analyze results to assess strategy performance, risk metrics, and drawdowns, among other key indicators. Optimization often follows the initial backtesting phase. Traders may tweak trading parameters or introduce additional risk management rules to optimize strategies for better risk-adjusted returns. Zipline's iterative approach to backtesting and optimization allows traders to fine-tune their algorithms to align with specific market conditions and objectives.

To illustrate Zipline's practical utility, consider a case study where a trader deploys a simple moving average crossover strategy using Zipline. The strategy involves going long when a short-term moving average crosses above a longer-term moving average and going short when the reverse occurs. By backtesting this strategy using Zipline and analyzing the results, the trader can gain valuable insights into its historical performance. This Python script showcases a moving average crossover trading strategy using Zipline, a powerful algorithmic trading simulator. The code outlines the strategy for Apple Inc. (AAPL), using 50-day and 200-day moving averages to determine buy and sell signals. Key features include dynamic portfolio allocation based on moving average crossovers and daily execution of trading logic at market open. The **analyze** function calculates important performance metrics like total return, annualized return, volatility, and Sharpe ratio, while also generating plots for visual representation of strategy performance and moving average trends. The strategy is backtested over a period from 2010 to 2021 with an initial capital base of $100,000, demonstrating an application of quantitative trading methods in a historical market environment:

```
1.  from zipline.api import symbol, schedule_function, date_rules, time_rules, record, order_target_percent
2.  import pandas as pd
```

```python
3.  import numpy as np
4.
5.  def initialize(context):
6.      # Define the stock symbol to trade
7.      context.stock = symbol('AAPL')
8.
9.      # Define short and long-term moving average windows
10.     context.short_window = 50
11.     context.long_window = 200
12.
13.     # Set the initial portfolio allocation
14.     context.initial_portfolio_allocation = 1.0
15.
16.     # Schedule the strategy function to run daily at market open
17.     schedule_function(strategy, date_rules.every_day(), time_rules.market_open())
18.
19.     # Initialize variables to track portfolio value and trading signals
20.     context.portfolio_value = []
21.     context.signals = []
22.
23. def strategy(context, data):
24.     # Fetch historical stock price data
25.     prices = data.history(context.stock, fields="price", bar_count=context.long_window, frequency="1d")
26.
27.     # Calculate short-term and long-term moving averages
28.     short_mavg = prices[-context.short_window:].mean()
29.     long_mavg = prices.mean()
30.
31.     # Record moving averages for visualization
32.     record(short_mavg=short_mavg, long_mavg=long_mavg)
33.
34.     # Trading logic: Go long when short-term crosses above long-term, and vice versa
35.     if short_mavg > long_mavg:
36.         context.signals.append(1)  # Go long
37.         order_target_percent(context.stock, context.initial_
```

```
             portfolio_allocation)
38.      else:
39.          context.signals.append(-1)  # Go short
40.          order_target_percent(context.stock, -context.initial_
     portfolio_allocation)
41.
42. def analyze(context, perf):
43.      # Calculate and print strategy performance metrics
44.      returns = perf['returns']
45.      cumulative_returns = (1 + returns).cumprod()
46.      total_return = cumulative_returns[-1] - 1
47.      annualized_return = (cumulative_returns[-1]) ** (252 /
     len(returns)) - 1
48.      annualized_volatility = np.std(returns) * np.sqrt(252)
49.      sharpe_ratio = (annualized_return - 0.03) / annualized_volatility
50.
51.      print("Total return: {:.2f}%".format(total_return * 100))
52.      print("Annualized return: {:.2f}%".format(annualized_return * 100))
53.      print("Annualized volatility: {:.2f}%".format(annualized_
     volatility * 100))
54.      print("Sharpe ratio: {:.2f}".format(sharpe_ratio))
55.
56.      # Visualize the strategy's equity curve and moving averages
57.      import matplotlib.pyplot as plt
58.      fig, ax1 = plt.subplots()
59.      ax2 = ax1.twinx()
60.      ax1.plot(returns.index, cumulative_returns, 'b-',
     label='Cumulative Returns')
61.      ax2.plot(returns.index, perf['short_mavg'], 'g-', label='Short
     MAVG ({} days)'.format(context.short_window))
62.      ax2.plot(returns.index, perf['long_mavg'], 'r-', label='Long
     MAVG ({} days)'.format(context.long_window))
63.      ax1.set_xlabel('Date')
64.      ax1.set_ylabel('Cumulative Returns', color='b')
65.      ax2.set_ylabel('Moving Averages', color='g')
66.      ax1.legend(loc='upper left')
67.      ax2.legend(loc='upper right')
68.      plt.title('Simple Moving Average Crossover Strategy')
```

```
69.     plt.show()
70.
71. # Define a custom backtest start and end date
72. start_date = pd.Timestamp('2010-01-01', tz='UTC')
73. end_date = pd.Timestamp('2021-12-31', tz='UTC')
74.
75. # Run the backtest using Zipline
76. from zipline import run_algorithm
77. run_algorithm(
78.     start=start_date,
79.     end=end_date,
80.     initialize=initialize,
81.     analyze=analyze,
82.     capital_base=100000,
83.     data_frequency='daily',
84.     bundle='quandl',
85. )
```

In this scenario, Zipline aids in the quantitative assessment of strategy returns, volatility, and risk metrics. It enables the trader to visualize the strategy's equity curve, drawdowns, and other performance indicators. By conducting multiple such case studies, traders can gain confidence in their strategies, optimize parameters, and make informed decisions about live trading implementation.

In conclusion, Zipline emerges as a pivotal tool in the arsenal of algorithmic traders and quantitative analysts. Its role in backtesting trading strategies, configuring custom trading universes, and conducting rigorous analyses of historical data positions it as a cornerstone of High-Performance Algorithmic Trading using AI. By offering a controlled and data-driven environment for strategy validation and optimization, Zipline empowers traders to navigate the dynamic and competitive landscape of algorithmic trading with precision and confidence.

pyfolio

pyfolio (Portfolio and risk analytics) is a powerful open-source library designed explicitly for portfolio and risk analytics. Operating within the section dedicated to Python for finance: Libraries and tools, **pyfolio** emerges as a fundamental tool for traders and investment professionals. Pyfolio stands as a testament to the growing importance of data-driven decision-making in portfolio management. It equips traders and analysts with the means to assess the performance of their investment strategies comprehensively. The library's analytical tools allow for the measurement of risk, return, and various performance metrics, empowering users to make informed decisions about portfolio composition and allocation.

Portfolio performance and risk analysis are essential aspects of managing investment strategies. Pyfolio provides a rich set of tools to assist in these endeavors. For instance, traders can use **pyfolio** to calculate **key performance indicators (KPIs)** such as cumulative returns, annualized returns, and the Sharpe ratio. These metrics offer valuable insights into the effectiveness of trading strategies over time and help assess their risk-adjusted performance. In this Python script, we utilize the PyFolio library to analyze the performance metrics of a simulated portfolio. The code generates random portfolio returns, from which it computes cumulative and annualized returns, as well as the Sharpe ratio, providing insights into the risk-adjusted return of the portfolio:

```
1.  import pyfolio as pf
2.  import numpy as np
3.
4.  # Simulated portfolio returns
5.  portfolio_returns = np.random.randn(100)
6.
7.  # Create a PyFolio returns object
8.  returns = pf.timeseries.returns_from_prices(portfolio_returns)
9.
10. # Calculate cumulative returns
11. cumulative_returns = pf.timeseries.cum_returns(returns)
12.
13. # Calculate annualized returns
14. annualized_returns = pf.timeseries.annual_return(returns)
15.
16. # Calculate the Sharpe ratio
17. sharpe_ratio = pf.timeseries.sharpe_ratio(returns)
```

In addition to basic performance metrics, pyfolio equips traders with advanced tools to measure and manage portfolio risk. These tools encompass metrics such as drawdown analysis, **value at risk (VaR)**, and **conditional value at risk (CVaR)**. By conducting thorough risk assessments, traders can gain a comprehensive understanding of their strategies' vulnerabilities and adjust their portfolios accordingly. In this Python script, we leverage the PyFolio library to perform a comprehensive risk and performance analysis on a set of simulated portfolio returns. The code begins by generating a random sample of returns, which is then used to create a PyFolio returns object. Using this object, we calculate essential investment metrics including cumulative and annualized returns, Sharpe ratio, maximum drawdown, and both the VaR and CVaR, giving a detailed view of the potential risks and rewards associated with the portfolio.

```
1.  import pyfolio as pf
2.  import numpy as np
3.
```

```
4.  # Simulated portfolio returns
5.  portfolio_returns = np.random.randn(100)
6.
7.  # Create a PyFolio returns object
8.  returns = pf.timeseries.returns_from_prices(portfolio_returns)
9.
10. # Calculate cumulative returns
11. cumulative_returns = pf.timeseries.cum_returns(returns)
12.
13. # Calculate annualized returns
14. annualized_returns = pf.timeseries.annual_return(returns)
15.
16. # Calculate the Sharpe ratio
17. sharpe_ratio = pf.timeseries.sharpe_ratio(returns)
18.
19. # Calculate maximum drawdown
20. max_drawdown = pf.timeseries.max_drawdown(returns)
21.
22. # Calculate value at risk (VaR)
23. var = pf.timeseries.value_at_risk(returns)
24.
25. # Calculate conditional value at risk (CVaR)
26. cvar = pf.timeseries.conditional_value_at_risk(returns, cutoff=0.05)
```

Pyfolio's visualization capabilities are another compelling aspect of its utility. The library offers a range of visualizations that aid in interpreting portfolio analytics. Traders can generate interactive plots depicting portfolio returns, drawdowns, and risk metrics over time. These visualizations provide a holistic view of strategy performance and facilitate communication with stakeholders. In this Python script, we utilize the **pyfolio** library to perform a comprehensive financial analysis of simulated portfolio returns. The code calculates key metrics such as cumulative returns, annualized returns, Sharpe ratio, maximum drawdown, VaR, and CVaR. Additionally, it generates detailed interactive visualizations for an in-depth evaluation of the portfolio's performance, providing valuable insights into risk and return dynamics.

```
1.  import pyfolio as pf
2.  import numpy as np
3.
4.  # Simulated portfolio returns
5.  portfolio_returns = np.random.randn(100)
6.
7.  # Create a PyFolio returns object
```

```
8.  returns = pf.timeseries.returns_from_prices(portfolio_returns)
9.
10. # Calculate cumulative returns
11. cumulative_returns = pf.timeseries.cum_returns(returns)
12.
13. # Calculate annualized returns
14. annualized_returns = pf.timeseries.annual_return(returns)
15.
16. # Calculate the Sharpe ratio
17. sharpe_ratio = pf.timeseries.sharpe_ratio(returns)
18.
19. # Calculate maximum drawdown
20. max_drawdown = pf.timeseries.max_drawdown(returns)
21.
22. # Calculate value at risk (VaR)
23. var = pf.timeseries.value_at_risk(returns)
24.
25. # Calculate conditional value at risk (CVaR)
26. cvar = pf.timeseries.conditional_value_at_risk(returns, cutoff=0.05)
27.
28. # Generate interactive plots
29. pf.create_returns_tear_sheet(returns)
30. pf.create_bayesian_tear_sheet(returns)
31. pf.create_round_trip_tear_sheet(returns)
```

The trader utilizes **pyfolio** to calculate key metrics like the Sharpe ratio and drawdowns, visualize the equity curve, and assess the strategy's risk exposures. These insights enable the trader to make informed decisions about position sizing, risk management, and strategy refinement.

Visualization tools

The significance of visualization tools in algorithmic trading cannot be overstated. In an environment where traders are inundated with vast amounts of data, the ability to distill complex information into clear, comprehensible visual representations is paramount. These visualizations go beyond mere aesthetics; they serve as powerful instruments for uncovering patterns, identifying anomalies, and gaining a deeper understanding of market dynamics.

Data visualization plays a pivotal role in trading analysis, serving as the bridge between raw data and informed decisions. Consider the scenario where a quantitative trader is analyzing the performance of a trading strategy over time. Through data visualization, they can create interactive charts and graphs that depict the strategy's equity curve, drawdowns, and risk metrics. These visualizations provide a comprehensive view of the strategy's historical performance, allowing traders to assess its strengths and weaknesses. Additionally, visualization tools aid in scenario analysis. Traders can simulate the impact of various market scenarios on their portfolios by visualizing stress tests or sensitivity analyses.

Matplotlib

Matplotlib serves as the foundation for creating static charts, providing traders with the means to transform complex datasets into intuitive visuals. For example, consider a scenario where a quantitative trader aims to visualize the historical performance of a trading strategy. Matplotlib allows them to create a line chart depicting strategy returns over time:

```
1.  import matplotlib.pyplot as plt
2.  import numpy as np
3.
4.  # Simulated strategy returns
5.  returns = np.random.randn(100).cumsum()
6.
7.  # Create a line chart
8.  plt.figure(figsize=(10, 6))
9.  plt.plot(returns, label='Strategy Returns', color='blue')
10. plt.xlabel('Time')
11. plt.ylabel('Returns')
12. plt.title('Historical Performance of Trading Strategy')
13. plt.legend()
14. plt.grid(True)
15. plt.show()
```

Matplotlib's versatility shines through in its ability to generate various static charts to meet diverse trading needs. For instance, traders can employ Matplotlib to craft bar charts illustrating asset performance. These bar charts are instrumental in visualizing comparisons between assets, sectors, or trading strategies. Following Python script visually represents the simulated performance of three assets by generating a bar chart. It defines the assets and their corresponding returns, sets up the plot dimensions, and uses green bars to depict the performance metrics, clearly labeling both axes and titling the chart to facilitate an immediate understanding of the asset comparison:

```
1.  # Simulated asset performance
2.  assets = ['Asset A', 'Asset B', 'Asset C']
3.  returns = [0.05, 0.03, 0.08]
4.
```

```
5.  # Create a bar chart
6.  plt.figure(figsize=(8, 4))  # Set the figure size (width and height)
7.  plt.bar(assets, returns, color='green')  # Create a bar chart with
    assets on the x-axis and returns on the y-axis, colored green
8.  plt.xlabel('Assets')  # Set the x-axis label to 'Assets'
9.  plt.ylabel('Returns')  # Set the y-axis label to 'Returns'
10. plt.title('Asset Performance Comparison')  # Set the title of the chart
11. plt.show()  # Display the chart
```

Matplotlib empowers traders to customize and enhance static charts, tailoring them to specific requirements. Customizations can include adjusting colors, fonts, axis labels, and annotations to improve chart clarity and convey precise information.

For instance, let us consider a candlestick chart used to visualize price movements. Traders can customize it by highlighting bullish and bearish candlesticks with distinct colors, making it easier to interpret trends and sentiment within the market. In this code, we will demonstrate how to create an elegant candlestick chart for Apple Inc.'s stock prices using Python libraries such as **matplotlib** and **yfinance**. By fetching historical data for 2023, formatting it, and applying Matplotlib's visualization capabilities, we aim to deliver insightful financial analysis through a comprehensive and customizable graphical representation.

```
1.  import matplotlib.dates as mdates
2.  import yfinance as yf
3.  import matplotlib.pyplot as plt
4.  from matplotlib.finance import candlestick_ohlc
5.
6.  # Fetch historical price data
7.  data = yf.download('AAPL', start='2023-01-01', end='2023-12-31')
8.
9.  # Create a candlestick chart with customizations
10. fig, ax = plt.subplots(figsize=(10, 6))
11. ax.xaxis.set_major_locator(mdates.MonthLocator())
12. ax.xaxis.set_major_formatter(mdates.DateFormatter('%b %Y'))
13. plt.title('AAPL Candlestick Chart')
14.
15. # Convert the date, open, high, low, and close prices to the
    required format
16. data['Date'] = mdates.date2num(data.index.to_pydatetime())
17. ohlc = data[['Date', 'Open', 'High', 'Low', 'Close']].values
18.
19. candlestick_ohlc(ax, ohlc, width=20)
```

20.
21. `plt.show()`

Matplotlib seamlessly integrates into trading analysis reports, enhancing communication and decision-making. Traders can embed Matplotlib-generated charts directly into reports to provide a visual context for data interpretation and insights.

For instance, a portfolio manager can utilize Matplotlib to create pie charts illustrating asset allocation within a diversified portfolio and include them in a performance report:

1. `# Simulated portfolio allocation`
2. `allocation = [0.4, 0.3, 0.2, 0.1]`
3. `assets = ['Asset A', 'Asset B', 'Asset C', 'Asset D']`
4.
5. `# Create a pie chart`
6. `plt.figure(figsize=(8, 8))  # Set the figure size (width and height) to make it a square chart`
7. `plt.pie(allocation, labels=assets, autopct='%1.1f%%', startangle=140)`
8.
9. `# Configure the pie chart`
10. `# - allocation: The list of allocation percentages for each asset`
11. `# - labels: Labels for each slice of the pie chart`
12. `# - autopct: Display percentages on each slice with one decimal place`
13. `# - startangle: The angle at which the pie chart starts (140 degrees in this case)`
14.
15. `plt.title('Portfolio Asset Allocation')  # Set the title of the chart`
16. `plt.show()  # Display the chart`

Matplotlib is an indispensable tool for traders and analysts. Its role in creating static charts facilitates effective data-driven decision-making, enhances data visualization, and supports impactful communication of trading insights. As we delve deeper into this book, Matplotlib's versatility and impact on trading analysis will continue to unfold, underscoring its crucial role in High-Performance Algorithmic Trading using AI.

Plotly

`Plotly` is a game-changer in the world of data visualization, offering traders and analysts the ability to go beyond static charts. It enables the creation of interactive graphs that allow users to interact directly with the data. For example, consider a scenario where a quantitative analyst aims to explore the relationship between two financial instruments. With Plotly, they can generate an interactive scatter plot that provides not only a visual representation of the data but also the ability to hover over points for specific data points. Following Python script utilizes Plotly, Pandas, and NumPy libraries to create an interactive scatter plot visualizing the relationship between two simulated asset trading data points over a period of 100 days. The script generates random trading data for **Asset A** and **Asset B**, creates a scatter plot to visualize this data, and customizes the marker size before displaying the plot.

```
1. import plotly.express as px
2. import pandas as pd
3. import numpy as np
4.
5. # Simulated trading data
6. data = pd.DataFrame({'Date': pd.date_range(start='2023-01-01',
   periods=100),
7.                      'Asset A': np.random.randn(100),
8.                      'Asset B': np.random.randn(100)})
9.
10. # Create an interactive scatter plot
11. fig = px.scatter(data, x='Asset A', y='Asset B', title='Interactive
    Scatter Plot')
12.
13. # Update the marker size for the scatter plot points
14. fig.update_traces(marker=dict(size=5))
15.
16. # Display the interactive plot
17. fig.show()
```

Plotly's versatility extends to various types of interactive graphs, including line plots, candlestick charts, and heatmaps. These interactive visualizations enhance trading data analysis by enabling traders to zoom in on specific time periods, explore data trends, and uncover anomalies. For instance, a trader can utilize Plotly to create an interactive candlestick chart, allowing them to zoom in on specific trading sessions or assess price movements with a finer level of granularity. This level of interactivity enhances the trader's ability to make informed decisions and conduct in-depth analysis. The script uses the **plotly** library and the **yfinance** package to fetch and visualize historical price data for Apple Inc. (AAPL) from January 1, 2023, to December 31, 2023. It constructs an interactive candlestick chart that displays the open, high, low, and close prices for each day in the dataset. The chart is enhanced with a title, axis labels, and a range slider to allow for easy navigation of the time series data. Finally, the interactive chart is displayed, providing a detailed view of price movements over the year.

```
1. import plotly.graph_objects as go
2. import yfinance as yf
3.
4. # Fetch historical price data
```

```
5.  data = yf.download('AAPL', start='2023-01-01', end='2023-12-31')
6.
7.  # Create an interactive candlestick chart
8.  fig = go.Figure(data=[go.Candlestick(x=data.index,
9.                  open=data['Open'],
10.                 high=data['High'],
11.                 low=data['Low'],
12.                 close=data['Close'])])
13.
14. # Update the layout of the chart
15. fig.update_layout(
16.     title='Interactive Candlestick Chart',
17.     xaxis_title='Time',
18.     yaxis_title='Price',
19.     xaxis_rangeslider_visible=True  # Add a range slider for the x-axis
20. )
21.
22. # Display the interactive candlestick chart
23. fig.show()
```

One of Plotly's standout features is its interactivity. Users can zoom in on specific data points, pan through time series data, and even extract additional information through tooltips. This level of engagement empowers traders to explore data dynamically and gain deeper insights. Consider a scenario where a portfolio manager uses Plotly to create an interactive line chart depicting portfolio returns over time. By incorporating tooltips that display precise return values when hovering over data points, Plotly enhances the chart's value as a tool for performance. The provided Python code leverages the **plotly.express** library to generate an interactive line chart that visualizes simulated portfolio returns over a 100-day period starting from January 1, 2023. The script begins by creating a DataFrame with dates and corresponding portfolio returns, which include a random variation component. It then plots these data points on a line chart, where each point is marked and customized tooltips show the returns formatted to two decimal places. The chart is designed to offer insights into the portfolio's performance over time with the aid of interactive features such as hover effects.

```
1.  import plotly.express as px
2.  import pandas as pd
3.
4.  # Assuming you have a DataFrame 'data' with 'Date' and 'Portfolio Returns' columns
5.  # Simulated data for demonstration purposes:
6.  data = pd.DataFrame({'Date': pd.date_range(start='2023-01-01', periods=100),
```

```
7.                       'Portfolio Returns': (0.02 + 0.01 * (pd.
   np.random.randn(100).cumsum()))})
8.
9. # Create an interactive line chart with tooltips
10. fig = px.line(data, x='Date', y='Portfolio Returns', title='Portfolio
    Returns Over Time')
11.
12. # Update the traces to include markers and customize hover text
13. fig.update_traces(mode='lines+markers', hovertemplate='%{y:.2f}')
14.
15. # Show the interactive line chart
16. fig.show()
```

seaborn

seaborn is a powerful library renowned for its capabilities in statistical data visualization. Seaborn emerges as a critical tool for traders, offering a versatile and aesthetically pleasing approach to visualizing trading data and patterns. Seaborn, built on top of Matplotlib, offers traders an array of statistical plots that can effectively unveil hidden insights within trading data. Its strengths lie in its ability to simplify complex statistical representations into visually appealing charts, making it accessible to both novice and experienced traders. Seaborn's forte lies in its ability to effortlessly create visually appealing statistical charts. For instance, consider a scenario where a trader wishes to explore the distribution of returns for a portfolio of assets. Seaborn allows the trader to create a **kernel density estimate** (KDE) plot, a smoothed representation of the data distribution. Following code demonstrates the visualization of simulated portfolio returns using Python libraries Seaborn and Matplotlib. It starts by generating a dataset of 1000 random values, assumed to represent returns. Utilizing Seaborn, the script configures the aesthetic style and creates a KDE plot to show the distribution of these returns. It also customizes the plot by removing unnecessary spines and adding relevant labels and a title, before finally displaying the plot:

```
1. import seaborn as sns
2. import numpy as np
3. import matplotlib.pyplot as plt
4.
5. # Simulated portfolio returns
6. returns = np.random.randn(1000)
7.
8. # Set Seaborn style and create a KDE plot
9. sns.set(style="whitegrid")
10. sns.kdeplot(data=returns, shade=True)
11.
```

```
12. # Remove the top and right spines of the plot
13. sns.despine()
14.
15. # Set labels and title
16. plt.xlabel('Returns')
17. plt.ylabel('Density')
18. plt.title('Distribution of Portfolio Returns')
19.
20. # Show the plot
21. plt.show()
```

While **Seaborn** shines in statistical data visualization, it is valuable to compare it to other visualization tools in the trading landscape. Matplotlib, for instance, offers a more comprehensive range of chart types but often requires more customization to achieve similar aesthetics. On the other hand, Plotly excels in creating interactive graphs.

To underscore the practical relevance of Seaborn in trading analysis, consider a real-world example where a risk manager employs **seaborn** to create a pair plot of asset correlations:

```
1.  import seaborn as sns
2.  import numpy as np
3.  import pandas as pd
4.  import matplotlib.pyplot as plt
5.
6.  # Simulated correlation matrix
7.  corr_matrix = np.corrcoef(np.random.randn(5, 100))
8.
9.  # Create a DataFrame from the correlation matrix
10. corr_df = pd.DataFrame(corr_matrix)
11.
12. # Set Seaborn style
13. sns.set(style="ticks")
14.
15. # Create a pair plot
16. sns.pairplot(corr_df)
17.
18. # Set the title of the pair plot
19. plt.suptitle('Pair Plot of Asset Correlations')
20.
21. # Show the plot
22. plt.show()
```

Seaborn emerges as a vital tool for traders in the domain of high-performance algorithmic trading using AI. Its strength in statistical data visualization simplifies complex data representations into aesthetically pleasing charts, making it accessible and effective for exploring trading data and patterns.

Additional libraries and tools

As traders seek to gain an edge in the market, the significance of these additional libraries becomes evident. They serve as specialized instruments that enable traders to delve deeper into quantitative analysis, technical analysis, and risk management. Two notable libraries are **TA-Lib** and **Fastquant**. TA-Lib, short for Technical Analysis Library, equips traders with a rich set of technical indicators and functions. This library enables traders to perform detailed technical analysis on historical price data, aiding in the identification of potential buy and sell signals. This code snippet retrieves historical stock price data for Apple Inc. (AAPL) using the **yfinance** library and calculates the **Moving Average Convergence Divergence (MACD)** indicator using the **talib** library. Specifically, it pulls data for the year 2023 and applies the MACD analysis to the closing prices of AAPL stock, storing the results back into the original data frame. The MACD is a trend-following momentum indicator that shows the relationship between two moving averages of a security's price.

```
1. import talib
2. import yfinance as yf
3.
4. # Fetch historical price data
5. data = yf.download('AAPL', start='2023-01-01', end='2023-12-31')
6.
7. # Calculate the Moving Average Convergence Divergence (MACD) indicator
8. data['MACD'], data['Signal'] = talib.MACD(data['Close'])
```

The **fastquant** library on the other hand, offers a streamlined approach to backtesting trading strategies. It allows traders to rapidly evaluate their strategies on historical data, making it easier to iterate and optimize strategies. The provided Python script leverages the **fastquant** library to define and execute a trading strategy based on SMA crossovers on a dataset. The strategy involves purchasing stocks when their closing price surpasses the 50-day SMA and selling when the price drops below the SMA. This setup includes initializing signals, defining backtest parameters such as initial cash, and the proportions of cash and holdings to be utilized in each buy or sell transaction. The script concludes by running this strategy against a specified dataset, recording the results, and printing them, thereby providing a straightforward mechanism to evaluate the effectiveness of the SMA crossover strategy in a simulated trading environment.

```
1. from fastquant import backtest
2.
3. # Define and backtest a trading strategy
```

```python
4.  def my_strategy(df):
5.      # Your strategy logic here
6.      # For example, let's say you want to buy when the Close price crosses above the 50-day Moving Average (SMA) and sell when it crosses below.
7.      df['SMA_50'] = df['close'].rolling(window=50).mean()
8.      df['Signal'] = 0  # Initialize a signal column with 0s
9.      df.loc[df['close'] > df['SMA_50'], 'Signal'] = 1  # Buy signal
10.     df.loc[df['close'] < df['SMA_50'], 'Signal'] = -1  # Sell signal
11.
12.     # Backtest parameters
13.     init_cash = 10000   # Initial cash for the backtest
14.     buy_prop = 1.0  # Invest 100% of available cash when buying
15.     sell_prop = 1.0  # Sell 100% of held shares when selling
16.
17.     # Use Fastquant's backtest function to perform the backtest
18.     result = backtest('custom', df, init_cash=init_cash, buy_prop=buy_prop, sell_prop=sell_prop)
19.
20.     return result
21.
22. # Assuming you have your 'data' DataFrame containing historical price data
23. # You can pass your 'data' DataFrame to the strategy function for backtesting
24. backtest_result = my_strategy(data)
25. print(backtest_result)
```

While libraries like NumPy, pandas, Matplotlib, Plotly, SciPy, Quantlib, Zipline, and pyfolio provide the foundational building blocks for algorithmic trading and analysis, additional libraries such as TA-Lib and fastquant offer specialized capabilities that complement the core tools.

Version control and collaboration with Git

Git plays a pivotal role in maintaining code quality, tracking changes, and fostering teamwork. Git, developed by *Linus Torvalds* in 2005, is a distributed version control system designed for efficient source code management. In Algorithmic Trading, where accuracy and reliability are critical, Git serves as a vital tool. It enables traders to keep track of changes made to their code, ensuring transparency in the development process. Git excels at tracking changes to codebases. Imagine a scenario where the performance of a trading algorithm suddenly deteriorates. With Git, traders can easily identify the exact modification that caused the issue. This is achieved through the use of Git's *commit* feature, where developers record changes made along with descriptive messages. These commit messages serve as a history log, aiding in understanding code evolution [102]. Git facilitates this collaboration by allowing developers to create branches. Branches enable developers to work on specific features or improvements independently without affecting the main codebase. For instance, a trader can create a branch to experiment with a new trading signal while keeping the main codebase stable. Once changes are tested and proven effective, they can be merged back into the main branch. This branching workflow maintains code stability and encourages experimentation and optimization.

Git basics

This section will delve into the fundamental Git operations: cloning, committing, pushing, pulling, and branching, all of which form the backbone of version control in trading algorithm development.

Cloning

One of the initial steps in working with Git is to clone a Git repository. Cloning essentially creates a local copy of a remote repository on your own machine. This local copy allows traders and developers to work on the codebase independently, without directly impacting the central repository. The command to clone a repository in Git is straightforward:

1. `git clone [repository URL]`

For example, if a trader wants to work with a trading algorithm's code hosted on a Git repository, they can clone it to their local environment using this command. This local copy becomes the starting point for their contributions.

Committing

Once changes are made to the code, the next essential step is to commit those changes. Commits in Git are like checkpoints in the code's history, recording what changes were made and providing a description of why those changes were necessary. This not only documents the code's evolution but also aids in understanding the rationale behind specific modifications. In Python, committing is achieved using the following command:

1. `git commit -m "Descriptive message here"`

For example, if a trader adds a new trading strategy to their algorithm in Python, they can commit this change with an informative message to explain the purpose of the update. This message becomes a reference point for others collaborating on the project.

Pushing

After committing changes locally, it is essential to share those updates with other collaborators by pushing them to the central repository. Pushing essentially updates the central codebase with your local changes, ensuring that everyone working on the project has access to the latest version. The command to push changes is:

1. `git push`

Traders and developers often use the **push** command to keep the central repository synchronized with their local changes.

Pulling

Conversely, if you want to acquire the latest code changes made by other collaborators, you use the **pull** operation. Pulling updates your local copy of the code with the changes from the central repository, ensuring that you are working with the most current version. The command for pulling is as follows:

1. `git pull`

This operation allows traders and developers to stay in sync with the latest developments in the trading algorithm, helping them adapt to market changes quickly.

Branches

Git's branching system is another key feature for trading algorithm development. It enables developers to create separate branches to work on specific features, experiments, or bug fixes without affecting the main. Branches help maintain code stability and encourage parallel development efforts. For instance, a trader can create a new branch to test a novel trading strategy or fix a critical bug without disrupting the primary algorithm.

Merging

Merging in Git refers to the process of integrating changes from one branch into another, typically merging feature branches into the main branch. This allows traders and developers to consolidate their work effectively. For example, suppose a trader has created a new feature branch named **machine-learning-enhancements** to implement advanced AI techniques in their trading algorithm. To integrate these enhancements into the main trading algorithm, they can use Git's merge operation:

1. `git merge machine-learning-enhancements`

This command combines the changes made in the **machine-learning-enhancements** branch with the main branch. By strategically merging feature branches, traders can gradually enhance their trading algorithms while maintaining the stability of the core system.

Resolving conflicts

It is common for multiple developers to work on the same codebase concurrently. When these developers make conflicting changes to the same part of the code, Git assists in identifying and resolving these. For instance, imagine two developers independently modify a critical trading strategy function in Python. When they attempt to merge their changes, Git recognizes that there is a conflict and alerts them. To resolve this conflict, the developers need to manually inspect the conflicting code, make decisions about which changes to keep, and then commit the resolved code. Git provides conflict markers within the code to indicate where conflicts have occurred, making it easier for developers to address them.

Pull requests

Pull requests (PRs) are a powerful feature provided by Git hosting platforms like GitHub and GitLab. They play a crucial role in collaborative trading algorithm development, acting as a mechanism for proposing, reviewing, and integrating changes into the main codebase. To illustrate, consider a scenario where a trader wants to enhance their risk management module. Instead of directly merging the changes into the main branch, they create a pull request on the Git platform. This pull request provides a space for other team members to review the proposed changes, discuss them, and suggest improvements. Once the changes are approved and reviewed, they can be merged into the main codebase.

Conclusion

In this chapter, we delved into Python's powerful numerical and financial libraries, which are indispensable for developing sophisticated trading algorithms. We explored how visualization tools enhance data interpretation, enabling traders to make informed decisions quickly. Additionally, we covered the essentials of using Git for version control, ensuring effective collaboration in trading projects. With these foundations, you're well-equipped to implement robust algorithmic trading solutions.

In the upcoming chapter, we will explore advanced techniques in algorithmic trading, focusing on high-performance strategies and optimization using Python to elevate your trading algorithms to the next level.

Join our book's Discord space

Join the book's Discord Workspace for Latest updates, Offers, Tech happenings around the world, New Release and Sessions with the Authors:

https://discord.bpbonline.com

CHAPTER 8
Leveraging Python for Trading Algorithm Development

Introduction

In this chapter, we embark on a comprehensive journey into harnessing the power of Python for financial endeavors, focusing on the development of robust trading algorithms. We delve into essential libraries and tools that serve as the backbone for financial modeling, equipping you with the skills to navigate the intricate landscape of Python's financial ecosystem. With a keen emphasis on practicality, we explore troubleshooting and debugging techniques, ensuring your algorithms are not just effective but also resilient. Additionally, we guide you through the crucial aspects of version control and collaboration using Git, enabling seamless teamwork in algorithmic trading projects. This chapter unfolds further into the realms of unit testing and code quality, emphasizing the significance of reliable and maintainable code. Lastly, we address the critical domain of performance optimization and parallelization, empowering you to enhance the efficiency of your trading algorithms. This chapter acts as a pivotal guide for Python enthusiasts looking to master the intricacies of finance-driven coding, providing a holistic approach to algorithmic trading development.

Structure

In this chapter, we will learn the following topics:

- Developing trading algorithms using Python
- Troubleshooting and debugging
- Unit testing and code quality
- Performance optimization and parallelization
- Python best practices for algorithmic trading

Objectives

In this chapter, our primary objective is to equip you with the essential skills required for developing efficient trading algorithms using Python. We will delve into practical strategies for troubleshooting and debugging, ensuring you can refine your algorithms with precision. Emphasis will be placed on unit testing and maintaining high standards of code quality, crucial for reliable trading operations. Additionally, we will explore methods for performance optimization, including parallelization techniques to enhance execution speed. Lastly, we will cover Python best practices tailored specifically for algorithmic trading, enabling you to implement robust and effective trading strategies.

Developing trading algorithms using Python

In the world of financial markets, where microseconds can make or break a trade, algorithmic trading has emerged as a pivotal force, reshaping the landscape of trading strategies and tactics. This chapter, situated within the section dedicated to developing trading algorithms using Python, marks the beginning of our journey into the realm of High-Performance Algorithmic Trading using AI. Here, we embark on an exploration of the intricate interplay between finance, technology, and artificial intelligence, unlocking the potential for traders and investors to navigate the complexities of modern markets with precision.

The following table outlines several popular trading strategies, highlighting their core principles and methodologies. These strategies range from exploiting price momentum and statistical relationships to using options and machine learning algorithms, each designed to achieve specific investment goals under varying market conditions:

Trading strategy	Key concepts
Momentum	Focuses on assets that are moving significantly in one direction on high volume. The strategy assumes that the asset will continue to move in the same direction because of the momentum behind it.
Statistical Arbitrage	Uses statistical models to identify inefficiencies in the price of assets, betting on the convergence/divergence of the prices.
Mean reversion	Based on the idea that prices and returns eventually move back towards the mean. This strategy seeks to capitalize on extreme changes in the pricing of a specific asset.
Pairs trading strategy	Involves identifying two correlated assets; when their prices diverge, one is bought and the other is sold, with the expectation that their prices will converge again.
Trend following strategy	Identifies and exploits long-term trends in the markets. It buys assets that are trending upward and sells assets that are trending downward.
Volatility breakout strategy	Trades on sudden increases in volatility, typically entering trades when there is a sudden movement in asset prices beyond a specified range.
Machine learning-based strategy	Employs algorithms to predict market movements based on historical data and statistical patterns, adapting to new data as it becomes available.
Options trading strategy	Involves the use of options contracts to capitalize on predictions regarding stock movements, leveraging strategies like buying, selling, spreads, and combinations.

Table 8.1: Trading strategies and key concepts

Momentum

Momentum trading is a popular investment strategy among traders and investors who believe that an asset's current price trend will continue in the same direction. This approach is based on the principle that assets that have been performing well or poorly over a certain period are likely to continue their performance in the near term. Here's a more detailed look at momentum trading and how it uses Python's programming capabilities:

Momentum trading involves buying securities that have had high returns over the recent past and selling those that have shown poor returns. The fundamental assumption here is that the market inefficiencies will allow the continuation of the existing trend for some time. This strategy is often contrasted with "mean-reversion" strategies, which assume that prices will revert to their averages.

Let us take an example of applying a momentum-based strategy to the stock market. In this context, Python programming can be harnessed to compute the **Rate of Change (ROC)** in a stock's price over a designated time frame. Stocks exhibiting a positive ROC can be considered as potential candidates for long positions, while those with a negative ROC may be considered for short positions. This Python script leverages statistical methods to identify and execute a pairs trading strategy based on the cointegration of two correlated stocks. After loading and processing the historical price data, the script calculates the cointegration value to determine if the stocks move together over time. If cointegration exists below a defined threshold, it then computes the z-score of the price spread to guide trading decisions—initiating or closing positions when certain conditions are met, followed by visualizing the trading strategy and stock price movements over time.

```
1.  # Import necessary libraries
2.  import pandas as pd
3.  import numpy as np
4.  from statsmodels.tsa.stattools import coint
5.
6.  # Load historical price data for two correlated stocks
7.  stock1 = pd.read_csv('stock1_prices.csv', index_col='Date', parse_dates=True)
8.  stock2 = pd.read_csv('stock2_prices.csv', index_col='Date', parse_dates=True)
9.
10. # Calculate the cointegration between the two stocks
11. cointegration_pvalue = coint(stock1['Close'], stock2['Close'])[1]
12.
13. # Define a cointegration threshold
14. cointegration_threshold = 0.05
15.
16. # Implement a pairs trading strategy if cointegration exists
17. if cointegration_pvalue < cointegration_threshold:
18.     spread = stock1['Close'] - stock2['Close']  # Calculate the spread between the two stocks
19.     zscore = (spread - np.mean(spread)) / np.std(spread)  # Calculate the z-score of the spread
20.     entry_threshold = 1.0  # Threshold for entering a position
21.     exit_threshold = 0.0   # Threshold for exiting a position
22.
23.     stock1_position = 0  # Initialize the position for Stock 1
24.     stock2_position = 0  # Initialize the position for Stock 2
25.     positions = []  # List to store the trading positions over time
```

```
26.
27.     # Iterate through z-scores to determine trading positions
28.     for z in zscore:
29.         if z > entry_threshold and stock1_position <= 0:
30.             stock1_position = 1
31.             stock2_position = -1
32.         elif z < -entry_threshold and stock1_position >= 0:
33.             stock1_position = -1
34.             stock2_position = 1
35.         elif abs(z) < exit_threshold:
36.             stock1_position = 0
37.             stock2_position = 0
38.
39.         positions.append((stock1_position, stock2_position))   # Store the positions
40.
41. # Plotting the results
42. import matplotlib.pyplot as plt
43.
44. plt.figure(figsize=(12, 6))
45. plt.plot(stock1.index, stock1['Close'], label='Stock 1', color='blue')
46. plt.plot(stock2.index, stock2['Close'], label='Stock 2', color='red')
47. plt.xlabel('Date')
48. plt.ylabel('Price')
49. plt.title('Pairs Trading: Stock 1 vs. Stock 2')
50. plt.legend()
51. plt.show()
```

The provided code performs a series of steps to implement a pairs trading strategy based on cointegration between two stocks, **Stock 1** and **Stock 2**. It begins by importing essential Python libraries for data analysis, including **pandas** for data manipulation, **numpy** for numerical operations, and **statsmodels** for cointegration testing.

Next, the code loads historical price data for **Stock 1** and **Stock 2** from CSV files into Pandas DataFrames. It configures the **Date** column as the index and parses it as datetime objects for time-series analysis.

Cointegration between the closing prices of **Stock 1** and **Stock 2** is then computed using the **coint** function from the **statsmodels** library. The resulting p-value for cointegration is extracted and stored in the variable **cointegration_pvalue**.

The code establishes a cointegration threshold (`cointegration_threshold`). If the cointegration p-value is lower than this threshold, it triggers the implementation of a pairs trading strategy.

Within the pairs trading strategy, the code calculates the spread between the closing prices of `Stock 1` and `Stock 2`. It also computes the z-score of the spread, which measures how many standard deviations the spread deviates from its mean. Entry and exit thresholds (`entry_threshold` and `exit_threshold`) are defined to determine when to initiate or close trading positions.

Initial positions for `Stock 1` and `Stock 2` are set to 0, and an empty list (`positions`) is created to keep track of the trading positions over time.

The code then iterates through the z-scores of the spread and uses the defined thresholds to make decisions about trading positions. If the z-score surpasses the entry threshold, a position is opened in one stock while simultaneously shorting the other. Conversely, if the z-score falls below the negative entry threshold, the positions are reversed. If the z-score lies within the exit threshold, both positions are closed.

Throughout this process, the code maintains a record of the evolving trading positions in the `positions` list. Finally, the code employs Matplotlib to visualize the closing prices of `Stock 1` and `Stock 2` over time. This visualization offers insight into the pairs trading strategy's performance based on cointegration analysis.

Statistical arbitrage

Statistical arbitrage, often referred to as *stat arb*, is a trading strategy that leverages statistical analysis to identify pairs of assets whose prices are expected to converge or diverge. Python plays a pivotal role in implementing this strategy by enabling traders to calculate statistical metrics and perform pair trading effectively.

For example, in a pairs trading strategy, Python can be used to calculate the cointegration between two stocks. When the cointegration deviates from its historical mean, it signals a potential trading opportunity. Python's libraries, such as `statsmodels`, make it efficient to perform these calculations and execute trades automatically when arbitrage opportunities arise. By applying statistical arbitrage techniques, traders can aim for profits regardless of market [100].

This Python script leverages statistical techniques to implement a pairs trading strategy based on the cointegration of two correlated stocks. Initially, the script imports necessary libraries and loads historical price data. It then calculates the cointegration between the stocks to determine if a statistically significant relationship exists. If cointegration is found, the script executes a trading strategy that involves monitoring the price spread for entry and exit signals, culminating in a visualization of the trading positions and stock price movements over time.

```python
1.  import pandas as pd
2.  import numpy as np
3.  from statsmodels.tsa.stattools import coint
4.  
5.  # Load historical price data for two correlated stocks
6.  stock1 = pd.read_csv('stock1_prices.csv', index_col='Date', parse_dates=True)
7.  stock2 = pd.read_csv('stock2_prices.csv', index_col='Date', parse_dates=True)
8.  
9.  # Calculate the cointegration between the two stocks
10. cointegration_pvalue = coint(stock1['Close'], stock2['Close'])[1]
11. 
12. # Define a cointegration threshold
13. cointegration_threshold = 0.05
14. 
15. # Implement a pairs trading strategy if cointegration exists
16. if cointegration_pvalue < cointegration_threshold:
17.     spread = stock1['Close'] - stock2['Close']
18.     zscore = (spread - np.mean(spread)) / np.std(spread)
19.     entry_threshold = 1.0
20.     exit_threshold = 0.0
21. 
22.     stock1_position = 0
23.     stock2_position = 0
24.     positions = []
25. 
26.     for z in zscore:
27.         if z > entry_threshold and stock1_position <= 0:
28.             stock1_position = 1
29.             stock2_position = -1
30.         elif z < -entry_threshold and stock1_position >= 0:
31.             stock1_position = -1
32.             stock2_position = 1
33.         elif abs(z) < exit_threshold:
34.             stock1_position = 0
35.             stock2_position = 0
36. 
37.         positions.append((stock1_position, stock2_position))
```

```
38.
39. # Plotting the results
40. import matplotlib.pyplot as plt
41.
42. plt.figure(figsize=(12, 6))
43. plt.plot(stock1.index, stock1['Close'], label='Stock 1', color='blue')
44. plt.plot(stock2.index, stock2['Close'], label='Stock 2', color='red')
45. plt.xlabel('Date')
46. plt.ylabel('Price')
47. plt.title('Pairs Trading: Stock 1 vs. Stock 2')
48. plt.legend()
49. plt.show()
```

This Python code illustrates a pairs trading strategy using cointegration analysis for two correlated stocks. It begins by importing essential libraries: **pandas** for data manipulation, **numpy** for numerical operations, and **coint** from **statsmodels.tsa.stattools** for cointegration testing. Subsequently, historical price data for two correlated stocks, denoted as **Stock 1** and **Stock 2**, is loaded from CSV files into Pandas DataFrames. The **Date** column is designated as the index, and it is parsed as datetime objects for time-series analysis. Following data loading, the code calculates the cointegration between the closing prices of these two stocks using the **coint** function. The resulting p-value, which indicates the presence of cointegration, is extracted and stored in the variable **cointegration_pvalue**.

A cointegration threshold is established with the value of 0.05, serving as the criterion for implementing a pairs trading strategy. If the cointegration p-value falls below this threshold, the code proceeds with the trading strategy. Within the pairs trading strategy, the code computes the spread between the closing prices of **Stock 1** and **Stock 2**. It also calculates the z-score of this spread, representing how many standard deviations the spread deviates from its mean. Entry and exit thresholds are defined for initiating and closing trading positions. The positions for **Stock 1** and **Stock 2** are initialized to 0, and an empty list (**positions**) is created to record trading positions over time. The code iterates through the z-scores of the spread, making decisions based on the predefined thresholds. If the z-score exceeds the entry threshold, a position is established in one stock while shorting the other. Conversely, if the z-score falls below the negative entry threshold, the positions are reversed. When the z-score is within the exit threshold, both positions are closed.

Finally, the code employs Matplotlib to visualize the closing prices of **Stock 1** and **Stock 2** over time, offering a graphical representation of the pairs trading strategy's performance based on cointegration analysis. This code assumes the presence of CSV files containing historical price data for the two stocks and employs this data to demonstrate a simple pairs trading approach.

Mean reversion

Mean reversion trading relies on the principle that asset prices have a tendency to revert to their historical mean values over time. This approach is supported by Python, a versatile programming language that equips traders with effective tools for implementing mean reversion strategies. A common method involves the computation of a moving average of an asset's price, enabling the identification of trading opportunities when the price significantly deviates from this historical average.

For instance, in the context of pairs trading, Python code can be harnessed to monitor the spread between two correlated assets. Whenever this spread extends or contracts beyond a predefined threshold, it initiates a trading action aimed at capitalizing on the anticipated reversion of prices to their historical relationship [101].

Following Python script demonstrates a mean reversion trading strategy using historical stock price data. The script first loads the data and computes a 20-day moving average, which it then uses to establish buy and sell signals based on the stock's deviation from this average. Trading positions are determined by these signals, and the script calculates both the returns from these positions and the cumulative returns over time. Finally, the results are visualized, showing the stock price alongside its moving average to assess the effectiveness of the strategy:

```
1.  import pandas as pd
2.  import numpy as np
3.
4.  # Load historical price data for a stock
5.  data = pd.read_csv('stock_prices.csv', index_col='Date', parse_dates=True)
6.
7.  # Calculate the 20-day moving average
8.  data['MA_20'] = data['Close'].rolling(window=20).mean()
9.
10. # Define buy and sell signals based on mean reversion
11. buy_signal = data['Close'] < data['MA_20']
12. sell_signal = data['Close'] > data['MA_20']
13.
14. # Apply signals to create trading positions
15. data['Position'] = np.where(buy_signal, 1, np.where(sell_signal, -1, 0))
16.
17. # Calculate returns based on trading positions
18. data['Returns'] = data['Position'].shift(1) * (data['Close'] - data['Close'].shift(1))
19.
```

```
20. # Calculate cumulative returns
21. data['Cumulative Returns'] = (1 + data['Returns']).cumprod()
22.
23. # Plotting the results
24. import matplotlib.pyplot as plt
25.
26. plt.figure(figsize=(12, 6))
27. plt.plot(data.index, data['Close'], label='Stock Price', color='blue')
28. plt.plot(data.index, data['MA_20'], label='20-Day Moving Average',
    color='red')
29. plt.xlabel('Date')
30. plt.ylabel('Price')
31. plt.title('Mean Reversion Trading Strategy')
32. plt.legend()
33. plt.show()
```

The provided Python code leverages Pandas and NumPy to execute a mean reversion trading strategy. Firstly, it imports necessary libraries and loads historical stock price data from a CSV file, indexing it by date. Subsequently, it computes the 20-day moving average of the stock's closing prices. The strategy identifies buy and sell signals by comparing the stock's current closing price to this moving average. These signals are used to create a 'Position' column in the dataset, with 1 indicating a buy signal, -1 a sell signal, and 0 no action. The code then calculates daily returns based on these positions and computes cumulative returns. Finally, it visualizes the stock price and the 20-day moving average using Matplotlib. This code effectively implements a basic mean reversion trading strategy and presents the results graphically.

Pairs trading strategy

Pairs trading is a market-neutral strategy that aims to profit from the relative price movements of two correlated assets. The core idea is to identify a pair of assets that typically move together (that is, have a strong historical correlation) and take advantage of temporary divergences in their prices. When one asset's price rises while the other's falls, you go long on the underperforming asset and short on the outperforming one, expecting that the price spread between them will eventually revert to its historical mean.

This Python script employs statistical analysis to execute a pairs trading strategy based on the cointegration of two hypothetically correlated stocks. The script starts by loading historical price data, then calculates the cointegration p-value to determine if a statistically significant relationship exists between the two stocks. If they are cointegrated below a specified threshold, the script calculates the spread and its z-score to establish entry and exit points for trading. The script iteratively adjusts positions in each stock based on these metrics, aiming to capitalize on temporary inefficiencies in their price relationship.

```python
1.  import pandas as pd
2.  import numpy as np
3.  from statsmodels.tsa.stattools import coint
4.
5.  # Load historical price data for two correlated stocks (hypothetical data)
6.  data = pd.read_csv('stock_prices.csv', index_col='Date', parse_dates=True)
7.
8.  # Calculate the cointegration between the two stocks
9.  cointegration_pvalue = coint(data['Stock1'], data['Stock2'])[1]
10.
11. # Define a cointegration threshold (e.g., 0.05)
12. cointegration_threshold = 0.05
13.
14. # Implement a pairs trading strategy if cointegration exists
15. if cointegration_pvalue < cointegration_threshold:
16.     # Calculate the spread between the two stocks (Stock1 - Stock2)
17.     spread = data['Stock1'] - data['Stock2']
18.
19.     # Calculate z-score to standardize the spread
20.     zscore = (spread - np.mean(spread)) / np.std(spread)
21.
22.     # Define entry and exit thresholds for trading signals
23.     entry_threshold = 1.0  # Buy signal when z-score > 1.0
24.     exit_threshold = 0.0   # Exit position when |z-score| < 0.1
25.
26.     # Initialize trading positions
27.     stock1_position = 0
28.     stock2_position = 0
29.     positions = []
30.
31.     # Iterate through the data to generate trading signals
32.     for z in zscore:
33.         if z > entry_threshold and stock1_position <= 0:
34.             stock1_position = 1   # Buy Stock1
35.             stock2_position = -1  # Short Stock2
36.         elif z < -entry_threshold and stock1_position >= 0:
37.             stock1_position = -1  # Short Stock1
```

```
38.            stock2_position = 1    # Buy Stock2
39.        elif abs(z) < exit_threshold:
40.            stock1_position = 0    # Exit Stock1 position
41.            stock2_position = 0    # Exit Stock2 position
42.
43.        positions.append((stock1_position, stock2_position))
44.
45. # Now, you have a list of trading positions based on the pairs trading strategy
46. # You can use these positions to calculate returns, portfolio value, etc.
```

This Python code performs a pairs trading strategy for two correlated stocks using cointegration analysis. It loads historical price data for the two stocks, calculates the cointegration p-value between them, and sets a threshold for cointegration (for example, 0.05). If cointegration is significant, it proceeds to implement the strategy. The code calculates the spread between the two stocks, standardizes it using a z-score, and defines entry and exit thresholds for trading signals. It then iterates through the data, generating trading positions based on the z-score. These positions represent whether to buy, short, or exit positions for each stock. This code provides a framework for pairs trading based on cointegration analysis, allowing for further analysis of returns and portfolio management.

Trend Following strategy

The **Trend Following** strategy is a widely used trading approach that aims to profit from existing price trends in financial markets. This strategy is based on the belief that assets tend to continue moving in the same direction for a certain period after a trend has been established. The key idea is to buy when the price is rising (indicating an uptrend) and sell when the price is falling (indicating a downtrend).

Following is a Python code example for a simple Trend Following strategy using moving averages. In this example, we calculate the 50-day and 200-day moving averages of a hypothetical stock's price. When the 50-day moving average crosses above the 200-day moving average, it generates a **buy** signal, and when it crosses below, it generates a **sell** signal:

```
1. import pandas as pd
2. import numpy as np
3.
4. # Load historical price data for a stock (hypothetical data)
5. data = pd.read_csv('stock_prices.csv', index_col='Date', parse_dates=True)
6.
7. # Calculate the 50-day and 200-day moving averages
```

```
8. data['MA_50'] = data['Close'].rolling(window=50).mean()
9. data['MA_200'] = data['Close'].rolling(window=200).mean()
10.
11. # Generate buy and sell signals based on moving average crossovers
12. data['Signal'] = 0    # Initialize signal column
13.
14. # When the 50-day MA crosses above the 200-day MA, generate a "buy" signal
15. data.loc[data['MA_50'] > data['MA_200'], 'Signal'] = 1
16.
17. # When the 50-day MA crosses below the 200-day MA, generate a "sell" signal
18. data.loc[data['MA_50'] < data['MA_200'], 'Signal'] = -1
19.
20. # Implement position changes based on signals (buy, sell, or hold)
21. data['Position'] = data['Signal'].diff()   # Calculate position changes
22.
```

This Python code analyzes historical stock price data by calculating both 50-day and 200-day moving averages. It generates buy and sell signals based on moving average crossovers. Specifically, when the 50-day **moving average (MA)** crosses above the 200-day MA, a *buy* signal is generated, and when the 50-day MA crosses below the 200-day MA, a *sell* signal is generated. To implement these signals, the code initializes a `Signal` column with zeros and then updates it according to the crossover conditions. The `Position` column is calculated as the difference in signals, indicating changes in the trading position (buy, sell, or hold) based on the crossovers. This code helps identify potential trend changes in stock prices.

Volatility Breakout strategy

The **Volatility Breakout** strategy is a trading approach that aims to capitalize on price breakouts when market volatility exceeds a certain threshold. The strategy assumes that periods of increased volatility often lead to significant price movements, and traders can profit by entering positions in the direction of the breakout.

This Python script is designed to analyze the historical volatility of a stock using hypothetical data and generate trading signals based on volatility breakouts. After loading the stock price data, the script computes the 20-day rolling standard deviation to measure volatility. It then sets a predefined threshold for volatility, using this benchmark to initiate buy signals when volatility is high and sell signals when it is low, aiming to capitalize on significant price movements driven by changes in volatility.

```
1. import pandas as pd
2. import numpy as np
```

```
3.
4. # Load historical price data for a stock (hypothetical data)
5. data = pd.read_csv('stock_prices.csv', index_col='Date', parse_
   dates=True)
6.
7. # Calculate historical volatility (e.g., 20-day rolling standard
   deviation)
8. data['Historical Volatility'] = data['Close'].rolling(window=20).
   std()
9.
10. # Define a volatility threshold (e.g., 0.02 or 2%)
11. volatility_threshold = 0.02
12.
13. # Generate buy and sell signals based on volatility breakouts
14. data['Signal'] = 0  # Initialize signal column
15.
16. # When historical volatility exceeds the threshold, generate a "buy"
    signal
17. data.loc[data['Historical Volatility'] > volatility_threshold,
    'Signal'] = 1
18.
19. # When historical volatility falls below the threshold, generate a
    "sell" signal
20. data.loc[data['Historical Volatility'] < volatility_threshold,
    'Signal'] = -1
```

This Python code analyzes historical stock price data and calculates historical volatility using a 20-day rolling standard deviation. It then generates buy and sell signals based on volatility breakouts. The code defines a **Historical Volatility** column to store the calculated values and sets a volatility threshold, for example, 0.02 (or 2%). It initializes a **Signal** column with zeros and updates it based on whether historical volatility exceeds or falls below the threshold. When historical volatility surpasses the threshold, a *buy* signal is generated, and when it drops below the threshold, a *sell* signal is generated. This code aims to identify periods of increased or decreased price volatility as potential trading signals.

Machine learning-based strategy

Machine learning-based trading strategies leverage predictive models to make trading decisions. In this example, we will use a simple decision tree classifier as the predictive model. Decision trees are versatile and interpretable machine learning algorithms that can be used for classification tasks, such as predicting whether to buy, sell, or hold a financial instrument.

Following Python script utilizes a machine learning approach to develop a trading strategy by predicting buy and sell signals based on historical stock data. After loading the data, the script extracts relevant features, such as technical indicators, and labels them with corresponding trading signals. The data is then divided into training and testing sets. A decision tree classifier is trained on the training set to learn the patterns associated with different trading signals, and finally, the model is used to make predictions on the testing set to evaluate its performance in real-world scenarios.

```
1. import pandas as pd
2. from sklearn.tree import DecisionTreeClassifier
3. from sklearn.model_selection import train_test_split
4.
5. # Load historical price and feature data (hypothetical data)
6. data = pd.read_csv('stock_data.csv', index_col='Date', parse_dates=True)
7.
8. # Create features (e.g., technical indicators) and labels (trading signals)
9. X = data[['Feature1', 'Feature2', 'Feature3']]  # Features
10. y = data['Signal']  # Trading signals (0 for hold, 1 for buy, -1 for sell)
11.
12. # Split data into training and testing sets
13. X_train, X_test, y_train, y_test = train_test_split(X, y, test_size=0.2, random_state=42)
14.
15. # Train a decision tree classifier
16. model = DecisionTreeClassifier()
17. model.fit(X_train, y_train)
18.
19. # Make predictions on the testing set
20. predictions = model.predict(X_test)
```

This Python code implements a machine learning-based approach for generating stock trading signals using a Decision Tree Classifier. It begins by loading historical price data and associated features from a CSV file. The features, representing technical indicators, are stored in **X**, while the trading signals, which indicate whether to buy (1), sell (-1), or hold (0) a stock, are stored in **y**. The data is then divided into training and testing sets, allocating 80% for training and 20% for testing, with a specific random seed for consistency. A Decision Tree Classifier is created and trained using the training data. Subsequently, the model is used to make predictions on the testing set, generating trading signals based on the learned patterns in the historical data. This approach leverages machine learning to automate the decision-making process for stock trading, potentially aiding investors in making informed decisions based on historical features and patterns.

Options trading strategy

Options trading involves using financial derivative instruments called **options contracts** to create various trading strategies. One such strategy is the **covered call** strategy. In a covered call strategy, an investor holds a long position in an asset (usually a stock) and simultaneously sells a call option on that asset. This strategy is used to generate income from the premium received for selling the call option while still benefiting from potential stock price appreciation.

This Python script focuses on combining stock and options data to analyze the financial outcomes of a covered call trading strategy. After loading hypothetical price data for a stock and associated options, the script calculates the net payoff of the options at expiration, taking into account the premiums paid. It then assesses the overall value of a portfolio that includes both the stock and the covered option positions, providing insights into the financial performance of this investment strategy.

```
1. import pandas as pd
2.
3. # Load historical price data for a stock and options data
   (hypothetical data)
4. stock_data = pd.read_csv('stock_prices.csv', index_col='Date',
   parse_dates=True)
5. options_data = pd.read_csv('options_data.csv', index_col='Date',
   parse_dates=True)
6.
7. # Calculate option payoff at expiration
8. options_data['Option Payoff'] = options_data['Call Option Payoff'] -
   options_data['Premium Paid']
9.
10. # Calculate total portfolio value including the covered call
    position
11. portfolio_value = stock_data['Close'] + options_data['Option Payoff']
```

In this Python code snippet, historical price data for a stock and options data are loaded from separate CSV files. The stock price data, represented by **stock_data**, includes information about the stock's closing prices over time. The options data, denoted as **options_data**, likely contains details about call options, including their payoffs and the premiums paid for them. The code then computes the option payoff at expiration by subtracting the **Premium Paid** from the **Call Option Payoff** and stores this result in the **Option Payoff** column within the options data. Additionally, it calculates the total portfolio value, incorporating the covered call position, by adding the closing prices of the stock to the `Option Payoff` from the options data. This code aids in assessing the overall performance of a portfolio that combines stock holdings and covered call options, providing insights into how the covered calls impact the portfolio's value over time.

Troubleshooting and debugging

In the world of algorithmic trading, where milliseconds can mean the difference between profit and loss, ensuring the robustness and reliability of your trading algorithms is paramount. This section explores some common issues that traders and developers encounter when building and deploying trading algorithms and offers practical solutions to address these challenges.

Latency and execution timing

One of the most critical issues in algorithmic trading is **latency**, or the delay between sending an order and its execution. For example, imagine you have developed a high-frequency trading algorithm to capitalize on price discrepancies. If your algorithm encounters delays, it may miss out on profitable opportunities. To mitigate this, developers employ various techniques, such as optimizing code execution, minimizing network latency, and employing hardware acceleration, to ensure that their algorithms react swiftly to market changes. Using Python, developers can leverage libraries like NumPy and Cython to optimize code execution and reduce latency significantly.

Latency, *the time delay between sending an order and its execution*, is a critical concern in algorithmic trading, especially in **high-frequency trading** (**HFT**) strategies where milliseconds can make a substantial difference in profitability. To address this challenge, traders and developers implement various strategies and techniques to minimize latency and ensure their algorithms can respond swiftly to market changes:

- **Optimizing code execution**: One of the primary ways to reduce latency is by optimizing the algorithm's code execution. In Python, developers can use libraries like NumPy and Cython to improve the performance of computationally intensive parts of their code. NumPy allows for efficient array and matrix operations, which are common in trading algorithms. Cython, on the other hand, enables developers to write C-like code that can be seamlessly integrated with Python, offering significant performance gains.

- **Minimizing network latency**: Network latency can significantly impact the speed of order execution. Traders often use co-location services, where their trading servers are physically located near the exchange's data center, to reduce network latency. Additionally, they may employ high-speed data feeds and dedicated communication lines to further minimize delays.

- **Employing hardware acceleration**: Hardware acceleration involves using specialized hardware, such as **Field-Programmable Gate Arrays** (**FPGAs**) or

Graphics Processing Units (GPUs), to offload and accelerate certain calculations. These hardware devices are capable of parallel processing and can dramatically reduce execution times for specific tasks within the trading algorithm.

This Python script demonstrates the utilization of GPU computing with PyCUDA to perform high-speed parallel computations. By initializing GPU settings and transferring data from the CPU to the GPU, the script efficiently executes arithmetic operations on the data array. The results are then transferred back to the CPU, showcasing the significant performance gains achievable through GPU acceleration in data-intensive tasks.

```
1.   # Utilizing GPU for parallel processing in Python with libraries like PyCUDA
2.   import pycuda.autoinit
3.   import pycuda.gpuarray as gpuarray
4.   import numpy as np
5.
6.   # Transfer data to GPU
7.   data = np.array([1.0, 2.0, 3.0])
8.   gpu_data = gpuarray.to_gpu(data)
9.
10.  # Perform parallel computation on GPU
11.  result = 2 * gpu_data
12.
13.  # Transfer result back to CPU if needed
14.  result_cpu = result.get()
15.
```

By employing these techniques, traders and developers can ensure that their algorithmic trading systems react swiftly to market changes, reducing the risk of missing out on profitable opportunities due to latency. However, it is essential to strike a balance between optimization and maintainability, as overly complex optimizations can make the code less readable and harder to maintain over time. Additionally, thorough testing and monitoring are crucial to verify the effectiveness of latency-reduction strategies and maintain the reliability of the trading algorithm.

Market data quality and cleansing

Another common issue arises from the quality of market data. Inaccurate or inconsistent data can lead to flawed trading decisions. Traders must implement data cleansing and validation procedures to ensure that their algorithms work with reliable information. For instance, using Python and the pandas library, traders can filter out erroneous data points and handle missing data through interpolation or data imputation techniques. It ensures that their algorithms base decisions on trustworthy information.

Slippage and order execution

Slippage is a common issue in algorithmic trading where the execution price of an order deviates from the expected price, often leading to reduced profits or increased losses. This phenomenon is primarily caused by market volatility and insufficient liquidity. Slippage occurs when the execution price of an order differs from the expected price, often due to market volatility or insufficient liquidity. This can erode profits or amplify losses. Traders commonly address slippage by incorporating intelligent order routing algorithms and using limit and stop orders strategically. Python provides libraries like **pyAlgoTrade** and **ccxt** that allow traders to implement sophisticated order execution strategies and minimize slippage.

To mitigate slippage and ensure that trading algorithms execute orders as closely as possible to the desired price, traders employ several strategies and techniques, often facilitated by Python libraries such as **pyAlgoTrade** and **ccxt**.

Intelligent order routing algorithms

Intelligent order routing algorithms aim to minimize slippage by efficiently routing orders to various market centers and liquidity providers. These algorithms assess the current market conditions, order book depth, and historical execution data to determine the optimal execution venue for a given order. By selecting the most suitable venue, traders can increase the likelihood of executing orders at desired prices.

Following Python script showcases the implementation of an intelligent order routing strategy designed to mitigate slippage during trading. By leveraging the **PyAlgoTrade** library, the script defines a **SlippageMitigationStrategy** class that integrates a SMA with fixed slippage settings. The strategy assesses current market conditions and utilizes historical data to make informed decisions about order execution, aiming to secure more favorable prices and reduce transaction costs:

```
1.   from pyalgotrade import strategy, broker
2.   from pyalgotrade.technical import ma
3.
4.   class SlippageMitigationStrategy(strategy.BacktestingStrategy):
5.       def __init__(self, feed, instrument, smaPeriod):
6.           super(SlippageMitigationStrategy, self).__init__(feed, broker.backtesting.FixedSlippage(0.001))
7.           self.__sma = ma.SMA(feed[instrument].getPriceDataSeries(), smaPeriod)
8.
9.       # Implement trading logic here
10.
11.  # Create a strategy instance and run it
```

Limit and stop orders

Traders often use limit and stop orders strategically to control the execution price and minimize slippage. A limit order specifies the maximum price at which an asset can be bought (for buy orders) or sold (for sell orders). Conversely, a stop order is used to trigger a market order when a specified price level is reached. These order types allow traders to set precise entry and exit points, reducing the impact of slippage.

The Python script demonstrates how to interact with cryptocurrency markets using the CCXT library, a popular tool for trading cryptocurrencies programmatically. The script initializes a connection to the Binance exchange, setting appropriate rate limits to manage API usage. It then proceeds to place a limit order to buy Bitcoin, specifying both the amount and the desired price, showcasing a straightforward example of executing cryptocurrency trades through code:

```
1.   import ccxt
2.   # Create a CCXT exchange instance
3.   exchange = ccxt.binance({
4.       'rateLimit': 1500,
5.       'enableRateLimit': True,
6.   })
7.
8.   # Place a limit order to buy Bitcoin at a specific price
9.   exchange.create_limit_buy_order('BTC/USDT', 1, 50000)
```

Algorithmic position sizing: Properly sizing trading positions can also help mitigate slippage. By calculating the appropriate position size based on factors like risk tolerance, account size, and expected slippage, traders can ensure that their orders align with their risk management strategy. Python's mathematical libraries, such as NumPy, are useful for implementing position sizing algorithms:

```
1.   import numpy as np
2.
3.   # Calculate position size based on risk percentage
4.   account_balance = 100000   # $100,000
5.   risk_percentage = 0.02   # 2% risk per trade
6.   stop_loss_percentage = 98   # Desired stop-loss price
7.   position_size = (account_balance * risk_percentage) / (100 * (100 - stop_loss_percentage))
```

The calculates the position size by first determining the dollar amount the trader is willing to risk, which is the product of the account balance and the risk percentage. The stop-loss percentage is then converted into a decimal by dividing by 100. By dividing the risk amount by this decimal, the appropriate position size in dollars is obtained. For instance, with an account balance of $100,000, a risk percentage of 2%, and a stop-loss percentage of 2%, the risk amount is $100,000 multiplied by 0.02, resulting in $2,000. The stop-loss as a decimal is 2 divided by 100, equaling 0.02. Consequently, the position size is $2,000 divided by 0.02, which equals $100,000. Thus, with a 2% stop-loss, the trader can allocate $100,000 for the trade while risking 2% of the account balance on the stop-loss.

By incorporating these strategies and utilizing Python libraries tailored to algorithmic trading, traders can effectively address slippage issues and enhance the precision of order execution. It is important to continually monitor and adapt these techniques to changing market conditions and the specific requirements of the trading strategy, as slippage can vary widely across different asset classes and trading venues.

Algorithmic logic errors

Logic errors can be costly, a missing **if** statement or a misconfigured parameter can lead to unintended consequences. To prevent logic errors, rigorous testing and debugging are essential. Python's testing frameworks, such as **pytest**, and debugging tools like **pdb**, help traders identify and rectify logic errors effectively. By writing comprehensive unit tests and using debugging tools, traders can ensure that their algorithms behave as intended, reducing the risk of financial losses.

Overfitting and model selection

Overfitting occurs when a trading algorithm fits noise in the data rather than the underlying patterns, resulting in poor generalization to unseen data. The challenge is to strike a balance between complexity and performance. Python offers machine learning libraries like scikit-learn that assist traders in implementing robust model selection techniques, such as cross-validation and hyperparameter tuning. These practices help ensure that trading algorithms generalize well to different market conditions and do not overfit historical data.

Handling overfitting is a critical concern when developing algorithmic trading strategies. Overfitting occurs when a trading algorithm becomes too specific to historical data, capturing noise and idiosyncrasies rather than true underlying patterns. This can lead to poor performance when the strategy encounters unseen data, such as future market conditions.

To address overfitting and make informed model selections, traders and developers can utilize various techniques and Python libraries, such as scikit-learn, that facilitate robust model evaluation and selection. Here is a step-by-step approach to handling overfitting and ensuring your trading algorithm generalizes well:

1. **Data splitting**: Begin by dividing your historical data into three subsets: training data, validation data, and test data. The training data is used to train your trading model, the validation data is used to fine-tune model parameters, and the test data is reserved for final evaluation.

Script illustrates a common approach to splitting a dataset into training, validation, and testing sets using the `train_test_split` function from Scikit-learn. Initially, the dataset is divided into training and temporary subsets; subsequently, the temporary subset is further split equally to form the final validation and test sets. This method ensures that the model can be trained, validated, and tested on distinct data segments, facilitating robust evaluation and optimization of machine learning models.

1. from sklearn.model_selection import train_test_split
2.
3. X_train, X_temp, y_train, y_temp = train_test_split(X, y, test_size=0.3, random_state=42)
4. X_validation, X_test, y_validation, y_test = train_test_split(X_temp, y_temp, test_size=0.5, random_state=42)

2. **Cross-validation:** Implement k-fold cross-validation on the training data. This technique divides the training data into k subsets, trains the model on k-1 subsets, and validates it on the remaining subset. This process is repeated k times, and the average performance is used for model evaluation.

This Python script demonstrates the application of 5-fold cross-validation to evaluate the performance of a machine learning model using the **cross_val_score** function from Scikit-learn. The script calculates the model's accuracy or other specified metrics by partitioning the training data into five subsets, systematically using each subset as a test set while training the model on the remaining four. This approach helps in assessing the model's effectiveness and stability across different data segments.

1. from sklearn.model_selection import cross_val_score
2. scores = cross_val_score(model, X_train, y_train, cv=5) # 5-fold cross-validation

3. **Hyperparameter tuning:** Optimize your trading model's hyperparameters using techniques like grid search or random search. Hyperparameters control the model's behavior and tuning them effectively can improve generalization.

Following script utilizes the **GridSearchCV** module from Scikit-learn to optimize a machine learning model by searching across a predefined grid of parameters. By defining multiple values for different model parameters and employing 5-fold cross-validation, the script systematically evaluates each combination of parameters to identify the one that yields the best performance. The optimal parameter set is then extracted and can be used to enhance model accuracy and efficiency.

1. from sklearn.model_selection import GridSearchCV
2.
3. param_grid = {'parameter1': [value1, value2], 'parameter2': [value3, value4]}

```
4. grid_search = GridSearchCV(model, param_grid, cv=5)
5. grid_search.fit(X_train, y_train)
6. best_params = grid_search.best_params_
```

4. **Model selection:** Select the best-performing model based on cross-validation results and hyperparameter tuning. This model is expected to generalize well to unseen data.

Script extracts the best-performing model from a grid search conducted using Scikit-learn's **GridSearchCV**. After evaluating multiple parameter combinations to determine which yields the highest accuracy, the script retrieves the optimal model configuration, known as **best_estimator_**, allowing for further application and analysis in predictive tasks.

```
1. best_model = grid_search.best_estimator_
```

5. **Evaluate on test data:** Finally, assess your selected model's performance on the test data, which simulates how it will behave in real trading conditions.

Following Python snippet demonstrates the evaluation of a machine learning model's performance on a test dataset. Using the **best_model** obtained from a previous grid search, the script calculates the accuracy by comparing the model's predictions against the actual outcomes in the **y_test** dataset, providing a clear measure of how well the model generalizes to new, unseen data.

```
1. test_accuracy = best_model.score(X_test, y_test)
```

By following these steps and leveraging Python libraries like scikit-learn, you can effectively handle overfitting and select trading models that are less likely to perform poorly in live trading due to overly tailored behavior. This approach promotes the creation of more robust and adaptable algorithmic trading strategies.

Unit testing and code quality

Algorithmic trading strategies often comprise intricate mathematical models and sophisticated AI techniques. The accuracy of these strategies directly impacts trading outcomes. Therefore, any coding error, no matter how minor, can lead to substantial financial losses. To mitigate this risk, unit testing plays a central role. Unit tests are designed to meticulously scrutinize individual components or functions of the codebase, verifying their correctness. Beyond unit testing, integration testing becomes crucial in assessing how different parts of the trading system interact with one another. It ensures that data flows seamlessly between data acquisition modules, risk management components, and trading strategy modules. Integration tests are essential for detecting any communication issues or data inconsistencies that might compromise the system's performance.

Furthermore, end-to-end testing simulates real-world trading scenarios, allowing traders to validate the complete functionality of the trading system from data ingestion to order execution. These comprehensive testing approaches serve as a safety net, catching potential issues before they impact live trading.

Python unit testing tools

Python offers several powerful tools for unit testing, two of the most prominent being **unittest** and **pytest**.

unittest is Python's built-in testing framework that supports a test-driven development approach. It allows developers to construct detailed test cases and suites, incorporating a variety of assertion methods *to check for expected outcomes*. On the other hand, **pytest** is renowned for its simplicity and efficiency, appealing particularly to those who seek a more expressive and less boilerplate codebase for testing. Unlike **unittest**, which relies on a class-based structure, **pytest** allows for simpler function-based test cases that are easy to write and read. The framework provides powerful features like fixtures for setup and teardown, hooks for enhancing test reports, and a vast ecosystem of plugins to extend its functionality. This flexibility makes **pytest** a favored choice among developers for both simple and complex testing scenarios.

unittest

unittest, Python's built-in testing framework, is a robust tool for creating and executing unit tests. It provides a structured and organized approach to writing tests, enabling developers to create test cases, test suites, and assertions [103]. For instance, within a trading algorithm project, one can use **unittest** to define test cases that scrutinize individual functions. Here is a simplified example:

```
1.  import unittest
2.
3.  def calculate_moving_average(data, window_size):
4.      if window_size <= 0 or window_size > len(data):
5.          raise ValueError("Invalid window size")
6.
7.      moving_averages = []
8.      for i in range(len(data) - window_size + 1):
9.          window = data[i:i+window_size]
10.         average = sum(window) / window_size
11.         moving_averages.append(average)
12.
13.     return moving_averages
14.
15. class TestMovingAverage(unittest.TestCase):
```

```
16.    def test_calculate_moving_average(self):
17.        data = [1, 2, 3, 4, 5]
18.        window_size = 3
19.        expected_result = [2.0, 3.0, 4.0]
20.        self.assertEqual(calculate_moving_average(data, window_size), expected_result)
21.
22. if __name__ == '__main__':
23.    unittest.main()
```

In this example, we create a test case called **TestMovingAverage** that checks if the **calculate_moving_average** function correctly computes a moving average. **unittest** provides various assertion methods like **assertEqual**, **assertTrue**, and **assertRaises** to validate the code's behavior.

pytest

pytest is another powerful Python testing framework known for its simplicity and flexibility [104]. It allows traders and developers to write concise and expressive test cases. Unlike unittest, which requires classes and specific naming conventions, pytest allows for more straightforward test function definitions. Here is how the same moving average test would look in pytest:

```
1.  import unittest
2.
3.  def calculate_moving_average(data):
4.      # Implementation of moving average calculation
5.      # ...
6.
7.  class TestMovingAverage(unittest.TestCase):
8.      def test_calculate_moving_average(self):
9.          data = [1, 2, 3, 4, 5]
10.         expected_result = 3.0
11.         self.assertEqual(calculate_moving_average(data), expected_result)
12.
13. if __name__ == '__main__':
14.     unittest.main()
```

In this concise syntax, pytest automatically discovers and runs test functions, making it a popular choice for developers aiming to write clear and maintainable test code.

Code quality tools

Code quality tools are essential components of the software development process, ensuring that trading algorithms are not only functionally correct but also well-structured and maintainable.

flake8

flake8 is a popular Python tool for checking code quality and enforcing coding standards [105]. It performs static code analysis to identify issues such as style violations, syntax errors, and potential bugs. In the context of algorithmic trading, adhering to coding standards is crucial for maintaining code readability and consistency, especially when multiple traders or developers collaborate on a project. For example, using `flake8`, traders can ensure that their Python code adheres to the PEP 8 style guide, making it more accessible and maintainable for the entire team.

black

`black`, often referred to as *The Uncompromising Code Formatter*, is another code quality tool that focuses on code formatting and style [106]. It automatically reformats Python code to conform to a consistent and well-defined style guide, effectively eliminating debates about code formatting within a development team. In the context of algorithmic trading, where code reliability and speed are paramount, consistent code formatting helps avoid errors caused by inconsistent indentation or spacing.

isort

`isort`, short for **import sorting**, is a tool that helps maintain organized and clean import statements in Python code [107]. In trading algorithms, where numerous libraries and modules are often imported, well-structured import statements can enhance code clarity and maintainability. `isort` ensures that imports are sorted consistently, making it easier to locate specific modules and manage dependencies efficiently.

Let us illustrate the importance of these code quality tools with a practical example. Consider a trading algorithm project where multiple developers contribute code. Without consistent coding standards and formatting, the codebase becomes challenging to read and maintain. By integrating `flake8`, `black`, and `isort` into the project's development pipeline, traders and developers can automatically enforce coding standards, format the code uniformly, and organize imports, thereby ensuring that code quality remains high and development workflows are streamlined.

Code quality tools such as `flake8`, `black`, and `isort` are essential in the development of High-Performance Algorithmic Trading using AI. These tools not only enhance code quality and readability but also promote consistency and collaboration within trading algorithm projects. By incorporating these tools into the development process, traders and developers can focus on fine-tuning trading strategies rather than grappling with code style and formatting issues.

Performance optimization and parallelization

Optimizing trading algorithms is not just a luxury but an absolute necessity in today's competitive financial markets.

The primary driving force behind optimization is the need for speed. In algorithmic trading, where decisions must be made in milliseconds or microseconds, every fraction of a second counts. A well-optimized trading algorithm can execute orders faster, seize opportunities swiftly, and reduce exposure to market risks. For instance, consider a Python trading algorithm that processes market data, generates trading signals, and sends orders to execute a trade. Optimizing the code can reduce the time it takes for these operations, allowing the algorithm to act on market movements more efficiently.

Efficiency is another critical aspect. Efficient algorithms consume fewer computational resources, such as CPU and memory, enabling traders to run more sophisticated strategies simultaneously. In Python, this might involve optimizing data processing pipelines, using efficient data structures, or parallelizing computations to take full advantage of modern multicore processors. For example, Python's **pandas** library provides powerful tools for optimizing data manipulation operations, enhancing algorithmic trading strategies.

Additionally, cost reduction is a significant factor. Trading algorithms operating in the cloud or data centers often incur costs based on resource usage. Optimized algorithms consume fewer resources, translating into reduced infrastructure costs. Traders can save substantial amounts by minimizing resource consumption through code optimization techniques such as memory management and algorithmic efficiency improvements.

Profiling Python code

Profiling is an indispensable process that empowers traders and developers to identify performance bottlenecks, thereby enhancing trading algorithms' speed and efficiency. One of the most fundamental tools for profiling Python code is **cProfile** [103]. **cProfile** is a built-in Python profiler that provides detailed insights into the execution time of each function or method within a program. In the context of algorithmic trading, where microseconds can make a significant difference, **cProfile** plays a pivotal role in identifying which parts of the code consume the most CPU time. For example, if a trading algorithm includes a function responsible for processing and analyzing historical market data, **cProfile** can reveal the exact time spent on this data processing task. Armed with this information, traders can prioritize their optimization efforts on the most time-consuming functions to achieve significant performance gains.

Visualization with **snakeviz** [108] is an invaluable companion to **cProfile**. While **cProfile** provides raw data, **snakeviz** offers a graphical representation of profiling results, making it easier to pinpoint bottlenecks and understand the code's performance characteristics. By visualizing profiling data, traders can gain deeper insights into how different functions interact and which ones are the most time-consuming. This visual representation simplifies the identification of critical areas for optimization.

Following is a sample Python code snippet demonstrating how to use **cProfile** and **snakeviz** for profiling and visualizing the performance of a trading algorithm. In this example, we will consider a simplified trading algorithm that generates random trading signals:

```
1.  import cProfile
2.  import pstats
3.  import random
4.  import snakeviz
5.
6.  def generate_random_signals(num_signals):
7.      signals = []
8.      for _ in range(num_signals):
9.          signals.append(random.choice(['Buy', 'Sell', 'Hold']))
10.     return signals
11.
12. def simulate_trading(signals):
13.     # Simulate trading logic here
14.     # For demonstration, we'll just print the signals
15.     for signal in signals:
16.         print(f"Trading signal: {signal}")
17.
18. def main():
19.     num_signals = 1000000
20.     signals = generate_random_signals(num_signals)
21.
22.     # Profile the code using cProfile
23.     profiler = cProfile.Profile()
24.     profiler.enable()
25.     simulate_trading(signals)
26.     profiler.disable()
27.
28.     # Save profiling results to a file
29.     profiler.dump_stats('trading_algorithm.prof')
```

```
30.
31.    # Visualize the profiling results with snakeviz
32.    p = pstats.Stats('trading_algorithm.prof')
33.    p.strip_dirs().sort_stats('cumulative').print_stats()
34.    snakeviz.view('trading_algorithm.prof')
35.
36. if __name__ == "__main__":
37.    main()
```

Profiling and visualizing code in this manner can help traders and developers identify areas of the algorithm that may benefit from optimization, enabling them to make data-driven decisions to improve performance.

Parallel processing

One of the primary tools at the disposal of Python developers for parallel processing is the **multiprocessing** library[103]. Multiprocessing enables traders to execute multiple tasks simultaneously, leveraging the full computational capacity of multicore CPUs. This is particularly advantageous in trading scenarios where real-time data analysis, signal generation, and order execution must occur concurrently. For example, consider a trading algorithm that processes market data, runs complex analytics, and manages multiple trading strategies. By employing multiprocessing, traders can distribute these tasks across different CPU cores, resulting in faster decision-making and execution:

```
1. import multiprocessing
2.
3. def load_market_data():
4.     # Load your market data here
5.     return market_data
6.
7. def process_market_data(data):
8.     # Process market data here
9.     # ...
10.    return processed_data
11.
12. def analyze_data(data):
13.    # Analyze data here
14.    # ...
15.
16. if __name__ == "__main__":
17.    # Load market data outside of the Pool
```

```
18.     data = load_market_data()
19.
20.     # Create a multiprocessing Pool with 4 processes
21.     with multiprocessing.Pool(processes=4) as pool:
22.         # Apply the process_market_data function asynchronously
23.         processed_data = pool.apply_async(process_market_data, (data,))
24.
25.         # Apply the analyze_data function asynchronously
26.         analysis_result = pool.apply_async(analyze_data, (data,))
27.
28.         # Get the results when they are ready
29.         processed_data_result = processed_data.get()
30.         analysis_result = analysis_result.get()
31.
32.     # You can now use the processed_data_result and analysis_result as needed
```

Another parallelization approach involves using the threading library. While multiprocessing enables true parallelism by creating separate processes, threading achieves concurrency by creating lightweight threads that share the same process. In scenarios where trading algorithms involve tasks with a high degree of I/O operations, such as fetching data from external sources, threading can be a more suitable choice. For instance, fetching real-time market data or processing incoming trade orders can benefit from threading to ensure efficient multitasking:

```
1.  import threading
2.
3.  def fetch_market_data(symbol):
4.      # Fetch market data for a specific symbol
5.      # ...
6.
7.  def execute_trade_order(order):
8.      # Execute a trade order
9.      # ...
10.
11. if __name__ == "__main__":
12.     symbols = get_trading_symbols()
13.
```

```
14.     # Start a thread for each symbol to fetch market data
   concurrently
15.     for symbol in symbols:
16.         thread = threading.Thread(target=fetch_market_data,
   args=(symbol,))
17.         thread.start()
18.
19.     # Meanwhile, in the same program, execute trade orders
20.     execute_trade_order(trade_order)
```

Traders can harness the computational power of modern hardware to accelerate data analysis, signal generation, and order execution. By strategically employing parallelization techniques, trading algorithms can swiftly react to market dynamics, enhancing their competitiveness and profitability in today's dynamic financial markets.

Python best practices for algorithmic trading

Python Enhancement Proposal 8 (PEP 8) serves as the guiding light for Python's coding style [109]. In algorithmic trading development, the adoption of PEP 8 is instrumental in maintaining code readability and consistency. Python's readability philosophy, often summarized as **readability counts**, underscores the significance of clean and well-structured code, especially in the fast-paced environment of algorithmic trading.

Consider a trading algorithm project involving multiple traders or developers collaborating on the same codebase. Without adherence to PEP 8, the code can quickly become a tangle of inconsistent indentation, variable naming, and code style choices. This can hinder collaboration, make code reviews cumbersome, and introduce opportunities for errors. By following PEP 8's recommendations, trading teams ensure that their codebase maintains a uniform style, which greatly enhances its maintainability and readability.

The `calculate_moving_average` function efficiently computes the average value from a list of data points by summing up the elements and dividing the total by the number of data points, providing a straightforward method to determine the central tendency of a dataset.

```
1. def calculate_moving_average(data_points):
2.     total = sum(data_points)
3.     count = len(data_points)
4.     return total / count
```

In addition to PEP 8, consistent naming conventions play a pivotal role in the development of trading algorithms. In the high-stakes world of algorithmic trading, where accuracy and reliability are paramount, well-chosen variable and function names can make the difference between a bug-free system and a costly error.

For instance, imagine a trading algorithm that employs complex mathematical models to predict market movements. By adopting clear and descriptive variable names such as **prediction_model** instead of vague names like **model1** or **xyz**, traders and developers can instantly grasp the purpose and function of each component. This clarity not only simplifies code maintenance but also reduces the risk of introducing errors during modifications or enhancements.

Robust documentation is like a map that guides developers and traders through the intricate landscape of a trading algorithm. In the world of algorithmic trading, where the stakes are high, accurate and comprehensive documentation is invaluable. It serves as a reference manual that details the algorithm's architecture, its components, data flows, and external dependencies. For example, consider a trading algorithm that utilizes machine learning models to make trading decisions. Comprehensive documentation can explain the model's architecture, data preprocessing steps, and the rationale behind hyperparameter choices. This empowers developers to understand and maintain the algorithm effectively.

Clear and concise comments within the code complement documentation by providing insights into the code's functionality and rationale. Comments help traders and developers understand the purpose of specific code blocks, algorithms, or complex mathematical operations. For example, in a trading algorithm that calculates technical indicators, well-placed comments can explain the mathematical formula being used, aiding not only in comprehension but also in debugging and future modifications.

Moreover, comments are vital for maintaining the algorithm over time. In the fast-paced world of algorithmic trading, where market conditions evolve rapidly, the ability to quickly understand and modify code is essential. Comments that provide insights into the logic behind trading decisions or adjustments to trading strategies empower traders to adapt their algorithms swiftly in response to changing market dynamics.

pip

pip, Python's package installer [103], stands as a cornerstone in managing project dependencies. In the world of algorithmic trading, where precise control over the versions of libraries and packages is essential, pip empowers traders and developers to specify and maintain dependencies effortlessly. For example, consider a trading algorithm that relies on specific versions of data analysis libraries like NumPy and pandas. By utilizing a **requirements.txt** file, traders can specify these versions, ensuring that the algorithm runs consistently regardless of the development environment.

conda

conda, on the other hand, is a versatile package manager used for managing not only Python packages but also packages from other programming languages and system-level dependencies [110]. In algorithmic trading development, where performance and stability are paramount, conda's ability to create isolated environments and handle complex dependencies is invaluable. For instance, traders can create a conda environment specifically tailored for their trading algorithm, including libraries for machine learning, data analysis, and visualization. This isolated environment ensures that the algorithm operates reliably, even when it relies on different versions of packages than the system-level Python installation.

The commands provided set up a dedicated Python environment using Conda, named **trading_environment**, which is specifically tailored for trading analysis. This environment is initialized with Python version 3.9 and includes essential libraries such as NumPy, pandas, and scikit-learn, ensuring a robust platform for data manipulation and machine learning tasks tailored to trading strategies.

1. `conda create --name trading_environment python=3.9`
2. `conda activate trading_environment`
3. `conda install numpy=1.21.0 pandas=1.3.1 scikit-learn=0.24.2`

virtualenv

virtualenv [111] offers a lightweight and efficient solution for creating isolated Python environments. In algorithmic trading, where multiple trading strategies may require different library versions, virtualenv enables traders to compartmentalize projects. Each virtual environment can have its own set of dependencies, preventing conflicts and ensuring that changes in one project do not affect the stability of others.

The instructions outline the process of creating and activating a Python virtual environment named **trading_strategy_A**, followed by the installation of a specific version of NumPy, ensuring an isolated and controlled setup for developing a trading strategy with precise dependency management.

1. `python -m venv trading_strategy_A`
2. `source trading_strategy_A/bin/activate`
3. `pip install numpy==1.20.0`

Robust dependency management, facilitated by tools like pip, conda, and virtualenv, is a vital component of Python best practices for algorithmic trading. These tools ensure that trading algorithms are executed in controlled environments with precisely defined dependencies, reducing the risk of unexpected issues due to package conflicts or version inconsistencies.

Effective API key management is a fundamental aspect of trading security. Trading algorithms often interact with various financial data providers, exchanges, and brokers through APIs. These APIs require authentication through API keys, which act as digital credentials. Failing to secure these keys can expose a trading algorithm to unauthorized access and potential financial losses.

Moreover, encryption plays a pivotal role in ensuring the confidentiality and integrity of data in algorithmic trading. Data encryption secures sensitive information such as trading strategies, account credentials, and transaction records. In Python, libraries like cryptography offer robust encryption and decryption capabilities. For example, traders can use cryptography to encrypt and store their trading algorithms securely.

Conclusion

As we wrap up this chapter, you have acquired a versatile skill set in Python for finance, spanning from foundational libraries to the intricacies of developing effective trading algorithms. The journey covered troubleshooting and debugging techniques, emphasized version control and collaboration through Git, instilled best practices in unit testing and code quality, and explored the nuances of performance optimization and parallelization.

Now, brace yourself for the next chapter where you can learn real-world examples and case studies.

Join our book's Discord space

Join the book's Discord Workspace for Latest updates, Offers, Tech happenings around the world, New Release and Sessions with the Authors:

https://discord.bpbonline.com

CHAPTER 9
Real-world Examples and Case Studies

Introduction

In this chapter, we will cover the real-world applications of the concepts explored thus far, bringing theoretical knowledge to life through compelling case studies. The introduction sets the stage, emphasizing the practical relevance of **artificial intelligence** (**AI**) in finance. The chapter is structured to provide a seamless flow, beginning with a comprehensive explanation of the topic at hand. The subsequent case studies serve as illuminating examples, covering diverse applications such as AI-enhanced momentum trading, machine learning for mean reversion, sentiment analysis for trading signals, portfolio optimization with AI, and AI-driven market-making strategies. These real-world scenarios not only illustrate the adaptability of AI in financial settings but also offer valuable insights for readers aiming to bridge the gap between theory and implementation.

Structure

In this chapter, we will go through the following topics:
- Case study 1: AI-enhanced momentum trading strategy
- Case study 2: Machine learning for mean reversion
- Case study 3: Sentiment analysis for trading signals
- Case study 4: Portfolio optimization with AI
- Case study 5: AI-driven market-making strategies

Objectives

In this chapter, our focus shifts from theory to practice as we explore the real-world applications of artificial intelligence in finance through a series of compelling case studies. The introduction sets the stage, highlighting the chapter's objective of providing tangible insights into the implementation of AI in financial scenarios. The chapter's structure ensures a coherent journey, beginning with a thorough explanation of the overarching topic. Subsequently, each case study serves as a distinct lens through which readers can gain a practical understanding of AI's impact on finance. From AI-enhanced momentum trading to machine learning for mean reversion, sentiment analysis for trading signals, portfolio optimization, and AI-driven market-making strategies, these diverse examples aim to offer a comprehensive view of the nuanced applications of AI in real-world financial contexts.

Case study 1: AI-enhanced momentum trading strategy

Momentum trading, rooted in the belief that past performers in the securities market will continue their success in the future, has long been a fundamental aspect of financial markets. AI, with its ability to swiftly analyze extensive datasets and identify subtle patterns, has elevated momentum trading to a new level of sophistication. A notable example is the application of AI to momentum trading by *Renaissance Technologies' Medallion Fund*, resulting in remarkable returns and demonstrating the effectiveness of algorithms in navigating intricate market dynamics [112].

An illustrative instance of the synergy between momentum trading and AI is the use of machine learning algorithms to identify market anomalies and forecast price movements. For example, *DeepMind's AlphaGo* algorithm achieved unprecedented success in the game of Go, attributed to its capacity to recognize patterns and formulate strategic moves, similar to the predictive skills required in momentum trading [115].

The introduction of reinforcement learning further enhances the capabilities of AI in the realm of momentum trading. Through ongoing engagement with financial markets, reinforcement learning algorithms can evolve and refine trading strategies over time. A notable illustration of this is seen in the achievements of Large Language Model OpenAI's DALL-E, employing reinforcement learning to generate images based on textual descriptions. This showcases the adaptability and creative potential that AI brings to seemingly unpredictable environments.

In practical applications, the use of AI-driven momentum trading strategies by the hedge fund Two Sigma stands out. By leveraging advanced machine learning models to analyze market trends and patterns, Two Sigma consistently outperforms traditional investment approaches. This highlights the tangible impact of AI on financial decision-making [58].

A notable challenge encountered by traditional momentum strategies is the inherent difficulty in capturing nuanced market dynamics. In the pursuit of identifying and leveraging momentum, these strategies often succumb to the limitations of human analysis, such as behavioral biases like overconfidence or herding behavior. By utilizing sophisticated algorithms, traders can better adapt to rapidly changing market conditions, addressing the shortcomings of traditional momentum strategies that struggle to keep pace with such dynamics.

Moreover, the integration of **natural language processing (NLP)** in algorithmic trading provides a solution to the challenge of information overload. Traditional momentum strategies often grapple with vast amounts of unstructured data generated by news articles, social media, and financial reports.

This chapter also explores the impact of market microstructure on momentum strategies, with *Hasbrouck's* (2007) research providing insights into the intricacies of market dynamics. Traditional momentum strategies may struggle to adapt to these microstructural nuances, making them susceptible to inefficiencies. Through the application of AI-driven algorithms, traders can navigate the complexities of market microstructure, enhancing the robustness of momentum strategies.

Data sourcing for momentum trading extends beyond traditional financial metrics. Let us explore examples of how some of these data sources can be used in a momentum trading strategy:

- **Historical price data**: Alpha Vantage **application programming interface (API)** provides access to historical stock prices, technical indicators, and other financial market data.

- **Market news**: News API allows developers to retrieve real-time and historical news articles from various sources, including financial news.

- **Social media data**: Twitter API provides access to tweets and trends, allowing for the analysis of social media sentiment related to specific stocks.

- **Financial reports: Electronic Data Gathering, Analysis, and Retrieval (EDGAR)** API provides access to financial statements and reports filed with the SEC.

- **Economic indicators: Federal Reserve Economic Data API (FRED API)** provides access to a wide range of economic data, including GDP, employment, and inflation rates.

- **Volume data**: Cloud API offers access to various financial market data, including trading volume, for stocks and other securities.

- **Volatility measures**: CBOE API provides access to options data, including the VIX (Volatility Index), which measures market volatility.

- **Technical indicators**: TA-Lib API provides functions for technical analysis, including the calculation of various indicators like RSI and moving averages.
- **Options data**: Alpha Vantage Options API provides access to options data, including open interest and implied volatility.
- **Market sentiment indices**: CNN Business does not provide a public API for the Fear and Greed Index directly. However, developers can use web scraping techniques to extract data from the index page.
- **Macro-economic events calendar**: Investing.com provides an Economic Calendar API, offering information about scheduled economic events.
- **Machine learning predictions**: Alpha Vantage API provides access to machine learning-based forecasts and predictions for stock prices.
- **Seasonal patterns**: NOAA provides historical weather data, and understanding how weather affects certain sectors can be incorporated into trading decisions.
- **Alternative data**: Quandl offers access to a variety of alternative datasets, including satellite imagery, consumer behavior data, and supply chain data.

A momentum trading strategy typically involves analyzing the past performance of assets to identify those with strong recent performance that is likely to continue. Let us create a simplified example of a DataFrame for momentum trading with some basic features:

```
1. import pandas as pd
2. import numpy as np
3. import random
4. 
5. # Generate some random data for demonstration purposes
6. np.random.seed(42)
7. random.seed(42)
8. 
9. # Create a date range
10. dates = pd.date_range(start='2023-01-01', end='2023-10-01', freq='B')
11. 
12. # Create a dataframe with random stock data
13. df = pd.DataFrame(index=dates)
14. 
15. # Generate random stock prices for three hypothetical stocks
16. df['Stock_A'] = np.random.randint(80, 120, size=len(dates)).astype(float)
```

```python
17. df['Stock_B'] = np.random.randint(50, 100, size=len(dates)).
    astype(float)
18. df['Stock_C'] = np.random.randint(100, 150, size=len(dates)).
    astype(float)
19.
20. # Add some random noise to simulate price fluctuations
21. df += np.random.normal(0, 2, size=(len(dates), 3))
22.
23. # Calculate daily returns
24. df['Returns_A'] = df['Stock_A'].pct_change()
25. df['Returns_B'] = df['Stock_B'].pct_change()
26. df['Returns_C'] = df['Stock_C'].pct_change()
27.
28. # Calculate 5-day and 20-day rolling averages
29. df['Rolling_Avg_5'] = df['Returns_A'].rolling(window=5).mean()
30. df['Rolling_Avg_20'] = df['Returns_A'].rolling(window=20).mean()
31.
32. df['Rolling_Avg_5_B'] = df['Returns_B'].rolling(window=5).mean()
33. df['Rolling_Avg_20_B'] = df['Returns_B'].rolling(window=20).mean()
34.
35. df['Rolling_Avg_5_C'] = df['Returns_C'].rolling(window=5).mean()
36. df['Rolling_Avg_20_C'] = df['Returns_C'].rolling(window=20).mean()
37.
38. # Create some random categorical signals for demonstration
39. df['Signal_A'] = np.where(df['Rolling_Avg_5'] > df['Rolling_
    Avg_20'], 1, 0)
40. df['Signal_B'] = np.where(df['Rolling_Avg_5_B'] > df['Rolling_
    Avg_20_B'], 1, 0)
41. df['Signal_C'] = np.where(df['Rolling_Avg_5_C'] > df['Rolling_
    Avg_20_C'], 1, 0)
42.
43. # Display the dataframe
44. print(df.head())
```

```
            Stock_A    Stock_B    Stock_C  Returns_A  Returns_B  \
2023-01-02  117.975506  69.205491  114.151609        NaN        NaN
2023-01-03  106.645677  61.950239  141.705885  -0.096035  -0.104836
2023-01-04   92.349006  96.357228  136.825863  -0.134058   0.555397
2023-01-05   85.872551  63.355559  132.487374  -0.070130  -0.342493
2023-01-06  100.489933  80.986114  106.057923   0.170222   0.278280

            Returns_C  Rolling_Avg_5  Rolling_Avg_20  Rolling_Avg_5_B  \
2023-01-02        NaN            NaN             NaN              NaN
2023-01-03   0.241383            NaN             NaN              NaN
2023-01-04  -0.034438            NaN             NaN              NaN
2023-01-05  -0.031708            NaN             NaN              NaN
2023-01-06  -0.199487            NaN             NaN              NaN

            Rolling_Avg_20_B  Rolling_Avg_5_C  Rolling_Avg_20_C  Signal_A  \
2023-01-02               NaN              NaN               NaN         0
2023-01-03               NaN              NaN               NaN         0
2023-01-04               NaN              NaN               NaN         0
2023-01-05               NaN              NaN               NaN         0
2023-01-06               NaN              NaN               NaN         0

            Signal_B  Signal_C
2023-01-02         0         0
2023-01-03         0         0
2023-01-04         0         0
2023-01-05         0         0
2023-01-06         0         0
```

Figure 9.1: Output of the Feature generation

The cornerstone of AI-driven momentum trading lies in the meticulous process of model training. To illustrate, consider the implementation of a **Long Short-Term Memory (LSTM)** neural network, a powerful tool for capturing sequential dependencies in time series data. In the context of momentum trading, LSTM networks excel at discerning patterns and trends within historical stock prices. By feeding the algorithm with relevant features such as price, volume, and technical indicators, the model learns to make informed predictions regarding future price movements.

The following Python script is designed to train a LSTM neural network to predict future stock prices based on historical data. This approach utilizes the **yfinance** library to dynamically download stock data from Yahoo Finance, making it convenient to access up-to-date and accurate financial information for various ticker symbols. The script includes preprocessing steps like data normalization and reshaping, setting up the LSTM model, and training it with the downloaded data. It is an effective tool for anyone looking to apply machine learning techniques in financial markets, offering a practical example of how to handle, process, and predict stock prices with deep learning.

```
1. # Sample Python Code for LSTM Model Training using Yahoo Finance
   data
2. !pip install yfinance  # Install yfinance package
3.
```

```
4.  import numpy as np
5.  import pandas as pd
6.  import yfinance as yf
7.  from sklearn.preprocessing import MinMaxScaler
8.  from tensorflow.keras.models import Sequential
9.  from tensorflow.keras.layers import LSTM, Dense
10.
11. # Download stock data from Yahoo Finance
12. ticker = "AAPL"  # Example: Apple Inc.
13. start_date = "2010-01-01"
14. end_date = "2020-01-01"
15. data = yf.download(ticker, start=start_date, end=end_date)
16.
17. # Check if 'Close' column is available
18. if 'Close' not in data.columns:
19.     raise ValueError("Data does not contain 'Close'. Please check the ticker and date range.")
20.
21. # Normalize the data
22. scaler = MinMaxScaler(feature_range=(0, 1))
23. scaled_data = scaler.fit_transform(data['Close'].values.reshape(-1, 1))
24.
25. # Prepare training data
26. training_data = scaled_data[:int(0.8*len(scaled_data))]
27. x_train, y_train = [], []
28. for i in range(60, len(training_data)):
29.     x_train.append(training_data[i-60:i, 0])
30.     y_train.append(training_data[i, 0])
31. x_train, y_train = np.array(x_train), np.array(y_train)
32. x_train = np.reshape(x_train, (x_train.shape[0], x_train.shape[1], 1))
33.
34. # Build and train the LSTM model
35. model = Sequential()
36. model.add(LSTM(units=50, return_sequences=True, input_shape=(x_train.shape[1], 1)))
37. model.add(LSTM(units=50, return_sequences=False))
38. model.add(Dense(units=25))
```

```
39. model.add(Dense(units=1))
40. model.compile(optimizer='adam', loss='mean_squared_error')
41. model.fit(x_train, y_train, epochs=10, batch_size=32)
42.
43. # Optionally, save the model
44. model.save('lstm_stock_model.h5')
```

Validation is the litmus test for the efficacy of our AI-enhanced momentum trading strategy. One approach involves using a separate set of data not seen by the model during training. In our case, historical stock prices withheld from the training set provide a robust validation dataset. Through backtesting, we can simulate the model's performance in real-world scenarios, evaluating its ability to generate profitable trading signals:

```
1.  # Sample Python Code for Model Validation and Backtesting
2.  test_data = scaled_data[int(0.8*len(scaled_data))-60:]
3.  x_test, y_test = [], []
4.  for i in range(60, len(test_data)):
5.      x_test.append(test_data[i-60:i, 0])
6.      y_test.append(test_data[i, 0])
7.  x_test, y_test = np.array(x_test), np.array(y_test)
8.  x_test = np.reshape(x_test, (x_test.shape[0], x_test.shape[1], 1))
9.
10. # Generate predictions on the validation set
11. predictions = model.predict(x_test)
12. predictions = scaler.inverse_transform(predictions)
13.
14. # Assess model accuracy
15. rmse = np.sqrt(np.mean(np.square(predictions - y_test)))
16. print(f"Root Mean Squared Error (RMSE) on Validation Set: {rmse}")
```

Embarking on the implementation of an AI-driven momentum trading strategy involves the integration of cutting-edge technologies, and Python stands as the vanguard. Let us consider the application of a **Gradient Boosting Machine (GBM)**, a robust ensemble learning technique, to predict price movements. The following code snippet showcases a simplified implementation using the popular **scikit-learn** library:

```
1. import numpy as np
2. import pandas as pd
3. import yfinance as yf
4. from sklearn.ensemble import GradientBoostingClassifier
5. from sklearn.model_selection import train_test_split
6. from sklearn.metrics import accuracy_score
```

```
7.
8. # Fetch historical stock data using yfinance
9. ticker = 'AAPL'  # Example ticker symbol for Apple Inc.
10. data = yf.download(ticker, start='2020-01-01', end='2023-01-01')
11.
12. # Calculate Simple Moving Average (SMA), Relative Strength Index
    (RSI), and Moving Average Convergence Divergence (MACD)
13. data['SMA'] = data['Close'].rolling(window=14).mean()
14. data['RSI'] = data['Close'].diff().apply(lambda x: np.where(x > 0,
    x, 0)).rolling(window=14).mean() / \
15.                data['Close'].diff().abs().rolling(window=14).mean() * 100
16. exp1 = data['Close'].ewm(span=12, adjust=False).mean()
17. exp2 = data['Close'].ewm(span=26, adjust=False).mean()
18. data['MACD'] = exp1 - exp2
19.
20. # Volume as a feature
21. data['Volume'] = data['Volume']
22.
23. # Create binary labels for trading signals (1 for Buy, -1 for Sell)
24. data['Signal'] = np.where(data['Close'] > data['Close'].shift(1), 1, -1)
25.
26. # Prepare data for training, dropping NaN values created by moving averages
27. data.dropna(inplace=True)
28. features = data[['SMA', 'RSI', 'MACD', 'Volume']]
29. X_train, X_test, y_train, y_test = train_test_split(features,
    data['Signal'], test_size=0.2, random_state=42)
30.
31. # Build and train the GBM model
32. model = GradientBoostingClassifier(n_estimators=100, learning_
    rate=0.1, max_depth=3, random_state=42)
33. model.fit(X_train, y_train)
34.
35. # Make predictions on the test set
36. predictions = model.predict(X_test)
37.
38. # Evaluate model accuracy
39. accuracy = accuracy_score(y_test, predictions)
40. print(f"Model Accuracy: {accuracy}")
```

The heart of assessing any trading strategy lies in the crucible of backtesting, a process that simulates the strategy's performance using historical data. In this chapter, we illuminate the backtesting results of our AI-enhanced momentum trading strategy. One crucial metric is the Sharpe ratio, which measures the risk-adjusted performance of the strategy. A higher Sharpe ratio indicates a better risk-return profile. The following code snippet demonstrates how to compute the Sharpe Ratio based on daily stock closing prices, providing a quantitative measure to compare the performance of different investments under varying levels of risk:

1. # Sample Python Code for Sharpe Ratio Calculation
2. daily_returns = data['Close'].pct_change()
3. sharpe_ratio = (daily_returns.mean() / daily_returns.std()) * np.sqrt(252) # Assuming 252 trading days in a year
4. print(f"Sharpe Ratio: {sharpe_ratio}")

In addition to the Sharpe ratio, the strategy's cumulative returns and maximum drawdown provide further insights. Cumulative returns showcase the overall profitability, while maximum drawdown signifies the largest peak-to-trough decline. These metrics collectively paint a comprehensive picture of the strategy's performance and guide traders in making informed decisions.

Despite the technological strides, real-time execution of AI-enhanced momentum trading strategies is not without its challenges. Latency, the time delay between order placement and execution, poses a significant hurdle. In the fast-paced world of financial markets, even milliseconds matter, and mitigating latency becomes paramount. This challenge necessitates continuous optimization of algorithms, leveraging techniques like parallel processing and optimizing code execution to enhance speed.

Addressing the dynamic nature of markets is another formidable challenge. Market conditions can shift rapidly, rendering pre-trained models less effective. Adaptive strategies that can recalibrate in response to changing market dynamics are crucial. Incorporating reinforcement learning techniques allows algorithms to adapt and learn from real-time data, offering a potential solution to the challenge of evolving market conditions.

Case study 2: Machine learning for mean reversion

Mean reversion, a cornerstone of algorithmic trading, embodies the principle that asset prices tend to revert to their historical average over time. Traditional mean reversion techniques, such as moving averages and Bollinger Bands, have long been employed by traders seeking to identify opportunities in market fluctuations. For instance, a trader observing the recent price movements of a stock might use a simple moving average to gauge whether the current price deviates significantly from the historical average. This provides a basis for predicting a potential mean reversion in the near future.

The use of AI and sophisticated algorithms has ushered in a new era of predictive analytics. In the context of mean reversion, machine learning models can analyze vast datasets and identify subtle patterns that elude traditional methods. For instance, a **support vector machine (SVM)** model can discern complex relationships between multiple variables, offering a more nuanced understanding of mean reversion dynamics [114].

The foundation of success lies in the quality of data and the precision of pre-processing techniques. Efficient data collection ensures that the models are fed with accurate and relevant information. Historical stock price data, for instance, serves as the bedrock for mean reversion strategies. Utilizing Python libraries like Pandas and Yahoo Finance API, traders can effortlessly gather and organize data. Pre-processing steps, such as handling missing values and normalizing data, are imperative for model robustness. By employing techniques like Min-Max scaling, the data can be standardized, preventing any single feature from disproportionately influencing the model. This example code demonstrates how to retrieve Apple Inc.'s stock price data from Yahoo Finance for the year 2022, clean the dataset by removing any missing values, and normalize it using Min-Max scaling to facilitate more effective data analysis techniques.

```
1.  import pandas as pd
2.  import yfinance as yf
3.
4.  # Collect historical stock price data for Apple Inc. (AAPL)
5.  stock_data = yf.download('AAPL', start='2022-01-01', end='2023-01-01')
6.
7.  # Display the first few rows of the data
8.  print(stock_data.head())
9.
10. # Handle missing values by dropping them
11. stock_data = stock_data.dropna()
12.
13. # Normalize the data using Min-Max scaling
14. stock_data_normalized = (stock_data - stock_data.min()) / (stock_data.max() - stock_data.min())
15.
16. # Display the first few rows of the normalized data
17. print(stock_data_normalized.head())
```

Selecting meaningful features is pivotal in enhancing the predictive power of mean reversion machine learning models. Beyond traditional indicators like moving averages, incorporating advanced features can amplify the model's ability to capture subtle market patterns. For instance, the **Relative Strength Index (RSI)** and **Moving Average Convergence Divergence (MACD)** are powerful indicators that can be computed using

Python libraries such as TA-Lib (Technical Analysis Library). These features provide insights into the momentum and trend strength, crucial for identifying potential mean reversion opportunities. In the following Python example, we utilize the **talib** library to compute two key technical indicators for stock analysis: the RSI and the MACD. These indicators are essential tools for traders to gauge market sentiment and make informed decisions based on the historical price data of stocks.

```
1.  import talib
2.
3.  # Ensure that you have loaded your stock data into a DataFrame named `stock_data`
4.  # and that it includes a 'Close' column with closing prices.
5.
6.  # Compute RSI (Relative Strength Index)
7.  stock_data['RSI'] = talib.RSI(stock_data['Close'], timeperiod=14)
8.
9.  # Compute MACD (Moving Average Convergence Divergence)
10. macd, signal, _ = talib.MACD(stock_data['Close'])
11. stock_data['MACD'] = macd - signal
12.
13. # Display the head of the DataFrame to see the computed columns
14. print(stock_data.head())
```

Leveraging libraries like Scikit-learn and Tensor Flow, traders can seamlessly train models. Cross-validation ensures the model's robustness by assessing its performance on different subsets of the data. Hyperparameter tuning becomes a critical step to fine-tune the model for optimal performance. Python's Scikit-learn provides tools like **GridSearchCV** to systematically explore a range of hyperparameters. This example demonstrates how to optimize a **RandomForestClassifier** using **GridSearchCV** in Python. This process involves defining the model, selecting a range of hyperparameters, and then performing grid search cross-validation to determine the best parameters for model training based on a predefined parameter grid. This method ensures that we identify the most effective combination of parameters for maximizing the predictive performance of the model on the training dataset.

```
1.  # Example Python code for model training and hyperparameter tuning
2.  from sklearn.model_selection import GridSearchCV
3.  from sklearn.ensemble import RandomForestClassifier
4.
5.  # Define the model
6.  model = RandomForestClassifier()
7.
8.  # Define hyperparameters to tune
```

```
9. param_grid = {'n_estimators': [50, 100, 200], 'max_depth': [None,
      10, 20]}
10.
11. # Perform grid search
12. grid_search = GridSearchCV(model, param_grid, cv=5)
13. grid_search.fit(X_train, y_train)
```

Traders can evaluate metrics such as accuracy, precision, and recall to gauge the effectiveness of mean reversion strategies. The comparison might reveal that machine learning models, with their ability to discern complex patterns, outperform traditional techniques in identifying and capitalizing on mean reversion opportunities. The following Python code snippet demonstrates how to evaluate a machine learning model's performance using scikit-learn by computing accuracy, precision, and recall metrics, and then visualizes the results using Matplotlib for a clear comparison:

```
1.  # Example Python code for results comparison using Matplotlib
2.  import matplotlib.pyplot as plt
3.  from sklearn.metrics import accuracy_score, precision_score, recall_
      score
4.
5.  # Evaluate model performance
6.  y_pred = grid_search.predict(X_test)
7.
8.  # Calculate metrics
9.  accuracy = accuracy_score(y_test, y_pred)
10. precision = precision_score(y_test, y_pred)
11. recall = recall_score(y_test, y_pred)
12.
13. # Visualize results
14. # (Matplotlib code not provided for brevity)
```

While the allure of machine learning in algorithmic trading is undeniable, the specter of overfitting looms large. Traders must grapple with the delicate balance between a model's complexity and its ability to generalize to unseen data. Overfitting occurs when a model learns noise in the training data rather than the underlying patterns. For instance, a trader implementing a complex neural network for mean reversion may find the model fitting too closely to historical data, resulting in poor performance on new market data. Through techniques like regularization and dropout, traders can mitigate overfitting concerns and ensure their ML models maintain predictive accuracy across various market conditions. This Python code snippet illustrates how to incorporate a dropout layer into a neural network using TensorFlow's Keras API, aimed at reducing overfitting. The example constructs a simple neural network model with a dropout rate of 0.5, and demonstrates the process of compiling and training the model on training data with validation:

```python
# Example Python code for implementing dropout in a neural network
from tensorflow.keras.models import Sequential
from tensorflow.keras.layers import Dense, Dropout

# Define a simple neural network with dropout layer
model = Sequential()
model.add(Dense(64, input_dim=num_features, activation='relu'))
model.add(Dropout(0.5))  # Dropout layer with a dropout rate of 0.5
model.add(Dense(1, activation='sigmoid'))

# Compile and train the model
model.compile(optimizer='adam', loss='binary_crossentropy', metrics=['accuracy'])
model.fit(X_train, y_train, epochs=10, batch_size=32, validation_data=(X_val, y_val))
```

In navigating the intricate landscape of algorithmic trading, the judicious choice between traditional and machine learning approaches, coupled with a keen awareness of overfitting challenges, can pave the way for strategies that not only capitalize on mean reversion but also withstand the test of dynamic market conditions.

Case study 3: Sentiment analysis for trading signals

Market sentiments, often intangible and elusive, wield substantial influence over financial markets. Investors, armed with a deep comprehension of sentiment dynamics, can anticipate market movements and strategically position themselves for optimal gains. Sentiment analysis provides a systematic approach to gauging these sentiments by analyzing textual data from diverse sources, such as news articles, social media, and financial reports. A classic example is the significant impact of Elon Musk's tweets on Tesla's stock prices, underscoring the critical role sentiments play in shaping market trends.

Traditional sentiment analysis methods, utilized predefined sentiment dictionaries to analyze the polarity of words within texts. For instance, a positive sentiment might be inferred from words like **profit** or **success**. These methods, while effective, faced challenges in handling nuanced language and context. The advent of AI has revolutionized sentiment analysis in trading. High-performance algorithmic trading systems, powered by advanced machine learning algorithms, can now process vast amounts of unstructured data with remarkable speed and accuracy.

One primary aspect is the utilization of diverse data sources, including news articles and social media feeds, to gauge market sentiments. For instance, utilizing the Python library **tweepy** allows traders to access Twitter's API for real-time tweet analysis. By harnessing this data, traders can gain insights into public perceptions of financial instruments. The code snippet below demonstrates a simple Python script to fetch tweets related to a specific stock symbol:

```
1. import tweepy
2.
3. # Set up Twitter API credentials
4. consumer_key = 'your_consumer_key'
5. consumer_secret = 'your_consumer_secret'
6. access_token = 'your_access_token'
7. access_token_secret = 'your_access_token_secret'
8.
9. # Authenticate with Twitter API
10. auth = tweepy.OAuthHandler(consumer_key, consumer_secret)
11. auth.set_access_token(access_token, access_token_secret)
12. api = tweepy.API(auth)
13.
14. # Define the stock symbol
15. stock_symbol = 'AAPL'
16.
17. # Fetch recent tweets related to the stock
18. tweets = api.search(q=stock_symbol, count=10)
19.
20. # Display the retrieved tweets
21. for tweet in tweets:
22.     print(tweet.text)
```

Once the textual data is obtained, effective pre-processing is crucial for meaningful sentiment analysis. NLP libraries such as NLTK in Python can be instrumental in tasks like tokenization and removing stop words. The following code snippet demonstrates a basic pre-processing pipeline for tweets:

```
1. import nltk
2. from nltk.corpus import stopwords
3. from nltk.tokenize import word_tokenize
4.
5. nltk.download('stopwords')
6. nltk.download('punkt')
7.
8. # Sample tweet
9. tweet = "Stock prices soaring! #BullMarket"
10.
```

```
11. # Tokenize the tweet
12. tokens = word_tokenize(tweet)
13.
14. # Remove stop words
15. filtered_tokens = [word for word in tokens if word.lower() not in
    stopwords.words('english')]
16.
17. print(filtered_tokens)
```

Creating a robust sentiment analysis model involves leveraging machine learning algorithms. The Python library **scikit-learn** provides powerful tools for this purpose. A simple following example demonstrates sentiment analysis using a Naive Bayes classifier:

```
1. from sklearn.feature_extraction.text import CountVectorizer
2. from sklearn.naive_bayes import MultinomialNB
3. from sklearn.model_selection import train_test_split
4. from sklearn.metrics import accuracy_score
5.
6. # Sample data (X: Text, y: Sentiment)
7. X = ["Stocks are rising!", "Market is uncertain.", "Economic
    downturn ahead."]
8. y = ["Positive", "Neutral", "Negative"]
9.
10. # Vectorize the text data
11. vectorizer = CountVectorizer()
12. X_vectorized = vectorizer.fit_transform(X)
13.
14. # Split the data for training and testing
15. X_train, X_test, y_train, y_test = train_test_split(X_vectorized, y,
    test_size=0.2, random_state=42)
16.
17. # Train a Naive Bayes classifier
18. classifier = MultinomialNB()
19. classifier.fit(X_train, y_train)
20.
21. # Make predictions on the test set
22. y_pred = classifier.predict(X_test)
23.
24. # Evaluate the model accuracy
25. accuracy = accuracy_score(y_test, y_pred)
26. print(f"Model Accuracy: {accuracy}")
```

Final step is translating sentiment scores into actionable trading signals. A simplistic example using a moving average strategy in Python with the **pandas** library is demonstrated as follows:

```
1.  import pandas as pd
2.  
3.  # Sample sentiment scores and stock prices
4.  sentiment_scores = [0.8, -0.5, 0.2, 0.9, -0.3]
5.  stock_prices = [100, 105, 98, 110, 95]
6.  
7.  # Create a DataFrame
8.  df = pd.DataFrame({'Sentiment': sentiment_scores, 'StockPrice': stock_prices})
9.  
10. # Create a moving average column
11. df['MA_Sentiment'] = df['Sentiment'].rolling(window=3).mean()
12. 
13. # Generate trading signals based on the moving average
14. df['Signal'] = df['MA_Sentiment'].apply(lambda x: 'Buy' if x > 0 else 'Sell')
15. 
16. print(df)
```

Case study 4: Portfolio optimization with artificial intelligence

Portfolio optimization stands as a critical facet of modern financial strategies, marrying risk and return to achieve an optimal balance. Traditional methods, often rooted in mean-variance analysis, have long dominated this field. In understanding portfolio optimization, a key point is recognizing the delicate equilibrium between risk and reward. Python code snippets can illustrate classical optimization techniques, such as the efficient frontier, showcasing the combination of assets that yields the highest return for a given level of risk:

```
1.  import numpy as np
2.  import matplotlib.pyplot as plt
3.  from scipy.optimize import minimize
4.  
5.  # Define expected returns and covariance matrix (replace with real data)
6.  returns = np.array([0.12, 0.18, 0.25])
```

```
7. covariance_matrix = np.array([[0.1, 0.03, 0.05], [0.03, 0.12, 0.07],
   [0.05, 0.07, 0.15]])
8.
9. # Objective function for minimizing negative Sharpe ratio
10. def objective(weights, returns, covariance_matrix):
11.     portfolio_return = np.dot(returns, weights)
12.     portfolio_volatility = np.sqrt(np.dot(weights.T,
    np.dot(covariance_matrix, weights)))
13.     return -portfolio_return / portfolio_volatility
14.
15. # Constraints: weights sum to 1
16. constraints = ({'type': 'eq', 'fun': lambda weights: np.sum(weights)
    - 1})
17.
18. # Initial weights
19. initial_weights = [1/3, 1/3, 1/3]
20.
21. # Minimize negative Sharpe ratio to find optimal weights
22. result = minimize(objective, initial_weights, args=(returns,
    covariance_matrix), method='SLSQP', constraints=constraints)
23.
24. # Optimal weights
25. optimal_weights = result.x
26. print("Optimal Weights:", optimal_weights)
```

Moving beyond classical methods, AI has emerged as a game-changer in portfolio construction. Machine learning models can process vast datasets to identify intricate patterns, providing a deeper understanding of asset behavior. Techniques like neural networks, as implemented in libraries, can adapt to nonlinear relationships within financial data. For example, a neural network-based model can capture subtle correlations between stocks that might escape traditional statistical methods.

Data requirements and normalization are pivotal considerations in AI-driven portfolio optimization. Quality and diversity of data sources (for example, historical prices, economic indicators) significantly impact model performance. Proper normalization methods, such as Min-Max scaling or Z-score normalization, ensure that features are on a comparable scale, preventing dominance by certain variables.

AI model design and training for optimization involve intricate processes. Reinforcement learning, a subset of machine learning, enables algorithms to learn optimal decision-making strategies through repeated interactions with the environment. Implementing a reinforcement learning model for portfolio optimization in Python requires defining states, actions, and rewards. This approach allows the algorithm to iteratively improve its decision-making prowess.

AI model design and training for optimization, reinforcement learning for portfolio allocation:

```
1.  import gym
2.  import numpy as np
3.  import tensorflow as tf
4.  from tensorflow.keras import layers
5.
6.  # Define a custom gym environment for portfolio allocation
7.  class PortfolioEnv(gym.Env):
8.      def __init__(self, returns):
9.          super(PortfolioEnv, self).__init__()
10.         self.returns = returns
11.         self.portfolio_value = 1.0
12.         self.current_weights = np.ones(len(returns)) / len(returns)
13.
14.     def step(self, weights):
15.         # Simulate portfolio returns and update portfolio value
16.         portfolio_returns = np.dot(self.returns, weights)
17.         self.portfolio_value *= (1 + portfolio_returns)
18.
19.         # Calculate reward (could be modified based on specific objectives)
20.         reward = portfolio_returns
21.
22.         return self.portfolio_value, reward, False, {}
23.
24.     def reset(self):
25.         # Reset portfolio value and weights for a new episode
26.         self.portfolio_value = 1.0
27.         self.current_weights = np.ones(len(self.returns)) / len(self.returns)
28.         return self.current_weights
29.
30. # Define a simple neural network model for portfolio allocation
31. model = tf.keras.Sequential([
32.     layers.Dense(64, activation='relu', input_shape=(len(returns),)),
```

```
33.     layers.Dense(len(returns), activation='softmax')
34. ])
35.
36. # Compile the model
37. model.compile(optimizer='adam', loss='mse')
38.
39. # Train the model using a custom gym environment
40. env = PortfolioEnv(returns)
41. observations = env.reset()
42. target_weights = np.array([0.4, 0.4, 0.2])  # Replace with target weights
43. model.fit(np.array([observations]), np.array([target_weights]), epochs=10)
```

Comparing AI-driven methods with classical techniques reveals both strengths and limitations. While AI excels in capturing complex patterns, classical methods often showcase simplicity and interpretability. Code examples can illuminate the distinctions, making it clear how different models handle various market conditions or shocks.

Robustness and consistency checks form the bedrock of any reliable portfolio strategy. Stress testing models against historical data or unexpected market events provides insights into their resilience. Real-world implementation concerns should not be underestimated. Transaction costs, liquidity constraints, and model deployment are crucial elements that demand attention. Python's financial libraries, like Pyfolio, aid in backtesting strategies and understanding their real-world viability.

Case study 5: AI-driven market-making strategies

Market making, as a cornerstone of financial markets, plays a pivotal role in maintaining liquidity and ensuring smooth trading operations. Traditionally, market making involved human traders who facilitated the buying and selling of financial instruments, profiting from the bid-ask spread. Traders relied on historical data, market indicators, and gut feelings to make split-second decisions. This approach, though effective to a certain extent, had its limitations, often leading to suboptimal outcomes in fast-paced and volatile markets.

The infusion of AI into market making ushered in a new era of efficiency and precision. AI-driven algorithms, powered by machine learning models, analyze vast datasets at speeds unattainable by human traders. A prime example is Citadel Securities, a market maker known for leveraging advanced algorithms to execute trades with remarkable speed and accuracy [115]. These algorithms, through continuous learning and adaptation, outperform traditional methods by identifying subtle patterns and exploiting market inefficiencies.

AI model development, training, and real-time adaptation form the crux of modern market-making strategies. Quantitative analysts and data scientists collaborate to design algorithms capable of processing real-time market information. These models undergo rigorous training using historical data, enabling them to recognize evolving market trends and adapt swiftly to changing conditions.

Let us delve into a simplified example of an AI-driven market-making strategy using Python. For the sake of brevity, we will focus on a basic market-making algorithm that employs a mean-reverting strategy:

```
1.  # Import necessary libraries
2.  import numpy as np
3.  import pandas as pd
4.
5.  # Generate sample market data
6.  np.random.seed(42)
7.  timestamps = pd.date_range('2023-01-01', '2023-01-31', freq='T')
8.  prices = np.random.normal(loc=100, scale=1, size=len(timestamps))
9.  market_data = pd.DataFrame({'Timestamp': timestamps, 'Price':
    prices})
10.
11. # Define a simple mean-reverting market-making strategy
12. def mean_reverting_strategy(data, window_size=10, spread=0.1):
13.     data['RollingMean'] = data['Price'].rolling(window=window_size).
    mean()
14.     data['UpperBound'] = data['RollingMean'] + spread
15.     data['LowerBound'] = data['RollingMean'] - spread
16.
17.     # Buy when the price is below the lower bound
18.     data['Signal'] = np.where(data['Price'] < data['LowerBound'], 1,
    0)
19.
20.     # Sell when the price is above the upper bound
21.     data['Signal'] = np.where(data['Price'] > data['UpperBound'],
    -1, data['Signal'])
22.
23.     return data
24.
25. # Apply the mean-reverting strategy to the market data
26. market_data = mean_reverting_strategy(market_data)
27.
```

```
28. # Simulate trading based on the signals
29. market_data['Position'] = market_data['Signal'].cumsum()
30.
31. # Visualize the strategy's performance
32. import matplotlib.pyplot as plt
33.
34. plt.figure(figsize=(10, 6))
35. plt.plot(market_data['Timestamp'], market_data['Price'],
    label='Market Price', alpha=0.5)
36. plt.plot(market_data['Timestamp'], market_data['RollingMean'],
    label='Rolling Mean', linestyle='--', color='orange')
37. plt.scatter(market_data['Timestamp'][market_data['Signal'] == 1],
38.             market_data['Price'][market_data['Signal'] == 1],
39.             marker='^', color='g', label='Buy Signal')
40. plt.scatter(market_data['Timestamp'][market_data['Signal'] == -1],
41.             market_data['Price'][market_data['Signal'] == -1],
42.             marker='v', color='r', label='Sell Signal')
43. plt.legend()
44. plt.title('Mean-Reverting Market-Making Strategy')
45. plt.xlabel('Timestamp')
46. plt.ylabel('Price')
47. plt.show()
```

As we delve into the future of AI in market making, the trajectory points towards even greater integration and sophistication. This example generates synthetic market data and implements a simple mean-reverting market-making strategy. The strategy buys when the price is below the lower bound and sells when the price is above the upper bound.

In a real-world scenario, the algorithm would need to be more sophisticated, incorporating machine learning models for dynamic parameter estimation and adapting to changing market conditions. Additionally, it would interface with a trading platform for executing orders and managing the portfolio.

Conclusion

In conclusion, this chapter illuminated the practical applications of AI in finance through detailed case studies, from enhancing momentum trading to machine learning for mean reversion and sentiment analysis. Exploring portfolio optimization and AI-driven market-making strategies, this chapter underscores the transformative power of AI in diverse financial scenarios. In the upcoming chapter, readers will delve deeper into intricate facets, gaining expertise in cutting-edge applications, and refining their understanding of the evolving landscape of artificial intelligence in finance.

Chapter 10
Using LLMs for Algorithmic Trading

Introduction

Large Language Models (**LLMs**) have emerged as a groundbreaking paradigm shift. This chapter delves into the pivotal role played by LLMs in the realm of algorithmic trading, unveiling their transformative potential in various aspects of financial analysis and decision-making. From harnessing the power of **Natural Language Processing** (**NLP**) for deciphering market sentiment to the creation of predictive models utilizing LLMs, this chapter explores the cutting-edge applications that LLMs bring to the table. Furthermore, it investigates the specific use case of **Generative Pre-trained Transformer** (**GPT**)-based models in sentiment analysis for trading purposes, shedding light on their effectiveness. Lastly, it delves into the crucial domain of risk management strategies enhanced by LLMs, highlighting their significance in shaping the future landscape of algorithmic trading.

Structure

In this chapter, we will learn about the following topics:

- Introduction to Large Language Models
- Integration of LLMs in algorithmic trading
- Natural Language Processing for market sentiment analysis
- Predictive modeling with LLMs

- Use of GPT for sentiment analysis in trading
- Risk management strategies with LLMs

Objectives

In this chapter, our primary objective is to provide a comprehensive understanding of the transformative role that LLMs play in the domain of algorithmic trading. We aim to introduce the concept of LLMs and their significance, setting the stage for a deeper exploration of their integration into algorithmic trading strategies. Through this chapter, we will elucidate how LLMs can be harnessed for NLP in market sentiment analysis, offering a nuanced perspective on their application. Furthermore, we will delve into the realm of predictive modeling with LLMs, demonstrating their capacity to enhance forecasting and decision-making in financial markets. Specifically, we will examine the use of GPT-based models for sentiment analysis in trading, elucidating their effectiveness and relevance. Lastly, we will explore the critical aspect of risk management strategies empowered by LLMs, emphasizing their pivotal role in optimizing trading outcomes.

Introduction to Large Language Models

LLMs such as the GPT series represent a significant advancement in the field of artificial intelligence, particularly in the realm of natural language processing (NLP). These models are essentially sophisticated algorithms that have been trained on extensive datasets consisting of vast amounts of text. This training enables them to recognize, interpret, and generate language that closely resembles human communication in both style and substance. One of the key features of LLMs is their ability to understand context and generate coherent, relevant text based on that understanding. They achieve this by analyzing the patterns, structures, and nuances in the language data they have been trained on. This deep understanding allows them to perform a variety of language-related tasks, such as answering questions, writing essays, translating languages, and even creating content like poems or stories.

The computational strength of LLMs lies in their specialized design, tailored to manage the intricacies of human language. They utilize a transformer-based architecture, a system that allows them to focus selectively on various segments of the input text. This approach aids in grasping the context and crafting appropriate responses, as described by Vaswani and colleagues in 2017[116]. It is this ability to perceive and apply contextual nuances that endow LLMs with their remarkably human-like text production capabilities.

LLMs have revolutionized various AI applications, encompassing areas such as natural language understanding, automated content generation, advanced language translation, and sentiment analysis. These developments have brought transformative changes across multiple sectors, including healthcare, education, and customer relations, through enhanced efficiency in processing language-based tasks. In the financial sector, especially in algorithmic trading, the application of LLMs has been groundbreaking. Their ability to analyze extensive financial news, market trends, and historical data aids significantly in predictive analysis and decision-making processes.

The journey of LLM development is marked by significant milestones. Beginning with early models such as **Long short-term memory (LSTM)**, which introduced the concept of processing sequential data, to the advent of transformer-based models like **Generative Pre-trained Transformer (GPT)** and **Bidirectional Encoder Representations from Transformers (BERT)**, there has been a dramatic enhancement in language processing and generation. The field reached a new zenith with the introduction of GPT-3 and its successor, GPT-3.5. These models, recognized for their advanced learning algorithms and comprehensive training datasets, have demonstrated exceptional proficiency in a wide array of language tasks. GPT-3.5 stands as a paragon of the latest advancements in LLMs. This model, trained on a vast array of text, showcases an unparalleled ability to produce text that is not only coherent and context-sensitive but also capable of engaging in sophisticated AI conversations. Its utility extends beyond basic text generation, encompassing areas like automated coding, creative content generation, and intricate data analysis.

Summarized overview of the key capabilities of various popular language models:

- GPT-3 by OpenAI:
    - Text generation: Creates coherent and contextually relevant text based on prompts.
    - Language translation: Capable of translating text between various languages.
    - Question answering: Provides answers to a wide range of questions.
    - Summarization: Can summarize long texts.
    - Conversation simulation: Engages in dialogue with users.
    - Code writing and debugging: Assists in writing and debugging computer code.
- **BERT by Google:**
    - Text classification: Categorizes text into predefined categories.
    - Named entity recognition: Identifies and classifies named entities in text.
    - Question answering: Provide specific answers from given texts.
    - Language understanding: Excels in understanding the context of a word in a sentence.
- **Text-To-Text Transfer Transformer (T5):**
    - Text generation: Generates text for a variety of tasks.
    - Summarization: Summarizes longer texts into concise versions.
    - Translation: Translates between languages.

- o Question answering: Answers questions based on context.
- o Text classification: Classifies text into different categories.
- **XLNet:**
  - o Language understanding: Better at understanding context compared to traditional models.
  - o Text generation: Generates high-quality text.
  - o Question answering: Effective in context-based question answering.
  - o Named entity recognition: Accurately identifies entities in text.
- RoBERTa by Facebook AI:
  - o Text classification: Highly effective in classifying text into categories.
  - o Sentiment analysis: Determines the sentiment expressed in text.
  - o Language understanding: Enhanced understanding of language nuances.
  - o Question answering: Answers questions with high accuracy.
- **ELECTRA:**
  - o Efficient language understanding: Performs well on language understanding benchmarks.
  - o Text classification and sentiment analysis: Effective in classifying text and detecting sentiment.
  - o Smaller and faster: More efficient training compared to models like BERT.
- **DistilBERT:**
  - o Optimized BERT: A smaller, faster, and more efficient version of BERT.
  - o Maintains most of BERT's capabilities: Effective for tasks like text classification, NER, and question answering.
  - o Resource-efficient: Requires less computational resources.
- **Bidirectional and Auto-Regressive Transformers (BART):**
  - o Effective at both understanding and generation tasks: Combines the capabilities of BERT and GPT.
  - o Text generation: Generates coherent and contextually relevant text.
  - o Summarization: Summarizes text effectively.
  - o Translation: Capable of translating languages.

These models represent the cutting edge of NLP and AI research, each with unique strengths and designed for various applications in understanding, generating, and interacting with human language. They continue to evolve, offering increasingly sophisticated capabilities for a wide range of language-based tasks.

Tools and libraries

Python offers several frameworks that are designed to work with LLMs, like GPT-4. Two prominent examples are:

- **Langchain**: Langchain is a versatile framework designed to streamline the integration of large language models into diverse applications. It simplifies the complex process of building language model-based applications by offering robust tools for managing conversations, implementing actions based on model outputs, and efficiently handling information flow. Key features of Langchain include its adept conversation handling, which ensures smooth interactions with language models, and its capability to produce actionable outputs, facilitating the implementation of model-driven actions. The framework's modular design offers significant flexibility, allowing for seamless integration of various components. Moreover, its compatibility with a wide range of language models makes it a universally applicable solution for developers looking to harness the power of advanced language AI in their projects.

- **Hugging Face Transformers**: Hugging Face is a renowned framework widely recognized for its work with LLMs. Central to its offering is the Transformers library, an extensive collection of pre-trained models that cater to a variety of NLP tasks such as text generation, translation, summarization, and more. Its key features include a comprehensive array of pre-trained models for diverse NLP applications, ensuring users have access to the latest in language model technology. The framework is designed for ease of use, greatly simplifying the utilization of state-of-the-art language models for developers and researchers alike. Hugging Face is also community-driven, which means it's regularly updated with the newest models and features, reflecting the latest advancements in the field. Additionally, it boasts extensive documentation and strong community support, making it an invaluable resource for those working in NLP and AI language modeling.

- **OpenAI's GPT API**: OpenAI's GPT-3 API is a prominent tool offering direct access to GPT-3, one of the most advanced language models currently available. This API facilitates easy integration of GPT-3's capabilities into a wide range of applications, encompassing text generation, translation, and numerous other uses. Key features of OpenAI's GPT-3 API include its straightforward approach to accessing GPT-3, allowing users to harness its sophisticated language processing abilities with minimal complexity. The API is designed for simple and seamless integration, making it suitable for various applications, from small-scale projects to large enterprise solutions. Additionally, it provides a scalable and managed service, ensuring reliability and adaptability for users who require the model to scale with their application's growing demands. This makes the OpenAI GPT-3 API an invaluable asset for developers and organizations looking to leverage cutting-edge language model technology in their digital solutions.

Integration of LLMs in algorithmic trading

Significant advancements in LLMs have brought about a profound transformation in algorithmic trading, offering an array of sophisticated analytical capabilities. These models possess the remarkable ability to effectively analyze and comprehend extensive volumes of unstructured data, encompassing various sources such as news articles, social media updates, and financial reports. This capacity proves indispensable when it comes to facilitating well-informed trading strategies. LLMs offer versatile integration possibilities within trading systems. One avenue involves leveraging predictive analysis, wherein the model thoroughly examines historical and live market data to generate forecasts regarding forthcoming price fluctuations. Another strategy involves the application of NLP techniques to decode financial news and social media trends, thereby evaluating prevailing market sentiment. Furthermore, LLMs can play a pivotal role in risk management by scrutinizing trading patterns and flagging potential risks associated with investment strategies. To illustrate, one practical application of LLMs involves the creation of a sentiment analysis tool using Python. This tool is designed to meticulously scan through news articles and social media content, discerning positive or negative sentiment pertaining to specific stocks. By doing so, it contributes significantly to the task of forecasting market trends and movements.

There have been noteworthy instances where LLMs made substantial contributions to trading decisions. One notable case involved a prominent hedge fund that harnessed an LLM-based system to analyze news and social media content. This empowered them to make profitable trades swiftly during a significant political event by rapidly comprehending the event's implications on the market. In another illustrative example, a trading firm adopted an LLM to construct a predictive model for stock prices, using earnings call transcripts as input data. This strategic move resulted in enhanced accuracy in their investment strategy, enabling them to make more informed and successful investment decisions.

The integration of LLMs in the scenarios described has significantly enhanced decision-making speed and accuracy within algorithmic trading, resulting in both increased profitability and reduced risk. By harnessing the predictive capabilities of LLMs, traders have been able to stay ahead of market trends and react swiftly to emerging information.

Incorporating LLMs into algorithmic trading offers a multitude of advantages. These encompass improved predictive accuracy, efficient data processing, advanced risk management, and enhanced automation and efficiency. Traders benefit from more accurate market predictions, greater insights from extensive datasets, improved strategies for managing risk, and streamlined trading processes with reduced manual intervention.

However, alongside these benefits come a set of challenges. Data privacy concerns arise due to the need to handle sensitive financial information, necessitating stringent measures to safeguard confidential data. Model interpretability is another challenge, as LLMs often operate as black-box models, making it difficult to understand their decision-making processes. Finally, the computational demands of running LLMs are substantial, which can be a barrier for smaller trading firms with limited resources, requiring significant investments in hardware and software infrastructure to meet these requirements.

In summary, while the incorporation of LLMs in algorithmic trading holds great promise, traders must navigate these challenges related to data privacy, model interpretability, and computational requirements to fully unlock the potential of these powerful tools in the trading landscape.

Natural Language Processing for market sentiment analysis

LLMs have become a fundamental tool for conducting sentiment analysis within the financial markets. These advanced NLP techniques play a crucial role in extracting valuable insights from the extensive pool of unstructured textual data sources, including news articles, social media updates, and financial reports. This capability is instrumental in gaining a comprehensive understanding of market sentiment and its dynamics.

The exploration of NLP techniques in sentiment analysis encompasses several crucial steps. Initially, the text data undergoes preprocessing, involving tasks such as tokenization (segmenting text into words or sentences), the removal of stop words (common words with little informational value), and stemming (reducing words to their base form). Once preprocessing is complete, the model utilizes techniques like **Named Entity Recognition** (**NER**) to identify and categorize important entities within the text, such as company names or stock tickers.

In a typical sentiment analysis model, a pre-trained LLM, such as BERT or GPT, is employed. These models are fine-tuned on financial texts, allowing them to capture the nuances of language specifically related to the financial domain. The model then evaluates the sentiment of the text, classifying it as positive, negative, or neutral, taking into account the context and the financial lexicon used within the text.

Sentiment analysis methodologies in the context of trading can be broadly classified into two main approaches: The lexicon-based approach relies on a predefined list of words that are associated with either positive or negative sentiments. Each word within the text is assigned a score based on this predefined list, and the overall sentiment of the text is determined by aggregating these scores. However, this method, while simple, often lacks sensitivity to context and nuances. In contrast, the machine learning-based approach, especially when leveraging LLMs, involves training a model on a labeled dataset where text samples are annotated with their corresponding sentiments. This approach is more sophisticated and has the capability to comprehend context, identify sarcasm, and interpret complex expressions, making it particularly well-suited for the analysis of financial texts where context and subtle nuances are crucial for accurate sentiment assessment.

Following code implement the sentiment analysis using the **transformers** library, a powerful tool for natural language processing. We'll load a pre-trained model from NLP

Town, specifically designed for multilingual sentiment analysis, and apply it to evaluate the sentiment of a text snippet, which in this case is an earnings report from a company. The process will demonstrate how to interpret the sentiment and confidence score generated by the model, providing a practical example of sentiment analysis in action.

```
1. from transformers import pipeline
2.
3. # Load a pre-trained sentiment analysis model
4. nlp = pipeline('sentiment-analysis', model='nlptown/bert-base-multilingual-uncased-sentiment')
5.
6. # Sample text
7. text = "The latest earnings report from Company X was beyond expectations, driving a positive outlook among investors."
8.
9. # Perform sentiment analysis
10. result = nlp(text)
11.
12. # Output the result
13. print(f"Sentiment: {result[0]['label']}, Confidence: {result[0]['score']:.2f}")
```

The Python code you provided uses the Hugging Face Transformers library to perform sentiment analysis on a given text using a pre-trained model called **nlptown/bert-base-multilingual-uncased-sentiment**. This model is designed for multilingual sentiment analysis. The code then prints the sentiment label and confidence score for the input text.

Predictive modeling with Large Language Models

Predictive modeling within the realm of algorithmic trading encompasses the utilization of statistical techniques and machine learning algorithms to predict forthcoming market trends, drawing insights from historical data. In the financial sector, this approach holds substantial significance, as it empowers traders and investors to make well-informed choices by foreseeing future market dynamics and price fluctuations. The precision of these forecasts assumes critical importance, as it can wield a substantial influence on investment strategies and overall returns.

LLMs such as GPT and BERT have brought about a significant transformation in the realm of predictive modeling within the trading sector. These models, owing to their advanced natural language processing capabilities, excel at deciphering and analyzing extensive volumes of unstructured textual data. This ability proves immensely valuable for comprehending market sentiments and trends effectively. LLMs are proficient in extracting patterns and insights from a wide array of sources, including news articles, financial reports, and social media content. In doing so, they provide a more nuanced perspective on market dynamics compared to traditional.

Market sentiment analysis using LLMs: LLMs can assess the sentiment expressed in financial news and social media content for the purpose of predicting stock market fluctuations. By efficiently processing substantial quantities of textual data, this model yielded valuable insights into the public's sentiment regarding specific stocks or sectors. Such insights served as pivotal indicators of the prevailing market. LLM has found application in the realm of predicting stock prices with heightened accuracy. These models undergo training using historical stock price data and are enriched with real-time market data and news feeds. As a result, they possess the capability to anticipate short-term price fluctuations, delivering essential insights to traders for informed decision-making. While LLMs offer significant advancements in predictive modeling, they are not infallible. Their predictions depend heavily on the quality and diversity of the training data. Market unpredictability, influenced by numerous variables, can affect the accuracy of these models. Additionally, LLMs may struggle with the contextual understanding of market-specific language, which can lead to inaccuracies in predictions.

Use of GPT for sentiment analysis in trading

The practical application of NLP for sentiment analysis in trading is not merely a theoretical concept; it has been successfully executed in various real-world scenarios. These case studies underscore the efficiency of sentiment analysis within the financial sector, particularly when harnessed in conjunction with LLMs.

One noteworthy instance revolves around a major investment bank that harnessed NLP techniques to conduct sentiment analysis, thereby informing their trading strategies. By scrutinizing earnings calls, financial news reports, and social media content, the bank achieved a precise assessment of market sentiment. This analytical approach translated into substantially improved trading performance, as sentiment analysis provided early indications of market trends, allowing the bank to capitalize on them before they became apparent to the broader market [117].

Another case involved a hedge fund that seamlessly integrated an LLM-based sentiment analysis system into its algorithmic trading platform. This system actively examined real-time news updates and social media discussions to evaluate the sentiment surrounding specific stocks and sectors. This real-time sentiment analysis empowered the fund to adapt its trading positions dynamically, effectively responding to shifts in market sentiment. The hedge fund reported amplified returns, attributing this success to the nuanced understanding of market sentiment facilitated by the LLM-powered analysis [15].

The provided Python code utilizes the **Tweepy** library to access Twitter's API for fetching tweets based on a specified search term (**YourSearchTerm**) and language preference (**en** for

English). It begins by configuring Twitter API credentials and establishing authentication. Subsequently, it interacts with the API to retrieve up to 100 tweets that match the given search criteria and stores them in a Pandas DataFrame named `df_tweets`. This DataFrame consists of a single column named **Tweet**, where each row contains the text content of an individual tweet. By executing this script with valid Twitter API credentials and a desired search term, you can extract relevant tweets and easily analyze and manipulate them using Pandas for various data-driven tasks.

The following code utilizes **tweepy**, a Python library for accessing the Twitter API, along with **pandas** for data manipulation, to retrieve tweets based on a specified search term and convert them into a DataFrame for further analysis:

```
1. import tweepy
2. import pandas as pd
3.
4. # X API 2 credentials
5. bearer_token = 'YOUR_BEARER_TOKEN'
6.
7. # Authenticate with X API 2
8. client = tweepy.Client(bearer_token)
9.
10. # Fetch tweets
11. query = "YourSearchTerm"
12. tweets = client.search_recent_tweets(query=query, max_results=100,
        tweet_fields=["lang"], expansions=["author_id"], user_fields=["username"])
13.
14. # Extract tweet texts
15. tweets_data = [tweet.text for tweet in tweets.data if tweet.lang == "en"]
16.
17. # Convert tweets to DataFrame
18. df_tweets = pd.DataFrame(tweets_data, columns=['Tweet'])
```

The provided Python code defines a function called **preprocess_tweet** designed to clean and standardize text data typically found in tweets. This function removes URLs, mentions (usernames), and the **#** symbol (commonly used for hashtags) from the input text using regular expressions. Additionally, it converts all text to lowercase for consistency. Subsequently, the code applies this preprocessing function to each tweet in a **pandas** DataFrame called **df_tweets**. It creates a new column named **Processed_Tweet** in the DataFrame to store the preprocessed versions of the original tweet texts. This preprocessing step is essential for data cleaning and standardization, ensuring that text data is in a uniform and sanitized format, which is often a prerequisite for further **natural language processing** (**NLP**) or text analysis tasks.

The provided code defines a Python function named **preprocess_tweet** that applies various preprocessing steps to clean raw tweet text, including the removal of URLs, mentions, and hashtags, as well as converting the text to lowercase. These preprocessing steps are then applied to each tweet in a **DataFrame** column, resulting in a new column containing the processed tweet text:

```
1. !pip install langchain
2.
3. from langchain.llms import OpenAI
4.
5. # Initialize LangChain with OpenAI (assuming you have access)
6. llm = OpenAI(api_key='YOUR_OPENAI_API_KEY')
7.
8. def analyze_tweet(tweet):
9.     # Here you can customize the analysis, e.g., sentiment analysis
10.    response = llm.invoke(f"What is the sentiment of this tweet? '{tweet}'")
11.    return response
12.
13. # Apply semantic analysis to each processed tweet
14. df_tweets['Analysis'] = df_tweets['Processed_Tweet'].apply(analyze_tweet)
```

The provided code utilizes the **LangChain** library, specifically the OpenAI interface, to perform semantic analysis on a collection of processed tweets stored in a Pandas DataFrame. It begins by initializing LangChain with your OpenAI API key.

Next, a function named **analyze_tweet** is defined to perform the semantic analysis on each tweet. Within this function, you have the flexibility to customize the type of analysis you want to perform on the tweet. In this example, it generates a query to LangChain, asking for the sentiment of the tweet. The generated query includes the processed tweet's text enclosed in single quotes.

Finally, the code applies the **analyze_tweet** function to each processed tweet in the **DataFrame**, creating a new column named **Analysis** to store the results of the semantic analysis for each tweet. This analysis could include sentiment analysis, but you can adapt it to perform various other types of semantic analysis depending on your specific needs. The **Analysis** column will contain the results of the customized analysis for each tweet, allowing you to gain insights and extract valuable information from the tweet data.

This Python script integrates sentiment analysis into tweet processing using OpenAI's capabilities, enabling comprehensive understanding of textual data for deeper insights:

```
1. from langchain.llms import OpenAI
2.
3. # Initialize LangChain with OpenAI (assuming you have access)
4. llm = OpenAI(api_key='YOUR_OPENAI_API_KEY')
```

```
5.
6. def analyze_tweet(tweet):
7.     # Here you can customize the analysis, e.g., sentiment analysis
8.     response = llm.invoke(f"What is the sentiment of this tweet? '{tweet}'")
9.     return response
10.
11. # Apply semantic analysis to each processed tweet
12. df_tweets['Analysis'] = df_tweets['Processed_Tweet'].apply(analyze_tweet)
```

The provided code counts and visualizes the distribution of sentiment types in a DataFrame of analyzed tweets. It first calculates the frequency of each sentiment type and stores this information in a Pandas Series. Then, using the **Matplotlib** library, it creates a bar chart where each sentiment type corresponds to a bar, making it easy to visualize the relative occurrence of different sentiments in the tweet data. The chart is titled **Tweet Sentiment Analysis**, with labeled axes showing **Sentiment** and **Count**. This visualization offers valuable insights into the sentiment patterns within the tweet dataset, aiding in the understanding of sentiment trends and variations.

Following code counting sentiment types and visualizing them using **matplotlib**, we can gain valuable insights into the prevailing sentiments expressed in tweets:

```
1.  # Example: Counting sentiment types
2.  sentiment_counts = df_tweets['Analysis'].value_counts()
3.
4.  # Visualization (using matplotlib)
5.  import matplotlib.pyplot as plt
6.
7.  sentiment_counts.plot(kind='bar')
8.  plt.title('Tweet Sentiment Analysis')
9.  plt.xlabel('Sentiment')
10. plt.ylabel('Count')
11. plt.show()
```

Risk management strategies with LLMs

LLMs, equipped with their advanced data processing capabilities, assume a pivotal role in the identification and evaluation of risks. Through the analysis of market news, financial reports, and social media content, LLMs have the capability to unearth concealed risk elements, thereby offering traders a comprehensive perspective on potential market challenges. This proactive risk assessment approach holds fundamental significance in the pursuit of minimizing losses and optimizing returns.

The predictive efficacy of LLMs in risk management arises from their remarkable capacity to swiftly process and comprehend extensive datasets, a task that poses challenges and consumes significant time for humans. Leveraging their deep learning algorithms, LLMs can identify subtle patterns and correlations within data, potentially signaling market risks such as economic downturns, geopolitical developments, or sector-specific vulnerabilities. This capability contributes to an improved predictive accuracy of risk models.

Incorporating risk factors identified by LLMs into trading algorithms requires a thoughtful approach. The initial step involves translating the qualitative insights furnished by LLMs into quantitative metrics that can seamlessly integrate with existing trading models. This translation process may encompass assigning risk scores to various market indicators or employing sentiment analysis techniques to quantify market sentiment. It is imperative to execute the integration of these insights meticulously, ensuring that the trading algorithm can interpret and respond to these risk indicators effectively.

In practical terms, implementing risk management strategies with LLMs entails several vital steps and considerations. Firstly, it is crucial to ensure that the LLMs are trained on high-quality, pertinent data. Inaccurate or biased data can lead to erroneous risk assessments. Secondly, the incorporation of LLMs into trading algorithms must be executed in a manner that accommodates continuous learning and adaptation, as market conditions are in a constant state of flux. Lastly, it is essential to strike a balance between automated decision-making and human oversight to mitigate the potential risks associated with excessive reliance on algorithmic predictions.

Conclusion

This chapter has meticulously delved into the role of LLMs in transforming the domain of algorithmic trading, with a particular focus on their integration and impact across various facets. The discussion has spanned the utilization of LLMs in NLP for a nuanced market sentiment analysis, showcasing how these advanced models interpret and analyze market-related data and news to inform trading decisions. Additionally, the chapter has explored the application of predictive modeling, demonstrating how LLMs can forecast market trends and movements with a high degree of accuracy, thereby offering traders a significant edge. Further, the chapter has shed light on the specific use of GPT in sentiment analysis, illustrating how these models parse vast quantities of textual information to gauge market sentiment, an invaluable tool in the trader's arsenal. Alongside, the text has discussed the strategic role of LLMs in enhancing risk management practices, enabling traders to devise more informed and robust strategies that mitigate potential losses while maximizing returns.

As we transition to the forthcoming chapter, the narrative will shift towards a forward-looking perspective. This segment is set to offer a comprehensive exploration of emerging trends within the realm of algorithmic trading, identifying the challenges that practitioners face in this dynamic environment, and pinpointing the opportunities that lie ahead.

By dissecting these aspects, the chapter aims to provide readers with a well-rounded understanding of the future trajectory of algorithmic trading, equipping them with the insights and knowledge necessary to navigate and excel in this innovative and competitive field. Through this, readers can anticipate an enriching journey into the next frontier of algorithmic trading, where AI's potential is continuously redefining the boundaries of what is possible in financial markets.

Join our book's Discord space

Join the book's Discord Workspace for Latest updates, Offers, Tech happenings around the world, New Release and Sessions with the Authors:

https://discord.bpbonline.com

CHAPTER 11
Future Trends, Challenges, and Opportunities

Introduction

In this chapter, we delve into the transformative effects of advanced technologies on the trading landscape, focusing on the integration and implications of **artificial intelligence (AI)** and **machine learning (ML)**, the cutting-edge developments, and the ethical dilemmas they bring. We explore the emerging trends in AI and ML that are revolutionizing trading strategies and operations, alongside the ethical considerations and potential pitfalls that accompany these advancements. Furthermore, we examine the impact of quantum computing on algorithmic trading, highlighting its potential to significantly enhance processing speed and efficiency. The role of blockchain technology and **decentralized finance (DeFi)** is also discussed, emphasizing their contribution to increased transparency and security in trading operations. Lastly, we address the evolving regulatory landscape, which aims to keep pace with the rapid advancements in AI-driven trading, ensuring a balanced ecosystem that fosters innovation while protecting market integrity and investor interests. This chapter sets the stage for a comprehensive understanding of how these technological advancements are reshaping the trading world, offering insights into their benefits, challenges, and the future direction of the industry.

Structure

In this chapter, we will go through the following topics:

- Emerging trends in AI and ML for trading
- Overcoming common challenges in AI-based trading
- Preparing for the future of algorithmic trading
- AI-based tools for alternative data analysis
- Ethical considerations and potential pitfalls
- Impact of quantum computing on algorithmic trading
- Role of blockchain and decentralized finance in trading
- Evolving regulatory landscape for AI-driven trading

Objectives

The primary objective of this chapter is to provide an in-depth exploration of the significant advancements and challenges at the intersection of technology and trading, specifically through the lens of AI and ML, quantum computing, blockchain, and DeFi. We aim to elucidate the emerging trends in AI and ML that are reshaping trading strategies, while also addressing the ethical considerations and potential pitfalls that these technologies entail. Furthermore, we will investigate the transformative impact of quantum computing on the efficiency and capabilities of algorithmic trading, as well as the role of blockchain and DeFi in enhancing the transparency and security of trading operations. Additionally, this chapter seeks to analyze the evolving regulatory framework tailored to AI-driven trading, highlighting the efforts to harmonize innovation with market fairness and investor protection. Through this exploration, readers will gain a comprehensive understanding of the current state and future prospects of technology-driven trading, equipped with the knowledge to navigate the complexities of this rapidly evolving landscape.

Emerging trends in AI and ML for trading

The integration of deep learning and neural networks represents a significant advancement in the field of algorithmic trading. This fusion has become increasingly influential in refining trading strategies within the financial sector. Deep Learning, particularly through the use of **Convolutional Neural Networks (CNNs)** and **Recurrent Neural Networks (RNNs)**, has proven instrumental in dissecting and understanding complex financial datasets. These models excel in detecting intricate patterns and enhancing the precision of predictions, which are critical in the fast-paced trading environment.

A practical example of this integration can be seen in the application of deep learning for stock price prediction. Traders, leveraging advanced programming languages like Python, have developed neural network models that utilize these deep learning techniques. A notable instance is the work of Brown and Smith [118], who employed TensorFlow, a leading deep learning framework, to construct a **Long Short-Term Memory (LSTM)** model for this purpose. Their model, which was trained on historical stock price data, showed an exceptional ability to understand and utilize temporal data. This capability is crucial in trading, where understanding past trends can provide insights into future market movements.

Such a model does not just offer theoretical benefits but also has real-world applications that enable traders to make more educated and timely decisions. This is especially important in an environment where market conditions can shift rapidly, and the ability to quickly adapt to these changes can mean the difference between profit and loss. The LSTM model by Brown and Smith is a testament to how the integration of Deep Learning in financial trading can lead to more adaptive and potentially more profitable trading strategies.

These advancements highlight a broader trend in the financial industry, where technology and data science are becoming increasingly important tools. As these technologies continue to evolve, they offer promising prospects for even more sophisticated and efficient trading strategies.

The field of predictive analytics has seen remarkable growth and innovation, particularly in its application to algorithmic trading and risk management. The integration of ML algorithms such as Random Forests and Gradient Boosting has revolutionized how traders approach market analysis. These sophisticated tools enable the analysis of complex datasets, including historical market data, sentiment from news sources, and macroeconomic indicators.

A practical example of this advancement is the use of the Random Forest model in Python, utilizing the Scikit-Learn library. This particular model allows traders to predict stock price directions by analyzing various features, including past price data, trading volume, and news sentiment. The ability to process and interpret such diverse data points enhances the decision-making process, making it more data-driven and informed. Research [119] provided valuable insights into the practical applications of predictive analytics in the financial sector. By employing Random Forest, traders can now integrate a multitude of factors into their predictive models, a necessity in the multifaceted trading environment of today. This comprehensive approach to data analysis and prediction significantly bolsters trading strategies, allowing for a more nuanced understanding of market dynamics.

The evolution of algorithmic trading frameworks has been a cornerstone in the advancement and fine-tuning of trading strategies. Open-source platforms, such as QuantConnect and backtrader, have revolutionized the landscape of algorithmic trading. These platforms have made it more accessible for traders to engage with historical data, utilize various built-in indicators, and apply complex trading logic. One of the key benefits of these platforms is the significant reduction in the time required to develop and test trading algorithms.

Taking QuantConnect as an example, traders can leverage Python code snippets to quickly prototype and test various trading strategies. This flexibility allows for the customization of algorithms, integration of technical indicators, and efficient backtesting. The ease of testing and refining strategies using these frameworks has opened up algorithmic trading to a broader range of traders, enhancing competition and innovation in financial markets. By using such platforms, traders can concentrate more on strategy development and less on the technical complexities of algorithm construction, allowing for a greater focus on responding to market changes and optimizing trading performance.

The table below summarizes the evolution of algorithmic trading frameworks, illustrating their impact on trading strategy development:

Feature	Impact on trading strategy development
Access to Historical Data	Enables thorough testing and validation of trading strategies
Built-In Indicators	Facilitates technical analysis and decision-making
Complex Trading Logic	Allows for the creation of sophisticated algorithms
Reduced Development Time	Speeds up the process from concept to execution
Customization	Provides flexibility to tailor strategies to specific needs
Efficient Backtesting	Ensures strategies are robust before live implementation

Table 11.1: Trading strategy development impact

TensorFlow and Keras are two of the most popular libraries in the field of AI and ML, offering powerful tools for building and deploying complex models that can analyze vast amounts of data to make predictions or decisions. When it comes to AI-based trading, these technologies can be leveraged to develop sophisticated algorithms capable of identifying profitable trading opportunities, managing risk, and executing trades at high speeds. Below, we explore TensorFlow and Keras in more detail and discuss how they can be utilized in the context of AI-based trading.

- **TensorFlow:**

    GitHub Link: **https://github.com/tensorflow/tensorflow**

    TensorFlow is an open-source platform developed by the Google Brain team that allows developers to create complex ML models. It is known for its flexibility, scalability, and comprehensive ecosystem that includes tools, libraries, and community resources. TensorFlow supports both CPUs and GPUs, making it suitable for a wide range of tasks, from developing simple models to deploying large-scale neural network systems.

- **Keras**:

    GitHub Link: **https://github.com/keras-team/keras**

    Keras, on the other hand, is a high-level neural networks API, written in Python that is capable of running on top of TensorFlow, CNTK, or Theano. It was developed with the aim of enabling fast experimentation with deep neural networks. Keras is known for its user-friendliness, modularity, and extensibility. It allows for easy and fast prototyping as well as running seamlessly on both CPUs and GPUs.

TensorFlow and Keras in AI-based trading

AI-based trading systems use algorithms to analyze market data and execute trades. These systems can process vast amounts of data, learn from historical trends, and make predictions about future market movements. TensorFlow and Keras can be used to build and train the models that power these systems. Here is how:

- **Data processing**: Trading algorithms require access to high-quality, real-time market data. TensorFlow and Keras can be used to preprocess this data, including normalization and transformation, making it suitable for model training and analysis. This preprocessing step is crucial for removing noise and ensuring that the input data is in a format that the models can work with effectively.

- **Feature engineering**: Feature engineering is the process of selecting, modifying, or creating new features from the raw data to improve the performance of machine learning models. In the context of AI-based trading, features might include price indicators, trading volumes, or even sentiment analysis from financial news. TensorFlow and Keras can be used to automate some aspects of feature engineering, helping to identify the most predictive features.

- **Model development and training**: TensorFlow and Keras excel in building and training complex models, including deep learning models that are particularly well-suited for identifying patterns in data. In trading, these models can be used to predict market movements, evaluate risk, or identify potential trading strategies. Keras makes it easy to experiment with different model architectures, while TensorFlow provides the scalability and performance needed to train models on large datasets.

- **Backtesting**: Before deploying an AI-based trading model, it is essential to test its performance on historical data. This process, known as backtesting, helps to evaluate the model's effectiveness and adjust its parameters for optimal performance. TensorFlow and Keras can be used to automate the backtesting process, allowing for rapid iteration and refinement of trading strategies.

- **Deployment**: Once a model has been developed and tested, it can be deployed to make real-time trading decisions. TensorFlow offers tools like TensorFlow Serving and TensorFlow Lite for deploying models in production environments, including on low-latency, high-throughput systems that are typical in trading applications.

Overcoming common challenges in AI-based trading

AI-based trading, leveraging artificial intelligence algorithms to make investment decisions, has revolutionized financial markets. However, it's not without its challenges. One common hurdle is data quality and quantity. AI models heavily rely on vast amounts of high-quality data to make accurate predictions. Obtaining clean and relevant data can be challenging, as financial markets are dynamic and data sources may be inconsistent or incomplete. Overcoming this challenge often involves rigorous data cleaning processes and utilizing advanced techniques like data augmentation to enhance dataset quality.

Another significant challenge in AI-based trading is model overfitting. AI models can sometimes perform exceptionally well on historical data but fail to generalize to unseen data. This phenomenon, known as overfitting, occurs when a model captures noise in the training data rather than true underlying patterns. To address this, traders employ techniques such as regularization, cross-validation, and ensemble methods to ensure their AI models generalize well to new market conditions. Additionally, ongoing monitoring and refinement of models are essential to adapt to changing market dynamics and prevent overfitting.

Risk management is paramount in AI-based trading, yet it poses another common challenge. AI models may generate signals with high confidence levels, but there's always a risk of unexpected market events causing significant losses. Moreover, AI systems can sometimes exhibit unexpected behaviors or biases, leading to erroneous trading decisions. To mitigate these risks, traders implement robust risk management strategies, including diversification, position sizing, stop-loss mechanisms, and stress testing. Furthermore, continuous monitoring and human oversight are crucial to intervene when AI systems deviate from expected behavior or encounter unforeseen scenarios.

Finally, regulatory compliance presents a persistent challenge for AI-based trading firms. Financial markets are subject to complex regulations aimed at ensuring fair and transparent trading practices, investor protection, and market stability. AI algorithms must comply with these regulations, which often require transparency, explainability, and accountability in algorithmic decision-making processes. Meeting regulatory requirements entails thorough documentation, audit trails, and governance frameworks to demonstrate compliance. Additionally, staying abreast of evolving regulatory landscapes and adapting AI systems accordingly is vital for long-term success in AI-based trading while navigating the regulatory maze.

Preparing for the future of algorithmic trading

Algorithmic trading, the use of computer programs to execute trades at speeds and frequencies beyond human capabilities, has become an integral part of modern financial markets. As technology continues to advance, preparing for the future of algorithmic trading becomes increasingly crucial. One key aspect of this preparation involves staying abreast of technological advancements and their implications for trading strategies. This requires ongoing education and adaptation to new tools and techniques. Moreover, risk management is paramount in the world of algorithmic trading. As algorithms execute trades automatically based on pre-defined criteria, the potential for rapid and unexpected market movements poses significant risks. Therefore, it's essential to develop robust risk management protocols that can identify and mitigate potential threats. This might involve implementing circuit breakers, position limits, or other measures to prevent catastrophic losses.

Additionally, regulatory oversight is becoming more stringent in response to the growing influence of algorithmic trading. Traders must ensure compliance with relevant regulations and industry standards to avoid legal repercussions. This includes understanding the impact of regulations such as MiFID II [128] or the Dodd-Frank Act [129] on algorithmic trading practices and adapting strategies accordingly. Failure to comply with regulatory requirements can result in fines, sanctions, or even the suspension of trading activities. Furthermore, the future of algorithmic trading will likely be shaped by advancements in artificial intelligence and machine learning. These technologies enable algorithms to analyze vast amounts of data and adapt their strategies in real-time, potentially leading to more sophisticated trading algorithms and strategies. Traders must stay informed about these developments and explore ways to incorporate AI and machine learning into their trading systems effectively. This might involve collaborating with data scientists or investing in AI-driven trading platforms to gain a competitive edge in the market. Ultimately, preparing for the future of algorithmic trading requires a proactive approach that combines technological innovation, risk management, regulatory compliance, and a willingness to adapt to changing market dynamics. By staying informed and agile, traders can position themselves for success in an increasingly complex and competitive trading environment.

Algorithmic trading is on the cusp of a transformative era with the emergence of quantum computing and generative AI. Quantum computing has the potential to revolutionize the speed and efficiency of data processing, enabling traders to analyze vast datasets and execute trades with unprecedented accuracy and speed. However, with this power comes the need for careful consideration of security protocols, as quantum computing also has the capability to break traditional encryption methods. Traders must stay informed about developments in quantum computing and explore how to leverage this technology while ensuring the security of their trading systems. Generative AI, another cutting-edge technology, holds promise for creating novel trading strategies and predicting market trends with greater precision. By generating synthetic data and simulating various market scenarios, generative AI algorithms can help traders identify profitable opportunities and optimize their trading strategies. However, like any AI technology, generative AI algorithms require extensive testing and validation to ensure their reliability and effectiveness in real-world trading environments. As quantum computing and generative AI continue to evolve, traders must adapt their approaches to algorithmic trading accordingly. This may involve investing in new hardware and software infrastructure to support quantum computing capabilities or partnering with AI experts to develop and implement generative AI algorithms. Additionally, traders must remain vigilant about the ethical implications of these technologies, including concerns about data privacy, algorithmic bias, and the potential for market manipulation.

AI-based tools for alternative data analysis

AI-based tools for alternative data analysis have emerged as powerful assets in various industries, offering unique insights and competitive advantages. Alternative data, which refers to non-traditional datasets like social media activity, satellite imagery, or sensor data, holds immense potential for uncovering trends, sentiments, and patterns not readily apparent through conventional methods. AI-driven tools play a pivotal role in harnessing this data by employing advanced algorithms to extract meaningful information.

One significant advantage of AI-based tools for alternative data analysis is their ability to process vast amounts of unstructured data rapidly. Traditional analysis methods often struggle with the sheer volume and complexity of alternative datasets. However, AI algorithms excel at handling unstructured data, employing techniques such as **natural language processing** (**NLP**) and computer vision to extract insights from diverse sources efficiently. This capability enables businesses to make data-driven decisions quickly and stay ahead in dynamic market environments.

Moreover, AI-driven tools enhance the accuracy and granularity of insights derived from alternative data sources. By leveraging machine learning models, these tools can identify subtle correlations, anomalies, and predictive signals within the data that might elude human analysts. Whether it's predicting consumer behavior, monitoring supply chain disruptions, or assessing investment opportunities, AI-powered analysis offers a deeper understanding of market dynamics and enables proactive decision-making.

Furthermore, the integration of AI-based tools for alternative data analysis fosters innovation across industries. Businesses can leverage these tools to uncover untapped market opportunities, optimize operations, and mitigate risks effectively. For instance, in finance, hedge funds utilize AI algorithms to analyze alternative datasets like satellite images of parking lots to gauge retail activity or sentiment analysis of social media posts to predict stock price movements.

Ethical considerations and potential pitfalls

The emergence of AI in the field of high-speed algorithmic trading has significantly transformed the financial sector. It has empowered traders to utilize sophisticated machine learning algorithms for swift, informed decision-making. The tenth chapter of the book specifically addresses Advanced Topics and Techniques, placing a notable emphasis on the Ethical Considerations and Challenges associated with this innovative area. In this part of the book, we will examine five critical aspects that highlight the ethical aspects of using AI in high-speed algorithmic trading and its impact on the finance sector:

- **Addressing bias and ensuring equity in AI-driven trading systems**: AI-based trading algorithms primarily use historical data for forecasting and executing trades. An ethical challenge surfaces when these algorithms unintentionally embed biases found in the historical data. This issue is exemplified by the case of Renaissance Technologies' Medallion Fund, as reported by Zuckerman in 2019 [37], where algorithmic trading strategies were seen to reinforce gender and racial biases, potentially leading to inequitable market practices. To counter this problem, it's crucial for traders to meticulously evaluate and rectify biases in their data sets. Implementing debiasing methods and continuously overseeing the decisions made by algorithms are essential steps to guarantee fairness in trading activities.

- **Clarity and comprehensibility in AI trading systems**: The inherent complexity of AI models often leads to a lack of clarity in their decision-making mechanisms. This becomes a significant issue in algorithmic trading, where the impenetrability of these models can lead to severe implications, particularly during unforeseen market fluctuations or system malfunctions. To mitigate these risks, it is essential for traders to integrate explainable AI methods. These techniques allow all involved parties to understand and have confidence in the logic driving the trading decisions, thereby improving responsibility and risk control in trading operations.

- **Safeguarding data privacy and security in AI trading**: The extensive data demands for AI-powered trading systems bring forth critical challenges in data privacy and security. It is imperative for traders to rigorously follow regulatory standards, like the **General Data Protection Regulation (GDPR)** established by the European Union in 2016, to protect their clients' sensitive information and preserve trust. Implementing robust data protection measures, such as encryption, access control, and auditing procedures, is vital for maintaining a secure environment in algorithmic trading.

- **Navigating regulatory compliance in AI-enabled trading**: AI-based algorithmic trading is governed by a complex array of financial regulations, encompassing rules against market manipulation and insider trading. Compliance is not just essential but mandatory. It is crucial for traders to rigorously abide by the regulatory landscape of their operating regions. This involves incorporating thorough compliance verifications and risk management strategies within their trading algorithms to ensure adherence to legal standards.

- **Promoting ethical investments and social responsibility through AI**: With the growing dominance of AI in algorithmic trading, there's a rising focus on ethical investment and AI-guided social responsibility. Modern investors increasingly prefer companies that adhere to ethical trading standards and prioritize **environmental, social, and governance (ESG)** principles. AI technologies are instrumental in assisting traders to pinpoint such ethical investment opportunities, allowing for the alignment of their portfolios with socially responsible goals.

Impact of quantum computing on algorithmic trading

The advent of quantum computing revolutionizes various sectors, with algorithmic trading being no exception. This section explores the profound impact of quantum computing on the field, focusing on quantum algorithms, enhanced computational capabilities, problem-solving, security implications, and quantum machine learning in trading.

Quantum algorithms in finance

The advent of quantum algorithms marks a pivotal shift in the world of finance, particularly in aspects of financial modeling and trading. *Orús, Mugel,* and *Lizaso* [120], in their insightful article in *Reviews in Physics,* underscore the profound capabilities of quantum algorithms. These algorithms are not just incremental improvements but represent a paradigm shift in computational capacity. Unlike traditional computers, quantum algorithms harness quantum mechanics to process complex calculations at an exponentially faster rate. This quantum leap in processing power opens up new horizons in the financial sector, especially in areas like risk assessment, portfolio optimization, and exploring arbitrage opportunities.

For instance, risk assessment in finance often involves simulating various market scenarios to evaluate the risk associated with different assets or investment strategies. Classical computers handle this by sequential processing, which can be time-consuming and less effective in capturing the complexities of financial markets. Quantum algorithms, on the other hand, can analyze numerous possibilities simultaneously, providing a more holistic and accurate risk analysis in a fraction of the time.

In the realm of portfolio optimization, quantum algorithms can efficiently sift through vast combinations of assets to identify the optimal portfolio mix. This process, known as the optimization problem in finance, is notoriously complex and resource-intensive. Quantum computing can navigate this complexity more effectively, finding solutions that maximize returns while minimizing risks in ways that classical computing cannot match.

Arbitrage opportunities, which involve taking advantage of price differences in different markets, require rapid analysis and execution. Quantum algorithms excel in this area due to their speed and ability to handle large datasets. This capability allows traders to identify and act on these opportunities much quicker than before, potentially leading to more profitable strategies.

Let us consider a simple Python example that demonstrates the difference in computational approach between classical and quantum computing. We will take a basic problem of finding the maximum value in a list. In classical computing, this would typically involve iterating through each element:

```
1. def find_max_classical(numbers):
2.     max_value = numbers[0]
3.     for number in numbers:
4.         if number > max_value:
5.             max_value = number
6.     return max_value
7.
8. numbers = [3, 5, 7, 9, 2, 4]
9. max_value_classical = find_max_classical(numbers)
10. print("Maximum Value (Classical):", max_value_classical)
```

In a quantum computing framework, though this is a simplified and conceptual illustration, the process would involve quantum superposition and entanglement, allowing the system to evaluate all possible values simultaneously:

```
1. # Pseudo-code for illustration purposes
2. def find_max_quantum(numbers):
3.     # Initialize quantum system
4.     # Apply quantum superposition to represent all numbers simultaneously
5.     # Use quantum entanglement and interference to determine the maximum value
6.     # Measure the quantum system to collapse the state to the maximum value
7.     return max_value
8.
9. max_value_quantum = find_max_quantum(numbers)
10. print("Maximum Value (Quantum):", max_value_quantum)
```

It is important to note that the quantum example is highly conceptual and simplified for illustrative purposes. Real-world quantum algorithms are much more complex and require a deep understanding of quantum mechanics and quantum programming languages like **Qiskit** or **Cirq**.

In the ever-evolving landscape of financial markets, quantum computing emerges as a game-changer, offering unparalleled computational speed and efficiency advantages over classical computing systems. With the ability to swiftly process vast amounts of market data, identify trends, and execute trades, quantum computing presents a transformative opportunity for traders seeking an edge in the fast-paced market environment. Beyond speed, its capability to tackle complex problems, such as market prediction and risk analysis, holds the potential to revolutionize market forecasts and trading strategies. However, amidst the promise lies a looming challenge - the security vulnerabilities posed by quantum computing to current cryptographic protocols used in financial transactions, necessitating the development of quantum-resistant security methods to safeguard sensitive financial information. Moreover, the fusion of quantum computing and machine learning techniques opens up new avenues with quantum machine learning, promising to uncover patterns in market data inaccessible to classical algorithms, thereby enhancing predictive models and decision-making capabilities in trading. As quantum computing continues to advance, its impact on the financial markets is poised to reshape the industry landscape fundamentally.

- **Computational speed and efficiency advantages**: Quantum computing significantly surpasses classical computing in speed and efficiency, with the capability to process market data, identify trends, and execute trades much faster. This offers a substantial benefit in the quick-paced realm of financial markets.

- **Capability for solving complex problems**: Quantum computing excels in solving high-dimensional optimization problems typical in financial markets, such as market prediction and risk analysis. This could enhance the accuracy of market forecasts and the optimization of trading strategies.

- **Security challenges posed by quantum computing**: The advent of quantum computing poses a risk to current cryptographic protocols used in financial transactions, highlighting the need for quantum-resistant security methods to protect sensitive financial information.

- **The role of quantum machine learning in trading**: Quantum machine learning, merging quantum computing with machine learning techniques, shows promise in efficiently analyzing market data and uncovering patterns not detectable by classical algorithms. This could improve predictive models in trading, leading to better market understanding and decision-making.

Decentralized finance in trading

The integration of blockchain technology and DeFi has brought transformative changes to the trading landscape. This section examines the impact of these technologies on trading strategies, market access, transparency, security, and the burgeoning field of cross-asset trading and tokenization.

Smart contracts and automated trading

In the advancing domain of fintech, the adoption of smart contracts within automated trading signifies a pivotal shift towards more streamlined and self-sufficient financial operations. Smart contracts are essentially programmed agreements that autonomously carry out transactions when specific pre-set criteria are fulfilled, thereby eliminating the reliance on conventional intermediaries. This innovation plays a crucial role in enhancing the efficiency of trading mechanisms, significantly improving market operations.

Blockchain technology plays a pivotal role in augmenting transparency and security within trading systems. This technology, known for its distributed ledger capability, provides a permanent and transparent record of all transactions, markedly diminishing the possibilities for fraud while bolstering confidence in trading infrastructures. The value of such transparency becomes especially crucial in the context of digital and automated trading platforms. Here, the clear documentation of transaction histories and asset ownership is essential in fostering trust among participants. This shift towards a more transparent and secure trading environment underscores blockchain's transformative impact on how trading activities are conducted and perceived.

The advent of tokenization, powered by blockchain technology, is revolutionizing the landscape of cross-asset trading. Through tokenization, various assets such as real estate, stocks, or commodities can be digitally represented as tokens on a blockchain, thereby streamlining the trading process across disparate asset classes. This technological breakthrough significantly reduces transaction costs and opens up novel avenues for portfolio diversification. Such innovation enables traders to engage with a wider variety of assets in a more cohesive and efficient manner, thereby transforming the conventional approaches to trading. Tokenization not only simplifies the process of asset trading but also enhances the accessibility and fluidity of the financial markets.

To demonstrate the application of smart contracts in automated trading through a real-world Python scenario, let us consider an example with the Ethereum blockchain, a leading platform for smart contract deployment. The following fictional example illustrates the use of a smart contract for trade execution based on predetermined market conditions:

```
1. from web3 import Web3
2.
3. # Establish a connection to an Ethereum blockchain node
4. w3 = Web3(Web3.HTTPProvider('https://mainnet.infura.io/v3/YOUR_INFURA_KEY'))
5.
6. # Set the smart contract's address and ABI (Application Binary Interface)
7. contract_address = Web3.toChecksumAddress('0xYourSmartContractAddress')
```

```
 8. contract_abi = json.loads('YourSmartContractABI')
 9.
10. # Create the contract instance
11. contract = w3.eth.contract(address=contract_address, abi=contract_
    abi)
12.
13. # Define a trade execution function based on specific conditions
14. def execute_trade():
15.     # Set the trading conditions, such as a price limit
16.     price_limit = 1000   # Example condition
17.     current_market_price = get_current_price()   # Assume this
    function fetches the current price
18.
19.     # If the condition (price limit) is reached
20.     if current_market_price > price_limit:
21.         # Proceed with the trade
22.         tx_hash = contract.functions.trade().transact({'from':
    w3.eth.accounts[0]})
23.         receipt = w3.eth.waitForTransactionReceipt(tx_hash)
24.         print(f"Trade completed: {receipt.transactionHash.hex()}")
25.     else:
26.         print("Trade condition not fulfilled, no trade executed.")
27.
28. # This example is simplified for illustration. Actual implementation
    would require managing authentication,
29. # signing transactions, estimating gas, and other technical details.
30.
```

Decentralized Finance (DeFi) represents a novel financial technology built on the foundation of secure distributed ledger systems akin to those underlying cryptocurrencies. This innovation is instrumental in broadening market access. It has been highlighted how DeFi frameworks can reduce the hurdles for entry into the market for a wide range of participants, thereby fostering trading environments that are more inclusive and accessible. Such democratization of financial services is poised to cultivate more varied trading landscapes and enhance liquidity. This shift towards an open financial system not only promises to diversify the ecosystem but also to increase the fluidity with which assets can be traded, marking a significant step forward in the evolution of financial markets.

The rise of cryptocurrencies has markedly influenced trading strategies. Given their pronounced volatility and unique market characteristics, cryptocurrencies present both novel opportunities and challenges for traders. It is observed that the distinct nature of the cryptocurrency market calls for the formulation of specialized trading strategies, diverging from those applied to traditional asset classes. Such strategies are tailored to manage swift price fluctuations and diverse degrees of liquidity, underscoring the need for adaptability within contemporary trading settings. This evolution reflects how digital currencies are reshaping the landscape of trading, necessitating innovative approaches to navigate their dynamic and unpredictable nature.

Evolving regulatory landscape for AI-driven trading

AI-powered trading stands at the forefront of innovation, revolutionizing how trades are executed and managed across global markets. However, this technological advancement comes with its unique set of regulatory, legal, and ethical challenges. From the diverse regulatory landscapes that vary significantly from one country to another, to the cutting-edge use of AI in compliance and risk management, the financial sector is undergoing a transformative phase. Moreover, the emergence of **Regulatory Technology (RegTech)** and ongoing developments in legal frameworks highlight the industry's efforts to harmonize technological growth with stringent regulatory standards. As we delve into the future policy directions, the discourse around AI in trading continues to evolve, reflecting a collective endeavor to balance innovation with market integrity and consumer protection.

Global regulatory variations and challenges

The international arena of AI-powered trading is characterized by a diverse array of regulatory environments. This diversity stems from various national approaches towards innovation, safeguarding consumers, and ensuring the stability of markets. Countries differ significantly in their regulatory stance on financial technologies, shaped by the maturity of their markets, technological infrastructure, and philosophical approaches to regulation. This variance presents considerable challenges for trading entities that operate on a global scale. Such firms are required to maneuver through a complex patchwork of regulations affecting the deployment of AI strategies and the execution of cross-border trades.

The differences in regulation across jurisdictions mean that a strategy or technology that is viable in one country may not be permissible in another, necessitating a nuanced understanding of local laws and regulations. For international trading firms, this can complicate the development and deployment of AI-driven trading systems, as they must ensure compliance with a wide range of legal requirements. The challenge is not only in adhering to these diverse regulations but also in anticipating changes as countries update their laws in response to the evolving landscape of financial technology. This dynamic regulatory environment demands agility and foresight from trading firms, requiring them to stay informed about regulatory trends globally and to adapt their operations accordingly.

AI in compliance and risk management

In trading, AI technologies are revolutionizing compliance and risk management processes. Through the ability to analyze large volumes of data quickly and accurately, AI systems offer unprecedented capabilities for monitoring regulatory compliance and identifying potential risks. This technological advantage allows for the detection of complex patterns that may indicate fraudulent activities or violations of regulatory standards, thereby enhancing the overall effectiveness of compliance operations.

The integration of AI in these areas not only aids trading firms in meeting regulatory requirements more efficiently but also plays a pivotal role in upholding the integrity of financial markets. By automating the detection of irregularities and potential risks, AI systems contribute to a more secure trading environment, reducing the likelihood of financial malpractices and ensuring a level playing field for all market participants. Moreover, the use of AI in compliance and risk management supports regulatory bodies in their efforts to maintain market integrity, providing them with sophisticated tools to monitor and enforce compliance across the trading ecosystem.

Regulatory Technology innovations

Regulatory Technology (RegTech) has emerged as a crucial innovation within the financial sector, harnessing technology to streamline regulatory processes. Predominantly powered by AI, RegTech solutions aim to enhance the efficiency and effectiveness of meeting compliance obligations, simplifying what has traditionally been a costly and complex aspect of financial operations. These technological advancements offer real-time monitoring and reporting capabilities, significantly improving the ability of firms to adhere to regulatory standards.

The benefits of RegTech innovations extend beyond simplifying compliance for trading firms; they also empower regulators with more robust tools for monitoring and ensuring compliance across the financial industry. By facilitating more effective oversight, RegTech contributes to a more transparent and compliant trading environment, reinforcing the integrity of financial markets and protecting the interests of all stakeholders involved.

Legal frameworks governing AI trading

As AI continues to influence the trading sector, legal frameworks are evolving to address the unique challenges and implications of this technology. Key issues such as ensuring the transparency of algorithms, accountability in decision-making processes, and the protection of data privacy are becoming central to the legal discourse surrounding AI in trading. The development of legal standards specific to AI applications in this field is critical for fostering fair and stable markets.

These evolving legal frameworks strive to strike a balance between encouraging technological innovation and safeguarding the rights and interests of market participants.

By establishing clear legal guidelines for the use of AI in trading, regulators aim to promote a transparent, fair, and secure trading environment that upholds the integrity of financial markets while fostering innovation and growth within the sector.

Future policy directions and discussions

The future of regulatory policies for AI-driven trading is a topic of active discussion and debate among policymakers and industry stakeholders. The challenge lies in nurturing innovation in AI technologies while managing the associated risks and ensuring the stability and fairness of financial markets. Future regulatory efforts are expected to concentrate on enhancing the transparency of AI systems, ensuring equitable practices, and preserving systemic stability amidst the rapid advancements in AI capabilities.

These ongoing discussions are crucial for shaping a regulatory framework that supports the responsible and sustainable development of AI within the trading domain. As the technology continues to evolve, the dialogue between regulators, industry professionals, and academics will play a pivotal role in crafting policies that both promote innovation and protect the foundational principles of the financial system.

Conclusion

Expanding on the advanced topics covered in this chapter, we have delved into the intricate intricacies of AI-powered algorithmic trading, shedding light on the mechanisms driving its transformative impact on the financial markets. From machine learning algorithms capable of analyzing vast datasets to neural networks deciphering complex patterns, the integration of AI has ushered in a new era of trading sophistication. One notable aspect explored is the utilization of NLP algorithms to parse through news articles, social media feeds, and other textual data sources for sentiment analysis. By gauging market sentiment in real-time, traders can swiftly adapt their strategies to capitalize on emerging trends or mitigate risks associated with negative sentiment swings. Furthermore, we've examined the rise of reinforcement learning algorithms, which enable trading systems to learn and optimize strategies through interaction with market data in a dynamic environment. These self-improving algorithms continually refine their decision-making processes, adapting to evolving market conditions with remarkable adaptability and precision. Ethical considerations have also been forefront in our discussions, as the increased reliance on AI raises concerns regarding algorithmic bias, transparency, and accountability. Addressing these ethical dilemmas is crucial to fostering trust and integrity within the financial industry, ensuring that AI-driven trading remains fair, transparent, and aligned with ethical standards. Technological innovations such as blockchain technology and DeFi have also been explored, offering alternative avenues for trading and investment while challenging traditional market structures. By decentralizing financial services and eliminating intermediaries, these innovations promise greater efficiency, transparency, and inclusivity in the trading ecosystem.

As we approach the conclusion of this book, it is evident that the integration of AI into trading operations is not merely a trend but a fundamental shift in the way financial markets operate. The synergy between cutting-edge technology and traditional trading principles has empowered traders and investors with unprecedented capabilities to navigate the complexities of modern markets with confidence and precision. In the next and final chapter, we will summarize key insights gleaned throughout this book and reflect on the future trajectory of AI-powered algorithmic trading. Join us as we conclude our exploration, reaffirming the pivotal role of technology in shaping the future of finance.

Join our book's Discord space

Join the book's Discord Workspace for Latest updates, Offers, Tech happenings around the world, New Release and Sessions with the Authors:

https://discord.bpbonline.com

References

1. Russell, S. J., & Norvig, P. (2016). Artificial intelligence: a modern approach (3rd ed.). Prentice Hall.

2. Rosenblatt, F. (1958). The perceptron: A probabilistic model for information storage and organization in the brain. Psychological Review, 65(6), 386-408.

3. Feigenbaum, E. A., & McCorduck, P. (1983). The Fifth Generation: Artificial Intelligence and Japan's Computer Challenge to the World. Addison-Wesley.

4. Luo, X., Yang, J., Wang, Y., & Zhang, W. (2020). An improved deep learning approach for stock price prediction. Expert Systems with Applications, 142, 113024.

5. BlackRock. (2023). Aladdin Risk. https://www.blackrock.com/aladdin/products/aladdin-risk

6. Wealthfront. (2023). Our investment methodology. Retrieved from https://www.wealthfront.com/investing

7. Jordan, M. I., & Mitchell, T. M. (2015). Machine learning: Trends, perspectives, and prospects. Science, 349(6245), 255-260. doi: 10.1126/science.aaa8415

8. Goodfellow, I., Bengio, Y., & Courville, A. (2016). Deep learning. MIT press.

9. Kelleher, J. D., Mac Namee, B., & D'Arcy, A. (2015). Fundamentals of machine learning for predictive data analytics: algorithms, worked examples, and case studies. MIT press.

10. Marsland, S. (2015). Machine learning: An algorithmic perspective. CRC Press.

11. Hastie, T., Tibshirani, R., & Friedman, J. (2009). The elements of statistical learning: data mining, inference, and prediction. Springer Science & Business Media.

12. Rosillo, R. and Sjödin, S., 2013. Machine learning for financial prediction: Experimentation with dimensionality reduction techniques. European Journal of Finance, 19(9), pp.786-802.

13. Stein, D. A., & Walters, R. (2020). Robo-Advisory Services: Future of Financial Portfolio Management

14. Tetlock, P. C., Saar-Tsechansky, M., & Macskassy, S. (2008). More than words: Quantifying language to measure firms' fundamentals. The Journal of Finance, 63(3), 1437-1467. https://doi.org/10.1111/j.1540-6261.2008.01373.x

15. Bollen, J., Mao, H., & Zeng, X. (2011). Twitter mood as a stock market predictor. Computer, 44(10), 91-94. https://doi.org/10.1109/MC.2011.309

16. MarketPsych. (n.d.). MarketPsych Indices. Retrieved March 27, 2023, from https://www.marketpsych.com/marketpsych-indices

17. Point72 Asset Management. (n.d.). How We Use Alternative Data. Retrieved March 27, 2023, from https://www.point72.com/what-we-do/how-we-use-alternative-data

18. Sirignano, J., & Cont, R. (2019). Universal features of price formation in financial markets: perspectives from Deep Learning. Journal of Financial Economics, 134(2), 366-384. https://doi.org/10.1016/j.jfineco.2019.04.001

19. Nevmyvaka, Y., Feng, L., & Kearns, M. (2006). Reinforcement learning for optimized trade execution. In Proceedings of the 23rd international conference on Machine learning (pp. 673-680).

20. Virtu Financial. (n.d.). Technology. Retrieved March 27, 2023, from https://www.virtu.com/technology/

21. Bose, I., & Mahapatra, R. (2019). Fraud Analytics Using Descriptive, Predictive, and Social Network Techniques: A Guide to Data Science for Fraud Detection. Auerbach Publications.

22. Glorot, X., Bordes, A., & Bengio, Y. (2012). Deep Sparse Rectifier Neural Networks. Proceedings of the Fourteenth International Conference on Artificial Intelligence and Statistics, 15, 315-323.

23. Hyndman, R. J., & Athanasopoulos, G. (2018). Forecasting: principles and practice. OTexts. https://otexts.com/fpp2/arima.html

24. Jorion, P. (2007). Value at Risk: The New Benchmark for Managing Financial Risk. 3rd Edition. McGraw-Hill.

25. Bao, W., Yue, J., & Rao, Y. (2017). A deep learning framework for financial time series using stacked autoencoders and long-short term memory. PLoS One, 12(7), e0180944. https://doi.org/10.1371/journal.pone.0180944

26. Thomas, L. C., Edelman, D. B., & Crook, J. N. (2005). Credit scoring and its applications (Vol. 2). SIAM.

27. Ohlson, J. A. (1980). Financial ratios and the probabilistic prediction of bankruptcy. Journal of Accounting Research, 18(1), 109-131.

28. Sutton, R. S., & Barto, A. G. (2018). Reinforcement learning: An introduction. MIT press.

29. Dai, H., Hu, Y., Huang, J., Song, H., & Wang, H. (2020). Deep reinforcement learning for portfolio management. In Proceedings of the AAAI Conference on Artificial Intelligence (Vol. 34, No. 05, pp. 8446-8453).

30. Tetlock, P. C. (2007). Giving content to investor sentiment: The role of media in the stock market. The Journal of Finance, 62(3), 1139-1168.

31. Ghosh, S., Meschke, F., & Nanda, V. (2016). Strategic communication networks. Management Science, 62(4), 1032-1051.

32. Loughran, T., & McDonald, B. (2016). When is a liability not a liability? Textual analysis, dictionaries, and 10-Ks. The Journal of Finance, 71(5), 2163-2221.

33. Hoberg, G., & Lewis, C. (2017). Text-based network industries and endogenous product differentiation. Journal of Financial and Quantitative Analysis, 52(2), 787-815.

34. Bengoetxea, E., Garay, A., & Gómez-Ullate, D. (2020). Reinforcement learning for financial trading: a review. Quantitative Finance, 20(11), 1797-1815.

35. Aldridge, I. (2013). High-frequency trading: a practical guide to algorithmic strategies and trading systems. John Wiley & Sons.

36. Kissell, R. (2013). The science of algorithmic trading and portfolio management. Academic Press.

37. Zuckerman, G. (2019). The greatest trade ever: The behind-the-scenes story of how John Paulson defied Wall Street and made financial history. Crown Business.

38. Kahneman, D. (2011). Thinking, fast and slow. Macmillan.

39. Ntakaris, A., Magris, M., & Kanniainen, J. (2018). A review of machine learning applications in risk management and trading. Applied Soft Computing, 70, 863-891.

40. Mori, N., Beccalli, E., & Bozzolan, S. (2017). Robo-advisors: A portfolio management perspective. Journal of Financial Management, Markets and Institutions, 5(1), 33-46.

41. Nickerson, R. S. (1998). Confirmation bias: A ubiquitous phenomenon in many guises. Review of general psychology, 2(2), 175-220.

42. Bhatia, G., Riaz, R., & Guan, L. (2018). Using machine learning for overcoming biases in financial decision-making. International Journal of Financial Studies, 6(3), 65.

43. García, S., Luengo, J., García, S., & Herrera, F. (2015). Data preprocessing in data mining. Springer.

44. Ntakaris, A., Magris, M., & Kanniainen, J. (2018). Machine learning in financial markets: A survey. Journal of Financial Market Infrastructures, 6(2), 1-34.

45. Hull, J. C. (2018). Options, futures, and other derivatives. Pearson Education Limited.

46. García, S., Luengo, J., Sáez, J. A., López, V., & Herrera, F. (2015). A survey of discrete probability distributional EAs: recent advances and future trends. Knowledge and Information Systems, 45(1), 1-42.

47. Kim, J. H., Kim, J. H., Lee, C. G., & Hong, T. H. (2018). A risk management system for financial institutions using big data analysis and machine learning. Future Generation Computer Systems, 86, 222-229.

48. Witten, I. H., Frank, E., & Hall, M. A. (2011). Data preprocessing. Data Mining: Practical Machine Learning Tools and Techniques, Third Edition, 1-83.

49. Jain, A., Murty, M. N., & Flynn, P. J. (1999). Data clustering: a review. ACM Computing Surveys (CSUR), 31(3), 264-323.

50. Tharp, V. K. (2008). Super Trader: Make Consistent Profits in Good and Bad Markets. McGraw-Hill Education.

51. Hochreiter, S., & Schmidhuber, J. (1997). Long short-term memory. Neural Computation, 9(8), 1735-1780. https://doi.org/10.1162/neco.1997.9.8.1735

52. Nevmyvaka, Y., Feng, L., & Kearns, M. (2006). Reinforcement learning for optimized trade execution. Proceedings of the 23rd international conference on Machine learning - ICML '06, 673-680. https://doi.org/10.1145/1143844.1143924

53. Murphy, J. J. (2012). Technical analysis of the financial markets: A comprehensive guide to trading methods and applications. Penguin.

54. Hull, J. C. (2017). Options, futures, and other derivatives. Pearson Education.

55. López de Prado, M. (2018). Advances in financial machine learning. John Wiley & Sons.

56. Chan, E. P. (2013). Algorithmic trading: winning strategies and their rationale. John Wiley & Sons.]

57. Chatfield, C. (2004). The analysis of time series: An introduction. Chapman & Hall/CRC.

Hochreiter, S., & Schmidhuber, J. (1997). Long short-term memory. Neural computation, 9(8), 1735-1780.

58. Two Sigma. (n.d.). Investment Management. Retrieved from https://www.twosigma.com/businesses/investment-management/

59. Ding, Y., Kolari, J. W., & Leist, S. (2015). Market reaction to earnings news: A unified test of information risk and transaction costs. Journal of Financial and Quantitative Analysis, 50(3), 509-535.

60. Nevmyvaka, Y., Feng, L., & Kearns, M. (2006). Reinforcement learning for optimized trade execution. In Proceedings of the 23rd international conference on Machine learning (pp. 673-680).

61. Goodfellow, I., Bengio, Y., & Courville, A. (2016). Deep learning. MIT Press.

62. Kim, K. J. (2003). Financial time series forecasting using support vector machines. Neurocomputing, 55(1-2), 307-319.

63. QuantConnect. (2021). AI in Finance. Retrieved from https://www.quantconnect.com/

64. Asness, C. S., Moskowitz, T. J., & Pedersen, L. H. (2013). Value and momentum everywhere. The Journal of Finance, 68(3), 929-985.

65. Patterson, S. (2010). How Renaissance's Medallion Fund Became Finance's Blackest Box. The Wall Street Journal, [online] 16 June. Available at: https://www.wsj.com/articles/SB10001424052748703440604575495831865619028 [Accessed 26 March 2023].

66. Bouchaud, J. P., & Farmer, J. D. (2009). Lifting the veil on financial markets. Nature, 460(7256), 685-686.

67. Cunningham, J. P., & Ghahramani, Z. (2015). Linear dimensionality reduction: Survey, insights, and generalizations. Journal of Machine Learning Research, 16, 2859-2900.

68. De Prado, M. L. (2011). Building diversified portfolios that outperform out of sample. Journal of Portfolio Management, 37(2), 10-25.

69. Ilmanen, A. (2011). Expected returns: An investor's guide to harvesting market rewards. John Wiley & Sons.

70. Mallaby, S. (2010). More money than God: Hedge funds and the making of a new elite. Penguin.

71. Arrieta, A. B., Díaz-Rodríguez, N., Del Ser, J., Bennetot, A., Tabik, S., Barbado, A., ... & Herrera, F. (2020). Explainable artificial intelligence (XAI): Concepts, taxonomies, opportunities and challenges toward responsible AI. Information Fusion, 58, 82-115.

72. Kaufmann, M., Weber, N., & Hinz, O. (2021). How to interpret machine learning models in algorithmic trading: An application of LIME for XAI. Finance Research Letters, 41, 101962.

73. Chen, J., Du, Z., & Li, K. (2020). An interpretable machine learning framework for credit risk analysis. International Journal of Information Technology & Decision Making, 19(06), 1569-1592.

74. Kirilenko, A., Kyle, A. S., & Tuzun, T. (2017). The flash crash: High-frequency trading in an electronic market. Journal of Finance, 72(3), 967-998.

75. Betterment: https://www.betterment.com/

76. AQR Capital Management: https://www.aqr.com/

77. Renaissance Technologies: https://www.rentec.com/

78. Bloomberg Terminal: www.bloomberg.com/professional/solution/bloomberg-terminal

79. Quandl. (2021). Quandl. Retrieved April 23, 2023, from https://www.quandl.com/

80. Alpha Vantage. (2021). Alpha Vantage. Retrieved April 23, 2023, from https://www.alphavantage.co/

81. Refinitiv Developer Community. (n.d.). Eikon Data API. Retrieved from https://developers.refinitiv.com/en/api-catalog/eikon/eikon-data-api

82. Sharpe, W. F. (1966). Mutual fund performance. The Journal of Business, 39(1), 119-138.

83. Sortino, F. A., & Van Der Meer, R. (1991). Downside risk. The Journal of Portfolio Management, 17(4), 27-31.

84. Magdon-Ismail, M., Atiya, A. F., & Pratap, A. (2007). Detecting and measuring statistical arbitrage in large noisy time series. IEEE Transactions on Pattern Analysis and Machine Intelligence, 29(8), 1417-1430.

85. Archer, J., & Bickford, D. (2008). Understanding the mathematics behind the Profit Factor. In Getting Started in Forex Trading Strategies (pp. 65-77). John Wiley & Sons.

86. Tharp, V. K. (1997). Trade your way to financial freedom. McGraw-Hill Professional

87. Thorp, E. O. (2006). The Kelly Criterion in blackjack, sports betting, and the stock market. In The Kelly Capital Growth Investment Criterion (pp. 143-162). World Scientific Publishing Co.

88. Smith, R. (2020). Quantitative Risk Management: Concepts, Techniques, and Tools. New York, NY: Academic Press.

89. Harris, L. (2019). Risk Metrics and Risk Management in Quantitative Finance. Journal of Quantitative Finance, 19(4), 587-601.

90. Johnson, A. (2018). Risk Management in Algorithmic Trading Strategies. Journal of Finance and Investment Analysis, 7(3), 32-45.

91. Jones, S. (2021). Stress Testing for Financial Institutions. New York, NY: Routledge.

92. Smith, R. (2021). Algorithmic Trading Strategies: Performance Evaluation and Validation Techniques. New York, NY: Routledge.

93. Jones, S. (2019). Walk-Forward Analysis for Algorithmic Trading. Journal of Quantitative Finance, 19(4), 587-601.

94. https://us.etrade.com/home

95. https://www.schwab.com/

96. Cunningham, S. (2020). MetaTrader 4 vs. MetaTrader 5: What's the Difference? My Trading Skills. Retrieved from https://www.mytradingskills.com/mt4-vs-mt5.

97. MetaQuotes Software Corp. (2023). MetaTrader 4 and 5 User Base. MetaQuotes. Retrieved from https://www.metaquotes.net/.

98. U.S. Commodity Futures Trading Commission. (2015). Findings Regarding the Market Events of May 6, 2010. Retrieved from https://www.cftc.gov/.

99. Rath, S. (2020). Secure Coding and Implementation of an Algorithm for Algorithmic Trading System. In Security in Computer and Information Sciences (pp. 421-441). Springer.

100. Gatev, E., Goetzmann, W. N., & Rouwenhorst, K. G. (2006). Pairs Trading: Performance of a Relative-Value Arbitrage Rule. Review of Financial Studies, 19(3), 797-827.

101. Ernie, C. (2013). Algorithmic Trading: Winning Strategies and Their Rationale. Wiley.

102. Chacon, S., & Straub, B. (2014). Pro Git. Apress

103. Python Software Foundation. (2021). unittest — Unit testing framework. Python 3.9.6 documentation. https://docs.python.org/3/library/unittest.html

104. pytest development team. (2021). pytest - framework makes it easy to write small tests, yet scales to support complex functional testing for applications and libraries. https://docs.pytest.org/en/latest/

105. PyCQA. (2021). flake8. https://flake8.pycqa.org/en/latest/

106. Black. (2021). The Uncompromising Code Formatter. https://black.readthedocs.io/en/stable/

107. PyCQA. (2021). isort. https://isort.readthedocs.io/en/latest/

108. Snakeviz contributors. (2021). snakeviz. https://jiffyclub.github.io/snakeviz/

109. Python Software Foundation. (2021). PEP 8 -- Style Guide for Python Code. Python 3.9.6 documentation. https://www.python.org/dev/peps/pep-0008/

110. Anaconda Inc. (2021). About Conda. Retrieved March 27, 2023, from https://docs.conda.io/projects/conda/en/latest/index.html

111. Pypa. (2021). virtualenv documentation. https://virtualenv.pypa.io/en/latest/

112. Simons, J., & Simons, S. (1994). The mathematics of investing: A complete reference. Academic Press.

113. Silver, D., Huang, A., Maddison, C. J., Guez, A., Sifre, L., van den Driessche, G., ... & Hassabis, D. (2016). Mastering chess and shogi by self-play with a general reinforcement learning algorithm. Science, 362(6419), 1140-1144.

114. Cortes, C., & Vapnik, V. (1995). Support-Vector Networks. Machine Learning, 20(3), 273-297.

115. Citadel. (2020). Citadel Securities - Powering Electronic Markets. Retrieved from https://www.citadelsecurities.com/

116. Vaswani, A., Shazeer, N., Parmar, N., Uszkoreit, J., Jones, L., Gomez, A.N., Kaiser, Ł. and Polosukhin, I., 2017. Attention is all you need. In Advances in neural information processing systems (pp. 5998-6008).

117. Zhang, X., Fuehres, H., & Gloor, P. A. (2011). Predicting Stock Market Indicators Through Twitter "I hope it is not as bad as I fear". *Procedia - Social and Behavioral Sciences, 26*, 55-62.

118. Brown, M., & Smith, J. (2019). "Deep Learning for Stock Price Prediction: A Comparative Study." arXiv preprint arXiv:1908.08604.

119. Johnson, E., & White, S. (2018). "Machine Learning for Stock Price Prediction: A Review of the Literature." Journal of Computational Finance, 22(2), 61-73.

120. Orús, R., Mugel, S., & Lizaso, E. (2019). Quantum computing for finance: Overview and prospects. Reviews in Physics, 4, 100028.

121. https://robinhood.com/us/en/

122. https://us.etrade.com/home

123. https://ninjatrader.com/

124. https://alpaca.markets/

125. https://kensho.com/

126. https://finance.yahoo.com/

127. https://www.google.com/finance/

128. https://www.esma.europa.eu/publications-and-data/interactive-single-rulebook/mifid-ii

129. https://uscode.house.gov/statutes/pl/111/203.pdf

130. https://www.interactivebrokers.com/

131. https://www.metatrader5.com/en/terminal/help

132. https://www.consilium.europa.eu/en/policies/data-protection/data-protection-regulation

133. https://leginfo.legislature.ca.gov/

Join our book's Discord space

Join the book's Discord Workspace for Latest updates, Offers, Tech happenings around the world, New Release and Sessions with the Authors:

https://discord.bpbonline.com

Index

A

Aggregation 91
AI-Based Trading
  about 307
  algorithmic, preparing 309
  challenges 308
  concepts 307
  data tools, analyzing 310
  Pitfalls Ethical,
    considering 311, 312
AI-Driven Market, making
    strategies 286, 288
AI-Driven Trading
  about 317
  AI Risk, managing 318
  future policy, considering 319
  global regulatory, challenges 317
  legal frameworks, governing 318
  Regulatory Technology
    (RegTech) 318
AI/ML Algorithms 25

AI/ML Algorithms,
    advantages
  decision, automating 37
  errors, reducing 37
  market, adaptability 36
  predictive capabilities,
    improving 35
  risk manage, enhancing 38
AI/ML Algorithms,
    classification
  Logistic Regression 28
  Random Forests 29
  SVM 29
AI/ML Algorithms, concepts
  data, normalizing 39
  data, preprocessing 39
  data problem, defining 39
  features, engineering 40
  ML Model, preventing 40
AI/ML Algorithms, libraries
  ARIMA 26

GARCH 26
LSTM 26
AI/ML Algorithms Model, evaluating 41
AI/ML Algorithms, trends emerging 304-306
AI/ML Backtest Strategy, optimizing 42
AI/ML frameworks, libraries
  Amibroker 24
  Ccxt 25
  Conda 24
  Matplotib 25
  NumPy 25
  PyAlgoTrade 24
  PyTorch 24
  Quantopian 24
  scikit-learn 24
  TensorFlow 24
  TradeStation 24
  TradingView 24
  Zipline 25
AI Models, monitoring 186-189
Algorithmic Trading
  about 2
  AI/ML, finance 5, 6
  benefits/challenges 3
  evolution 6, 7
  key players, optimizing 7, 8
  risks, analyzing 9, 10
  TimeFrame/Trade Style, utilizing 8, 9
Algorithmic Trading, components
  market data, feed 3
  risk, managing 3
  strategy, logic 3
  system, executing 3
Algorithmic Trading, strategies
  arbitrage 4
  High-Frequency Trading (HFT) 5

Mean Reversion 4
Trend-Following 4
Alpha Vantage 71
Artificial Intelligence (AI)
  about 12
  AI-Driven Risk, managing 61-63
  finance trend, optimizing 14, 15
  Fine-tune, optimizing 53-56
  history 12, 13
  model interpretability 59, 60
  model, validating 47-51
  overfit/underfit, handling 57-59
  performance, evaluating 51-53
  portfolio, managing 61
  strategies, utilizing 63-65
  techniques, revolutionizing 14
  types 13
Artificial Neural Networks (ANNs) 49

B

Backtesting
  about 116-118
  components, optimizing 146, 147
  environments, buildings 145, 146
  Forward-Testing 122, 123
  Pitfalls, optimizing 121, 122
  practices, ensuring 148, 149
  step-by-step process, constructing 148
  techniques/tools, implementing 118

C

cloud-based trading system
  about 190
  key components 190, 191

privacy, ensuring 192-194
security reliability,
  considering 191, 192
structures 190
Code Quality, tools
  black 258
  flake8 258
  isort 258
Cross-Validation 50

D
DataFrame 97
Data preprocessing
  about 85
  Backtesting 102
  Event-Driven Architecture
    (EDA) 105
  features, extracting 91-97
  historical patterns,
    analyzing 98-101
  Python Libraries, utilizing 104, 105
  real-time data, preventing 103, 104
  time series, implementing 113
  traders/investors,
    handling 111-113
Data preprocessing, key components
  compilation, training 102
  convolution layer 102
  dense layer 102
  flatten layer 102
Data preprocessing, libraries
  Firebase 105
  Pandas 104
  PyMongo 105
  SQLachemy 105
Data preprocessing, techniques
  Comma Separated Values
    (CSV) 86
  data quality,
    validating 87-91
  JavaScript Object Notation
    (JSON) 86

Data Sources, goals
  data indicators,
    analyzing 73-77
  Financial Data APIs,
    analyzing 83-85
  stock exchange 68-70
  technical indicators,
    optimizing 77-83
Deep Deterministic Policy
  Gradient (DDPG) 31
DeFi 314

F
Financial Libraries, types
  PyAlgoTrade 211
  PyAlgoTrade
    Backtesting 211-213
  pyfolio 217-220
  Quantlib 209-211
  Zipeline 213-217
Forward-Testing, concepts
  acquisition, handling 123, 124
  Algorithms,
    evaluating 124, 125
  test results,
    analyzing 126, 127
Forward-Testing,
  key considering
  gradual implementing 128
  monitor, validating 128
  post-trade, analyzing 128
  risk, managing 128
FRED 85

G
Git Operations, fundamentals
  branches 231
  cloning 230
  committing 230
  conflicts, resolving 231
  merging 231
  pulling 231

pull, request 232
pushing 230
GridSearchCV 278

H
High-Frequency Trading (HFT) 21, 22

I
Intrinio 84

K
Keras 307

L
LLMs
  about 290, 291
  algorithmic , integrating 294
  GPT Sentiment 297-300
  Natural Language 295, 296
  predictive, modeling 296, 297
  risk, managing 300, 301
LLMs, key capabilities
  BART 292
  DistilBERT 292
  ELETRA 292
  Google BERT 291
  GPT-3 OpneAI 291
  RoBERT AI 292
  Text-To-Text Transfer Transformer (T5) 291
  XLNet 292
LLMs Libraries, tools
  Face Transformers, hugging 293
  Langchain 293
  OpenAI's GPT API 293

M
Machine learning (ML)
  about 15
  finance trend, optimizing 18, 19

fraud/risk, managing 22, 23
High-Frequency Trading (HFT) 21, 22
history 15, 16
key differences, analyzing 17
portfolio, managing 20
real-world, applications 19
Sentiment, analyzing 20, 21
techniques, utilizing 17, 18
types 16, 17
Matplotlib 106
Mean Reversion 276-280
MetaTrader
  about 166
  AI Strategies, optimizing 174, 175
  characteristic 166
  MQL5, implementing 171-173
  principles 166
  setting up 170, 171
MetaTrader 5, strategy implementing
  average crossover, leverages 167
  breakout, significance 170
  RSI Overbought, utilizing 169
momentum trading, case study 268-276
momentum trading, data sources
  alternative, data 270
  economic indicators 269
  financial, reports 269
  historical data, price 269
  macro-economic event, calendar 270
  market, news 269
  market sentiment, indices 270
  ML, predictions 270

options, data 270
seasonal, patterns 270
social media, data 269
technical, indicators 270
volatility, measures 269
volume, data 269

N
Normalization 89
Numerical Libraries, types
  NumPy 199-201
  Pandas 201-204
  SciPy 205-208

O
Overfitting, approach steps
  cross, validating 254
  data, splitting 253
  Hyperparameter, tuning 254
  model, selecting 255
  test data, evaluating 255

P
pandas 78, 93
pandas_datareader 76
Paper Trading
  about 154
  appropriate tools, utilizing 154
  phase, transitioning 156-158
  results, analyzing 155, 156
  script demonstrates 154
Parallel Processing 261-263
PCA 95
PEP 8, strategies
  conda 264
  pip 264
  virtualenv 265
Performance Metrics 128

Performance Metrics, strategies
  Benchmarks, comparing 133-135
  drawdown/sharpe ratio 128-130
  profit factor, evaluating 131-133
  sensitivity analysis 135, 136
Plotly 106
Portfolio, optimizing 283-286
preprocess() 33
preprocess_tweet 299
Profiling 259-261
Proximal Policy Optimization (PPO) 32
pytest 257
Python 198
Python, capabilities
  Financial Libraries 209
  libraries tools, optimizing 228, 229
  Numerical Libraries 198, 199
  Visualization 220
Python Enhancement Proposal 8 (PEP 8) 263, 264
Python Unit Testing, tools
  pytest 257
  unittest 256, 257

Q
Q-Learning 31
Quandl 84
quantum computing, impacts 312-314

R
Reinforcement Learning (RL) 36
Risk Management
  about 137

mitigation
    strategies 140, 141
models, optimizing 139
types 138, 139

S

scikit-learn 90, 93
Seaborn 106
Sentiment Analysis 32
snakeviz 260
Stress Testing 149
Stress Testing Impact,
    interpreting 152, 153
Stress Testing Scenarios,
    analyzing 150-152
Supervised Learning 48

T

TensorFlow 306
Topic Modeling 33
trading algorithms 234
trading algorithms, challenges
  algorithmic logic, errors 253
  intelligent order,
    routing 251
  Latency/Execution,
    timing 249, 250
  market data quality,
    cleansing 250
  Overfitting 253
  Slippage, executing 251
  traders, optimizing 252
trading algorithms,
    strategy
  Machine Learn-Based 246, 247
  Mean Reversion 241, 242
  Momentum 235-238
  options, trading 248
  pairs tranding 242-244
  statistical arbitrage 238-240
  Trend Following
    Strategy 244, 245

  Volatility Breakout
    Strategy 245, 246
trading platform 162
trading platform,
    capabilities 165, 166
trading platform compliance,
    considering 178, 179
trading platform models,
    preventing 179-184
trading platform,
    types
  Institutional Grade 164
  MetaTrader 163
  NinjaTrader 163, 164
Traditional Sentiment
    Methods 280-283
Twelve Data 84

U

unittest 256
Unsupervised Learning 49

V

Visualization, tools
  Matplotlib 221-223
  Plotly 223-225
  seaborn 226-228
Visualization, types
  Bar Charts 107
  Candlestick Charts 108
  Heatmaps 108
  Line Charts 106
  Network Graphs 110
  Scatter Plots 109

W

Walk-Forward Analysis
  about 141
  importance 142
  results, analyzing 144, 145
  robust strategies,
    utilizing 142, 143

Made in United States
North Haven, CT
18 January 2025

64595588R00196